FRANK LLOYD WRIGHT

His Life and His Architecture

FRANK LLOYD WRIGHT

His Life and His Architecture

ROBERT C. TWOMBLY

A WILEY-INTERSCIENCE PUBLICATION

JOHN WILEY & SONS, New York · Chichester · Brisbane · Toronto

Library of Congress Cataloging in Publication Data

Twombly, Robert C.
  Frank Lloyd Wright, his life and his architecture

  "A Wiley-Interscience publication."
  Bibliography: p.
  Includes index.
  1. Wright, Frank Lloyd, 1867–1959.   2. Architects—
United States—Biography.   3. Wright, Frank Lloyd,
1867–1959—Influence.   I. Title.
NA737.W7T95   720'.92'4 [B]   78-9466
ISBN 0-471-03400-2

Printed in the United States of America

10 9 8 7 6 5 4

Preface

Authors rarely have the chance to redo books, to correct errors (hopefully without making too many new ones), to restate opinions with the benefit of accumulated experience, and to rethink everything conceptually. I am grateful to William Dudley Hunt, Jr., architectural editor, and to John Wiley & Sons for the opportunity. And I am grateful to architect/professor David Roessler for his conversations and criticisms over the years, for his drawings in this edition (see appendix), for his loan of photographs (some of which appear here), and for his company on those architectural trips that for Frank Lloyd Wright aficionados never seem to end.

Several other people helped in more specific ways: Ruth and Stewart Twombly of Concord, New Hampshire; Dione Neutra of Los Angeles; Louis and Joan Clark of Rochester, New York; Barry Bragg of Ottawa; Reid Addis of Providence; John Sergeant of the University of London; Don Kalec of the Frank Lloyd Wright Home and Studio Foundation in Oak Park, Illinois; Annette Carnow of the Oak Park Public Library; Adolph Placzek, Director of Avery Library at Columbia University in New York; Marsha Peters of the Rhode Island Historical Society; C. Ford Peatross of the Library of Congress; Lillian McCann and Frank Jewell of the Chicago Historical Society; Christine Schelshorn of the State Historical Society of Wisconsin; Annette Fern and Daphne C. Roloff of The Art Institute in Chicago; Gladys Hartmann of Teaneck, New Jersey; and members of the staffs at a number of Wright's buildings. Without their contributions this book would be the worse. And might not have been at all but for editor Susan Braybrooke in New York City.

After I completed the manuscript of *Frank Lloyd Wright: An Interpretive Biography* in 1971, and especially after Harper & Row published it in 1973, I thought I had given the man enough of my time. People asked me to lecture about him, which led to further articles, and to write reviews, and I was forever adding to my clipping file, why, I did not know, since I was supposed to be—and was in fact—doing other things.

But Frank Lloyd Wright is a compelling man. Once bitten by his bug one finds it difficult to regain immunity. Like William Faulkner's people, he "endured," but he also triumphed, and we are all the better for it. He triumphed over hostility, indifference, boredom, and the ignorance of well-meaning people—and he continues to triumph over saccharine cultism—to herald an individuality and a vision of social harmony to which most of his words and his deeds were directed. There is much about the man not to like, much to object to, but his life's goal was to bring about a more humane world through architecture, and that cannot be faulted. Because he was intensely socially conscious, dedicated to making America a better place by abolishing insensitive government and monopoly capitalism, he stands apart from most architects, indeed, from most public figures. He also lived with such flair and his life had such drama that he was, and continues to be, fascinating. Like a good book he is difficult to put down.

No important new repositories of material have come to light since research on this biography was (temporarily) completed in 1971. The Frank Lloyd Wright Foundation in Scottsdale, Arizona, keeps its files closed to any but approved scholars, whose publications have not been particularly illuminating. On the other hand, the holdings at Avery Library, the Chicago Art Institute, and at the State Historical Society of Wisconsin continue to grow; together with the Public Library and the new Frank Lloyd Wright Home and Studio Foundation in Oak Park, they somewhat ease the burden for scholars. I undertook additional research for this book, particularly in published sources from the 1930s, 1940s, and 1950s, and I examined old material in new ways. The result is a richer text throughout, several new subdivisions for topics not previously considered, a major reorganization including three new chapters, and many more illustrations.

Real estate developers continue to eat away at the Wisconsin valley Frank Lloyd Wright loved so much. One of their principal instigators is Taliesin Associated Architects, heirs to Wright's name and his practice, who designed massive recreational facilities all around his home. Almost within sight of Taliesin is its gatehouse for The Wintergreen ski resort, possibly one of the ugliest buildings in the state, an insulting reference to Wright, but a telling indication of the firm's abilities. Helped by its design insensitivity and by several of its own structures,

FRANK LLOYD WRIGHT

His Life and His Architecture

1867–1893

CHAPTER ONE

Nearly Everything
to Learn

Frank Lloyd Wright's early years were nomadic and unsettling. Before he was eleven he lived in six towns in four states from Massachusetts to Iowa while his restless father searched for a better situation. In his early teens he worked summers to supplement family income, and when his parents divorced he left high school to take a job. He started college but after two unproductive semesters moved to Chicago where he worked for three employers in a year. A week before his twenty-second birthday he married his eighteen-year-old fiancée, his first romantic attachment. Despite a provincial background and lack of formal training, Wright by his mid-twenties acquired the social and architectural credentials necessary to become an upper middle class professional.

□ □ □

Like the wandering pioneer of American folklore, Frank Lloyd Wright's father willingly subordinated family stability and familiar surroundings to a relentless search for personal fulfillment. William Russell Cary Wright was born a minister's son in 1825 at Westfield, Massachusetts, a few miles from Springfield. A precocious young man, he entered Amherst College in 1839 at age fourteen intending to study music and law. Although he registered for both his freshman and sophomore years, he completed neither, left the college in 1840, and moved with his brother, the Reverend Thomas G. Wright, to Claremont, New Hampshire, in 1847. That October he enrolled as a senior at Madison University (later renamed Colgate), from which he graduated in 1849. On his first job as a "piano forte teacher, and organist" in Utica, New York, he married Permelia Holcomb, a native of nearby Litchfield, in 1851. The newlyweds moved to Hartford, Connecticut, where Wright supported himself by teaching while he read law, entering the bar in 1857. After eight years in Hartford his wanderlust could no longer be denied, and William C. Wright joined that inexorable westward migration, arriving at Lone Rock, Wisconsin, to hang out a lawyer's shingle sometime in 1859.[1]

His residential choice was apt, for Lone Rock immediately recognized him as a potential leader, as a well-educated man with talents useful to the community and conducive to personal success on the frontier. Wright was ambitious and aggressive and made friends easily; he was universally liked and respected. Within a year he was appointed Commissioner of the Richland County Circuit Court, testimony to his political as well as legal acumen, then announced his candidacy for county school superintendent, winning the enthusiastic endorsement of a local newspaper. "Probably no better man could be selected," the editor insisted. "His friends speak very highly of him. . . ."

William C. Wright's defeat did not prevent him from trying again, and winning, in 1863. During his two-year tenure, Permelia Holcomb Wright died in 1864, leaving William a widower with three children. The chances are that he had already met Anna Lloyd Jones, who lived just seven miles away, at Hillside.[2]

About Frank Lloyd Wright's mother there is very little reliable information. Anna was born in Wales in 1842, migrated with her family to New York City in 1844, and trekked to Milwaukee and then to Ixonia, Wisconsin, in 1845. After a few years, probably in 1855 or 1856, Anna's family moved again, to the tiny farming settlement of Hillside in the Helena Valley across the Wisconsin River from Spring Green. The Lloyd Joneses, a tightly knit Unitarian clan with eleven children (four born in Wisconsin), quickly became one of the largest and most prosperous families in the south-central part of the state. It was probably the reverence at home for books and learning that directed Anna to teaching, one of the few careers open to young women at the time that had also attracted two of her sisters. Riding and walking across the sparsely populated countryside to one or another rural school, sometimes through fierce winter storms, must have fired in Anna a sense of mission that her commitment to education had already kindled. But it also awakened her to the forms and processes of nature, as her

Figure 1.1 Anna Lloyd Wright, date unknown. From Maginel Wright Barney, *The Valley of the God-Almighty Joneses.* With the permission of Hawthorne Books.

children later recalled. "Nature and knowledge," her daughter Maginel wrote, "those were her early and abiding passions."[3]

The superintendent of schools interviewed job applicants and lectured annually at the Richland County Teachers' Institute, so Anna may well have met her future husband when their professional paths crossed. This gifted, versatile, mature, and well-educated man, who numbered among his ancestors James Russell and Amy Lowell and Phoebe and Alice Cary, must have impressed the bookish, comparatively provincial, but strong-willed Anna, seventeen years his junior. Despite "some misgivings" among the Lloyd Joneses, Anna and William were married on August 17, 1866, when he was forty-one and she twenty-four (Fig. 1.1). By this time William C. Wright had entered politics as a minor official in the Republican party and as deputy United States revenue collector. But his career as a politician was even shorter-lived than his legal practice, for Wright was establishing a reputation as an orator in connection with his emergence as a preacher. During his first marriage he had begun to ride the thirty-five-miles round trip each Sunday to the Richland Center Baptist Society where he was ordained in August 1863. With his new wife eight months pregnant in May of 1867, the Wrights moved from Lone Rock to preside over construction of the Society's new building. Just as they were settling in, Anna gave birth to the first of her three children, her only son, Frank Lloyd, on June 8, 1867. Daughters Mary Jane and Margaret Ellen (Maginel) followed in 1869 and 1877.[4]

Throughout his life Frank Lloyd Wright consistently maintained that his architectural career was prenatally chosen for him by his mother, who did not confide this to William. But the younger Wright also freely admitted that his lifelong attraction to Bach and Beethoven was stimulated by his father who, he recalled many times, taught him to make structural comparisons between music and buildings. William's relationship with his son was never close—"he never made much of the child,"[5] the architect said—ending when Frank was seventeen, but his impact was profound and enduring. Indeed, in one of Wright's last publications, in 1957 when he was ninety, he recounted as he often had his love–hate attraction to his father: love for William's music and for the esteem in which his peers held him, hate for his indifference and authoritarian manner.[6] Although young Wright owed his artistic inclinations as much to his father as to his mother, Anna has received more attention, while William's career and parental influence have been neglected.

The elder Wright was a man of many talents—a practicing lawyer, music teacher, politician, educator, and clergyman—constantly looking for new outlets. In Lone Rock, Reverend Wright established a reputation for excellence in public speaking at a time when skillful oratory was universally admired. The prize of delivering the eulogy for Abraham Lincoln in April 1865 was presumably given to the town's most able speaker; and, according to one observer, Wright made "an appropriate and eloquent address which. . .was highly praised by all who heard it." After January 1866, when his term as school superintendent ended, he devoted himself to the Richland Center Baptist Society. A month after his son's birth in 1867, William C. Wright gave his first local concert—for the benefit of the church building fund—establishing himself as both musician and preacher, as he would again in other communities. His "musical attainments [are] well known," the town's newspaper editor reminded his readers, and the concert was "equal to the best entertainment ever given here."[7]

Despite local enthusiasm for his diverse talents, William C. Wright found Richland Center too confining, perhaps too unprofitable. Community largesse dispensed at occasional "donation parties" to supplement his meager salary was hardly sufficient recognition of his worth. So to salvage his pride and with an eye toward greener pastures, the family moved in March 1869 to McGregor, Iowa, where Wright had bought into a department store's music section. But the flattering reputation preceding him had little to do with business matters: "Our city has reason to be glad," the McGregor *Times* commented, "that so valuable a gentleman has been added to its religious, musical, and social lists." Wright plunged into civic and religious affairs, preaching "very acceptably when requested to do so," directing a musical group, and contributing to the annual Thanksgiving Festival.

William C. Wright excelled at everything but turning a profit. "He cared nothing for money," his daughter remembered; he "had no financial sense whatever." Unable to support his family from the department store, he returned to preaching. Everyone in McGregor understood that he was "not professionally a clergyman," but after delivering a much-admired funeral oration over a locally prominent citizen, he was soon made temporary pastor of the Baptist Church, a position he held for the next two years. His congregation thought him "as unassuming and plain a Christian as walks or talks," whose sermons were "highly commended by those who are competent to judge. . . ." People came to "expect something original, practical, and unhackneyed from Mr. Wright," his friend the newspaper editor wrote. "He is a plain speaker and for that we like him." Many people in McGregor thought of the Wrights as "valued friends" and were therefore somewhat stunned to learn in May 1871 that the minister was leaving:

There are few clergymen who have so strong a hold upon their congregation as the reverend gentleman has, and we happen to know that there are none who do not rejoice at the success which his people have had in persuading him to remain.[8]

But the decision to stay was quickly reversed, and when the Wrights actually left McGregor two months later in July 1871, most of the town felt the loss:

The people. . .have not submitted willingly to the decision which has taken from us this excellent man. They love him. . .and separate from him with regret, and will ever follow him with their kindest wishes to whatever field of labor he may be called.[8]

Frank Lloyd Wright and his sister Maginel Wright Barney depicted their father as a moody man, subject to frequent periods of depression and withdrawal. "Failure after failure added to failure," the architect wrote, produced "the inveterate and desperate withdrawal on his part into the arid life of his studies, his books, and his music, where he was oblivious to all else." Maginel remembered that "he was often away for long stretches—teaching or preaching?—I don't even know." This picture was certainly accurate for the 1880s, when Maginel noticed something "wrong between my father and mother."[9] But during the 1860s and 1870s William seemed contented enough, at least on the surface. He was admired by his neighbors, beloved for his preaching and music, and a welcome participant in community activities. Reclusiveness came later, perhaps after gestation through a long period of repeated personal and financial frustrations.

The Wrights left McGregor as optimistically as they had left Richland Center. After a few months with the Lloyd Joneses at Hillside, they moved to Pawtucket, Rhode Island, where William assumed the pastorate of the High Street Baptist Church in December 1871. Had William been more practical and a man less certain of his own abilities, he might never have taken the job. The original High Street Church had burned down in 1868, leaving the new minister the thankless responsibility of presiding over what seemed an endless series of fund raisers designed to rebuild the church and rescue the congregation from an embarrassing debt. But the church was apparently beyond salvation, for shortly after Wright left the pulpit in January 1874, the structure was sold to the town as a high school. Despite his financial failures, Wright was applauded as "a workman that need not be ashamed—earnest, unwearied, successful, as far as circumstances permitted."[10]

In Pawtucket, William C. Wright displayed the varied talents and amiable personality that had made him popular elsewhere. His public lectures—some religious, some not—revealed a continuing interest in politics when he thanked God for President Ulysses Grant's 1872 reelection, and a moderate interest in reform when he discussed "the responsibility of public carriers for human life and safety." He gave his first addresses on temperance and Ancient Egypt, dependable lecture topics thereafter, and was elected to various offices and committees of the Rhode Island Baptist State Convention and the Providence Baptist Association, in both of which he was quite conspicuous from 1872 to 1874. He received the honor, in fact, of writing the Circular Letter for the 1873 convention on the topic, "How Shall Our Efficiency [as Churches] be Increased?" Not the least of his accomplishments was "'Tis Sweet to Meet, and Each Other Greet," a song he published as sheet music and sold through newsdealers as a five-cent supplement to *The Social Times*, a church paper he launched to raise money. "The song is well worth double the price of the paper," the *Pawtucket Gazette and Chronicle* decided, "and we wish a copy of it might be found in every family."

Many of William C. Wright's activities and most of his lectures and sermons were covered by the local newspaper. Talks on "The Art of Happiness" and "Honest Blunders" received enthusiastic reviews. His 1872 Thanksgiving lecture was "of more than the usual interest": with many a "fitting allusion. . .beautifully shown," it was "admirable in spirit, in conception, in execution, and in delivery," the editor said, "and the congregation, on retiring from the sanctuary, evidently felt it had been good to be there. . . ." But praise and press coverage were not enough. Despite his lecturing, William C. Wright was nearly insolvent; the church could not pay an adequate salary, at times no salary at all. The embarrassment for strong-willed Anna and proud William must have been intense when 100 members of the congregation descended unannounced on their home to present her with "useful and seasonable articles" and him with "a quantity of *greenbacks*." Subsequent newspaper coverage in humorous detail must have been equally trying.

Little wonder that Wright tendered his resignation early in December 1873, that the High Street Baptist Society voted unanimously not to accept it, and that Wright insisted, effective January 1874. Before the Wrights left Pawtucket, a second church group called at their home to give William fifty dollars and Anna forty. At this point the Wrights disappeared from the historical record until August, when they returned for a week to gather their possessions and to announce that William had received a call from the First Baptist Church in Weymouth, Massachusetts, where he would begin duties on September 6. That church, the editor of the Pawtucket paper stated in his farewell to the minister, "will find in Mr. Wright a Christian heart and an earnest worker in his Master's cause." When Wright returned to Providence on September 16 to preach the annual sermon before the Baptist Association, he was listed among "visiting brethren" from the "Boston North" meeting.[11]

Weymouth was the first town Frank Lloyd Wright remembered, at least the first he wrote about. He was seven years old when he moved into the "modest, gray, wooden house near a tall white-brick church" where he pumped organ bellows to the point of exhaustion so his father could practice (or meditate). He also recalled Miss Williams' private school, excursions to Nantucket Island, and clambakes somewhere on Narragansett Bay (which he may have confused with living in Pawtucket). His most important memory, certainly in light of his architectural career, came as a result of his mother's visit to the 1876 Centennial Exposition in Philadelphia's Fairmount Park where she saw a display of Froebelian games and toys.[12] Friedrich Froebel (1782–1852), a German educational theorist and reformer who pioneered the "kindergarten" concept, had used wooden blocks, cards, and paper of pure geometric forms and primary colors in programmed exercises to channel childrens' play toward a knowledge of composition, relationships, and nature itself. The toys could be stacked, folded, arranged, and manipulated endlessly in two- and three-dimensional constructions resembling furniture, buildings, and entire city plans. Froebel also taught that natural objects could be expressed through basic geometry. In Boston, Anna Wright discovered book and toy sellers who handled Froebel's materials, and a number of schools based on his principles. She bought the "gifts," as they were called, for her own kindergarten, where Mary Jane and Frank spent hours experimenting with building methods. In order to play correctly, young Wright was forced to experience shapes and colors, and their spatial and interrelationships, a lesson in bold non-Victorian construction possibilities he never forgot.[13]

Meanwhile, William C. Wright's Weymouth career followed the usual pattern. He quickly established a reputation for musical excellence, befriended the newspaper editor, and helped form a literary circle. He was associated with the Massachusetts Total Abstinence Society and the local Reform Club, more than likely another temperance group. He convinced a wealthy parishoner who had been instrumental in Wright's move to Weymouth to install a pipe organ in the Baptist Church. "He had some wonderfully interesting musical Sundays," one member recalled, but they were "not entirely to the satisfaction of his congregation." Perhaps his habit of "seat[ing] himself at the piano, and throwing back his head, with its snow-white hair, sing[ing] and play[ing] to us some song of his choosing" disquieted puritanical worshippers sensitive to ministerial decorum, especially on the Sabbath. Chroniclers of local history do not agree whether Wright resigned in October 1877 or was fired, but when he left the pulpit the church took up a special collection since it had been unable to pay his salary.

Wright turned to lecturing and music as alternative sources of income. His talk on abstinence at the Universalist Church was his first foray outside the Baptist fold, while his addresses to the Women's Christian Temperance Union on "Curiosities of Egypt" and "Reigns of the Ptolemies and Cleopatra" were as well attended as his musicales, one of which was "the most brilliant display of home talent ever witnessed in town." But his triumphs left him unsatisfied, not to mention insolvent. Anna had been homesick for some time, and probably at her urging William decided to return to Wisconsin. After a farewell sermon at the Universalist Church and a testimonial dinner at the Reform Club in April 1878, the Wrights were accompanied to the railroad station by a large group of well-wishers, citizens of a fifth town (in nine years) that had wanted him to stay.

The William C. Wrights traveled directly to Wisconsin to spend the spring and summer with the Lloyd Joneses, substantiating Frank Lloyd Wright's recollection that he was eleven when he first worked on his Uncle James' farm. Although the date of William's next move is uncertain, he was cited in an August 1878 newspaper as a resident of Madison and as pastor of the Liberal (Unitarian) Church of Wyoming, another hamlet outpost of the Lloyd Jones clan, near Hillside. He had certainly secured this position and its associated responsibilities through the influence of Anna's brother, Jenkin Lloyd Jones, a prominent Chicago clergyman and Missionary Secretary of the Western Unitarian Conference embracing Wisconsin. "The State work," Jones wrote in *Unity*, the journal he edited, "has been put in the hands of Mr. Wright who has energetically pushed missionary enterprises, ministering fortnightly to the little society at Wyoming, and visiting other places," namely, Edgerton, Richland Center, Lone Rock, and Bear Creek. Before the year was out Wright, who was said to have been "recruited" from the Baptists sometime after May 1878, was appointed secretary of the Wisconsin Conference of Unitarians and Independent Societies.

Although his services were "heartily" commended to the officers of the American Unitarian Association, Wright did not find his new religious affliliation any more financially rewarding than the old one. Even with proceeds from the music studio he opened in Madison by March 1880, he could not support his family and was forced back to the lecture platform and the pulpit in other denominations to supplement his income. In October 1881 he opened a series of meetings at the Spring Green Congregational Church. "As a lecturer, Mr. Wright is one of the best," a local paper observed, "and none should fail to hear him." But many did, for even though his talk on Ireland "was without doubt one of the best we ever attended," the turnout was "very small." Nevertheless, Wright spoke to the Congregationalists periodically until late 1884, meanwhile continuing his Unitarian functions into the summer of 1885.[15]

Frank Lloyd Wright was now conscious enough of his surroundings to have clear memories, some of which he recorded in his autobiography. He and his sister Maginel both remembered his close friendship with Robert M. "Robie" Lamp (for whom he designed a house in 1904). Frank, Robie, and their friends engaged in the usual boyish activities; they "invented" things, published a one-sheet neighborhood newspaper, and had lots of parties and after-dinner singing sessions. Frank was popular among young people but shy around girls. He had a tendency to fantasize, and in his attic "sanctum" read, drew, and painted frenetically, retreating for hours at a time into *Arabian Nights* or the plans for a daring new kite. His father taught him to play viola in the family orchestra, supplemented on occasion by young musicians from the neighborhood. Frank was at once withdrawn and outgoing, physically active, and intellectually comtemplative. In short, he seems to have had a relatively normal adolescence.[16]

From sources other than memoirs it is possible to reconstruct additional aspects of young Wright's Madison years—especially important ones for him as it turned out. His family lived at the corner of Gorham and Livingston Streets on the East Side, about a block from the Second Ward Grammar School he attended during the late 1870s and early 1880s. Spotty evidence shows he went to Madison (now Central) High School from October 1884 through March 1885, though he may have enrolled earlier. His grades were not outstanding: "average" in rhetoric and botany, both good and poor in physics, and poor to average in algebra, which he failed once. Most of Madison's school records for the period have been lost or destroyed, but there is nothing anywhere to indicate that he graduated from high school, which may explain why young Wright was admitted to the University of Wisconsin on "Jan. 7, 1886 as a Special Student."

During the months between March 1885, when he is known to have last attended high school, and January 1886, when he started college,

Frank Lloyd Wright took a job in the newly opened architectural office of Allan D. Conover, a University of Wisconsin professor of civil engineering, who was also the Madison city engineer and a consultant to the State Railroad Commission. Wright was familiar with hard work, having spent every summer since 1878 on one or another uncle's farm "adding tired to tired," as he put it. But the job with Conover, for which he apparently dropped out of high school, was necessary because of financial difficulties in his family resulting from dramatically changed circumstances. Wright always depicted his childhood as having been much poorer than his sister Maginel did, but in 1885 things were clearly deteriorating.[17]

In April, William C. Wright filed for divorce, without any contest whatsoever from Anna. Claiming she was insulting, extravagant, ignored her household duties, and was money hungry, William also objected most vehemently to her refusing "me intercourse as between husband and wife." For two years, he claimed, she had deserted him in every way but physically removing herself from home. She had told him she hated the very ground he walked on, that she would never again live with him as a wife. Although his suit focused only on the period since 1883, Wright contended that "our married life has been unhappy from the start" because Anna was jealous of her three step-children (who had long since left home). "Many times," he said, "I had thought on the subject of a divorce but. . .for the sake of our children. . .I would never bring the case into court." But now "I [can] endure it no longer." Anna made no defense, saying only she did not love her husband. On April 24, 1885, the court ruled that William C. Wright had indeed discharged his obligations to his wife, "that all the allegations of the complaint are true," and granted him a divorce. After deeding the house to Anna, William left Madison. His son never saw him again.[18]

Imcompatibility between Anna and William was deep-rooted. She had come from a prosperous, tightly knit immigrant family. Her husband, settling far from his old-line New England relatives, could not recreate for her the sense of camaraderie and united purpose that had characterized her youth. It was difficult for her to adjust to frequent moves from one small town and one poor church to another, waiting for her husband—who was on the verge of middle age when they married—to find what he wanted. She had once admired William's dedication to things of the spirit—to music, ideas, and learning—but she came to see them as evidence of self-indulgence, irresponsibility, and lack of concern for the family's welfare. For him she had abandoned a teaching career, raised three young children from his first marriage, and entered an alien religious denomination, receiving, she believed, little in return. William's unceasing restlessness contributed to an unstable home atmosphere, in sharp contrast to her childhood. Even her return to Wisconsin did not save the marriage, as it was probably designed to do, but indeed might have made it seem worse in comparison to life at Hillside.

The family's financial situation was another factor contributing to its eventual breakup. The move to Madison was undoubtedly prompted in part by a promise of assistance from the Lloyd Joneses. (Jenkin had certainly secured Wright's position with the Unitarians.) The summers that Frank Lloyd Wright, his sisters, and sometimes his entire family spent with his aunts and uncles were presumably designed to ease money problems. (After the divorce Anna's brothers agreed to support her and the children.) Even though William had held three jobs simultaneously in Madison—music teacher, Unitarian missionary, and lecturer—he could not provide the financial security Anna had expected since childhood. It was not that the Wrights were poverty stricken; they owned their own home, after all. But Anna's aspirations were high while William's did not seem to include material comfort. No doubt this contributed to her hostility and to his feeling that she was extravagant, insensitive, and overly critical.

A kind of tragic pattern emerges from even the little that is known of William C. Wright's story. He was never able to stay where he was most appreciated; every small town he lived in praised him enthusiastically and counted him a valuable asset, but none could satisfy his own sense of worth. A proud and talented man, he believed his abilities warranted a larger and more prestigious audience, that his status and reputation should have been greater than they were. But life never lived up to his expectations. The inability of small Midwestern towns to satisfy led him back East. But further disappointments, financial and professional, took him on a second westward migration, not with the optimism of youth this time but with the burdens of family, desperation, and old age (see Fig. 1.2). By 1885 at age sixty, he knew success had passed him by. He had disappointed Anna but, even worse, he had disappointed himself. William Wright lived in a world of unfulfilled ambitions, reaching for elusive dreams, his daughter Maginel wrote, that "remained a shadow all his life."[19] His career was poignant proof that the safety valve of the American West was sometimes closed.

Children usually detect uneasiness between their parents. When discontent burst to the surface of his family's life, the sensitive Frank Lloyd Wright must have been aware of it. He could not have been

Figure 1.2 William C. Wright, 1904. Courtesy University of Wisconsin Archives.

oblivious to the breakdown in parental relations after 1883, when he turned sixteen. He must have noticed that his mother "hated the very ground" his father walked upon. He must have been puzzled by his father's moodiness and withdrawal. But nineteenth-century teenagers were even more likely than today's to brood about such things rather than confront their parents directly, and many times young Frank could hardly be pulled from the security of his attic "sanctum." It was Anna, of course, who answered all the questions he finally asked about his parents' life together and his father's disappearance, apparently to his satisfaction, for he accepted her version of the episode without reservation. And her interpretation, most likely in self-defense, departed significantly from the facts.[20]

After years of suffering through financial hardship and William's self-absorption and lack of interest in her and the children, Anna told her son, she reluctantly asked him to leave, hoping he would find the initiative to change his ways. Instead, he took the opportunity to walk out, leaving her family "deeply grieved, shamed." She never stopped believing William would return and wondered what "crime" she had committed to be "punished" so cruelly. In actuality, of course, Anna had been the defendant against a lonely and frustrated husband who had apparently clung to a deteriorating relationship long after it was salvageable. But Anna, unsympathetic, proud, and unwilling to admit her part in the breakup, told her son that *she* was the plaintiff, charging William with desertion in the desperate hope he would come back. Emotionally broken, she suffered the public disgrace of a divorce, Anna said, in court and forever after.

Frank Lloyd Wright accepted this version for a number of reasons. He never saw his father again after 1885. Except for periods of several months at a time, he continued to live with or near his mother until her death in 1923 and had ample opportunity to absorb her interpretation without hearing his father's side of the story, But more important, he had a *need* to accept Anna's views because they so easily (and so perfectly) acted as a psychological anchor in his own life.

In 1926, when he wrote the sections of his autobiography dealing with his parents, Wright was a fugitive from the law avoiding arrest under the Mann Act (see Chapter Seven). Since 1909 he had been involved in a series of highly publicized love affairs. He had been divorced once, married twice, lived with three women, and was linked with yet a fourth companion. Far from apologizing or feeling remorse for his behavior, he believed himself persecuted by an intolerant society. Until she died, his mother was one of the few people who seemed to understand, was sympathetic, and remained loyal and supportive. Not only had she given him land to build a home for his first paramour, but she later shared that home with him and his second. Just as Anna had suffered through her "persecution," so had he been publicly condemned for doing what he felt was right. Just as she had been "punished" for her courage, so had he been ostracized for acting openly and honestly. As Wright saw it, he and his mother has suffered similar, unjust fates, and the parallel between their lives was a certain solace. Identifying with Anna's interpretation of her marital difficulties gave him a crutch to lean on during his own.[21]

Despite Anna's continuing presence, William C. Wright had a considerable impact on his son. Much has been inferred about the influence on Wright of the English cathedral pictures Anna reputedly placed in young Frank's nursery and of the Froebel games she gave him in Weymouth. Critics searching for childhood sources of Wright's architectural inspiration have stressed the Froebel system, partly because Wright acknowledged it himself and partly because of the powerful geometry of his designs. There is little doubt that Wright's kindergarten experiences were every bit as crucial to his aesthetic development as his later work with Louis Sullivan (see pages 19–24). But critics invariably overlook Wright's obligation to music, which in his autobiography he discussed *before* any other source of inspiration. While position on a page may not indicate priority of importance, it is likely that Wright's sensitivity to structure, form, and composition owed as much to music as to other influences. In adult life music was a constant source of relaxation and a major activity at his architectural school. He often urged clients to include space for pianos and, without being asked, actually designed in one plan a wedge-shaped addition on a house façade to accommodate a baby grand.[22] Wright often compared music to architecture: "an edifice—of sound!" was a favorite metaphor. There are clear parallels between the horizontal progression of his designs—"plasticity," he called it—and the rhapsodic flow of Beethoven, his favorite composer, and between his geometric, and Bach's musical, symmetry.

The influence of William C. Wright's music must have been profound if in the 1950s the architect could tell his sister:

I dreamed of Father during my nap. Just this afternoon. I was in a dark place. . .in the Weymouth Church, the chamber for the organ bellows. I was pumping away and pumping away. Father was playing Bach. I heard it, Sis, in the dream, very distinctly, every note as he used to play it. My God, Bach required a lot of air! I had to pump like the devil, and woke up tired![23]

Although the negative associations of paternal tyranny and back-breaking labor ("in a dark place"!) remained throughout Wright's life, they were overshadowed by the happy memories of the music he had helped create as a boy and of playing viola in the family orchestra. Equally exciting, Wright recalled, was Victor Hugo's comparison of Gothic cathedrals with musical forms, a comparison he might not have appreciated but for his father. Anna's Froebelian kindergarten was undoubtedly a significant factor in Wright's attraction to architecture, but his father's music was at least of comparable importance.

That William C. Wright's legacy to his son stemmed in part from his failures as a parent and from his absence, not his presence, in the household does not make it any the less profound. That the boy had a mother to sustain him did not obviate his father's impact. William's scholarly habits, reinforced by Anna's interests, certainly encouraged Frank to take intellect seriously, but it was his father's frequent withdrawals into himself that forced the youngster (not unwillingly) to rely on his own resources. Letting his imagination wander, he began to develop creative abilities, learning early in life the meaning of independence and personal responsibility. The atmosphere William Wright created, furthermore, was probably as influential as his personality. His insensitivity and authoritarian manner helped weaken family mutuality, while his constant wandering compounded its instability. Later on, Frank Lloyd Wright's architecture made obvious and sustained attempts to correct these very conditions (see Chapter Two).

As an adult, Wright evidenced a number of his father's personality traits. Both men were exceptionally restless, always discontent with their living arrangements, constantly moving from one locale to another. The architect, moreover, was never satisfied with his own homes, forever tearing down, redesigning, and rebuilding them. Neither had a common sense of economic practicality; the elder Wright was financially inept, the younger an impulsive spendthrift (possibly in reaction). Both were highly ambitious, allowing personal fulfillment to take precedence over family obligations; both regarded children as intrusions on their work. Son like father placed a premium on privacy, to which Frank devoted considerable attention in his own and his clients homes, especially after 1911 (see Chapters Six, Seven, and Nine). Both men found it essential periodically to withdraw into personal retreats—in the mind or in the study—invariably to emerge eager to perform for appreciative audiences. Frank Lloyd Wright was only seventeen when he saw his father for the last time, but he always remained his father's son.

After the divorce in 1885, probably with the assistance of his employer, Professor Allan D. Conover, Wright entered the University of Wisconsin. According to his transcript, he studied a "scientific" curriculum but in his first semester, from January through March 1886, took only French, for which he was not given a grade. In his September-to-December term he received "average" marks in descriptive geometry and drawing, the only courses he carried. As a "member of the class of 1889," he joined the "U. W. Association of Engineers" and Phi Delta Theta fraternity. Almost nothing else is known of Wright's college year—his only one—which ended in December 1886. He continued working part-time at $35 a month in Professor Conover's architectural office, doing odd jobs on various building projects including a minor supervisory role on the University's Science Hall for which Conover was in part responsible.[24]

Wright received additional experience during 1886 from a source close to the Lloyd Jones family. Joseph Lyman Silsbee, a prominent Chicago architect of Queen Anne residences, designed All Souls

Church for Wright's Uncle Jenkin in June 1885. Early in 1886 Silsbee produced a plan for the Joneses Unity Chapel at Helena (really Hill-side), Wisconsin. The building was completed in August, and its rendering, published in the January 1887 *Annual* of All Souls Church (Fig. 1.3), bore the signature "F. L. Wright, Del[ineator]," who had more important responsibilities on the job than that. According to William C. Gannett, a noted Unitarian divine and Lloyd Jones friend, the chapel's three-room interior was "looked after" by "a boy architect belonging to the family."[25] It is therefore likely that when young Wright moved to Chicago early in 1887, after his fall semester in college, he knew where to find a job.

Wright claimed in his autobiography that, reluctant to exploit a family connection, he took a position with Silsbee only as a last resort, failing to find work at five other architectural offices. And even then, he wrote, Silsbee did not know who he was.[26] But at nineteen, with college not to his liking, financial difficulties at home, and an entree into the profession, there is every reason to believe that Wright went directly to Silsbee who knew him from work on Unity Chapel the year before. If Wright had absorbed only a smattering of his father's ambition or the Lloyd Jones drive for achievement, he would have been impatient to begin his career. Indeed, as soon as he took the job with Silsbee, he began moving along the clearly marked path to professional recognition. With his employer's acquiescence or with his en-

Figure 1.3 Unity Chapel (1886), Hillside, Wisconsin. From *Fourth Annual, All Souls Church, 1887.*

couragement, Wright published a sketch of a second Unitarian Chapel, at Sioux City, Iowa, in the June 1887 *Inland Architect and News Record* (Chicago), his first in a professional journal.

Wright's first five published renderings, in fact, appeared under his own name, not Silsbee's. There were four designs for his Helena Valley relatives—Unity Chapel (1886), two houses in *The Inland Architect* (August 1887 and February 1888), and the Hillside Home School (1887) in Uncle Jenkin's *Unity* (September 10, 1887)—and a fifth for the Sioux City chapel. It was common at the time for delineators and draughtsmen to moonlight, to accept independent work outside their employers' offices. Most architects objected, but apparently not Silsbee, at least in Wright's case. Perhaps as a favor to the Lloyd Joneses or because he especially liked the young man or recognized his budding talent, Silsbee gave Wright a good deal of latitude, permitting, maybe even encouraging, him to seize every opportunity to publicize his name.

There are three possible explanations for Wright's somewhat independent status in 1887. One is that the work he published as his own was really for Silsbee who let Wright take the credit. The second is that Silsbee allowed or encouraged his young employee to accept outside jobs, particularly for his own relatives but also at Sioux City. The third possibility is that Wright actually tried to establish himself as an independent architect or delineator in his own employ. The evidence for this is that the Sioux City chapel and one Helena residence were signed by "F. L." or "Frank L. Wright, Archt, Chicago, Ill." In addition he was listed in the 1887 *Lakeside City Directory* as an "architect," although in subsequent years he used the word "clerk." A sixth early drawing from the February 1888 *Inland Architect* of an Edgewater, Illinois, house for J. L. Cochrane, and a seventh for the same real estate development published later in the year, both signed by Silsbee and by Wright as "Del[ineator]," can be used to support either the first or the third possibilities.[27]

Precise conclusions about Wright's occupational arrangements during his first year or two in Chicago are further complicated by the fact that at no time did the city directory list him at Silsbee's address. His first entry, in 1887 as an "architect," was at Room 88, 175 Dearborn Street, the office of William W. Clay. In his autobiography Wright recalled that after "a few months" at Silsbee's he had gone to "Beers, Clay, and Dutton" for higher pay but, finding the work too advanced for him at that stage of his career, returned to his original employer "in a few weeks." The problem here is that the Beers, Clay, and Dutton partnership was not formed until 1890 or 1891, meaning that

Wright must have worked for Clay alone. In the 1888 directory "Frank L." was listed as a clerk without a business address, and in 1889 as "Frank," a clerk, at 66 North Clark Street where there were no architectural offices. Most historians believe that his two stints with Silsbee came to about a year in all, making it February 1888 when he signed on with Dankmar Adler and Louis H. Sullivan. But here again the city directory raises doubts. In 1887 and 1888 Adler and Sullivan were located in Room 56 of Adler's Borden Block on Randolph Street, moving in 1889 to the 16th floor of the firm's new Auditorium Building (1887–1889). Not until 1890 would Sullivan and Wright (listed as a "designer") both appear at that same address. Of course there is the possibility—based on the presumed design date of the Falkenau Houses discussed below—that in 1888 or 1889 the young "clerk" was working for Adler and Sullivan but not in their office.[28]

Whatever his occupational situation, those first few months in Chicago proved to be excellent training for Wright. Silsbee stimulated his interest in residential architecture, so much so that the influence of his skillfully conceived plans continued to appear in Wright's work until 1900. The office atmosphere must also have been exciting. Silsbee's employees included George W. Maher and George Elmslie, later prominent in their own right, as well as Cecil C. Corwin, with whom Wright became quite friendly. With these kinds of associates and the independence Silsbee permitted, Wright learned so quickly that by November 1887 he executed a commission of his own, the Hillside Home School (Fig. 1.4) for his aunts Ellen and Jane. Silsbee gave him time off to supervise construction.[29] At the age of twenty Wright had a building to his credit, testimony to the quality of training he had received in Madison and in Chicago.

Wright remembered working on plans for the Auditorium in Sullivan's Borden Block office, meaning that he could have left Silsbee's as late as the early part of 1889 before Sullivan moved into his new quarters. The Auditorium was a monumental project, and Wright was presumably hired as one of several new employees to develop detail sketches. Since beginning his career in 1879 Sullivan had designed a number of commercial structures which made him one of the city's most respected architects. During Wright's tenure he went on with Adler to produce some of his best work: the Schiller Building (1891–1892) and the Transportation Building for the 1893 Columbian Exposition in Chicago, the Wainright Building (1891) in St. Louis, and many more. These were exciting and supremely creative times for Sullivan as he approached the apogee of his career, and an exceptional opportunity for Wright who absorbed invaluable philosophical knowl-

Figure 1.4 Hillside Home School (1887), Hillside, Wisconsin. Courtesy State Historical Society of Wisconsin.

edge from countless conversations with "der Lieber Meister," as well as incomparable architectural training under the tutelage of both Sullivan and his brilliant engineer partner, Dankmar Adler.

But the relationship was not entirely that of master and pupil. Quickly recognizing Wright's rapidly developing abilities, Sullivan set him designing the few residential commissions the firm accepted to please its commercial clients. During business hours Wright worked on the theatres, warehouses, hotels, and office buildings that were Adler and Sullivan's *forte,* rising from a sketch developer to a draughtsman to head draughtsman with his own office by 1891 or 1892. At night—at the home he built for himself in 1889 at 428 Forest Avenue in suburban Oak Park after living in boarding houses at 3921 Vincennes Avenue in 1887 and 29 Thirty-Seventh Street in 1888—Wright designed the single and multiple residences Sullivan assigned. The design of the four Victor Falkenau party-wall houses (1888) in Chicago, one authority concludes, "constitutes the turning-point in the quality of Adler & Sullivan's domestic architecture." Their clean and simple forms, almost abstract decoration, and relaxed horizontality were the marks of a new distinction for which Sullivan, devoted to commercial work and to his philosophy of ornamentation, had little responsibility.

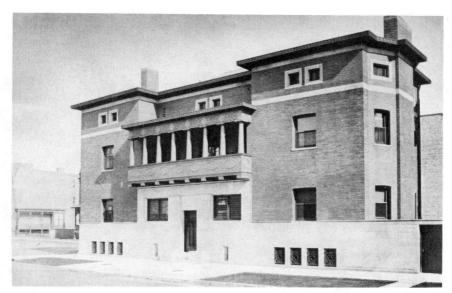

Figure 1.5 Charnley House (1892), Chicago. From *American Architect and Building News*, December 31, 1892.

As the rendering stated, the Falkenau houses came not from Sullivan's pen but from a new hand on the architectural scene, that of "Frank L. Wright."

Of the six or so houses Wright produced for Sullivan from 1888, presumably, until late 1892 or early 1893 when he left the firm, the most startling was for James Charnley (1892) in Chicago (Fig. 1.5). It was unlike anything built anywhere else, a thoroughly modern building with a clean horizontally oriented façade composed of broad, flat surfaces and deep contrasting reveals. Its exterior was a straightforward expression of its open, interpenetrating, horizontal and vertical interior spaces. The design, a specialist on Wright's early years contends, "was a spontaneous manifestation of a new and unfettered concept," toward which Sullivan "offered little or nothing of practical value."[30] Wright's success in this venture, his rapidly increasing interest and skill in residential architecture, and his struggle to meet the payments on his new home led him to moonlight. During the year or two after 1890 he designed approximately ten houses without his employer's knowledge (see Fig. 1.6). When Sullivan discovered the "bootlegged" ventures, as Wright called them, late in 1892 or early in 1893, his attitude was much different than Silsbee's. He disapproved angrily. Wright walked out or was fired and opened his own office in

Figure 1.6 George Blossom House (1892), left, and Warren McArthur House (1892), right, Chicago. Photo by author.

Room 1501 of the Schiller Building—a recent Sullivan opus on which he had worked—allowing his five-year contract to lapse.[31] For a time he shared the suite with Cecil Corwin, former office manager at Silsbee's, and did his draughting in Oak Park where he built a studio in 1895.

Wright's relationship with Sullivan was personally and professionally complex. Sullivan was thirty-one and a bachelor early in 1888 when the twenty-year-old Wright (Fig. 1.7) joined his firm. He came there in the first place because he correctly believed it to be the most exciting and progressive office in the city. For his part, based on the drawings Wright brought when he applied for the job and on their many late-night conversations, Sullivan saw exceptional promise in the young man. He also came to think of him as the son he never had, in the end an ungrateful one, while Wright apparently adopted Sullivan as a substitute father figure. But the father–son bond was never very stable because in some ways Wright was Sullivan's equal, even his superior. The Charnley House showed Wright to be the more imaginative residential architect with a great deal to teach the teacher, had he wanted to learn. (From 1893 to his death in 1924, Sullivan designed only two homes: for Henry Babson [1907] in Riverside, Illinois, and for Josephine Crane Bradley [1909] in Madison, Wisconsin, both of which

Figure 1.7 Frank Lloyd Weight, ca. 1889. With the permission of the Frank Lloyd Wright Home and Studio Foundation, Oak Park, Illinois.

reveal clear indebtedness to Wright's work after 1901.) If Sullivan grew jealous of Wright's unfolding talent, Wright became impatient with Sullivan's paternalistic and professional restrictions. Judging by the violent and abrupt end to their previously close relationship, and by their mutual refusal to see each other until after 1908 when Wright acknowledged his debt to Sullivan in a well-publicized magazine article,[32] the two suffered something akin to a family quarrel: both were so emotionally hurt that neither could take the first step toward reconciliation. The point was certainly reached when the one could no longer admit the other's importance, neither the senior architect at the top of the professional world nor the junior draughtsman eager for his own recognition. Wright had outgrown Sullivan's capacity to teach him. The time had come to go it alone. And so they parted, temporarily estranged.

The twenty-five-year-old architect launched his independent practice in 1893 with impressive credentials. As a delineator with Silsbee, one of Chicago's most popular practitioners, and as a draughtsman with Sullivan, then at the pinnacle of the profession, Wright had designed about twenty-five buildings on his own, of which twenty were executed, including seventeen residences, a hotel remodeling, a school, and a boathouse.[33] The Charnley House (1892) and others, including the home for Allison Harlan (1892) in Chicago, were remarkably fresh, notable for their crisp lines, broad clean surfaces, and their bold simplicity. Wright's several published renderings and his professional contacts enhanced his reputation, while his entry in the widely advertised competition for the Milwaukee Public Library and Museum in November 1893 also brought him useful publicity.[34] Most of Wright's buildings were derivative in grammar and style, but they were known to be thoughtfully designed and carefully executed. His architectural career at the end of 1893 looked promising indeed.

Wright's social life also acquired new dimensions after his arrival in Chicago. At Silsbee's he had met Cecil Corwin, who like their employer and the other draughtsmen was a minister's son. Wright later remembered that Corwin had the air of a cultured and sophisticated gentleman, qualities attracting the youngster from small-town Wisconsin. Perhaps the boy who had grown up with books, Bach, and Beethoven was destined to enjoy the finer things of life. For with Silsbee as a model and Corwin as a mentor, Wright began to attend concerts, improve his wardrobe, and, when he could afford it, dine in the better restaurants. Cecil's values were "similar to mine," Wright recalled, "yet he was different. And so much more developed. . . . So I began to go to school to Cecil." As a member of his Uncle Jenkin's All Souls Church he was introduced to the liberal Unitarian upper middle class, the source, as it turned out, of several early clients. He also met Catherine Lee Tobin, daughter of a prosperous businessman from the fashionable Kenwood district on the South Side. After a year or more of Wright's persistent wooing, the couple married on June 1, 1889, when he was twenty-one and she eighteen, moving into his newly designed home in a relatively unsettled section of suburban Oak Park, immediately west of Chicago.

Wright's marriage to Catherine is not without significance beyond the importance usually attached to such events. As his background indicates, Wright had come to Chicago with a noticeable lack of social experience. If he was not without a feeling for music and the arts, he had never before traveled in the urban upper middle class circles familiar to Corwin, Silsbee, Sullivan, and Uncle Jenkin. As far as women were concerned, Wright was less than a beginner, if that is possible. In his autobiography he recalled his lack of social poise, indeed, his colossal bumbling at a college dance where he was so shy that "the sight of a young girl would send him like a scared young stag, scampering back into his wood." In his later years Wright may have considered himself something of a ladykiller, and in his auto-biography exaggerated his early shyness to dramatize the rapidity with which he achieved rapport with the opposite sex (or to imply, in view of his several affairs, that he was not entirely a cad). Yet there is much truth in his claim to unfamiliarity with women.

For one thing he apparently rushed toward marriage with the first girl he ever seriously considered. Toward Catherine, it seems, it was love at first sight, and having made up his mind to marry her Wright would not be deterred, by her reluctance or by her parents' natural concern. Despite his inexperience and her youth, Catherine was a particularly apt choice. She understood the rules of etiquette and the social conventions of the very people who he knew hired architects. If the "social instinct" had been "left out of my education," as Wright correctly stated, it was hardly so with Catherine. As an independent girl she had long been trusted by her parents with considerable freedom. "Everything revolved around her," he noted. "Not only was she accustomed to having her own way but to having it without any trouble whatever." If the beginning of social poise involves learning to ma-nipulate one's family, Catherine was well schooled. As "a very sensible girl," furthermore, she forced Wright to save money and even before their marriage helped manage his finances. Unlike Wright, "she was sensitive and careful about things." "Where people were concerned," he admitted, "I had nearly everything yet to learn." To all indications, Catherine was just the person to navigate him through the unfamiliar waters.[35]

With Catherine to guide him socially, and with excellent architec-tural credentials and contacts, Wright launched his career in a rapidly growing metropolis, an ideal place for a young man with manifest skills in residential, and experience in commercial, design. By 1893 his buildings demonstrated that his apprentice years with Conover, Silsbee, and Sullivan had been fruitful. At least two—the houses for Charnley and Harlan—showed unusual verve and talent; the rest were carefully conceived and executed. Little about Wright at this time showed rebelliousness or eccentricity. To most people he was simply a "rising young architect of Chicago."[36]

NOTES

1 Biographical data on William C. Wright during his pre-Wisconsin years is in Abbie Whitaker, Comp., "A Copy of a Small Part of the Genealogy of the Wright Family," Jane Lloyd Jones Collection, Manuscripts Division, State Historical Society of Wisconsin (SHSW), Madison; *The First Half Century of Madison University, 1819-1869* (New York: Sheldon & Co., 1872), 295; Elmer Smith, Ed., *Colgate University: General Catalogue*, I (1937), 94; *Biographical Record of Amherst College Alumni*; Otis F. R. Waite, *History of the Town of Claremont, New Hampshire* (Manchester, N.H., 1895), 113; *Utica City Directory for 1851-52* (Utica, N.Y., 1851), 147.

2 *Richland County Observer* (Richland Center, Wis.), June 11, November 19, 1861; June 20, 1862; August 27, September 10, 24, October 1, November 19, 1863; *The Richland Zouave* (Richland Center, Wis.), October 19, 1861. Unless otherwise noted, all local newspapers used in this study are on deposit at SHSW. Also see James H. Miner, Ed., *History of Richland County, Wisconsin* (Madison: Western Historical Assoc., 1906), 169.

3 For sparse and somewhat unreliable information on Anna Lloyd Wright, see Frank Lloyd Wright, *An Autobiography* (New York: Duell, Sloan and Pearce, 1943 ed.), Book 1; Maginel Wright Barney, *The Valley of the God-Almighty Joneses* (New York: Appleton-Century, 1965), Ch. 7, quote from p. 62; and *The Weekly Home News* (Spring Green, Wis.), December 10, 17, 1885. *The Home News* is invaluable for Lloyd Jones family history. Also see *History of Iowa County, Wisconsin* (Chicago: Western Historical Society, 1881), 939; and George and Robert M. Crawford, Eds., *Memoirs of Iowa County Wisconsin*, I (Northwestern Historical Assoc., 1913), 261-262.

4 *Richland County Observer*, April 7, 28, May 19, 1864; March 2, May 11, 1865. On young Wright's correct birth date see Thomas S. Hines, Jr., "Frank Lloyd Wright—The Madison Years: Record versus Recollection," *The Wisconsin Magazine of History*, 50 (Winter 1967), 109-119. The 1867 birth date is corroborated by a copy from a page of Wright's wife Catherine's family record in the Frank Lloyd Wright Collection, Avery Library, Columbia University, New York, N.Y.

5 Frank Lloyd Wright, *An Autobiography*, 11.

6 "Architecture and Music," *The Saturday Review,* 40 (September 28, 1957), 72–73.

7 *Richland County Observer,* April 20, 27, 1865; October 1, 1866; *The Live Republican* (Richland Center, Wis.), May 16, July 4, 11, 18, 1867. For other aspects of Wright's career in town, see the *Richland County Observer,* August 27, 1861; June 30, 1864; February 9, 16, November 23, 1865; *The Live Republican,* February 7, 14, 1867; *The Richland Center Republican,* November 28, 1867; March 19, May 7, 1868; *Richland County Republican* (Richland Center, Wis.), May 21, 1868; January 14, 28, April 15, 1869.

8 Wright's McGregor career can be traced in *The Times* of that community (on deposit at the newspaper office): March 3, April 21, May 28, July 21, September 1, November 10, 17, 24, 1869; June 22, August 10, 1870; March 29, May 4, 1871. The two long quotations are from the May 17 and July 5, 1871, issues. Maginel's financial assessment is in M. W. Barney, *God-Almighty Joneses,* 63 (see note 3).

9 F. L. Wright, *An Autobiography,* 51; M. W. Barney, *God-Almighty Joneses,* 66.

10 Robert Grieve, *An Illustrated History of Pawtucket* (Pawtucket: The Gazette and Chronicle Co., 1897), 226–227; *Pawtucket Gazette and Chronicle,* November 24, 1871; October 4, 1872; January 23, 1874, on deposit at the American Antiquarian Society, Worcester, Mass., and at the Rhode Island Historical Society, Providence. Also see Richard M. Bayles, Ed., *History of Providence County, Rhode Island,* II (New York: W. W. Preston and Co., 1891), 76.

11 For the remainder of the Pawtucket years see the *Gazette and Chronicle,* April 6, October 18, 25, November 22, 28, December 6, 1872; February 7, March 7, 21, 28, April 4, 18, September 5, 12, 19, October 24, 31, December 12, 25, 1873; January 2, 23, August 28, September 4, 1874. On Wright's larger Baptist affiliations see *Forty-Seventh Annual Report of the Rhode Island Baptist State Convention* (Pawtucket: Nickerson & Sibley, 1872), 7, 19, 20, 26, 59, 60, 62, 63, 66; *Minutes of the Rhode Island Baptist Anniversaries, 1873* (Pawtucket: Nickerson & Sibley, 1873), 38, 69; and *Minutes. . .1874,* 36–37, 42. Wright's circular letter—his only known publication—is in *Minutes. . .1873,* 49–52.

12 F. L. Wright, *An Autobiography,* 11–16, quote from p. 11.

13 On the Froebel exercises see Grant Manson, "Wright in the Nursery: The Influence of Froebel Education on the Work of Frank Lloyd Wright," *The Architectural Review,* 113 (June 1953); Rich L. MacCormac, "The Anatomy of Wright's Aesthetic," *ibid.,* 143 (February 1968); Stuart Wilson, "The 'Gifts' of Friedrich Froebel," *Journal of the Society of Architectural Historians,* 26 (December 1967).

14 On the Weymouth years see its *Weekly Gazette:* September 4, October 30, December 4, 1874; June 11, September 24, October 8, 1875; October 12, 26, 1877; March 1, 15, 22, 29, 1878, on file at the Tufts Library, Weymouth. Also see Gilbert Nash, Comp., *Historical Sketch of the Town of Weymouth* (Weymouth: Weymouth Historical Society, 1885), 122; Howard H. Joy, Ed., *History of Weymouth Massachusetts*, 4 vols. (Weymouth: Weymouth Historical Society, 1923), I, 279–280; II, 864–865; *100th Anniversary—First Baptist Church of Weymouth* (1954); Records of the First Baptist Church, ledger pages 85–86. Unusual help and courtesy in gathering Weymouth material was extended to me by Mrs. Joan S. Green, Tufts Library.

15 *The Inter-County Times* (Spring Green and Lone Rock, Wis.), April 30, July 9, 1878; *The Times* (Spring Green, Wis.), October 28, 1881; *The Dollar Times* (Spring Green, Wis), August 12, 1879; *Spring Green News*, November 4, 11, 1881; January 13, 27, February 10, 24, April 21, June 14, 21, 1882; *The Weekly Home News*, August 28, October 9, 1884. Wright was first listed in the *Madison City Directory* in 1880. On Wright's Unitarian associations see *Unity*, the organ of the Western Unitarian Conference, edited by Jenkin Lloyd Jones: 3 (June 1, 1879), 194–196; 4 (December 1, 1879), 299; 4 (December 16, 1879), 314–315; 5 (June 16, 1880), 128; 7 (March 1, 1881), 11; 7 (May 16, 1881), 106; 8 (September 16, 1881), 271; 9 (August 13, 1882), 234; 14 (September 1, 1884), 274; 15 (May 23, 1885), 140; 15 (July 11, 1885), 241.

16 F. L. Wright, *An Autobiography*, 30–38; M. W. Barney, *God-Almighty Joneses*, 70–74.

17 See T. S. Hines, Jr., "The Madison Years," 113–116. On Conover see *Madison, Past and Present, 1852–1902* (Madison: Wisconsin State Journal, 1902), 139.

18 On the divorce see T. S. Hines, Jr., "The Madison Years," 111–112, which quotes State of Wisconsin, Circuit Court for Dane County, "William C. Wright *vs.* Anna L. Wright," April 1885. After leaving Madison the peripatetic William C. Wright renewed his law practice in Wahoo, Nebraska, lived in Omaha from 1890 to 1892, directed the Central Conservatory of Music in Stromsberg, Nebraska, until 1895, then wandered from St. Joseph, Missouri, to Des Moines to Perry, Iowa, to York, Nebraska, before arriving in Pittsburgh in 1902 where he died on June 16, 1904, at age 79: Smith, *Colgate University: General Catalogue*, 1 (1937), 94. He was buried at Richland Center, Wisconsin, where a rather impressive monument marks his grave.

19 M. W. Barney, *God-Almighty Joneses*, 64.

20 Anna's version is in F. L. Wright, *An Autobiography*, 48–51.

21 Wright's relations with women from 1909 through the 1920s will be discussed in Chapters 4, 5, and 7.

22 The Quentin Blair House (1953), Cody, Wyoming: verbal communication between Mrs. Blair and the author, August 1965.

23 M. W. Barney, *God-Almighty-Joneses*, 12.

24 T. S. Hines, Jr., "The Madison Years," 115–117.

25 The rendering of Unity Chapel, Wright's first published drawing, appeared in *Fourth Annual, All Souls Church, 1887* (Chicago, January 6, 1887); his role in the construction is mentioned in William C. Gannett, "Christening a Country Church," *Unity*, 17 (August 28, 1886), 356–357. The design and erection of this important building in Wright's career can be followed in *Unity*, 16 (October 3, 1885), 62–63; 17 (June 5, 1886), 193; 17 (June 12, 1886), 222; 17 (July 31, 1886), 314; 17 (August 7, 1886), 327; and in *The Weekly Home News*, August 20, 1885.

26 F. L. Wright, *An Autobiography*, 65–68. Also see Susan Karr Sorell, "Silsbee: The Evolution of a Personal Architectural Style," and "A Catalog of Work by J. L. Silsbee," *The Prairie School Review*, 7 (Fourth Quarter 1970), 5–13, 17–21.

27 There is a peculiar fascination among scholars with Wright's first year in Chicago. For the latest views and reproductions of his first seven published drawings, see Wilbert A. Hasbrouck, "The Earliest Work of Frank Lloyd Wright," *The Prairie School Review*, 7 (Fourth Quarter, 1970), 14–16; Eileen Michels, "The Early Drawings of Frank Lloyd Wright Reconsidered," *Journal of the Society of Architectural Historians*, 30 (December 1971), 294–303; and Curtis Besinger, "Comment on [Michel's article]," *ibid.*, 31 (October 1972), 216–220.

It has not been emphasized sufficiently that Wright's rendering of the Hillside Home School in *Unity* (September 18, 1887), minus a porch and with a redrawn tree, is the same as the Helena Valley house from the February 1888 *Inland Architect*. By publishing the drawing a second time with only the slightest changes, Wright seems to have been quite entrepreneurial about advertising his name.

28 See F. L. Wright, *An Autobiography*, 73–74, and *The Lakeside Directory of Chicago* for 1887 through 1891. Beers and Clay had different addresses, and there was no mention of an architect named Dutton, until the partnership was first listed in 1891, the year the firm's projects began to appear in *Inland Architect*.

29 *The Weekly Home News*, November 10, 1887, also remarked, somewhat prophetically, that "Mr. Wright is an able young artist, and if all had a 'barrel of money' with which to carry out his attractive mansion and cottage plans they might be happy yet."

Construction of the Hillside Home School, an historically curious if not important building since it was Wright's first, can be traced in *The Weekly Home News*, July 7, August 18, November 10, 1887; *Unity*, 20 (September 3, 1887), 6–7; 20 (September 10, 1887), 13. The earliest informative description appeared in *Unity*, 21 (August 18, 1888), 328–329: "the building does credit to the young architect nephew who planned it," while possibly the first published photographs are in an intriguing item in possession of SHSW entitled *Hillside Calendar, 1895*, a folder with views of the school and surrounding countryside and with hand-drawn decorations "Made by

Frank Lloyd Wright." SHSW also has *The Hillside Home School: Eight Years, 1895–96* (and similarly titled pamphlets for other years), including photographs of the reception room, parlors, and gymnasium, and of Unity Chapel, perhaps the first depiction of that structure.

More than one report noted that the Hillside Home School was already too small when it opened in the fall of 1887. Ground was broken for a new wing in 1888, and for a gymnasium and separate teacher's cottage in 1892. Although there is no way to be sure that Wright designed the additions, the local paper observed in December 1892 that "the gymnasium appliances are so arranged that they can be raised to the ceiling when not in use, and the hall can be used for dancing," just the sort of facility the young architect might have dreamed up. See *Unity*, 21 (August 18, 1888), 328–329; *The Weekly Home News*, September 8, December 15, 1892.

30 Grant Manson, "Sullivan and Wright: An Uneasy Union of Celts," *The Architectural Review*, 118 (November 1955), 297–300. For Wright on Sullivan see F. L. Wright, *An Autobiography*, 89–104, 107–109, 110–111.

31 It is still not exactly clear when Wright opened his own office. His friend, Robert C. Spencer, Jr., reported in 1900 that Wright secured the commission for the William H. Winslow House (River Forest, Ill.) "in the third year of his independent practice": "The Work of Frank Lloyd Wright," *The Architectural Review*, 7 (June 1900), 65. Most sources date this commission 1893, which would mean that Wright was working for himself in 1890 or 1891. (Perhaps Spencer was referring to the "bootlegged" homes Wright designed around that time.) Actually, the Winslow commission was first announced in June 1894 in *The Inland Architect* and in the Oak Park, Illinois, *Reporter* on June 8, moving the start of Wright's independent career ahead to 1891 or 1892. Even this date seems too early, yet Spencer was in a position to know.

Grant C. Manson, who has researched the early years most thoroughly, maintains that Wright opened his own office in 1893. From 1890 to 1892 he was listed in the *Lakeside City Directory* of Chicago at 1600 Auditorium Building—Adler and Sullivan's. In the 1893 directory Wright's address changed to the Schiller Building, his office as an independent: *Frank Lloyd Wright to 1910: The First Golden Age* (New York: Reinhold Pub. Corp., 1958), 215. When his drawings for municipal boathouses won a Madison, Wisconsin, competition in May 1893, Wright was described as "a former Madison boy, now a Chicago architect," without mention of Sullivan: *Wisconsin State Journal*, May 12, 1893. The conclusion seems to be that Wright had opened his own office at 1501 Schiller no later than May 1893.

32 "In the Cause of Architecture," *The Architectural Record*, 23 (March 1908), 155–222.

33 For compiling Wright's designs on a year-by-year basis, Henry-Russell Hitchcock, *In the Nature of Materials: The Buildings of Frank Lloyd Wright*,

1887–1941 (New York: Duell, Sloan and Pearce, 1942), 107–130, is more accurate than Olgivanna Lloyd Wright, *Frank Lloyd Wright: His Life, His Work, His Word* (New York: Horizon Press, 1967), 206–222, a highly doctored list. I have used this study to compute the number of Wright's designs during certain time periods, making allowance for its many errors in attributing dates. At appropriate places in the text, notes, and bibliography I have made additions and corrections.

34 Young Wright, who thought that "the site and purpose of the [Milwaukee Library and Museum] afforded a most excellent opportunity for the exercise of the highest skill in architecture," struck a dissenting note in his first known interview when he "expressed surprise at the inexperience shown by many of the plans": *The Milwaukee Journal,* November 21, 1893.

35 Wright's comments on Corwin are in F. L. Wright, *An Autobiography,* 67–69, 75; the quotation is on page 70. On Catherine and other women see *ibid.,* 48, 77–78, 85–89. Their marriage date is confirmed by a copy of a page from Catherine's family record in the FLW Collection, Avery Library.

36 *The Weekly Home News,* April 12, 1888.

1893–1901

CHAPTER TWO

The Art and Craft of Success

I n his early years of independent practice, Frank Lloyd Wright plotted a prudent course. Although he followed proscribed avenues to professional recognition, he did not attempt to launch a career by berating his colleagues. Critical of the architectural establishment at times, he was not particularly rebellious. He was as interested in the nature of the family and a philosophy of architecture as he was in acquiring wealth and fame. In 1901, when he integrated his metaphysical probings with his understanding of family life, he produced a startling synthesis called the "prairie house" which soon became immensely consequential for international architecture. Before then, he proceeded with all deliberate speed.

□ □ □

Frank Lloyd Wright consciously or unconsciously chose a mate who could guide him through the intricate social webs and priorities imposed by his profession. Similarly, by instinct or design, he moved to an expanding upper middle class community that needed and could appreciate his services. Wright accurately described Oak Park, Illinois, as a suburb "which denies Chicago." It held a high opinion of itself: its residents were *Oak Parkers*, not Chicagoans, though many worked in the city. Oak Parkers were white, Protestant, provincial, exclusive, and prosperous. Dissociating themselves from urban corruption, they were happy that Austin Street, separating the city from their "dry" suburb, was the point, as Congregational minister Bruce Barton put it, where "the saloons stop and the church steeples begin."[1]

In 1893, about the time Wright opened his practice, his immediate neighborhood was singled out as an example of Oak Park's progress and expansion. Houses had never gone up so rapidly, a local newspaper boasted; but they were occupied so quickly that there was often a shortage. One of Wright's own designs, in fact, was mentioned as typical of the community's dramatic growth.[2] His buildings were soon very typical indeed in Oak Park, where by 1901 he had built eighteen and by 1909, twenty-nine. Today the houses lining the streets of his neighborhood constitute a museum of his architecture; at the time they represented excellent publicity in a profession ethically bound not to advertise.

Wright faced a number of social obligations in the suburbs he could not, and chose not, to ignore. He was careful, in fact, to observe important upper middle class conventions. Living in a fashionable community, he joined the tennis club in adjacent River Forest, even more fashionable. The year after he opened his practice he began speaking to civic organizations, and in 1900 appeared in print for the first time. He contributed to Oak Park's newspapers, competed in the annual Chicago Horse Show, dined at the best restaurants, and wore expensive clothes. He became an art connoisseur, loading his home with rugs, vases, and hangings, particularly from the Orient. He patronized the theatre, concerts, and museums, often in parties with well-to-do clients, some of whom accompanied the Wrights to Japan in 1905 on their first trip abroad. Wright joined the esoteric Caxton Club, devoted to the admiration and preservation of rare books and bindings, and was a charter member of Daniel H. Burnham's and Hamlin Garland's Cliff Dwellers, a "congenial Chicago 'club,'" Wright called it, for artist and literary folk. He kept expensive riding horses and, as soon as automobiles were readily available, drove only the latest and best models. In view of his subsequent antiurban diatribes it is important to note that during these years and for another decade no one enjoyed metropolitan pleasures more than Frank Lloyd Wright.

Catherine Wright gave teas, luncheons, and afternoon musicales. She joined and spoke to local cultural associations, ran her own kindergarten—still something of an avant-garde endeavor in the 1890s— and with her husband was a member of All Souls Unitarian Church. As fashion dictated, she summered in Wisconsin where Wright joined her on weekends and of course sent some of her children to Hillside, the progressive boarding school run by Ellen and Jane Lloyd Jones. She was known in Oak Park as an excellent hostess. The Wrights' most signal observances of the social amenities, in fact, maximizing their good name in the community, were their parties. Father had "clam-bakes, tea parties in his studio, cotillions in the large drafting room," his son John remembered. "There were parties somewhere all of the time and everywhere some of the time." Wright's mother and sisters, who lived next door on Forest Avenue, held their own parties in his children's playroom. People liked to gather around him, leaving little doubt of his popularity. As a local newspaper remarked in 1901, "Mr. Wright is held in high esteem by his neighbors."[3]

So too was his architecture. Far from being ridiculed and rejected, as he often insisted, his buildings were well received from the start. The façade of Wright's own 1889 home may have had "no particular character," a critic for The House Beautiful, soon an influential Mid-western magazine concluded in 1897, but inside everything "appears to the best effect. . . . There is no discordant note to break the restful feeling induced by the interior." Two years later when another re-viewer for the same publication returned to inspect Wright's 1895 studio, he could hardly contain his enthusiasm: "It is refreshing to come in contact with a genius so fresh, so truthful, and so full of vitality." The prestigious Architectural Review, commenting in 1900 on photographs of Wright's work in The Inland Architect, praised it as "extraordinarily interesting. One may condemn," it added, "but one is driven to admire. Here is originality and unquestionable genius. Good or bad. . .the work is full of intense personality."[4]

From 1893 through 1901, Wright produced seventy-one designs of which forty-nine were built, an average of eight commissions and five and one half completions a year. Among the latter were three apart-ment projects in Chicago, a golf clubhouse for River Forest, and a scattering of boathouses and stables. Francisco Terrace (1895), built for Chicago real estate speculator Edward C. Waller, was a two-story block around an interior court entered through a beautiful Sulli-vanesque arch, an imaginative venture in multiresidence architecture intended for young married couples. Although most of his work was homes in the greater Chicago area, he received commissions from as far away as Buffalo, Los Angeles, and Texas. His reputation was pri-marily regional but his publication in 1901 of two articles in Ladies Home Journal indicated that this would not be true for long.

From the beginning Wright took a familiar route to architectural recognition. He did not pretend that talent alone would get him ahead; it was important to make connections. But he also valued the stimulation of vigorous colleagues. Like other young professionals he was quick to associate with an organization, in his case the Chicago

Architectural Club. As soon as he did so in 1894, he was put on a committee with Irving K. Pond and W. B. Mundie to select the winner of an "Art Club" competition in Classic or Renaissance style. Naturally eager to display his work, he participated in the Club's annual exhibitions in 1894, 1895, 1898, and 1900. In 1899 he spoke on "The Practical Nature of the Artistic," and in June with several members he attended the founding convention of the Architectural League of America in Cleveland. With James Gamble Rogers he judged the 1901 competition for "A United States Embassy in a European Capital," the same year the Club printed his now famous speech, "The Art and Craft of the Machine," delivered at Jane Addams' Hull House on March 6.[5] Despite all these activities, Wright never joined the Chicago Architectural Club. But he used it well.

Newcomers to the profession traditionally enter competitions in the hope of instant fame, and Wright was no exception. His 1893 entry for a Milwaukee library and museum failed to win, but he was selected the same year to design two boathouses for Madison, Wisconsin, although only one was built. In 1898 he submitted a drawing to the Luxfer Prism Company's $2000 contest for an office building but withdrew it when he, along with Daniel H. Burnham, W. L. B. Jenney, and William Holabird, was placed on the judging panel. Although Robert C. Spencer, Jr., eventually won, Wright's scheme was published anonymously in *The Inland Architect*, where illustrations of his work appeared on the average of once a year. Wright also spoke to both civic and professional groups. His first lecture seems to have been in 1894 before the University Guild of Evanston, Illinois, to which he returned two years later. In October 1897 he gave one of the regular Sunday evening talks at Hull House. Between 1893 and 1901 he lectured publicly at least six times.[6]

If the notion that Wright consistently avoided organizational activities is not entirely accurate, neither is the companion assertion that he always worked alone. After he left Adler and Sullivan he shared offices in 1894 and 1895 with Cecil Corwin in Room 1501 of the Schiller Building. Corwin left the city in 1895, the same year Robert C. Spencer, Jr., moved into Room 1503 next door. Wright did his designing in Oak Park, and whether he ever collaborated, especially with Spencer who agreed with many of his ideas, is unknown. In 1898 Wright, Spencer, and George R. Dean were selected by the Central Art Association "to design a home which may be considered typical of American architecture" for the Trans-Mississippi Exposition.[7] Wright and Dwight H. Perkins developed a new All Souls Church for Jenkin Lloyd Jones in 1898–1899 but both later dissociated themselves from the project.

Spencer, Perkins, and Myron Hunt joined Wright to open a common business office in Room 1107 of Steinway Hall on Van Buren Street in 1897, but in 1898 Wright moved by himself to 1119 in The Rookery (1888), a Burnham and Root opus in which Daniel Burnham still practiced. Wright moved again in 1899 to Room 1104 but by 1901 was back in Steinway, this time in 1106 quite near Perkins and Spencer (Hunt had left) who now shared space with Adamo Boari and Arthur H. Niemz. Although the young architects apparantly designed separately, "it was a lively association," a noted historian has written, "with all participating in each other's work." Along with several more Steinway tenants and others not in the building Wright helped form "The Eighteen," a dinner group meeting regularly for a number of years around the turn of the century. Their stimulating and mutually supportive ideas helped Wright formulate his theories which, more than anyone else's, served as the philosophical basis of "The New School of the Middle West," as he later called this group of friends.[8] Wright may have returned to Steinway precisely to strengthen these ties but he also came to enter "into copartnership with [Webster Tomlinson with] studios in Oak Park" (Fig. 2.1). Scholars disagree on whether the two actually collaborated during their several months association, but since they shared a studio, it is possible they did.[9] Finally, in 1906, Wright and two other members designed new quarters for the River Forest Tennis Club. Usually the lone wolf in his later self-assessments, Wright was quite happy not to have started that way.[10]

His professional reputation reached enviable heights in 1900. His thirteen drawings (including three of All Souls Church with Perkins) in the Thirteenth Annual Exhibition of the Chicago Architectural Club were deemed by *American Architect and Building News* "a very attractive group of houses." Robert C. Spencer, Jr., wrote that of all the work on display, Wright's was "the most unique and interesting individual architectural effort."[11] He appeared in print for the first time in May when his letter on the debate over whether architects should place "progress before precedent" was included in an article by George R. Dean in *The Brickbuilder*. The next month *Brickbuilder* published the full text of his speech, "The Architect," delivered in Chicago to the Second Annual Convention of the Architectural League of America.[12]

But the most important event of the year was Spencer's feature article in the June 1900 issue of *Architectural Review* entitled "The Work of Frank Lloyd Wright." Dozens of illustrations and plans showed his efforts in their very best light, and the text praised him

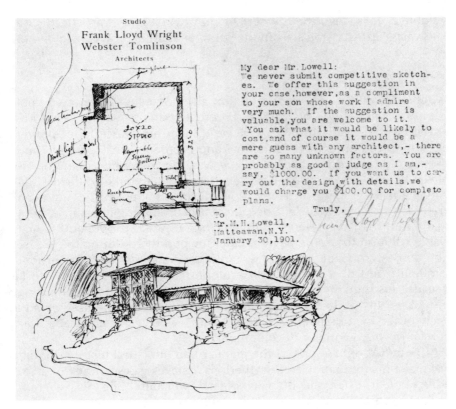

Studio
Frank Lloyd Wright
Webster Tomlinson
Architects

My dear Mr. Lowell:
We never submit competitive sketches. We offer this suggestion in
your case, however, as a compliment
to your son whose work I admire
very much. If the suggestion is
valuable, you are welcome to it.
You ask what it would be likely to
cost, and of course it would be a
mere guess with any architect, - there
are so many unknown factors. You are
probably as good a judge as I am, -
say, $1000.00. If you want us to car-
ry out the design, with details, we
would charge you $100.00 for complete
plans.

Truly,

To
Mr. M. H. Lowell,
Matteawan, N.Y.
January 30, 1901.

Figure 2.1 Frank Lloyd Wright to M. H. Lowell, January 30, 1901, during Wright's brief partnership with Webster Tomlinson. Courtesy Avery Library, Columbia University.

exuberantly. "Few architects have given us more poetic translations of material into structure than Frank Lloyd Wright," Spencer testified. "To those who understand and know him best," he was, though barely thirty-three years old, "a perpetual inspiration."[13] This high praise in a leading journal gave Wright's career an immense boost and may in fact have led in 1901 to his publication of two illustrated articles in *The Ladies Home Journal* and of a third—a scheme for a small bank—in *The Brickbuilder*.[14] His 1901 speech at Hull House, where he had been a member of the Chicago Arts and Crafts Society since its founding in 1897, together with the magazine articles by and about him, has led one scholar to note "the authority with which he already spoke in these early years."[15] If "authority" somewhat exaggerates Wright's influence, it is nevertheless certain that by 1901 he was one of the Midwest's fastest rising stars in the younger architectural constellation.

□ □ □

Behind Wright's growing reputation giving it a substance to compel attention was a body of work and a creative mind that made an important leap forward in 1901. For it was then he announced the "prairie house," pronounced it a functional and aesthetic breakthrough, and proceeded to build it. Nineteen one was the year when many of his ideas, beliefs, and even guesses jelled in a remarkable synthesis, signaling the beginning of a new episode in his life and in American architecture. That episode, a decade of artistic and intellectual ferment that Grant Manson called Wright's "Golden Age," produced his first viable solution to problems he repeatedly pondered during the 1890s: how to design residences that would preserve and strengthen proper family life and how best to utilize modern technology in that effort. Because his thinking on the nature of the family was confused during the 1890s, his early homes sometimes contradicted themselves and each other in fundamental ways. But his work in that decade was crucial for his own later development.

Although Wright is one of the giants of architectural history, he did not make his reputation from cathedrals, palaces, skyscrapers, or state edifices. Corbusier had his Chandigarh, van der Rohe his Seagram Building, and Walter Gropius his Bauhaus, and they all had much more. But in Wright's canon it is not a handful of magnificent monuments that is most striking (although that handful is a large one) but a continuous and almost compulsive effort to build the perfect house.

During his seventy-two-year career, an overwhelming number of his almost eight hundred designs, close to six hundred, were residences. His first executed building in 1887 was a "home school," and virtually his last commission, accepted a week before he died in 1959, was for a meager $3000 summer cottage.[16] After his Usonian homes of the late 1930s and early 1940s, Wright could make no further *conceptual* contributions to the sociology of residential design and with his several multimillion-dollar commissions in the 1950s did not need the small fees from houses. The reason for his continuing interest—despite his international reputation and his many lucrative projects—lies elsewhere, in an autobiographical as well as a professional imperative.

His early and perpetual fascination with residential architecture had several sources. J. L. Silsbee's encouragement and Louis Sullivan's decision to turn his few house commissions over to Wright may have stirred an interest compounded by his obvious talent and quick successes in the field. The growing demand for homes among Chicago's rapidly expanding upper middle class during the 1890s when he was starting out was surely important. But the major impulse was probably more a personal instinct than a tactical consideration: his own family history played a central role in his attraction to residential work. It is quite likely that his disrupted late adolescence helped stimulate an interest in the nature of the family and that his subsequent marital frustrations kept that interest alive.

Frank Lloyd Wright's childhood had been a contradictory mixture of family patterns and relationships. In his immediate household, his minister father was very much a detached disciplinarian of Victorian mold, insisting on order, decorum, and dignity at home while keeping distant from his children. Both of Wright's parents, with their strong religious attitudes, believed in the sanctity of the household, Anna in a real sense, William as an abstraction. But their divorce during Wright's mid-teens dramatized the hostilities, even hatreds, that lurked beneath the surface, hatreds the Victorian family was loathe to admit. The experience, illuminating as well as shattering for young Wright, who may have been forced even then to contemplate the nature of the institution, was entirely in keeping with the character of his own nuclear family.

For one thing, Wright's father devoted increasingly greater attention to his career than to his wife and children, leaving his son relatively free to pursue his own interests. The family, furthermore, was notably disunited. Although Frank had three stepsiblings (the oldest could not have been over fifteen at Frank's birth) and two sisters, he never mentioned the former and hardly mentioned the latter in his autobiographical writings. As he described it, his family had only three members: a withdrawn, imperious father; a warm, loving mother; and himself. His parents seemed to exist only for him. While this may be nothing more than another example of his legendary ego, it also reveals that Wright remembered his family as a fragmented collection of independent individuals rather than as members of a mutually supportive group.

The principle lesson Wright seems to have learned from his early years was self-reliance. Anna encouraged it but William made it necessary. In his autobiography he described things *he* did, alone or with friends, but hardly anything his family did together, a significant omission for what it tells about his childhood. When his parents divorced in 1885, he and his mother grew closer, forcing him to assume adult responsibilities as the only male in the household. After his move to

Chicago and until her death in 1923, Anna depended heavily on her son, his 1889 marriage notwithstanding. These obligations helped Wright develop a sense of self even stronger than when his father's real and symbolic absences from home left him to his own devices. His early independence and his family's household atmosphere may have encouraged him at times to seek the safety of personal withdrawal, but he came to understand that withdrawal could develop into the kind of reclusiveness that had destroyed his family's character. When Wright began to design homes he purposefully emphasized the importance of group togetherness.

Wright was fortunate to have had intimate childhood contact with another kind of family, one saturated with the mutuality and supportiveness lacking at home. The Lloyd Joneses, with whom he summered, presumably from 1878 to 1886, were a large, prosperous group with vigorous Welsh traditions and a strong feeling of camaraderie. They valued their individuality but not at the expense of group loyalty. As free-thinking Unitarians of decided intellectual bent on the American frontier, they assumed a collectively defensive posture symbolized by their motto, "Truth Against the World." The Lloyd Joneses became political, social, and economic leaders in their part of Wisconsin, working, worshipping, and living so closely together that they and their neighbors referred to them in Old World terms as a "clan." Wright believed his summers at Hillside to have been the best part of his youth, of crucial importance for his later development. Until 1909, after which personal difficulties forced him into isolation (at Hillside, significantly; see Chapters Five and Six), he maintained close ties with his maternal relatives whose jealously guarded individuality depended upon the strength of an extended family unit as it confronted humanity and nature.

If Wright called upon his own experience (as he undoubtedly did, though probably not consciously) when he turned to residential architecture, he had two models upon which to draw. The Lloyd Joneses offered him security, happiness, and comfort made possible by mutual respect, loyalty, and harmony: a fellowship among equals insofar as that was possible in Victorian America. His nuclear family, on the other hand, warned him of the disintegration that could occur when group needs were overwhelmed by individual aspirations. The house he built for himself and his bride in Oak Park in 1889 and his first important residential commission in private practice, the William H. Winslow House (1894) in River Forest, Illinois, were responses to both legacies.

The Oak Park home was set as far back on its lot as possible, emphasizing the detachment and privacy the William Wrights and Lloyd Joneses both cherished. But on the inside, Frank Lloyd Wright paid symbolic tribute and provided ample space for the kind of group events that characterized his Hillside relatives. The Winslow House was also set back and similarly arranged inside. In these two early and significant homes, in fact, both of which were occasions for maximum self-expression since he was designing for himself and for a close friend, Wright emphasized family togetherness more than personal independence, as if reassuring himself that the breakup of 1885 would not be repeated. He was trying to recreate architecturally the positive features of the Lloyd Jones experience while minimizing the negative aspects of his own family background.

When a visitor enters the Oak Park house from the front porch (s)he immediately confronts on the far side of the living room a fireplace with inglenooks on either side (Fig. 2.2). There, at the core of the house, at its physical center, in fact, was the traditional hearth for family gatherings. But in Wright's plan the recessed fireplace with

Figure 2.2 The principal public spaces of the Frank Lloyd Wright House (1889) in Oak Park, showing fireplace and inglenooks. From the John Lloyd Wright Collection. Courtesy Avery Library, Columbia University.

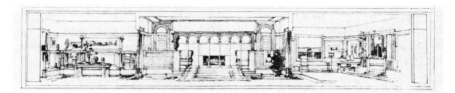

Figure 2.3 Rendering of the principal public spaces of the William H. Winslow House (1894) in River Forest. From *The Architectural Review,* June 1900.

flanking seats was hardly a family corner; it was too small, too formal, too centrally located. It was more a symbol than a functional requisite but, like the inglenooks and fireplace at the Winslow House, an especially important one. As Norris Kelly Smith has perceptively noted, the Winslow reception hall "affirms the sacredness of hearth and home. The room seems hardly to have been designed for family use. . . . Yet it is the most formal, the most carefully articulated room in the house [see Fig. 2.3]. Behind a delicate wooden arcade, [something like] a rood screen before an alter," is a large fireplace. "It looks as if it were intended for the celebration of some solemn family ritual," Smith concludes, "affirming the sacramental nature of the institution of marriage."[17] The Oak Park house gave a similar impression.

Both of these fireplace–inglenooks were symbolic affirmations of an old, important value: family togetherness in a specific and benevolent place. It was not by accident that Wright placed this arrangement where visitors would be sure to see it, as if to measure the residence against an ideal of domesticity, or that he used it several times during the 1890s. He often referred to the fireplace as the "heart" of the house, meaning the spiritual not the functional center. In Oak Park and River Forest he did not intend these areas for constant or intimate use; they were designed to make a point. Calling up memories of the farm and the close-knit family of yesteryear, the sacramental inglenooks reminded hustling suburbanites of the love and holiness marriage and the family represented.

Another impression that struck visitors to both houses is the impossibility of moving straight ahead; the fireplaces block forward progress, forcing people right or left. In the Winslow House, there is a library to the left, while to the right the living room, like the library a large airy space, leads to the dining room, the porch, and an unbuilt pavilion. The intent was similar in Oak Park, except that, in the plan he finally arrived at in his 1894 remodeling, Wright provided a rear parlor past the living room to the left and a side entrance–stairwell–hall combination opening to the dining room on the right. In both homes it was possible to walk through the entire ground floor in either direction and return to the starting point without retracing steps. Continuously circulating space with its sense of adventure could draw visitors into and around the house, through exceptionally wide doorways, encouraging participation in family life. For residents it meant that no one would be quite out of touch with the others. Rich ornament and leaded windows indicated well-developed tastes and sumptuous life styles. Architectural symmetry—the façade and plan fairly balanced left and right—suggested orderliness, specifically placed functions, and traditional family organization. But freely circulating space, extended vistas, and unique design aspects revealed a degree of experimentalism and a public statement of individuality unusual for the period—an individuality of the family as a unit, however, not of its members as separate entities.

During the winter of 1896–1897, Wright and William H. Winslow printed a limited edition of William C. Gannett's sermon, *The House Beautiful,* a book that if carefully read further illuminates the young architect's objectives in residential design.[18] Gannett was a Unitarian minister Wright admired, a family friend since childhood who had written about Wright's work on the Hillside Unity Chapel. It is clear from the preface that Wright was sympathetic to the author's philosophy and, judging from his elaborate hand-drawn page decorations, that he was willing to devote a great deal of time to "our first work," as he wrote Gannett, "for the sake of the work yet to be undertaken."[19] By this Wright probably meant that in his own residences he hoped to achieve the ideal of domesticity Gannett articulated in print. *The House Beautiful* urged its readers to make their homes simple and unpretentious. It abhorred gaudiness, blatant materialism, and conspicuous consumption, advocating functional ornament harmonious with the general design scheme. A gracious, beautiful home, Gannett had said, would foster self-respect and encourage an atmosphere of love and warmth for its residents. Fundamentally a spiritual entity, the house was "a building of God, not made with hands."

In "The Dear Togetherness," the last chapter of the book, Gannett enunciated views central to Wright's own thinking. The feeling of the house, the author contended, should be "like a constant love-song without words, whose meaning, is 'We are glad that we are alive together.'" It was an ambiance made possible by "many self-controls, of much forebearance, of training in self-sacrifice. . . ." Such discipline led not to domestic austerity but to cheer, peace, trust, delight, and finally to "a higher beauty. . .swiftly wrought by love within each soul,—the enlargement of powers, the virtues greatened, the meanness abated, and that unselfishness of each one for the other's sake, which really makes one a stronger, nobler self." Love was the shaping force in Gannett's ideal, but it was both a cause and a result of family happiness, "since home relations [were its] well-springs. . . ." This romantic, idealized, Victorian clarion call for therapeutic domesticity— sentiments he had heard Gannett express many times—touched the exposed nerves of Wright's family deficiencies at precisely the time he was having his own children and opening his residential practice. It was what the Winslow and his own house were all about.

Despite his propensity for purple prose, Gannett was not a rank sentimentalist. He urged his audience to use the latest construction techniques: pressed stone exteriors, fibrous slab interiors instead of mortar and lath, and iron ribbing instead of rafters and beams. The modern house should get its heat directly from a municipal steam plant, should have electricity and "telephones" piping music from "a distant capital." Equally important was family living style. Only fresh food shipped in daily would suffice. "Taste" would be apparant everywhere—in pictures, flowers, music, color schemes, draperies, table decorations, furniture arrangements, service, and the homeowners' clothes. Gracefulness, too—a harmony of colors, a song to children before bed, a good morning to God. Superfluousness should be removed and the "verys" banished.

Books should also be pervasive; introductions to "the noblest company that all the generations have generated," books were excellent furnishings. A quality newspaper reporting politics, business, thought, knowledge, and humanity but not divorce, murder, prizefights, or "the shames of low city life" was an essential accessory. Also necessary were a dictionary, an encyclopedia, and an atlas. And then there were the guests: "as important a part of the furnishings as their chairs. . . . People must look forward to going" to the house beautiful. "True hospitality is not in the effort made to entertain but in the depth of welcome. Guests love to come for people, not for things." Gannett's suggestions were close to Wright's personal and architectural values, and his goals were very much those of his young admirer. There is little doubt that the clergyman stated many of the architect's own feelings and that his influence on Wright's professional development was profound.

Despite his sympathy for Gannett's ideas, Wright was not completely satisfied. Gannett's emphasis was on togetherness, begging the question of the family's relations with the larger community. Wright was intensely concerned with this issue, and in his own home and the

Figure 2.4 Rear façade of the Winslow House (enclosed porch added after 1894). Photo by author.

Winslow House gave an architectural solution to what was basically a social problem.

As they face the street both structures are simple and symmetrical, suggesting orderly and traditional family functions, clearly expressed in the interiors as well by their formal room arrangements. But the face shown to the public on the façade is not necessarily the one reserved for the family, as the rears of these dwellings reveal. In back, the Winslow House is ordered and orderly, to be sure (Fig. 2.4). A broad, central chimney overlooks a porch, the dining room with bedroom above, and the kitchen facilities. Squarely in the middle, a rounded dining bay centered under the chimney protrudes into the yard. These elements are clean and balanced left and right, matching the front's clarity. But to the left of the rear porch is a free-standing wall that in plan opened on an arbor leading to a pavilion. As built, the wall served only to shelter the unroofed porch (since enclosed). To the right, almost as tall as the chimney, is an octagonal stairwell, exterior only on the second and third stories, by no means balancing the dormer window piercing the attic roof on the left. The street façade is memorable for its simplicity and cleanliness of line (Fig. 2.5), but the rear is busy and active—almost fussy—in its menagerie of geometric shapes, protrusions, and individualisms. One thing is clear:

Figure 2.5   Street façade of the Winslow House. Photo by author.

the face—the self-image—that the Winslow House shows the street is entirely different from the one reserved for the family in back. The façade promises visitors a placid restful interior and is in fact exceptionally inviting. But the rear acknowledges the functional complexity, indeed, the tensions contained within a family's life.

Wright's own Oak Park home makes a similar statement (Fig. 2.6). Facing the residential side street, it is straightforward, symmetrical, even conventional, but in the rear it is a study in contrast and complexity. Wright seemed to bow to Victorian insistence on family regularity in front while letting undisguised functional reality influence the arrangement where it was most private. When he built his multifaceted and unusually complex studio in 1895, it faced busy Chicago Avenue, not his neighbors. He had also expanded his residence the year before, adding a magnificent barrel-vaulted playroom and larger dining facilities. He could have built on the front where there was much more space, but choosing to preserve the orderly façade, he tucked the additions in the limited areas at the side and rear. Since the studio dramatically altered the house in 1895, Wright could not have been overly concerned with preserving its original appearance in 1894. He seems therefore to have thought it important to assure his suburban neighbors that his family was indeed unexceptional. In doing so he further confused the rear of the house, another way of saying that life grew more complicated as children grew more numerous.

Figure 2.6 Forest Avenue façade of the Frank Lloyd Wright House and Studio. Anna Wright lived in the building on the right. From the John Lloyd Wright Collection. Courtesy Avery Library, Columbia University.

Throughout the 1890s and into 1900, Wright's residences continued to be influenced by J. L. Silsbee and the prevailing house styles of the period, as historian Vincent Scully has demonstrated rather well.[20] But virtually every design was in some way uniquely his own. Sometimes Wright failed badly, as in the odd and awkward houses for George and Rollin Furbeck (1897 and 1898) in Oak Park with forbidding decorative colonnade and irrelevant rounded towers (Fig. 2.7). Usually he was more restrained, but even his obvious successes, such as the Winslow House, were not without flaw. Now in its ninth decade, it is still the freshest and most striking home in its upper middle class neighborhood of post-World War Two vintage. Yet it is jarring and unharmonious in its parts, has a strangely stark façade, and lacks the repose characteristic of Wright's later work. Largely because his purposes were quite different when designing its front and rear, he made it almost two separate buildings—dazzlingly beautiful but thematically dissonant.

Taken as a whole his residential ventures of the 1890s were carefully conceived but revealed a fundamental uncertainty about how best to provide architecturally for the family as a social institution. When Wright created dichotomous front and rear façades he was in effect giving outsiders an interpretation of interior events entirely different from the "truth" reserved for insiders, in the process sacrificing architectural harmony for unnecessary detail, visual titillation, and vaguely dishonest posing. When he combined simple, symmetrical exteriors with more complicated interiors or united the quasi-religious

Figure 2.7 The Rollin Furbeck House (1898), Oak Park. Photo by author.

with the avant-garde, he wavered between orthodox and progressive concepts of family life. And when he opened interior space he expanded the possibilities for multifunctional, more informal usage, but his striking geometry, luxurious details, traditional room designations, and squarish floor plans assumed orderly and familiar activities. Separate articulation of individual units—stairwells, playrooms, dining bays, libraries—indicated specific places for specific things or a fixed pattern of living. But stating the importance of each so vigorously also pointed the family toward a melange of activities without enumerating priorities, except that group spaces always received the most attention.

Despite their contradictions and shortcomings, the early homes reveal the direction of Wright's thinking. Drawing on the experience of the William C. Wrights and the Lloyd Joneses, stimulated by *The House Beautiful,* and conscious of his own growing family (with five children by 1901), the young architect took greater pains to provide for group solidarity than for individual interests. Whether it was a symbolic inglenook, a formal entryway, a playroom for his children, or his many exquisite dining and living rooms, his most elaborate efforts were areas of group activity. During this period he devoted less consideration than he did later to private retreats and quiet corners. The Lloyd Jones family was his paramount model, William C.

Gannett's philosophy his guiding sentiment. Wright understood the family to be a tightly knit group within a larger community from which it withdrew occasionally (but did not reject) for its own sustenance. More concerned at this stage of his life with family unity than personal freedom, he assumed that the former made the latter possible.

If Wright leaned heavily on his own past when confronting the nature of the family, he looked to the present and future when dealing with his second major concern as the twentieth century opened. Believing that machinery would radically alter the appearance of buildings and substantially increase design options, he was captivated by new construction methods and technological changes, leading him to formulate his own architectural philosophy including a theory of aesthetics. In his two earliest speeches that survive, "The Architect" (1900) and "The Art and Craft of the Machine" (1901), he stated the theoretical underpinnings for the practical applications offered in his 1901 *Ladies Home Journal* articles, "A Home in a Prairie Town" and "A Small House with 'Lots of Room in It.'" With these publications Wright assembled the philosophical and architectural weapons necessary to launch a devastating assault on the contemporary residence.

"The Architect" described the doldrums in which he found the profession, while "The Art and Craft of the Machine" suggested a remedy. In the earlier speech, delivered in 1900 to the Second Annual Convention of the Architectural League of America in Chicago, Wright reminded his colleagues that in this country commerce had triumphed over art. The lust for money had reduced the architect to a servant of the business community. Unwilling to sacrifice assured financial success for the less tangible benefits of individuality and experimentalism, he slavishly reproduced European styles, catering to uninformed public demand. Having "degenerated to fakir," Wright charged patronizingly, the architect "panders to silly women his silly artistic sweets." While in years gone by he had been the master of creative effort, making "imperishable record of the noblest in the life of his race in his time," he now modeled commercial buildings after Greek temples and luxury homes after Louis XIV palaces, all because the businessman and his wife "knew what they wanted." No longer an independent spirit, the architect had become a salesman, peddling prepackaged "styles" from the files of huge "plan-factories." At the height of the industrial revolution in America, Wright was painfully aware that the new corporate elite had usurped the status of the professional, reducing him to an employee at its beck and call.

But there was still hope. Common sense—that hallowed American attribute—would prevail. The public would gradually learn that a bad American original was preferable to a good European copy because it was honest. As the taste and the artistic sensibilities of the nation matured, and at this time Wright was sure they would, America would develop a native architecture, and architects would regain their independence. In that noble effort he and his young colleagues would play a central role. They would

Help the people to feel that architecture is a destroyer of vulgarity, sham, and pretense, a benefactor of tired nerves and jaded souls, an educator in the higher ideals and better purposes of yesterday, to-day, and to-morrow.

Such an art only is characteristic of the better phase of commercialism itself, and is true to American independence, America's hatred of cant, hypocrisy, and base imitation.

When once Americans are taught in terms of building construction the principles so dear to them at their fireplaces, the architect will have arrived.[21]

To interpret the best in national ideals, to transcribe them into structure, and to awaken the public to its own cultural heritage was a large order for any profession. But it would happen when greed gave way to the spiritual and aesthetic renaissance Wright glimpsed over the horizon.

His optimism in 1900 was based on his own instincts, his faith in America's good sense and capacity for spiritual growth, and on the missionary potential of a group of younger Midwestern architects with whom he was associated, that is, his Steinway Hall neighbors and members of "The Eighteen" not yet known as the "Prairie" or "Western" School. By contrast, "The Art and Craft of the Machine," delivered in March 1901 at the Arts and Crafts Society of Jane Addams' Hull House, was programmatic although it sacrificed little by way of rhetorical flourish. In 1900 Wright had prophesied the revitalization of architecture, and now he told how it would happen. "In the machine lies the only future of art and craft," he informed his audience. Artists must change their attitudes toward the new technology. Instead of blaming it for the destruction of traditional craftsmanship, they must seize the machine as the characteristic tool of the modern age and with it create an art vital to the life of the times.

Architects had so far totally misconceived and misused machinery. Instead of exploring new techniques to create an aesthetic appropriate to the twentieth century, they used technology to design buildings reminiscent of ancient Greece and Rome, Tudor England, or Renaissance France. Fakery, imitation, and sham, Wright charged, flooded the land, bearing absolutely no practical relevance to modern living. "Badgered into all manner of structural gymnastics," wonderful new materials were forced to look "real," that is, old. Steel beams, for example, the structural reality of a high-rise office building, were buried under tons of ornamental and nonbearing masonry, making the finished product resemble a Greek temple rather than a sleek engine of modern enterprise. Lying about its function and its construction materials, such a building used the latest technologies symbolically to reject the modern age. Wright also cited mass-produced carved wood as a further illustration of technological chicanery. By substituting an imitation of handcraft for the genuine article, builders debauched honored skills and negated the machine's capacities. Employed to produce myriads of "elaborate and fussy joinery of posts, spindles, jig-sawed beams and braces, butted and strutted, to outdo the sentimentality of the already over-wrought antique product," nineteenth century craftsmanship was being transformed into twentieth century frauds.

The time had come, Wright insisted, to learn from the machine, to assert control over it. The central and primary lesson of modern technology was *simplicity*. New methods reemphasized old truths, for example, that the beauty of wood "lies first in its qualities as wood," not in how it could be carved and twisted to approximate something else. "No treatment that did not bring out these qualities . . . could be plastic," he continued. "The machine teaches us . . . that certain simple forms and handling are suitable to bring out the beauty of wood and certain forms are not; that all wood-carving is apt to be a forcing of the material, an insult to its finer possibilities. . . ." Intrinsically, wood had unparalleled artistic properties—markings, texture, color, grain—that the machine "by its wonderful cutting, shaping, smoothing, and repetitive capacity" had "emancipated." Modern methods could create "clean strong forms that the branch veneers of Sheraton and Chippendale only hinted at, with dire consequences."

New technology had also enabled iron and steel, with an attractiveness all their own, to open new doors of aesthetic expression. And cement, a plastic covering, allowed the architect "to clothe the structural form with a simple, modestly beautiful robe where before he dragged in. . .five different kinds of materials to compose one little cottage. . . ." Multitudes of processes—metal casting, electroglazing, and more—"are expectantly awaiting the sympathetic interpretation of the master mind. . . ." These new techniques and materials, Wright thought, could again reveal the essential nature of the design process, opening unlimited potential for the imaginative architect. The resulting aesthetic breakthrough would be "organically consistent," that is, "in conception and composition. . .the essence of refinement in organization."[22]

To suggest machinery as the solution to architectural lethargy in 1901 was provocative though not revolutionary but, as Wright stated it, still an abstraction. A month before the Hull House speech, however, he had taken the first steps toward a practical demonstration by publishing in the February *Ladies Home Journal* the renderings and plans for a new kind of residence embodying the techniques he had described. He followed this in July with a second illustrated article in the same magazine and by announcing that he would build eight model homes to prove the efficacy of his ideas. Although the building project never materialized, before the year was out he began construction on the first prairie buildings. What he was beginning to call "organic architecture" had begun to take shape in wood, stone, and mortar.

"In keeping with a high ideal of family life together," he told the February 1901 readers of *The Ladies Home Journal* (Fig. 2.8) in much the same language as Gannett had used in his *House Beautiful,* he offered "a simple mode of living." The rendering of "A Home in a Prairie Town" showed a low, decidedly horizontal, two-story building with unusually long stretches of unadorned cement walls and straight, clean lines. Seemingly without applied trim, it was actually highly decorated with leaded windows, flower boxes, plantings, dark strips of wood, and the shadows of its own projections. Broad, overhanging eaves and gently sloping hip-roofed porches and portes-cochere recalled the lines of prairie terrain. "Firmly and broadly associated with the site," Wright explained, the new home "makes a feature of its quiet level." Interior sectional views revealed that every element, including custom accessories, built-in furniture, and integral decorations, could best be fabricated by the machine techniques Wright had described. In the text of this and the July article, "A Small House with 'Lots of Room in It,'" he listed the innovations, refinements, and simplicities made possible by intelligent use of technology. Moldings, paint, varnish, drain pipes, and several other "necessities" had been eliminated. After explaining the plans and specifying the costs—$7000 for the "Prairie" and $5800 for the "Small" House—Wright declared himself ready to accept orders.[23]

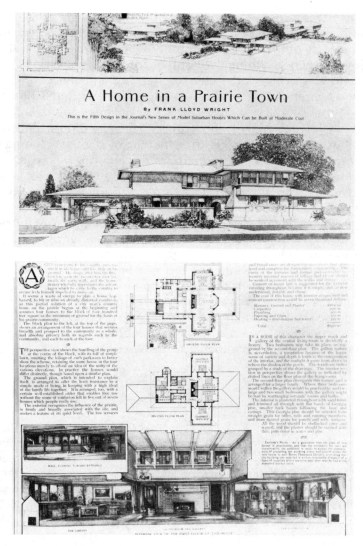

Figure 2.8 "A Home in a Prairie Town," *The Ladies Home Journal,* February 1901, announcing the prairie house.

The same month as the second *Ladies Home Journal* article Wright announced financial backing to implement the "quadruple block" scheme shown in "A Home in a Prairie Town."[24] On two four-hundred-foot-square blocks in Oak Park, Wright said he would erect eight houses, four on a block, each commanding an entire side and sharing common acreage with its three neighbors to the rear in the center.

The eight-home "colony" would serve the purpose, he said, of show-ing that his ideas were practical and of integrating buildings with site and with each other "in a community where everything will be in harmony and where nothing offensive to the eye shall exist." This "architectural surprise," the best of the city and the country com-bined, was intended as a showcase for his "Art and Craft of the Machine" theories as depicted in *The Ladies Home Journal*.

Unfortunately for Wright, the "colony" remained on paper. But his proposals were taken up in 1901 by a handful of clients including Frank Thomas, who wanted a prairie house at the far end of Forest Avenue, the architect's own street, and by Ellen and Jane Lloyd Jones, who had decided to expand their Hillside Home School.[25] During the next decade Wright refined and improved the experiment started here; 1901 was only a beginning. But in a very fundamental way it was also an end to a decade or more of architectural wandering. During the 1890s it was unclear just where Wright's ideas were taking him, but it was certainly a place he himself did not know. In 1887 his school-teacher relatives had given him his first opportunity, and in 1901 their needs and his again coincided. The prairie house, that great synthesis of art and science, of theory and practice that brought Wright inter-national recognition, owed an immense debt to a neighbor down the block and to two maiden aunts in rural Wisconsin.

NOTES

1 Wright's comment on Oak Park is in *Two Lectures on Architecture* (Chi-cago: The Art Institute, 1931), reprinted in *The Future of Architecture* (New York: Horizon Press, 1953), 188. For Bruce Barton's comment see *Oak Leaves* (Oak Park, Ill.), June 30, 1906. All Oak Park newspapers used in this study are in that city's public library.

2 Wright's neighborhood was evaluated in *The Reporter* (Oak Park, Ill), April 14, 1893; also see *The Vindicator* (Oak Park), September 3, 1897.

3 The Oak Park years are described in Frank Lloyd Wright, *An Autobiogra-phy* (New York: Duell, Sloan and Pearce, 1943 ed.), 109–120; in John Lloyd Wright, *My Father Who is on Earth* (New York: G. P. Putnam's Sons, 1946), *passim*; and Maginel Wright Barney, *The Valley of the God-Almighty Joneses* (New York: Appleton-Century, 1965), 133–134. Passports for the 1905 trip are in the FLW Collection, Avery Library. Also see *The Caxton Club, 1908–1909* (Chicago: The Fine Arts Building, 1908–1909); *The Re-porter*, March 30, 1899; and Frank Lloyd Wright, *Genius and the Mobo-cracy* (New York: Duell, Sloan and Pearce, 1949), 72.

On Catherine Wright, in addition to the books cited above, see *The Weekly Home News,* June 15, 1893; September 30, November 11, 1897; February 14, 1901; *The Reporter,* July 14, 1893; January 11, June 28, 1900.

On parties see J. L. Wright *My Father,* 43; *The Reporter,* January 11, 1900. His neighbors' assessment is in *The Reporter,* July 19, 1901; also see *ibid.,* August 23, 1900.

4 "Successful Homes," *The House Beautiful,* 1 (February 15, 1897), 64–69, including four photographs; Alfred H. Granger, "An Architect's Studio," *ibid.,* 7 (December 1899), 36–45, with eleven illustrations; *The Architectural Review,* 7 (June 1900), 75, not the article by Robert C. Spencer, Jr., cited in footnote 13.

5 On Wright's club activities see *The Brickbuilder,* 3 (September 1894), 181–182; *The Inland Architect,* 24 (September 1894), 17; *ibid.,* 24 (December 1894), 48; and most especially the variously titled annual exhibition catalogs on file at Avery Library and other architectural archives. Also see H. Allen Brooks, *The Prairie School: Frank Lloyd Wright and His Midwest Contemporaries* (Toronto: University of Toronto Press, 1972), 37–38.

6 On the Milwaukee Library competition see *The Milwaukee Journal,* November 15, 21, 1893; and on the Madison boathouses see *Wisconsin State Journal,* May 12, 13, 25, June 15, 16, August 9, 1893. The Luxfer design appeared in *The Inland Architect,* 30 (January 1898), 63–64.

The full texts of "Architecture and the Machine," delivered in 1894 to the Evanston University Guild, and of "Architecture, Architect, and Client," read to the same group in 1896, are not available, but there are excerpts in Frederick Gutheim, Ed., *Frank Lloyd Wright on Architecture: Selected Writings, 1894–1940* (New York: Duell, Sloan and Pearce, 1941), 3–6.

"A paper read by Mr. Frank B. [sic] Wright upon The Use of Machinery, was followed by a most valuable and spirited discussion": *Hull-House Bulletin* (November 1897). This speech was called to my attention by Ms. Rosemarie Scherman, Stony Point, New York, a biographer of Jane Addams.

7 *The Brickbuilder,* 7 (May 1898), 107. If the plan for this home was ever completed it has not been included in lists of Wright's work.

8 For the All Souls Church project see *The Brickbuilder,* 7 (November 1898), 240, and *ibid.,* 8 (January 1899), 17–18. On the Steinway group see Brooks, *The Prairie School,* 28 and following. "The Eighteen" included Wright, Spencer, Perkins, Hunt, James Gamble Rogers, Howard Van Doren Shaw, Hugh Garden, J. K. Cady, Frank W. Handy, Arthur and George Dean, Arthur Heun, Irving and Allen Pond, Alfred Granger, Richard E. Schmidt, and probably Webster Tomlinson. The eighteenth may have been Walter Burley Griffin, Adamo Boari, Birch B. Long or Arthur R. Niemz all tenants at Steinway around this time. Also see the *Lakeside City Directory,* 1895–

1901. Wright left Steinway by 1902, and was thereafter unlisted in the *Directory* except for 1908 when he briefly kept an office in Room 1020 at 203 Michigan Avenue, one floor above Solon S. Bemen, noted designer of Pullman, Illinois.

9 On the Wright-Tomlinson partnership see *The Brickbuilder,* 10 (January 1901), 20; *The Inland Architect,* 37 (March 1901), 16; and *The Reporter,* January 24, 1901. In *Frank Lloyd Wright to 1910: The First Golden Age* (New York: Reinhold Pub. Corp., 1958) 46, Grant C. Manson disagrees with Henry-Russell Hitchcock's assertion in *In the Nature of Materials: The Buildings of Frank Lloyd Wright, 1887–1941* (New York Duell, Sloan and Pearce, 1942), 111–112, that the two architects actually designed together, arguing that Tomlinson was Wright's office manager and business agent.

10 The original River Forest Tennis Club opened July 4, 1905 and burned to the ground July 23, 1906. Vernon S. Watson, Charles E. White, Jr.—an employee of Wright's—and the architect himself immediately drew plans for a new clubhouse which opened September 23, 1906. See *Oak Leaves,* April 27, 1907.

11 *Annual of the Chicago Architectural Club Being the Book of the Thirteenth Annual Exhibition* (1900); *American Architect and Building News,* 68 (April 14, 1900), 13; Robert C. Spencer, Jr., "Work of the Younger Architects," *Brush and Pencil,* 8 (May 1901), 118.

12 George R. Dean, "'Progress Before Precedent,'" *The Brickbuilder,* 9 (May 1900), 96–97; "The Architect," *ibid.,* 9 (June 1900), 124–128.

13 Robert C. Spencer, Jr., "The Work of Frank Lloyd Wright," *The Architectural Review,* 7 (June 1900), 61–72, plus foldouts; quotations from pages 61 and 72.

14 "A Home in a Prairie Town," *The Ladies Home Journal,* 18 (February 1901), 17; "A Small House with 'Lots of Room in It,'" *ibid.,* 18 (July 1901), 15; "The Village Bank Series. V," *The Brickbuilder,* 10 (August 1901), 160–161.

15 F. Gutheim, *Selected Writings,* 25.

16 Wright to Willard Jones, April 2, 1959, FLW Collection, Northwestern University Library, Evanston, Illinois.

17 Norris Kelly Smith, *Frank Lloyd Wright: A Study in Architectural Content* (Englewood Cliffs, N.J.: Prentice-Hall, 1966), 70–71. The plan of the Winslow House is in Spencer, "The Work of Frank Lloyd Wright," foldout; for Wright's own home see "For Sale at Oak Park. A Forest Avenue Property and a Chicago Avenue Property," a brochure designed by Wright when he put the house and studio up for sale in 1925, in the John Lloyd Wright Collection, Avery Library.

18 *The House Beautiful* was reprinted in J. L. Wright, *My Father,* quotations in the following paragraphs from pages 157, 166–169.

19 Wright to William C. Gannett, December 27, 1898, Gannett Collection, Rush Rhees Library, University of Rochester, Rochester, New York.

20 "Conclusion: Frank Lloyd Wright," *The Shingle Style and the Stick Style: Architectural Theory and Design from Richardson to the Origins of Wright* (New Haven: Yale University Press, 1971 rev. ed.), 155–164.

21 "The Architect," *The Brickbuilder,* 9 (June 1900), 124–128, long quotation from page 126. Olgivanna Wright in *Frank Lloyd Wright: His Life, His Work, His Word* (New York: Horizon Press, 1967), 207, says her husband read three papers in 1900: "The Architect," "The Philosophy of Fine Art," and "What is Architecture?" In *Selected Writings,* 6, Gutheim says "The Philosophy of Fine Art" was read to the Architectural League of America in 1900, reproducing most of it (pp. 6–21). "The Architect" as published in *Brickbuilder* coincides almost exactly with "The Philosophy of Fine Art," a manuscript copy of which is in the John Lloyd Wright Collection at Avery Library. I have therefore concluded that Gutheim gave the wrong title to the speech before the Architectural League and that "The Architect" and "The Philosophy of Fine Art" are different versions of the same paper which may have been read to more than one audience. There is no other record of "What is Architecture?"

22 F. L. Wright, "The Art and Craft of the Machine" was originally published in the *Chicago Architectural Club Catalogue of the 14th Annual Exhibition* (1901).

23 See note 14 for full citations.

24 "New Idea for Suburbs," *The Reporter,* July 18, 1901.

25 It might be useful here to establish the correct dates for Wright's work at Hillside. The Romeo and Juliet windmill, consistently assigned to 1896, was actually designed and constructed around September 1897: *The Weekly Home News,* September 23 and 30, 1897.

    The Hillside Home School's second building is usually dated 1902 and sometimes 1903 or 1904. But it was actually designed in 1901: "The plans have been drawn and sent from the studio of Frank L. Wright, architect, Chicago," *The Weekly Home News* reported on October 17, 1901, "and. . .construction will begin at once." The cornerstone was laid in April 1902 and the building completed approximately April 1903: *ibid.,* April 24, 1902, and February 19, 1903.

1901–1909

CHAPTER THREE

A Radically Different Conception

No one in 1901 could have anticipated Frank Lloyd Wright's accomplishments in residential architecture by 1909. No one could have foreseen the mature prairie house. But during the decade his work brought him as many commissions as he could fill, partly because it spoke so directly to the needs of upper middle class suburbanites. In his own and in the public's mind he was associated with a group of progressive midwestern architects known as the "Prairie School," but most authorities would not dispute Vincent Scully's assertion that "all the significant ideas were his own, and the development of their common style was totally dependent on him."[1] Even before 1909 the prairie house became a bold, daring, but popular and marketable structure. Although it appeared to be "radical," it was actually familiar and reassuring. Making the avant-garde accessible was part of Wright's genius.

□ □ □

The twentieth century in America opened amidst a wave of national self-scrutiny. The muck that had given a protective covering to the economic and social misery caused by industrialization and corporate consolidation was being raked away. Protest and reform swept the land and drifted into literature, where the social realism of Stephen Crane, Jack London, and Theodore Dreiser exposed the brutalization of working people, and into painting, where John Sloan, Robert Henri, and others depicted the seamier side of urban life. Even though Frank

Lloyd Wright's prairie houses were designed for comfortable to affluent people, they too were considered "reformist" since everything
about them implied discontent with the architectural and social status
quo. And there was much for him to be unhappy about. The typical
turn-of-the-century house for the upper middle to upper classes—the
sort of building to set the style and attract attention in the professional
literature—had in many ways lost touch with fundamentals.

Residential architecture had long ago evolved beyond simple shelter, even in comparatively young America. People like eighteenth
century John Hancock, one of the richest in the colonies, and the
early nineteenth century merchants, built their homes with simple
elegance, stating their social standing only with restraint. But by the
1880s, in an era of unparalleled opulence and unmitigated acquisitive-
ness, while the new industrial elite scrambled frantically to shed its
crude image by imitating the social behavior of European aristocrats,
the meaning of dwellings changed significantly. Still living places and
family centers, of course, they also became, perhaps primarily, symbols of status, stages for entertainment, and statements of wealth—
indices of success as measured by conspicuous display of imported
culture. The socially conscious were as apt to be concerned with
public opinion as with their own needs and comfort when they built
their houses. Social pressure could force an upwardly mobile businessman in one of Edith Wharton's novels to order a "complete architectural meal; if he had omitted a style, his friends might have
thought the money had given out."[2] For the elite and those clamoring
to join it, a home was as much a social investment as a place to live.

Patrons of architecture lavished enormous sums on reproductions
of medieval castles, ornate melanges of European styles, or elaborate
ensembles of "artistic" forms. Colonies of estates for "robber barons"
sprang up in Newport, Rhode Island, Deal, New Jersey, Lenox, Massachusetts, and other summer watering holes, as well as along the
Prairie, Fifth, and Woodward Avenues in the major cities. Together
they formed little architectural Leagues of Nations—French Second
Empire here, English Tudor there, Italianate Revival down the block—
even within a single structure. Reproductions and variations of foreign
styles did not seem to Wright an authentic expression of *American*
culture unless, of course, America had none, nor did he find them
appropriate to their time, place, or to the national ideals of practicality
and egalitarianism. The irony is that by the third quarter of the twentieth century, awash in a sea of faceless, dehumanized, and impersonal
buildings, the department stores of design Wright found so objectionable were admired for their variety, personality, and character.

At the highest economic levels during the late nineteenth century, society architects like Richard M. Hunt could make fortunes from a single family. The Vanderbilts, for example, ordered Gothic mansions to demonstrate their membership in America's capitalist aristocracy. Hunt's townhouse for W. K. Vanderbilt (1881), a fussy, elaborate Fifth Avenue chateau, was surpassed in pretentiousness and grandeur by his Loire-type castle for G. W. Vanderbilt (1895) in Asheville, North Carolina, one of the most monumental private residences in all America. The not-quite-so-rich, in their envy and haste, could be even gaudier. The now legendary William Carson House (1886) by Joseph and Samuel Newsom for a Eureka, California, lumberman, with towers, dormers, brackets, pillars, and something-or-other filling every available space in more ways than can easily be imagined, adds insult to insult, write two architectural historians, "until its swagger betrays a man of wealth who wistfully hoped to acquire prestige through foreign forms, no matter how grossly mishandled. . . ."[3] Homes like these, usually with less pretense and a bit more restraint, were built all over America. Eclecticism, whether direct imitation or, as was usually the case, interpretive adaptation, was the dominant mode of architectural expression. Its apologists thought they were injecting taste and literacy into the burly industrial atmosphere of the late nineteenth century.

Chicagoans may have been more artistically sophisticated than William Carson in Eureka, California, but they, too, expressed their aspirations in architecture. Aware that theirs was not the first among American cities—that Chicago trailed New York in wealth, power, and prestige—North Side and Prairie Avenue plutocrats pursued social equality with their own extravagant paeans to the godhead of eclecticism. The McCormicks and the Cudaheys, the Ryersons, Fields, Armours, and Potter Palmers vied to outdo each other and their New York counterparts.[4] In the East, where commercial and cultural ties with Europe were strongest, eclecticsm had a certain validity. But in the heartland of America, it was conspicuously inappropriate and noticeably foreign, at least Wright thought so. Chicago houses, not those for the superrich but for the comfortably well-to-do, as he himself exclaimed, "were fantastic abortions, tortured by features that disrupted the distorted roof surfaces from which attenuated chimneys like lean fingers threatened the sky." Interiors were chopped up into "box-like compartments. . .and 'Architecture' chiefly consisted in healing over the edges of the curious collections of holes that had to be cut in the walls for light and air" and movement. As long as their buildings were "fashionable," he thought, most people cared no more about them than horses cared about stables. The typical Chicago home at the turn of the century, Wright believed, "*lied* about everything."[5]

Dwellings like these also disturbed Wright because they were unrelated to their physical environment, something that other people noticed. Norwegian-born novelist Ole E. Rolvaag wrote that ubiquitous gabled frame houses "seemed strangely conspicuous in the bare, level landscape; one could not help wondering if they really belonged here." Willa Cather also expressed serious reservations. She remembered a dwelling with "sharp-sloping roofs to shed the snow. It was encircled by porches, too narrow for modern notions of comfort, supported by the fussy, fragile pillars of that time, when every honest stick of timber was tortured by the turning-lathe into something hideous." In order to build "suitable to the prairie," a Sinclair Lewis character remarked, one would need an "entirely new form of architecture."[6]

Wright's new forms had their origins at least as far back as 1892. With considerable backing and hauling he had struggled for a decade to create an alternative to eclecticism. In retrospect it is easy to trace a direct progression from the James Charnley (1892) and William Winslow (1894) houses to the prairie house, as if Wright had moved straight toward a predetermined goal, a view he repeatedly offered in his writings. But this interpretation reduces his achievement to a mechanical process, minimizing the considerable difficulties he confronted. It was clear during the 1890s that Wright was uncomfortable with prevailing styles, disliked the general run of interior arrangements, and was disturbed by what he saw around him. But no one, least of all he, knew where his efforts would lead. No one in 1893 or even in 1900 could have predicted the mature prairie house. Not until after 1901, when the new designs defined his work and he produced no other kind, did the distance he had traveled or his destination become apparent.

As late as 1900 Wright was still leaning on precedent, incorporating elements from the work of J. L. Silsbee, Louis Sullivan, and Henry H. Richardson into his own. There was, for example, the Frederick Bagley House (1894) in Hinsdale, Illinois (Fig. 3.1), depending on the authority either "Dutch Colonial" or Suburban Richardsonian, with its detached octagonal library, gambrel roof, gables, inset porch with Ionic columns, and elliptical attic window, a feature of many Richardson buildings. Wright built a Tudor half-timber in 1895 for Nathan Moore in Oak Park (Fig. 3.2), the same year he pierced Chauncey William's steeply pitched roof in River Forest (Fig. 3.3) with dormer windows and lined the entrance with "picturesque" uncut boulders. His Oak Park house for George Smith (1899) was one of several with precipitous

Figure 3.1 The Frederick Bagley House (1894) in Hinsdale, Illinois. Photo by author.

roofs and sharply skirting eaves to which he added flaring ridgepoles in the Japanese-flavored S. A. Foster House (1900) in Chicago (Fig. 3.4). Wright continued to borrow from historic styles even after the turn of the century, but he never imitated directly.

Figure 3.2 The Nathan G. Moore House (1895) in Oak Park, remodeled by Wright in 1924. Photo by author.

Figure 3.3 The Chauncey H. Williams House (1895) in River Forest, Illinois. Photo by author.

Mixed with the more traditional efforts of the 1890s were a number of designs that in retrospect seem prophetic. Lacking the coherence of the prairie house, they nevertheless included many of its features. The James Charnley House (1892), already discussed, was notable for its clean brick façade and for its concrete string course under the widely spaced windows of the third story. The Chicago home for Allison Harlan (1892) had an overhanging, gently hipped roof, ample

Figure 3.4 The S. A. Foster House (1900) in Chicago. Photo by author.

front windows, and an absolutely plain curved brick wall—itself an important part of the streetside composition—enclosing a front terrace. At the Municipal Boathouse (1893) in Madison, Wisconsin, Wright painted the underside of the broad eaves to match the upper walls, making the two flow together, and edged it all with contrasting color. In the William Winslow House (1894) he dramatized the flaring hip roof and brought the string course from the Charnley House down under the second story windows. All these devices made little reference to conventional styles but had the effect of emphasizing horizontality and the impression of simplicity.

By 1894 Wright was increasingly relying on these and other reductionist strategies. The 1894 stables for Winslow, the 1894 projects for Orrin Goan in La Grange, Illinois, and for A. C. McAfee in Chicago, his own 1895 Oak Park Studio, the 1896 Heller House and Devin project in Chicago, the design for E. C. Waller (Fig. 3.5) and the Golf Club (both 1898 in River Forest), and the 1900 Joseph Husser House and Robert Eckart project in Chicago (Fig. 3.5) and River Forest, respectively, were all horizontally oriented with gently sloping roofs, overhanging eaves, and trim in contrasting color around the upper story which was sometimes covered by a fenestrated frieze. All featured broad expanses of unadorned surfaces and dispensed with many unnecessary encumbrances. Along with other early commissions, such as the 1900 Harley Bradley and Warren Hickox houses in Kankakee,

Figure 3.5 Projects for Robert Eckart (1900) and for E. C. Waller (1898) in River Forest, Illinois. From *The Annual of the Chicago Architectural Club Being the Book of the Thirteenth Annual Exhibition* (1900).

Illinois (Fig. 3.6), they were distinctive enough to bear the architect's own "signature," as Grant Manson has put it.[7] But occasional rounded arches, elaborate friezes, gratuitous columns and sculpture, the Spanish flavor of the Husser House, the unnecessary colonnade at the Heller House, and the sharp peaks and heavy-handed trim at Kankakee clearly distinguish them from the harmoniously resolved prairie houses they anticipated.

But in 1901 Wright synthesized it all—the lessons of his own family history, his technical expertise, his dissatisfaction with conventional

Figure 3.6 The Harlan Bradley (top) and Warren Hickox Houses (both 1900) in Kankakee, Illinois. From *The Architectural Record,* July 1905.

housing, his philosophy of design, and his experiments with residential aesthetics. The February *Ladies Home Journal* article, the first hint of what was coming, found material expression that year in the Frank Thomas House (Oak Park) and in one of a seemingly inexhaustible number of thematic variations, the F. B. Henderson House in Elmhurst, Illinois. According to his autobiography, which describes the prairie house as well as anything else, Wright based his new concept on the conviction that dwellings should serve human needs and reflect human size without being showpieces, status symbols, or museums (all of which his buildings have since become). His purpose was to develop an aesthetic and functional fusion of environmental, cultural, and technological necessities for an architecture appropriate to time, place, and clientele.

So, he wrote, "I brought the whole house down in scale [Fig. 3.7]. . . . Walls were now started at the ground on a. . .water table that looked like a low platform under the building. . .[and] stopped at the second-story window-sill to let the bedrooms come through above in a continuous window series below the broad eaves of a gently sloping,

Figure 3.7 The F. B. Henderson House (1901), Elmhurst, Illinois. Photo by author.

overhanging roof." The climate being what it was, he continued, "violent in extremes. . ., I gave broad protecting roof-shelter to the whole. . . .The underside of roof-projections was flat and usually light in color to create a glow of reflected light that softly brightened the upper rooms. Overhangs had double value: shelter and preservation for the walls. . ., as well as this diffusion of reflected light. . . ." Usually having two or three levels, prairie houses looked lower and longer than they were. Unbroken sweeps of horizontal trim in contrasting colors, low-pitched or in some cases flat roofs with extensive overhangs, free-standing terrace walls, and open porches or portes-cochere under broad eaves thrust the building laterally beyond its central massing. "The house began to associate with the ground," Wright explained, "and became natural to its prairie site." He often placed a large urn with plantings at a conspicuous spot symbolizing an integral relationship between architecture and nature.

The *outside* of the house, he continued, "was all there, chiefly because of what happened *inside*." The wall, redefined as a screen, was no longer an obstacle to the flow of space. Rejecting what he described as "boxes beside boxes or inside boxes," he declared the "whole lower floor as one room, cutting off the kitchen as a laboratory, putting the servants' sleeping and living quarters next to the kitchen but semi-detached, on the ground floor [Fig. 3.8]. Then I screened

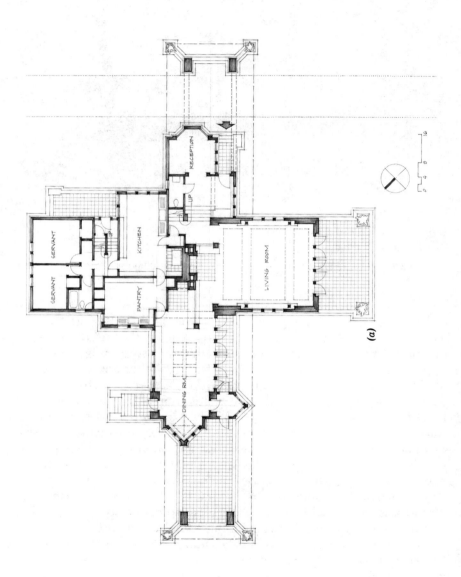

LIVING ROOM

RECEPTION

UP

KITCHEN

SERVANT

SERVANT

PANTRY

DINING RM.

(a)

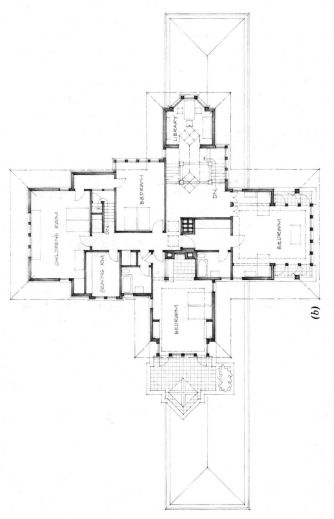

(b)

Figure 3.8 Plans of the Ward Willitts House (1902) in Highland Park, Illinois. Drawn by David Roessler and used with his permission.

various portions of the big room for certain domestic purposes like dining, reading, receiving callers." He reduced the number of doors except in the upper stories, where he retained his sleeping "boxes." Interior trim took on psychological as well as decorative importance. "The ceilings. . .could be brought down. . .by way of the horizontal bands of plaster on the walls themselves above the windows and colored the same as the room-ceilings," he explained. By bringing the "ceiling-surfaces and color down to the very window tops," he encouraged a sense of lowness, intimacy, and integration—many things becoming one, he often said—further enhanced by running a strip of contrasting trim around the room above the doors and windows to add a feeling of movement, continuity, and flow. Openings were now tied together, ceiling and walls united.[8]

Completing his insistence on architectural unity, in a total rejection of Victorian decorating notions which filled every space with stylistically unrelated "objects d'art," Wright built in as much furniture as possible, covered radiators and lighting with grilles to match the leaded windows, carpeting, lampshades, and fireplace equipment he designed, while outside he supervised the landscaping. The entire project, in other words, from cabinet hardware to site plan, was ideally a single unified conception. Everything worked together in relation to every other thing. To bring order out of chaos, as he frequently put it, was very much in keeping with an impulse of the times, when politicians were streamlining governmental and electoral procedures, corporate managers rationalizing and consolidating business practices, and when municipal reformers were "cleaning up" urban blight and corruption. Like Wisconsin's Robert M. La Follette, whom he knew well, Wright was modernizing his own bailiwick. In simplifying the home, making it more orderly, efficient, and rational, by taking it, in short, into the twentieth century, Frank Lloyd Wright was very much a "progressive."

Wright continued to design prairie houses until 1913, becoming increasingly excited by unusual and dramatic sites, so that his homes were not necessarily built on the prairie, suggesting, perhaps that a more accurate nomenclature is in order. He easily adapted his plans to the gently sloping shores of Lake Delavan, Wisconsin, where he built five homes from 1900 to 1905.[10] One of his most imaginative efforts was the 1905 Thomas P. Hardy House (Fig. 3.9), a pavilion format in Mediterranean tradition, jutting out daringly from the steep bluffs over Lake Michigan at Racine, Wisconsin. For another challenging situation that year he perched the W. A. Glasner House (Fig. 3.10) in Glencoe, Illinois, on the edge of a steep ravine, with a bridge and

Figure 3.9 The Thomas P. Hardy House (1905), Racine, Wisconsin. Photo by David Roessler.

teahouse projected (in plan) over a subsidiary crevice. He also began to use materials native to their region, a factor he repeatedly stressed later; the second Hillside Home School (1901) utilized local timber and fieldstone. But throughout the period Wright's designs generally called for wood, brick, or plaster regardless of locale.

As the decade proceeded and Wright grew more certain of his abilities, his architecture became bolder and more daring. Several of the early prairie houses were noticeably squat, were terminated somewhat abruptly, and sat rather steadfastly, even broodingly, on their sites, lacking flair and adventure. His two full-fledged prairie homes that first year, for Frank Thomas in Oak Park and F. B. Henderson (Fig. 3.7) in Elmhurst, for example, seem cramped and confined in comparison to the *Ladies Home Journal* design to which the Thomas House at least was closely related. A number of early dwellings with short overhangs and relatively inconspicuous windows had blocklike, rather unimaginative façades (Fig. 3.11), looking introspective, tentative, somewhat afraid literally or symbolically to stretch beyond their sturdy massing, although the impulse is there. They are more static than active, more reserved than outgoing. They represent trial balloons for a new idea, not the confident assertion of a proven thesis.

Figure 3.10 The W. A. Glasner House (1905) in Glencoe, Illinois. From *Frank Lloyd Wright Ausgeführte Bauten* (1911).

Figure 3.11 The J. J. Walser, Jr., House (1903) in Chicago. Photo by author.

Figure 3.12   The Isabel Roberts House (1908) In River Forest, Illinois. Photo by author.

But many of Wright's later designs exude a confidence, a daring, a willingness to take calculated risks. The Illinois homes for Avery Coonley in Riverside (1907), Isabel Roberts in River Forest (1908), and Frank H. Baker in Wilmette (1909) are among the many designs uninhibited by the hesitancy of inexperience. With eaves overhanging further, shelf-roofed porches and portes-cochere flung wider, and with a greater number of windows more emphatically and rhythmically expressed (Fig. 3.12), the mature homes seem to reach beyond their physical and psychological boundaries. Yet longer and therefore looking lower than their earlier versions, they nestle into the ground for strength and protection. Their successful resolution of a number of architectural dichotomies, moreover, further contributes to their sophistication. For example, they are at once active and static: while firmly and obviously rooted to site, they also reach beyond themselves. Anchored resolutely to the ground, looking as though nothing could rip them from their moorings, they offer a safe and secure harbor to the family battered about on the uncharted seas of modern life. With their extensions and openings embracing humanity and nature, they face life optimistically, accepting uncertainty without fear.

A comparison of two excellent prairie designs, the Arthur Heurtley

Figure 3.13   The Arthur Heurtley House (1902) in Oak Park. Photo by author.

House (1902) in Oak Park and the Frederick C. Robie House (1907) in Chicago, illustrates Wright's growing confidence and skill. The Heurtley House is a simple rectangle (Fig. 3.13). Widely spaced projecting brick bands on the exterior create an impression of solid stone, making it seem more monolithic than it actually is. A second-level porch under abbreviated eaves and behind substantial piers, first-floor front windows deeply recessed across a terrace from a low wall, and an entrance tucked in the dark alcove of a Richardsonian arch do not, even on the sunniest days, relieve the blocklike, seemingly impenetrable façade. The house guards its openings jealously and with its weighty look appears to withdraw within its stonelike walls, a precaution hardly necessary in refined Oak Park. Since the Heurtleys were not particularly happy together, inwardness and solidity may have been Wright's way of making them focus attention on each other without external distractions. Or, its social conservatism may simply have resulted from timidity about a new architectural concept at this early stage of the prairie genre.

Five years later Wright could afford to take chances. The Robie House, at an intersection one block from Chicago's busy Midway Plaissance, might easily have retreated from urban distractions but unlike its predecessor reaches out to face the city with confidence (Fig. 3.14). During a period of his life when he energetically pursued

Figure 3.14 The Frederick C. Robie House (1907) in Chicago. Photo by author.

urban pleasures, Wright designed a house that transformed a banal setting into an aesthetic playground, a building with few rivals even today in its architectural drama and adventure. The Robie House appears longer and lower than it actually is because its roofs—cantilevered so impossibly beyond its walls—and its emphatic uninterrupted trim unite to create an overwhelmingly horizontal attitude and because its extended fenestration, running the length of the second story, is punctuated by strong vertical mullions that accentuate the whole. The house leaps out beyond its confines and with incredible cantilevers soars off into space, yet its insistent horizontal lines keep it securely earthbound.

With its contradictory tendencies the Robie House remains in a state of perpetual tension. Its almost unbounded energy and the aggressive individuality of its several members threaten to tear the building asunder, yet its parts are subtly and resourcefully woven together. The light and shadow of its complex façade, at first glance only a complicated assortment of pieces, quickly resolves into a geometrical composition of supremely sensible proportions, an architectural chorus made even more harmonious when roof snow highlights the several components. The broad central chimney is another unifying device, acting as a massive stave to anchor the building to site and lock the pieces in place. The Robie House is clearly a dynamic structure, one that changes unexpectedly with the seasons and from each angle of vision, a reflection of the ebb and flow of natural and urban life.

Yet the house is obviously a safe, secure family place—strong, sheltering, and protective. With a long wall guarding the terrace from intruders but permitting social intercourse and with the family and bedrooms elevated to the second and third stories overlooking the street, the house stipulates independence without withdrawal. As Frederick Robie himself remembered, "I wanted to. . .look out and down the street to my neighbors without having them invade my privacy,"[11] a statement of measured civility. The hovering roofs, overhangs, and enclosed terraces, even the nooks and crannies forcefully articulated on the exterior, clearly state that deep within this architectural *tour de force* was a family confident enough to cope with its stimulating effects. The Robies were that kind of people and years later remembered the excitement of living there. This house, one of the most remarkable in Wright's entire career, was not a building he could have designed in 1902. It was the bold confident statement of a mature artist, vivid evidence that he was fully exploiting the possibilities of the prairie house concept.

Wright's path from architectural hesitancy to daring was not a straight one. Like the backing and hauling of the 1890s, many of his mature prairie ideas were hinted at earlier in the decade, while remnants of his tentativeness continued to appear later on. Robie characteristics were already evident in the Ward Willitts House (1902) in Highland Park, Illinois, for example (Fig. 3.15), and the Darwin D. Martin House (1904) in Buffalo, which were flung with controlled verve over the land. But not a few of the later homes, for P. D. Hoyt (1906) in Geneva, Illinois, Stephen Hunt (1907) in La Grange, Illinois (Fig.

Figure 3.15 The Ward Willitts House (1902) in Highland Park, Illinois. From *The Architectural Record,* July 1905.

Figure 3.16 The Stephen M. B. Hunt House (1907) in La Grange, Illinois. Photo by author.

3.16), and G. C. Stockman (1908) in Mason City, Iowa, to name but three, are boxy, squat, and self-contained in the Heurtley manner, although generous eaves and livelier trim mark their maturity over the Thomas and Henderson homes. So it is not that the prairie house evolved from one thing into another but that, over time, Wright's growing confidence and skill enabled him—clients and circumstances permitting—to state the prairie house philosophy with greater power.

□ □ □

The prairie house was simultaneously modern and old-fashioned: modern because its aesthetics and technology were new and old-fashioned because Wright's social objectives were in many ways traditional. The prairie house can best be understood in the context of its time, place, and the clients for which it was built. Leonard K. Eaton has demonstrated that prairie house owners were not conspicuously atypical members of their class. As independent businessmen likely to own their own moderate-sized manufacturing concerns, and as conservative Protestant Republicans, they frowned on eccentric social behavior, liberal causes, and protest literature.[12] In a period of "progressive" reform, they clung to nineteenth century values and like others in the rapidly growing metropolis felt themselves engulfed by sweeping changes not entirely to their liking. In the midst of rapid social reorganization and economic consolidation, the simpler world they had known was disappearing. It is therefore possible that their attraction to the prairie house was as strongly emotional and psychological as it was conscious and rational, for Wright's designs satisfied needs and wishes murkily understood but deeply felt by large numbers of city dwellers and satisfied them more fully, in fact, than conventional styles. The prairie house appealed to an apprehensive upper middle class by emphasizing in literal and symbolic ways the security, privacy, shelter, family mutuality, and other values some people found increasingly important in a period of urban dislocation and conflict.

Rapid industrialization and urbanization in late nineteenth century America created a disorienting situation. Armies of working class immigrants from Europe and from American farms and small towns helped escalate social tensions and instabilities in the cities. Newcomers of all classes, having lost their roots, found their places of residence determined not by family tradition or landholding but by unpredictable and insecure market situations. Vast impersonal corporations assumed control over the lives of laboring people, over white collar workers and executives, and over self-employed businessmen and professionals whose livelihoods depended upon the whims of an incomprehensible and seemingly capricious economic system. The depression of the 1890s, the most devastating in American history to that point, exacerbated the general uneasiness as even more people began to sense their helplessness. Few individuals could count on uninterrupted upward mobility, permanent employment, or a secure future for their children. Even the upper middle class, especially people like Wright's clients who did not possess inherited wealth, faced the specter of possible downward mobility and the loss of everything.

The expanding metropolis also weakened family connections. When parents no longer employed their offspring in their own enterprises, children were forced to make their way alone. Success became dependent on market conditions, not personal skills. The individual on his own, not the family as a group, became the primary economic unit. The civic and social demands of the city further weakened kin ties, especially for the middle class. With the father absent from home most of the day, the mother involved in voluntary associations, and the children in school with access to large numbers of neighborhood playmates, the family's time together decreased. "The social literature of the last half of the nineteenth century abounded in references to the instability of the family," one observer notes, "and practically predicted the extinction of family organization, at least in its present form."[13] In that kind of social climate, the family's physical encasement took on special importance for those whose resources allowed the luxury of choice. "Homes may be an *emotional bulwark* against the threats and insecurities of a too-big, too-fast, too-complicated world where one must compete, man against man, for his place in the sun," write urbanologists Charles Abrams and John P. Dean. "The high-tension currents of the job and the fears of the future are transformed into an extra need for the 'home' as a security."[14] Sociologist Richard Sennett argues that in the unknowable and potentially dangerous urban situation of the late nineteenth century, the family became a retreat, a shield against the destructive impact of the bureaucratic, overwhelming, industrial city.[15]

As much as any other American metropolis, Chicago experienced the crises and dislocations of maturing corporate capitalism. Indeed, its spectacular revival after the great fire of 1871 may have exaggerated the growing pains felt everywhere. Jane Addams' Hull House, standing in the midst of some of the nation's worst slums, called attention to the immigrant's plight and to social injustice and economic privation. Chicago had witnessed some of the bloodiest and most protracted labor–capital disputes in American history: the Haymarket Riot of 1886 and the Pullman Strike of 1894 were still alive in local memories after 1900. Poised at the crossroads of the Middle West, the city was a center of populism, socialism, and progressivism, and was of course the site of William Jennings Bryan's inflammatory "Cross of Gold" speech—which Wright witnessed, by the way—in 1896. United States Steel, the first billion dollar corporation, formed the same year in which Wright announced the prairie house, dominated the eastern approaches to the city at Gary, Indiana. At a time when novelist Frank Norris identified the railroad as the grasping "octopus" of business and politics, Chicago was the rail capital of the nation. Upton Sinclair's *The Jungle* (1906) exposed the venality, vulgarity, and sheer horror of the local meat-packing industry. Chicago was the dynamo of America, "Hog-butcher for the world. . . .City of the Big Shoulders," Carl Sandburg would soon write,[17] an exhilarating but disconcerting fact for its residents.

□ □ □

Forty percent of Wright's houses between 1901 and 1909 were in Illinois, mostly in greater Chicago, and several more were summer homes for his urban clientele. Although it looked different from other styles, the prairie house was familiar and reassuring in several important ways. The general public did not perceive Wright and his work to be totally exceptional but instead saw them in the context of the Prairie School—some of "The Eighteen" and others who began to follow Wright's lead after 1902 or so—and in relation to other architects and other manners of expression. The artistically informed considered the prairie movement and its contemporary Colonial Revival, for example, as equally legitimate attempts to create a distinctly American architecture, independent of historical influence. In retrospect the special importance of Wright's work is clear, but at the time its social and cultural milieu had a certain homogenizing effect, reducing it for the client to one of several styles from which to choose. When the professional journals and local newspapers singled Wright out for special mention, it was as often for his beautiful creations as for his innovative efforts.

Although Wright's façades were unmistakably novel, he gave his clients familiar interior programs: a living room, dining room, kitchen, reception hall, two or three bedrooms, servants' quarters, and, depending on special interests, a music room or a library. He may have articulated these spaces differently than other architects and interwoven them more closely, but the room designations themselves were traditional. If therefore, as historian H. Allen Brooks contends, the typical Prairie School client was unaware of what he was getting and remained oblivious to architectural sophistication, particularly the manipulation of interior space so central to Wright's achievement,[18] then he or she was probably attracted to the many features prairie houses shared with other styles. This analysis complements the findings of a 1954 study by the International Council on Building Research that a family's judgment about its home was an overall assessment, not a set of reactions to specific factors such as room size or traffic patterns.[19] The outside of the house was presumably not of special importance in the residents' assessment of its worth. It could have been that Wright's clients overlooked the unique to seize upon the familiar aspects of the prairie house, aspects he designed with particular reverence, and that they hired him *in spite of,* not because of, his unusual façades and subtle interiors.

Even Wright's "radically different conception," as he labeled the prairie house in 1908,[20] began to take on a certain familiarity and therefore safety if enough of them appeared in the same place. Most suburban architecture was imitative, differing only in trim, detail, and placement of elements; in essentials most homes for the same sort of people in the same neighborhood looked very much alike. And so it was with Wright in a way. A significant number of his prairie house clients hired him because they were relatives, friends, or business associates of earlier clients, because they lived nearby and saw his work, or knew it was becoming fashionable. He had five homes on the same road in Delavan Lake, Wisconsin, for example, all summer houses for Chicagoans built within five years of each other. In Oak Park, Wright erected or remodeled twenty-nine structures between 1889 and 1909, including a dozen grouped within a block or two of his own. He received four commissions in Buffalo from executives of the Larkin Company, a mail order business for which he designed administrative offices in 1904 after erecting an Oak Park house in 1903 for W. E. Martin, brother of Darwin D. Martin, a company official. The Martins first went to Wright after seeing his own studio and then, in 1905, rehired him to design their E-Z Polish Factory in Chicago. His Hillside relatives commissioned him three times between 1887 and 1901, and his Uncle Jenkin Lloyd Jones at All Souls Church, once. The list of clients who met him at All Souls, in fact, or at Hull House is a long one. Others saw his work when visiting their relatives or through other informal connections. Mrs. Harvey P. Sutton from McCook, Nebraska, put the matter quite concisely: "Having seen a plan you drew for Chas. Barnes, and being favorably impressed," she notified her future architect in 1905, "[I] write to see if you can do something for me."[21] Wright developed a kind of coterie, a group who chose him in part because others had done so and because he had a certain vogue.

His appeal, however, was not merely a matter of social connections, although they certainly helped. What the prairie house did for the client was the main thing. Post-Civil War homes, urban historian Sam Bass Warner remarks, revealed a "strong contemporary interest in private family life," and Richard Sennett writes that the need for privacy was crucial "as a means of quelling the fear and uncertainty men experienced in these new urban places. . . . So the first bulwark against the industrial city lay in the conditions of privacy vis-à-vis the outer world and nonprivate intimacy within the family itself."[22] The prairie house met these needs perfectly, much better than other styles, for one of its obvious themes was detachment from the community as a basis for close association among residents. Wright achieved the first part of this duality—privacy vis-à-vis the larger community—in a number of imaginative ways.

Although the prairie house had more window space than its neighbors, it was protected by shelf roofs or overhanging eaves, difficult to see under but not restricting the view out. Doorways were usually placed behind walls, in deep recesses, or around corners, rarely visible from the street; the difficulty in finding them could discourage casual approach. Terraces, verandas, and gardens, themselves enhancing privacy as intermediaries between public and private zones, were often screened by strategic plantings, so that even the family's outside ac-

Figure 3.17 Second level terrace of the Robie House (1907), running outside the living and dining rooms. Photo by author.

tivities were shielded from prying eyes. Although prairie houses gained additional seclusion from nestling along the ground, their main floors were sometimes raised higher above grade than usual (Fig. 3.17), enabling clients like Robie to have the privacy he wanted but still to survey street life. With openings and appendages guarded from actual and visual penetration but with a clear view of surroundings— with increased vista, in fact, due to greater fenestration—and with overhanging eaves and hovering roofs thematically emphasizing privacy, Wright's residences were like manor houses for an urban gentry, with an image closer to reserve than to hospitality. Unlike his homes of the 1920s and 1930s, they did not turn from the street to face the interior of the lot, but neither did they invite the neighbors to call. Their social statement was quite different from the large-windowed dwellings common in small-town Victorian America where pulling the shades insulted the neighbors. The prairie house drew on the newer metropolitan notions that home life was not to be intruded upon except by invitation, that it was separate though not totally withdrawn from the rest of the community, and that contact with the outside world should be at the residents' discretion.

Detachment from surroundings could well enhance, in Sennett's words, "non-private intimacy within the family," another major motif of the prairie house. "The fragmentation. . .of the many private worlds, experienced outside in the city," he notes, "was replaced by an overwhelming sense of intimacy within the house," by an increase in "absolute face-to-face relations with each other." Thus, "someone uneasy in the large world found in the home a situation of most direct and unimpeded contact with other people."[23] The prairie house seemed intentionally designed to accommodate these needs, placing an obvious premium on family togetherness. The "open plan" (Fig. 3.18) that became associated with Wright's name merged living, dining, and other common rooms, uniting the family more often than had been possible where each function was treated as a discrete entity. Wright turned the entire first floor (excluding kitchen and servants' quarters) into a single large space, separating activities by suggestion, screening, and subdivision rather than walls and doors. This brought the family physically together more often: people could be seen and their presence felt from one end of the house to the other most of the time, although the materials he used tended to absorb noise.

Prairie house space was multipurpose; it minimized the singularity of an event's location but increased the importance of the time it was performed, entirely in keeping with modern urban life in which space is a luxury and time jealously watched. With the floor plan more open, children could not be isolated (except in their bedrooms, of course, or if there was a nursery), nor could household functions be kept apart. The dining area might become a sewing room between meals and the parlor a noisy playroom all day. Uniting the family and its activities could work in two different but not necessarily exclusive directions: toward increased parental authority over children who were now easier to supervise, or toward greater mutuality and tolerance among family members who came together more often. The fact that prairie houses are still eagerly sought as private homes three quarters of a century later (Fig. 3.19) suggests successful adaptation to permissive post-World War Two concepts of child rearing. But even if they were intended to support more traditional family structures and authority patterns, they invariably served Wright's and his clients' intention of increasing contact among family members.

His clients were undoubtedly also attracted by the striking embodiment of shelter, strength, and security in the prairie house. Wright had entertained the idea, he wrote in 1936 of his early work, that "*shelter* should be the essential look of any dwelling," so he covered his homes with low-spreading roofs and generously projecting eaves. Lying close to the ground, stretching out as if to embrace as much land as possible, the prairie house was protected literally from the

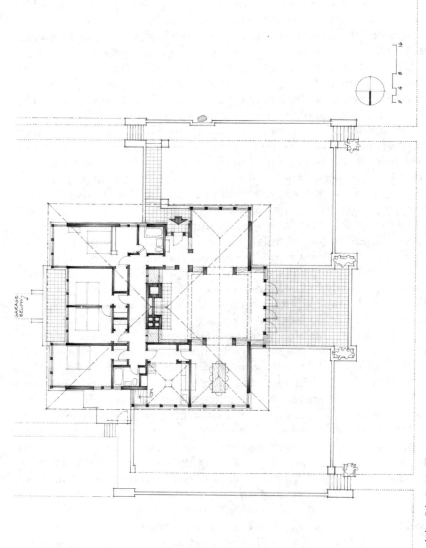

Figure 3.18 Plan of the Edwin H. Cheney House (1904) in Oak Park. Drawn by David Roessler and used with his permission.

Figure 3.19 The flow of space in the recently refurbished Edward E. Boynton House (1908) in Rochester, New York, looking from the dining and living rooms to the street-side terrace. Photo by Sue Miller, courtesy Mr. and Mrs. Louis M. Clark, Jr.

elements and symbolically from other dangers by its land and its plantings, its roofs, and its overhangs. It was a conspicuously strong and sturdy edifice, its mass and materials conveying a sense of durability, an impression enhanced by the broad chimney that staked it firmly to the ground. Wright himself appreciated the "sense of shelter" in the look of it, he wrote years later in his autobiography. It is noteworthy that he used the phrase "sense of shelter" rather than "shelter" alone, for it was the tone and feeling of his buildings as well as their design features that appealed to upper middle class buyers. Low ceilings, protected doors and windows, narrow hallways, massive hearths, and rich earth tones worked to create a warm, convivial atmosphere. The subtleties of interpenetrating spaces and the long vistas down halls through rooms to the outdoors could be fully appreciated only after extensive and intimate contact in a kind of symbiotic relationship between building and resident, subtleties a casual visitor could not understand. Wright's vigorous houses seemed to reinforce egos, encouraging inhabitants to rise to their challange. From outside, the complexities and power of the façade suggested that deep within lived a sturdy family approaching life on its own terms. "The sense of architecture as human shelter is a very fine sense," Wright wrote, perhaps with his business clients in mind, "common sense, in fact."[24]

His houses also appealed to members of the upper middle class through their literal and symbolic associations with nature and the land, a sought-for harmony Wright avidly encouraged. "The horizontal line [is] the line of domesticity," he wrote, enabling his homes to "lie serene beneath a wonderful sweep of sky" and avoid a struggle between architecture and the environment in which the residence, particularly the eclectic revivals of the period, had become a battleground. Wright proposed a working partnership with nature, "a more intimate relationship with out-door environment." He increased the number of windows that even in rain could stay open under broad eaves, usually casement windows that gave a greater sense of regulating nature's impact. Emphatic horizontal trim paid homage to and interpreted the lay of the land. All the various outreaching features pulled the outdoors within the building's grasp. Oversized urns and built-in window boxes made greenery a permanent part of the façade. Stained and waxed wood, brick, plaster, and rough-cut fieldstone in at least one case replaced paint, varnish, wallpaper, and other "unnatural" finishings. Gentle hip roofs cherished the snow for its insulating value, and instead of gouging the earth with a cellar excavation, the prairie house usually left it unscathed under its concrete slab foundation. All this was intended to eliminate visual and psychological barriers between outside and in, to create harmony between the two, so that humanity, nature, and architecture might unite in peaceful oneness. "Any building for humane purposes should be an elemental, sympathetic feature of the ground," Wright explained, "complementary to its nature-environment, belonging by kinship to the terrain."[25] As urbanization progressed and as society increasingly mythologized its rural past, people looked for ways to "get back" to nature. Moving to a suburb such as Oak Park was one way; purchasing a prairie house was even better.

Merging exterior with interior space was one of several methods Wright employed to create a holistic architecture, an ideal in part intended to alleviate confusions of urban life. The union of household members was part and parcel of the unity of design down to the last detail or, in the case of the Oak Park "colony," up to the entire neighborhood. Social and design unity also inferred "a yearning for

simplicity," as he once wrote, "a search for quiet."[26] Historian Vincent
Scully observes that Wright's impetus toward holism was expressed in
two opposite but very American ways: by emphasizing the permanence and stability that most people desire, seen in his solid massing
and blocklike building cores; and by stating the movement, expansion, and dispersal so typical of the national culture in his continuous
trim, interpenetrating spaces, far-flung appendages, and distant vistas.
"In this synthesis of opposites," Scully concludes, "Wright's intention
was to mesmerize the fragmented individual into a state of serenity
and peace, the 'Great Peace' of sheltered but continuously expansive
space to which he himself so often referred."[27] Americans were restless but wanted roots, were adventuresome but approached the unknown cautiously, took risks to make money but were socially conservative, and were ruthless in business but loved their families. The
prairie house resolved these behavior and value conflicts in a symbolic, architectural, and atmospheric synthesis that his clients were
somehow able to grasp. This attempt at sense making, at bringing
order out of confusion, at harmonizing contradictory social values
made Wright's work especially appealing to aggressive upper middle
class homeowners.

It is almost a commonplace that when people feel their institutions
threatened and their values questioned they sometimes elevate them
to the highest moral plane, sanctifying them at precisely the moment
they are least able to perform their traditional functions. Norris Kelly
Smith, whose views on the sacramental nature of William Winslow's
entry hall were quoted earlier, has noticed quasi-religious motifs in
the way Wright handled prairie house dining. He "consistently treats
the occasion as if it were liturgical in nature," Smith observes. "His
severely rectilinear furniture set squarely within a rectilinear context,
makes these dining rooms seem. . .like stately council chambers [Fig.
3.20]. . . . They declare unequivocally that the unity of the group requires submission and conformity on the part of its members."[28] A
few of Wright's prairie façades, furthermore, were precisely symmetrical, attesting to an exacting order and regularity for interior events.
Even his infrequent use of these formal devices reveals his capacity
for exalting certain family functions to the level of ritual and sacrament
"in keeping," he wrote when he announced the prairie house, "with
a high ideal of family life together."[29]

Smith goes on to argue that the real issue in Wright's prairie work
was freedom versus order, the problem of providing for authority and
submission within the family while at the same time preserving individual liberty. His conclusion is that Wright failed to hold this dichot-

Figure 3.20 The dining room in the Edward E. Boynton House (1908) in Rochester, New York. Photo by Sue Miller, courtesy Mr. and Mrs. Louis M. Clark, Jr.

omy in successful resolution, ultimately—in his dining rooms, in places like the J. Kibben Ingalls House (1909) in River Forest and in other rigidly symmetrical prairie residences—allowing the symbols of order and formality to dominate his work.

Something must be said about Wright's familiarity with social convention. Wright made it a point to know his clients well, and he listened to their advice. Contrary to legend, he did not browbeat them into accepting his plans; indeed, during most of the prairie period, his ideas about social life largely coincided with theirs. Before the era of the cocktail party, the backyard barbecue, and the buffet meal, dining was a crucial expression of social form. The dinner party, a most elaborate ritual for the hostess, was planned with meticulous care. Her ability to perform with finesse and to direct her servants with grace was an important measure of her social standing. Every effort was made to have things "just so." The intricate rules and procedures for the affair were well known to participants and, of course, to their architects. Wright gave many dinner parties himself, and thoroughly understood that dining rooms were obliged to express the sociology of dignified and orderly entertainment in which everyone—men and women—participated.

But vests that had been straightened at the table were sometimes unbuttoned after dinner when guests retired to the living room, perhaps breaking into smaller groups (by sexes) for conversation, musical entertainment, coffee, liqueurs, and cigars. Accommodating a multiplicity of events simultaneously, living rooms often played a less stately role than dining rooms in the dynamics of early twentieth century entertainment. Wright designed them accordingly, for more informality, to provide for the less ritualized aspects of a family's public and private existence. What Smith interprets as Wright's uncertainty in architectural expression—the order versus freedom dichotomy—may actually have indicated his grasp of social reality. Taken by themselves, his dining rooms do indeed imply the supremacy of order, formality, and tradition. In the context of the open plan and the disintegrating pressures of urban life, however, they emphasize occasions for sharing and group cohesion, but only occasions. Wright had no particular commitment to parental authority or child submissiveness, but he did value family mutuality. His dining rooms enhanced it in one way, his living rooms in another.

Wright's flamboyant image in later years, together with his technological and aesthetic modernity, obscures the fact that he was a product of Victorian America. Despite his futuristic architecture he was dedicated to preserving a preurban family. He was perfectly willing to provide it with startling new surroundings and yet not to change it in any fundamental way but to strengthen it against assault. Near the end of his life, in 1954 at age 87, he continued to speak nostalgically of the rural family he himself revered:

Back in farm days there was but one big living room, a stove in it, and Ma was there cooking—looking after the children and talking to Pa—all gemütlich if all was orderly, but it seldom was; and the children were there playing around. It created a certain atmosphere of a domestic nature which had charm and which is not, I think, a good thing to lose altogether.[30]

This is a homey recapitulation of determining prairie house characteristics: multifunctional interpenetrating spaces, an intimate atmosphere, and family mutuality. Recreating the best of the past was as much his goal in architecture as developing a new aesthetic. In fact, the two were one. It was probably this familiar feeling in his houses, albeit in modern dress, that attracted clients. With its occasional sanctification of the family, its motifs of strength, security, and durability,

Figure 3.21   The F. F. Tomek House (1907) in Riverside, Illinois. Photo by author.

its insistence on group mutuality and privacy, and its close association with nature and other cherished social and cultural values, the prairie house appealed to members of the metropolitan upper middle class anxious about a way of life they had adopted but not yet made their own.

□ □ □

A list of Wright's oustanding prairie homes would be too long to read and too redundant with eulogy to hold attention. Especially memorable, perhaps, are the homes (not already mentioned) for Susan Lawrence Dana (1903, 1905) in Springfield, Illinois; Edwin Cheney (1904) in Oak Park; W. R. Heath (1905) in Buffalo; A. P. Beachy (1906) in Oak Park; F. F. Tomek (1907) in Riverside, Illinois (Fig. 3.21); E. E. Boynton in Rochester and E. A. Gilmore in Madison, Wisconsin (both in 1908); and Elizabeth Gale (1909) in Oak Park (Fig. 3.22). There were many, many more. One way to measure Wright's success is to consider his total output. Only twice prior to 1901 (in 1896 and 1900) had he received as many as eleven commissions in a year. But once he developed the prairie house, he never failed to equal or surpass that figure before he left Oak Park in the fall of 1909. From 1893 through 1900, he had secured an annual average of eight commissions, of which he executed four. But from 1901 through 1909 he built approx-

Figure 3.22   Elizabeth Gale House (1909) in Oak Park. Photo by author.

imately 90 of 135 commissions, or fifteen designs and ten completions yearly. If anything, the prairie house became more popular as it grew more daring. From 1901 through 1904, he built eight of twelve buildings annually, but from 1905 through 1909, his output rose to eleven of seventeen. Although the vast majority of his structures were in the Midwest, especially Greater Chicago, he was also hired for work in California, Montana, Tennessee, New York, Kentucky, Virginia, Colorado, Quebec, and Ontario.[31] His architecture in name and in fact was regional, but it could have been built anywhere. By 1910 it was known all over the world.

NOTES

1   Vincent Scully, *American Architecture and Urbanism* (New York: Frederick A. Praeger, 1969), 126.

2   Edith Wharton, *The House of Mirth* (1905; New York: Charles Scribner's Sons, 1961, ed.), 159–160.

3   John Burchard and Albert Bush-Brown, *The Architecture of America: A Social and Cultural History* (Boston: Little, Brown, 1966 abr. ed.), 110, photo following page 178.

4   See the illustrations in John Drury, *Old Chicago Houses* (Chicago: The University of Chicago Press, 1941).

5   "In the Cause of Architecture," *The Architectural Record*, 23 (March 1908), 157; Frank Lloyd Wright, *An Autobiography* (New York: Duell, Sloan and Pearce, 1943 ed.), 139.

6   Ole E. Rolvaag, *Giants in the Earth* (New York: Harper & Brothers, 1927), 355; Willa Cather, *A Lost Lady* (New York: Alfred A. Knopf, 1923), 10; Sinclair Lewis, *Main Street* (New York: Harcourt, Brace, 1920), 140.

7   Grant C. Manson, *Frank Lloyd Wright to 1910: The First Golden Age* (New York: Reinhold Pub. Corp., 1958), 60; most of the structures discussed in the preceding paragraphs are illustrated in Robert C. Spencer, Jr., "The Work of Frank Lloyd Wright," *The Architectural Review,* 7 (June 1900).

8   Frank L. Wright, *An Autobiography*, 141–145.

9   Wright said little about his political views, but he was an admirer of the La Follettes, of Franklin D. Roosevelt for a while, and Adlai Stevenson, and an archenemy of Joseph R. McCarthy. These relationships will be discussed later in the text.

   Robert M. La Follette (1855–1925), governor and senator from Wisconsin, sent his three children to the Hillside Home School at the same time Wright's sons Frank Lloyd, Jr. (later known simply as Lloyd) and John Kenneth attended. La Follette also spoke there on occasion and once asked Andrew Carnegie to give it money. Another connection with Wright was that in 1904, the same year the architect designed a home in Madison for his childhood friend "Robie" Lamp, Lamp worked in La Follette's gubernatorial reelection campaign.

   For these relationships, see Florence Fifer Bohrer, "The Unitarian Hillside Home School," *The Wisconsin Magazine of History,* 38 (Spring 1955), 151–155; *The Weekly Home News,* November 1, 1906; La Follette to Carnegie, April 20, 1903; Ellen and Jane Lloyd Jones to La Follette, August 10, 1904; and La Follette to Lamp, October 20, 1904, all in the La Follette Collection, State Historical Society of Wisconsin (SHSW).

   La Follette's Weekly Magazine, 1 (August 28, 1909), 11, had this item, written by a member of the class in rhetoric at the Hillside Home School where "life. . .is spent in close contact with Nature:"

TO THE PASQUE FLOWER

I walked upon the hill one day
To rocky ledges far away
And there from out the warming ground
A wind-blown fur-cloaked flower found.

Its sturdy stalk upheld a cup
Whose azure-tinted face turned up
Drank in the vigor of the light
And gave it back in beauty bright.

Oh, little flower whose power for good
Has triumphed over wind and flood
Would that I might have thy power
To triumph over wind and shower.

By Frank Lloyd Wright, Jr.

10 For information on some of these homes see the *Delavan* (Wis.) *Enterprise*, April 10, 24, May 1, July 10, 1902.

11 Fred C. Robie, Jr., "Mr. Robie Knew What He Wanted," *The Architectural Forum*, 109 (October 1958), 126–127.

12 Leonard K. Eaton, *Two Chicago Architects and Their Clients: Frank Lloyd Wright and Howard Van Doren Shaw* (Cambridge: The M.I.T. Press, 1969).

13 Glenn H. Beyer, *Housing and Society* (New York: Macmillan, 1965 ed.), 53.

14 "Housing and the Family" in Ruth A. Anshen, Ed., *The Family: Its Function and Destiny* (New York: Harper & Row, 1949), 472.

15 Richard Sennett, *Families Against the City: Middle Class Homes of Industrial Chicago, 1872–1890* (Cambridge: Harvard University Press, 1970), especially Chapters 6, 7, 10, and 11.

16 Olgivanna Lloyd Wright, *Our House* (New York: Horizon Press, 1959), 26.

17 Carl Sandburg, "Chicago," *Chicago Poems* (New York: Henry Holt and Co., 1916).

18 H. Allen Brooks, *The Prairie School: Frank Lloyd Wright and His Midwest Contemporaries* (Toronto: University of Toronto Press, 1972), 25.

19 Cited in John Mogey, "Family and Community in Urban–Industrial Societies," in Harold T. Christensen, Ed., *Handbook of Marriage and the Family* (Chicago: Rand McNally, 1964), 524–525.

20 "The exteriors of these structures will receive less ready recognition perhaps than the interiors," Wright wrote in his 1908 article, "In the Cause of Architecture," cited in note 5, "because they are the result of a radically different conception as to what should constitute a building."

21 Mrs. Harvey P. Sutton to Wright, January 1905, in Don L. Morgan, "A Wright House on the Prairie," *The Prairie School Review*, 2 (Third Quarter, 1965), 6.

22 Sam Bass Warner, *Streetcar Suburbs: The Process of Growth in Boston, 1870–1900* (New York: Atheneum, 1971 ed.), 146; R. Sennett, *Families Against the City*, 195.

23 R. Sennett, *Families Against the City*, 194–195.

24 "Recollections—The United States, 1893–1920," *Architect's Journal* (London), 84 (July 16, August 6, 1936), reprinted *The Natural House* (New York: Horizon Press, 1954), 16; F. L. Wright, *An Autobiography*, 142; *Modern Architecture: Being the Kahn Lectures for 1930* (Princeton: Princeton University Press, 1931), reprinted *The Future of Architecture* (New York: Horizon Press, 1953), 119.

25 "A Home in a Prairie Town," *The Ladies Home Journal*, 18 (February 1901); "In the Cause of Architecture," *1908*; Introduction to *Ausgeführte Bauten und Entwürfe von Frank Lloyd Wright* (Berlin: Ernst Wasmuth, 1910).

26 F. L. Wright, *Modern Architecture* in *The Future of Architecture*, 130.

27 Vincent Scully, "The Heritage of Wright," *Zodiac*, 8 (1961), 9.

28 Norris Kelly Smith, *Frank Lloyd Wright: A Study in Architectural Content* (Englewood Cliffs, N.J.: Prentice-Hall, 1966), 70–71, 74.

29 "A Home in a Prairie Town," 1901.

30 Frank Lloyd Wright, *The Natural House* (New York: Horizon Press, 1954), 165–166.

31 Compiled from Olgivanna Lloyd Wright, *Frank Lloyd Wright: His Life, His Work, His Word* (New York: Horizon Press, 1967), 207–209. Dates of Wright's designs given incorrectly above and elsewhere can be corrected and verified from newspaper sources. The Scoville Horse Fountain in Oak Park, often dated 1903, was actually designed and built in 1909: *Oak Leaves*, July 31, 1909. The Elizabeth Gale House in Oak Park, sometimes attributed to 1904, was also designed and built in 1909: *ibid.*, June 12, December 11, 1909.

1901–1909

CHAPTER FOUR

Thinking and Working Along Original Lines

During the prairie years Frank Lloyd Wright made his reputation on the basis of residential work. But he also produced a number of outstanding public buildings. He attracted a good deal of attention, usually favorable, which helped generate an audience for his writing, considerable comment in the architectural press, and a following of young practitioners called the Prairie School, some of whom worked in his own Oak Park studio. He was much in demand as a speaker and with his wife Catherine was prominent in local social circles. To all indications Wright had made it to the top of his profession by 1909 and would stay there indefinitely.

□ □ □

One of Wright's most important and lasting achievements was to adapt his architectural grammar, philosophy, and technology to non-residential situations. By basing his designs on formats suitable to machine production, he found it possible to create a public architecture similar in style and feel to domestic work. Not that his churches and office buildings resembled houses—although several public structures did, in fact, look that way—but his social purposes, design features, and stylistic "trademarks," so to speak, were adaptable to different occasions. As social statements and as the art and craft of machinery, his public and private buildings were not so very dissimilar and were not intended to be. Thus, in commercial design he occasionally expressed internal organization and authority relationships in familial terms. The Larkin Administration Building (1904) in Buffalo and Unity Temple (1905–1906) in Oak Park, for example, were conceived as part-time homes for extended families as, of course, was the Hillside Home School.

The similarities in style, aesthetic expression, and proportion between Wright's public and private buildings are fairly obvious. The Tennis Club (1906) and the real estate office for E. W. Cummings (1907) in River Forest, the Pettit Mortuary Chapel (1906) in Belvidere, Illinois, and even something as small as the 1907 garage for George Blossom (Fig. 4.1) for whom Wright had built a Chicago house in 1892 (see Fig. 1.6) are so similar to prairie houses on the exterior that the uninformed might take them as residences. (In a way, of course, some were: for the dead, for the court set, and for the chauffeur.) The slab-roofed project for the Yahara Boat Club (1902) at Madison, Wisconsin, bears similarities to the Richard Bock Studio House (1906) in Maywood, Illinois, an idea that appeared again in "A Fireproof House for $5,000" published in the April 1907 *Ladies Home Journal* and in the 1909 Elizabeth Gale House in Oak Park. The significance of Wright's achievement was that it was not necessary for him to shift styles every time a new architectural problem arose. He had never been comfortable with the notion that a bank, for example, should be in one style (Classic Revival was a favorite), a church in another (Gothic was common), and a school in yet another. Since similarities among structures were all grist for the machine's mill, their differences would not be lost in a singular mode of expression. The fact that his public buildings sometimes bore striking resemblances to his homes did not mean that Wright was unable or unwilling to differentiate among various life functions or had a limited architectural vocabulary. It simply meant he had created a kind of Esperanto of design, a language comprehensive enough to speak to many possibilities.

The Hillside Home School, the Larkin offices, and Unity Temple were his three best known nonresidential buildings during the prairie decade. Of the three, the Home School most appropriately resembles a prairie house. All illustrate the many possibilities of his architectural language, and the near-unanimous praise they received indicates how much his work was admired. The Hillside Home School, fashioned from local timber and fieldstone for his aunts Ellen and Jane Lloyd Jones, was one of the first prairie buildings. Nestled into a gently sloping site, with overhanging eaves nearing the ground at points, it emphasized the reverence for nature his aunts hoped to instill in their students.

The Lloyd Jones sisters had opened the school in 1887 primarily for

Figure 4.1 Garage (1907) for the George Blossom House (1892), Chicago. Photo by author.

their thirty or more nieces and nephews, but its progressive atmosphere and individualized instruction soon attracted nationwide attention. It was coeducational with small, informal classes (many held outdoors) and an unusually high teacher–student ratio. The staff placed a premium on hikes, picnics, nature study, and the like, but hunting, fishing, and killing animals was prohibited, one of the school's few rules. Among the rare formalities were Friday afternoon dance classes conducted by "Professor" Kehl from Madison, for whom Wright designed an academy in 1912, and Sunday services at Silsbee's Unity Chapel where the aunts, uncles, and teachers presided. Little wonder Wright sent his two eldest sons, Frank Jr. and John Kenneth, to Hillside.

Wright's objective was to link art with nature for residential and pedagogical purposes. Long parallel lines of horizontal roof and trim, a spacious open interior, and native materials, all of which symbolically recapitulated nearby topography, were embellished by excellent craftsmanship, the most modern equipment, and leaded windows (Fig. 4.2). Susan Lawrence Dana of Springfield, Illinois, soon to hire Wright herself, donated the art and science rooms and their furnishings, all in the very best taste. With a number of architectural innovations,

Figure 4.2   The Hillside Home School (1901), Spring Green, Wisconsin. Source unattributable.

these features lent themselves to the appreciation of art, culture, and intellect in a beautiful natural setting.[1]

Far from being too avant-garde (or being ridiculed, as Wright liked to claim about his prairie designs), the Hillside School was locally praised as "a beautiful and ideal building" precisely because it was "something out of the ordinary." Its planning and construction were eagerly followed and commented upon each step of the way. In a short column for the village paper the reporter called it "delightful," "elegant," and "convenient" and, at an apparant loss for words, said it was "beautiful" seven times. If a structure's worth can properly be measured by the responses of those who use it, the Home School was an overwhelming success. As one gentleman commented, it was "a great joy to be in."[2]

In common with Unity Temple, the controversial five-story Larkin Administration Building bore its closest similarities to the prairie house in the interior where its trim, fixtures, atmosphere, and its physical organization suggested that the work experience should not be totally dissociated from life at home or, in more modern parlance, that the roles people perform should not be psychologically divisive. With a large main floor for the clerical force lit artificially and through sky-lights and with balconies around the perimeter for additional workers and supervisors who could observe the staff below (Fig. 4.3), the

Figure 4.3 Interior of the Larkin Administration Building (1904), Buffalo. From *The Inland Architect*, July 1907.

Larkin Building institutionalized hierarchical patterns of authority with analogies to the Victorian family. The architect's stated intention, in fact, was to encourage "a family gathering under conditions ideal for the body and mind," a simulated "family home" that would uplift workers and profit the owners.[3] Thus, there was a brick-paved recreation area on the roof and a restaurant and conservatory—with ferns and flowers visible from the main floor—on the top story. The structure was sealed to shut out noise and dirt from nearby railroads and industry. It featured custom-made office furniture and was air cooled and fireproofed. Its semidetached stairwells—a fire safety measure—were articulated as four massive pylons on the exterior corners (Fig. 4.4).

Figure 4.4   The Larkin Administration (1904), Buffalo. From *The Inland Architect,* July 1907.

Russell Sturgis, a prominent architectural critic of the day, acknowledged the Larkin Building was comfortable, futuristic, eminently practical, and exceptionally well planned, but deemed it hopelessly ugly. Architect Charles E. Illsley, on the other hand, commenting for *Inland Architect,* praised its many advances in the science of fireproofing, its desks with chairs attached on pivots for easy movement, and several other innovations. "Never before were the essentials of a modern office building, viz.: safety and light, with elbow room, ventilation and convenience more fully provided," he wrote, "nor more skillfully and beautifully combined for the daily toil of 1,800 clerks and officials." The exterior, he continued, "is such a wide departure from tradition that views must differ." They did, but the prestigious *Architectural Review* considered it "about as fine a piece of original and effective composition as one could expect to find."[4] Three officers of the Larkin Company must have agreed since they commissioned Wright to design their homes.

Unity Temple consists of two massive cubes, the larger an auditorium connected by an entrance hall to the church's community and secular activities in the smaller cube. Its poured concrete exterior seemed to Wright the most "natural" way to express its boxlike shapes. The symbolic importance of the cubes and their mutual relationship was clearly stated (Fig. 4.5): the spiritual aspects of Unity's work took precedence over the secular, housed in the smaller space, but the two were inseparably united by the sturdy bond of the entrance hall, itself set back from the building line and hidden by the auditorium from the main thoroughfare. The reporter for *Oak Leaves,* a local newspaper, congratulated Wright for making Unity "indescribably beautiful" (see Fig. 4.6). "The eye and mind were rested and the soul uplifted," he wrote, and then in a paean of unrestrained praise

Figure 4.5 Unity Temple (1905–1906), Oak Park. From *The Inland Architect,* December 1908.

Figure 4.6 Sanctuary in Unity Temple (1905–1906), Oak Park. From *The Inland Architect*, December 1908.

exclaimed: "it has the magic of grandeur to steal the carnal sense and inspire the spirit of reverence and desire for larger service." Parishioners may have been unaware of the nobler and more esoteric aspects of Wright's achievement, but they agreed that Unity Temple provided "superb surroundings" for their affairs, that it was "an edifice in which all can take pride. . . ."[5]

Wright designed several other nonresidential buildings during the decade. A partial list will show the range of his abilities. In 1901 there were additions to the River Forest Golf Club and an exhibition pavilion for the Universal Portland Cement Company in Buffalo. The year 1905 saw the little gem of a bank for Frank L. Smith in Dwight, Illinois, the E-Z Polish Factory in Chicago for Darwin D. Martin, and a striking, delicate, gold-leaf lobby and balcony remodeling in Burnham and Root's Rookery where Wright once had a suite. He designed a real estate office in River Forest, an Oak Park shop, and an exhibition pavilion for the Larkin Company in 1907; Brown's Bookstore in Chicago in 1908, another exquisite little store; and in 1909 the Chicago art galleries for W. Scott Thurber and the City National Bank and Hotel in Mason City, Iowa. Other nondomestic designs were never built: a boat club, stations for the Chicago & Northwestern Railway, another factory and an art gallery, an inn, a town hall, and more. Given the opportunity there was virtually nothing he would not attempt in his own pioneering style.

□ □ □

Even Wright's most provocative buildings received enthusiastic approval among laymen and professionals. Although his work looked and was constructed differently from conventional styles, and was in that sense radical, it was not incomprehensible to perceptive observers. Like many another artistic or intellectual breakthrough, his was arduously arrived at, but its practical application made immediate common sense. His buildings were, in short, more efficient than their more traditional counterparts, inside and out. They appealed to a generation whose heroes—businessmen and reformers—had successfully eliminated obstacles to personal achievement or had rationalized governmental and industrial processes.

A perusal of the architectural press from 1901 to 1909 shows that prairie buildings were not ridiculed and abused, as Wright later claimed, but were taken seriously and favorably commented upon. Chicago's *Inland Architect,* for example, which H. Allen Brooks says was unfriendly to the prairie movement, published over a dozen illustrations of Wright's work from 1901 until its demise in December 1908.[6] Critic F. W. Fitzpatrick revealed in its pages that by 1905 he had changed his mind about the "new style." Much of the early prairie work, he said, was "to say the least amusing," especially Wright's 1901 Thomas House (misnamed Rogers): "That sort of thing is simply exotic. His later work is far saner and loses nothing in artistic daintiness." Fitzpatrick went on to say that in more recent years prairie architects, including Wright, produced much that was "absolutely new, particularly in domestic architecture, of which we may be proud." By 1909 Fitzpatrick was prepared to admit in *The Western Architect* (Minneapolis) that although their work was sometimes more arty than practical and much too horizontal, "it is sane, and smacks of this age." For its part, *The Inland Architect* concluded its life in December 1908 by reprinting a long description of Unity Temple from the church's brochure which, needless to say, was very complimentary.[7]

American Architect and Building News in New York underwent a similar transformation. "When one sees the seriously beautiful work, even in domestic architecture, that is being done . . . notably in the East," its reviewer wrote of the 1902 Chicago Architectural Club's exhibition, "one is ashamed of the trivial spirit . . . here among us. There is a set of younger men here in Chicago who foster all this sort of thing," especially Frank Lloyd Wright. But by 1907, G. B. Ford praised him without reservation in the same journal. "What a home-like and cozy feeling is evoked by the use of big simple roofs, as in the house for F. W. Little at Peoria," he marveled, "or by the happy grouping of broad horizontal lines as in the house for Mr. Coonley at Riverside, Illinois, . . . or by the exceptionally artistic grouping of windows in the house for Mr. Hardy at Racine, Wisconsin."[8] As Wright's work grew more daring and assertive, it turned hostility into praise, in a sense redefining the terms by which architecture was judged. But even reviewers who liked it focused on details and superficialities, rarely on its underlying philosophy. Wright would soon rebel against that kind of compliment.

Elsewhere he fared even better. *The House Beautiful* in Chicago had been friendly since it began publication in 1897. It featured his prairie homes in June, July, and August 1906, and when Robert C. Spencer, Jr., began a regular column, additional illustrations of his friend's work appeared from time to time. Spencer boosted Wright elaborately in "Brick Architecture in and around Chicago" in the September 1903 *Brickbuilder*. In December 1909, *The International Studio*, reviewing the Thurber Galleries (Fig. 4.7), said "the light itself is perfectly diffused and so softened as to have the effect of daylight," the highest praise an art magazine could give an architect. Harriet Monroe, commenting for the *Chicago Examiner* on the Architectural Club's 1907 exhibition, thought Unity Temple and the Larkin Building to be "without grace or ease or monumental beauty," but she praised the "graceful. . .lines and masses" of the Coonley, Glasner, and Hardy houses.[9]

The most favorable appraisals came from Boston's *Architectural Review* and from New York's *Architectural Record*. "Deeply interesting" was the *Review*'s 1903 comment on prairie work—brilliant and illuminating, straightforward and quintessentially American. In 1907 it said that the Larkin Building was "absolutely in the line of creative architecture," and in March 1908 Thomas Tallmadge noted the aesthetic importance of Wright's leaded glass windows. In April the editor urged his subscribers to read carefully Wright's "In the Cause of Architecture," the most important feature, he said, in the March 1908 *Record*. *The Architectural Record*'s first editorial endorsement had appeared in August 1905. The "Work of Frank Lloyd Wright—Its Influence" proclaimed his buildings to be important "not only because of their

Figure 4.7 The W. Scott Thurber Galleries (1909), Chicago. From *The International Studio*, December 1909.

outstanding qualities but because of the influence they have had. Mr. Wright, indeed, stands more prominently than does any other Western [residential] architect." Even though it was absolutely uncompromising, original, conspicuous, and "so experimental in origin and so startling in effect, [his work] remains on the whole so legitimate—so free from arbitrary and capricious qualities." It was quite rare, said *The Record*, to find any group of designs so completely consistent. "He himself has feeling," embodies it in his forms, and awakens it "in the people. . .he serves. His work consequently is sufficiently popular. . .; and whatever its influence has been in the past, it will be even more efficacious in the future."[10] Wright could have hardly said it better.

He also gained stature from public showings. The Chicago Architectural Club gave him his own room in its 1902 exhibition, and in a separate sixteen-page section of the catalog printed twenty-two illustrations headed by a specially drawn title page. This was Wright's last entry in the club's annual until 1907 when he again had his own space, designed by him for an unprecedented thirty-four pieces. No Chicago architect including Sullivan had ever been so honored. Harriet Monroe wrote that Wright's low-browed, slant-roofed, unobtrusive houses with groups of windows and broad verandas nestling under the eaves "seem to grow out of the ground as naturally as the trees, and to express our hospitable suburban life, . . . of indoors and outdoors, as spontaneously as certain Italian villas express the . . . life of those old gorgeous countries."[11] He was invited to submit twelve drawings to the 1907 exhibition of the Architectural Club in Pittsburgh where one critic admired the way Wright's houses blended into their settings, how their vines and window boxes added color to the facades. But most of all he liked their "predominant sentiment of hominess, of livableness."[12] Wright was also asked to participate in the first annual exhibition of the Minneapolis Architectural Club in 1909. And when Professor Emil Lorch from the University of Michigan took his architectural students on a tour of Chicago in 1908, he made it a point to visit "Oak Park to see the concrete church designed by Mr. Frank Lloyd Wright."[13]

Wright had invested a considerable amount of time, thought, and energy in the development of his architecture. Much more than a way of making a living, it was fundamentally an emotional commitment and an extended intellectual exercise. In his first major essay for an architectural magazine, Wright discussed his work in just those terms. "In the Cause of Architecture" in the March 1908 *Architectural Record* was optimistic and self-congratulatory. Its title, which Wright would use more than fifteen times through 1928, indicated that he saw his work in a broad context and, as the text made clear, that it represented the revitalization of architectural art. Embellished by eighty-seven illustrations not counting those in advertisements, "In the Cause" was his most comprehensive statement since the 1901 Hull House speech, another building block in the philosophical edifice later known as "organic architecture."[14]

"Radical though it may be," Wright began, "[my work] is dedicated to a cause conservative. . ."; it is "a declaration of love" for the spirit of that "elemental law and order inherent in all great architecture," a law and order most readily observed in nature, particularly plant and animal forms. Since great buildings had always been based on nature's motifs, he claimed, their careful study would yield "a sense of the organic," by which he meant at this time "a knowledge of the relation between form and function." But nature's secrets could only be discovered by diligent contemplation. Like many of his contemporaries in arts and letters, Wright believed that reality and truth were not to be found on the surface of things, at best a set of illusions and at worst a deception. The truth in things was hidden, recoverable only after extensive probing, but it *was* discernible and it yielded valuable lessons. For the architect the patient analysis of nature would reveal the true meaning of function and structure. Japanese artists were among the very few who had learned to derive building forms from a close observation of nature's principles, he maintained, and Louis Sullivan had also been aware of its bounty. So, in 1908 Wright admitted to three sources of inspiration: the art of Nippon, his "Lieber Meister," and nature itself.

Good architecture, of course, was not literal reproduction but the translation of natural principles into form and method. In the broadest sense Wright meant that a design might be "deduced from some plant form that has appealed to me," such as the sumac for the Susan Lawrence Dana House (1903) in Springfield, Illinois. One house might "flare outward, opening flowerlike to the sky," while another "droop[s] to accentuate artistically the weight of the masses." Nature was also his mentor in other ways. Just as flowers, birds, and the human hand, for example, were perfectly functional and carried their own decoration, so architectural trim ought not to be applied as an afterthought but should grow organically from the structure itself in the form of doors, windows, and other functional requisites. The incorporation of natural principles into design would be even more difficult than it was, Wright thought, were it not for technology—the "modern opportunity." Never before had the architect so many tools, materials, and processes capable of interpreting and applying natural characteristics.

Wright's emphasis on nature in this and later writing in no way contradicted his 1901 "Art and Craft of the Machine." On the contrary, the two became companion cornerstones in his architectural philosophy. Depending on each other for their integrity, nature would inform and machinery execute a totally new architecture in an historically unprecedented synthesis. Indeed, the machine's capacities were best utilized when they translated natural principles into structural forms.

Extensive contemplation of nature and the machine had led him, he wrote, to formulate six architectural propositions upon which he had based his work for the last decade. Simplicity and repose, he noted first of all, defined art as surely as they did natural forms. For architecture this meant a building "should contain as few rooms as will meet the conditions which give it rise. . . ." Doors and windows should be "integral features of the structure, and if possible act as its natural ornamentation"; too much detail turned houses into "mere notion stores, bazaars, and junk shops." Appliances and fixtures should be designed into the building, pictures incorporated into the general scheme as decoration, and furniture built in. "The whole," he wrote, "must always be considered as an integral unit."

The second proposition was that "there should be as many kinds (styles) of houses as there are kinds (styles) of people and as many differentiations as there are different individuals." Thirdly, "a building should appear to grow easily from its site and be shaped to harmonize with its surroundings. . . ." If the environment was not particularly interesting, the structure should be "as quiet, substantial, and organic" as possible. The prairie, of course, had its own natural beauty—"a quiet level"—which he tried to capture and accentuate in his work.

Fourthly, he believed that natural colors—"the soft, warm, optimistic tones of earths and autumn leaves"—were easier to live with, were "more wholesome and better adapted in most cases to good decoration." Next, Wright urged home builders not to force materials but to respect their individual properties and to preserve their natural qualities. The sixth and last proposition was more a statement of faith than a rule to live by. "A house that has character stands a good chance of growing more valuable as it grows older while a house in the prevailing mode, whatever that mode may be, is soon out of fashion, stale, and unprofitable." He obviously considered the prairie house an eternal verity, not a passing fancy.

Wright thought of his buildings as problem-solving mechanisms, with floor plans being the functional, and elevations the aesthetic, solution to the problem of designing a satisfactory residence for American conditions. The difficulty was to harmonize the elevation with the plan, to integrate them so that look and livability complemented each other in keeping with the modern age. As nearly as possible, he wrote, a house should be the "grammatical expression" of an "organic integrity," a compleat design, and insofar as it had style (not a style) it would state present-day conditions honestly. A building must therefore be the best possible expression of an *idea* about how modern life is lived, given the prevailing level of sociological, technological, and cultural awareness. Any architectural statement necessarily carried political implications, as Wright clearly understood, because a building reflected, as well as shaped, social life.

Analyzing the cultural significance of technology more thoroughly than he had at Hull House seven years before, Wright maintained that since machinery now performed so many construction tasks, greatly increasing aesthetic consistency, there had arisen a "modern opportunity, to make of a building, together with its equipment, appurtenances, and environment . . . a complete work of art. . . ." Architecture based on the new technology would be "more valuable to society as a whole. . .because discordant conditions [of construction], endured for centuries, are smoothed away." As the "average of human intelligence rises steadily," enabling the individual homeowner to make better decisions, the architectural forms he or she selected would accommodate living styles more accurately and comfortably than the various revival styles because machine-made products truly express, and are the expressions of, modern circumstances. Authentic indigenous architecture, he insisted, would ultimately bring about true democracy: "the highest possible expression of the individual as a unit not inconsistent with a harmonious whole." The individual citizen bore the same relation to organic society as a single aspect of a Wright design to the entire project: His or her (its) significance could be achieved and articulated only by finding a functional place within the social (architectural) whole. In democracy, as in architecture, he believed, individuality meant "richer variety in unity."

"In the Cause of Architecture" was also Wright's most contemporary statement of the way in which the prairie house had evolved. He described his thought processes, the history of his architectural notions, the reaction of clients, contractors, and workmen. He listed what he believed were his practical and aesthetic innovations, discussed the significance of his achievements, and named his most helpful assistants and draughtspeople. He reiterated again and again that his goal was even more unity and harmony in building. Although he was quite certain that future work "shall grow more truly simple, more expressive with fewer lines, . . .more articulate with less labor, more plastic, more fluent, although more coherent, more organic," he promised to continue the search for more efficient technology, for cleaner and more virile modes of expression. As his "understanding and appreciation of life matures and deepens," his work would "prophesy and idealize the character" of his clients even more accurately. It would become "as pure and as elevating in its humble way as the trees and flowers are in their perfectly appointed way. . . ." If Wright derived intense satisfaction from what he had already accomplished, he fully expected even greater rewards as his skills developed further. The publication of "In the Cause" in a prominent New York magazine signaled that Frank Lloyd Wright had indeed arrived.

□ □ □

Not the least of his achievements was to gather in his Oak Park studio a number of exceptionally talented employees, several of whom went on to their own successful careers. Drawn to Wright by his pioneering work, his philosophy, and his popularity, they contributed to a creative atmosphere unmatched in Wright's later life or in many other architectural offices, for that matter. In some ways the studio continued the spirit of "The Eighteen" and of the Steinway loft. As the pressure of work reduced his contact with the Chicago Architectural Club after 1902, the studio became a hothouse for the budding Prairie School movement, the anvil on which progressive design ideas were hammered out. Even before Wright closed it in 1909, former employees were spreading his ideas around the Middle West, making the Prairie Movement for a number of years prior to World War One the most exciting and imaginative development in American residential design since the nation's beginning.

Studio employees came and went depending on the availability of work. Some stayed a few weeks, others several years. Some had only the simplest responsibilities, others contributed significantly to the finished projects. Wright did not keep accurate records, so it is difficult to know with certainty everyone who worked with him or when they were there. But "In the Cause of Architecture" listed several "members. . .of our little university of fourteen years' standing" (from 1893 when he opened his office until 1907 when he wrote the piece). There was Marion Mahony, who worked there eleven years or more; William Drummond, seven years; Barry Byrne, five or six years; Isabel Roberts, five years; George Willis, four; Walter Burley Griffin, four; Andrew Willatzen, and Charles E. White, Jr., three; Harry Robinson, two; Erwin Barglebaugh, Robert Harden, and Albert McArthur, one year or less. Others were George Elmslie, Francis Sullivan, Hugh M. Garden, John S. Van Bergen, A. C. Tobin (Wright's brother-in-law), and several more, including a number of sculptors, among them Richard Bock.

In 1904 and 1905, Wright designed the Larkin and Unity buildings, and from 1905 through 1909 received some eighty-four commissions, almost seventeen a year. Because he was unable to supervise every detail of each design in the studio or at the site, around 1904 certain assistants were apt to be given greater responsibility. There were two general ways this happened. One was that after Wright "carefully conceived" a project "in my own mind," he wrote in 1908, he assigned it to someone to follow "its subsequent development through all its phases in drawing room and field, meeting with the client himself on occasion, gaining an all-round development impossible otherwise." The alternative was group participation on a commission. In one well-documented case and therefore probably in others, different members of the staff advised the client at various stages, depending upon the office workload. Those writing to Harvey P. Sutton in McCook, Nebraska, between 1905 and 1908, each in response to questions requiring precise knowledge of the project, included the architect himself, and Griffin, Drummond, Tobin, Byrne, and Roberts, Wright's secretary, who also helped design ornamental glass.[15]

The major activity at the studio was, of course, draughting, which permitted little individual creativity. But when it came to rendering, that is, preparing final drawings for clients, exhibitions, and publications, assistants had latitude to add personal touches and even develop personal styles. Wright was fortunate to have Marion Mahony (who married Walter Burley Griffin in 1911) as his principal renderer after about 1905. "Her brilliant draftsmanship and unusual artistic skill," Allen Brooks states, enhanced the quality of Wright's 1907 exhibition at the Chicago Architectural Club and served her well in association with Griffin.[16] Wright depended upon his assistants' advice, judgment, and skills—Mahony did chairs, tables, and sculptural ornament for several projects—but he alone was responsible for all designs. Barry Byrne and others have testified to the stimulating atmosphere at the studio. "The value of training under Wright," Byrne remembered, "lay in. . .seeing top grade talent, or shall I say genius, function. There was no one around him that in any way approached him in ability."[17]

About six or seven employees at the studio, Allen Brooks says, "ultimately made significant contributions" to the Prairie School or later with other kinds of work, including Mahony, Griffin, Byrne, Elmslie, Drummond, Sullivan, and Van Bergen. Walter Burley Griffin, the most famous, is best remembered for Canberra, the Australian federal capital, while Barry Byrne went on to design a number of important churches after World War One. George Elmslie and William Drummond were for several years prominent in the Prairie Movement. Least known are Francis C. Sullivan and John S. Van Bergen. "A devoted promoter of Wright's work in Canada," Sullivan produced impressive houses and public buildings out of Ottawa before his decline due to personal problems after 1916. Van Bergen did excellent residences in and around Chicago, very much in Wright's manner, to be sure, but some of the strongest and most striking of the prairie genre. Marion Mahony, obscured by Griffin's shadow after she married him, designed two major planned communities and a number of other buildings after his death.[18] And although Charles E. White, Jr., continued practicing, he achieved greater fame writing architectural columns for homemaking magazines.

The Prairie School, of course, included many who never worked with Wright. Some knew him professionally, were trained by or knew

Louis Sullivan, or were influenced by journals, exhibitions, and the work itself. Collectively, their output, scattered through large cities and small towns mostly in the Middle West, was particularly popular until World War One. The reasons for the movement's decline have been discussed elsewhere and are not at issue here. The point is that after 1902 or so, Wright, his studio employees during and after their tenure with him, and a number of other architects constituted the cutting edge of American design for a decade and a half. The Oak Park studio, "that extraordinary atelier in American architectural history," one authority calls it,[19] generated and stimulated a body of designers whose buildings are still popular and influential. If one were to pin-point the single place in America where architectural innovation was being pursued most avidly between 1902 and 1909, it would have been the studio at 951 Chicago Avenue, Oak Park, Illinois.

□ □ □

Next door and connected to it, at 428 Forest Avenue, was the residence of Frank Lloyd Wright's burgeoning family. After he married Catherine Lee Tobin in June 1889, their children came quickly and on

Figure 4.8 The Wright Family, ca. 1903 in Oak Park (left to right): Frank Lloyd Wright (who took the picture), his mother Anna holding her grandson Llewelyn, Frances, Catherine, David, Catherine Tobin Wright to the rear of her son John, unidentified woman (possibly Maginel Wright, the architect's sister), and Frank, Jr. From the John Lloyd Wright Collection, courtesy Avery Library, Columbia University.

Figure 4.9 Catherine Tobin Wright, ca. 1908. Courtesy Frank Lloyd Wright Home and Studio Foundation, Oak Park, Illinois.

schedule (Fig. 4.8). Frank Lloyd Wright, Jr. (later known simply as Lloyd), was born in March 1890, followed by John Kenneth (later known as John Lloyd) in December 1891. Then, at approximate two-year intervals, came Catherine, David, and Frances and, after a five-year gap, Llewelyn, the youngest and last.[20] By 1903, after fourteen years, just as Wright's practice was about to explode in size and intensity, there were six children. Wright would soon complain of the extent to which family interfered with his work, but it was Catherine (Fig. 4.9) who bore the burden of caring for the flock. Yet despite the undoubted demands on her time and energy, she remained quite active socially and in community affairs.

Like many other upper middle class women of the time, Catherine Wright had few institutional outlets for her talents. Raising children and running their kindergarten were not completely satisfying. So she joined the cultural and literary organizations that in communities like hers were inevitably dominated by women looking for something constructive to do. She regularly attended and contributed to the local Scoville Institute, for example, where in 1907 she and Mamah Cheney (wife of a Wright client) read a paper on the "Life and Short Poems of Goethe." During a vacation at Hillside she presented "A Tribute to [George] Washington" before the Home School gathered at Unity Chapel. She was also a member of Unity Club, a social group at the Temple, of Jenkin Lloyd Jones' Abraham Lincoln Center, and was Art Committee chairwoman at Oak Park's Nineteenth Century Club, where on one occasion she reviewed "The Servant in the House," a play from which she read "beautifully and impressively" enough to leave her audience with "a feeling of peace and charity."[21]

But there lingers the nagging suspicion about Catherine that her literary and cultural activities were not entirely her own doing. She had been but eighteen at marriage, and with the immediate responsibility of a rapidly growing large family, she had not attended college or had any other career training. If she had guided Wright socially during their early years together, he soon outstripped her both artistically and socially. As time passed she seemed to look to him increasingly for intellectual affirmation. Trapped by her children, she followed Wright's lead, investigating few subjects in which he was not also interested. Goethe, for example, was one of her husband's favorites, as was the theatre, so much so that in 1907 during an exceptionally busy year he took time to write an article for *Oak Leaves*, a local paper, on an appearance by Donald Robertson at William Winslow's home prior to a series of plays the actor was about to stage in Oak Park.[22] Catherine also acted as Wright's stand-in if necessary. When the Nineteenth Century Club "felt the subject of Oak Park was hardly complete without . . . Frank Wright, who is thinking and working along original lines [,] Mr. Wright consented to state some of his guiding principles, which were read and admirably explained by his wife."[23]

On their trip to Japan from February to April 1905, Catherine seemed to be following her husband's wishes once again. It was probably not her idea to go there; most couples take their first overseas excursion to Europe. But Wright had been impressed with the country ever since he saw its buildings at the 1893 Columbian World Exposition. For a year after their return, they were virtual proselytizers for things Nipponese. Wright read a paper on "The Art of Japan" to the River Forest Women's Club in February 1906, two months before Catherine spoke to the Nineteenth Century Club, showing pictures and a model residence she brought back. In March the Wrights threw "a Japanese social" at their home under the auspices of Unity Club, with lantern slides, prints, curios, music, and tea served by "young ladies in Japenese costume." Wright had invested heavily in Japanese art, and in March 1906 exhibited 213 Hiroshige prints at the Art Institute in Chicago. Catherine seemed to enjoy this phase of their life together but does not appear to have initiated any of it. She expressed no opposition to living in Wright's shadow, doing what he wanted to do and going where he wanted to go, or even acting as his surrogate.[24]

Despite what he said later, Wright took pleasure in his children. He and his sons enjoyed hosing each other down on the front lawn, much to their neighbors' amusement. They took cold baths together with considerable splashing and horseplay, and when the boys were older he taught them to box. Wright encouraged all his children to learn a musical instrument. Lloyd played the cello, John the violin, Frances the piano, David the flute, and Llewelyn guitar and madolin. Daughter Catherine sang, her mother played the piano, and Wright tried to. Soon there was a little family orchestra going, giving Wright as much pleasure as the one he remembered fondly from his own childhood. The children were boisterous, to say the least, often spilling out noisily from their beautiful playroom into the front yard; the Wrights' end of Forest Avenue was not very quiet. Occasionally the youngsters, dirty faces and all, burst into the studio while their father was conducting business. But even "a fashionable, fastidious client from the North Side," he recalled, "was highly amused" by the goings-on. "And so must I have been," he added, "for I've never forgotten. . . . Those children!"[25]

Wright remained especially close to his maternal relatives. His mother Anna and his sister Maginel lived next door at 424 Forest Avenue even after he left Oak Park.[26] Frank Lloyd, Catherine, and their children were constant travelers to Hillside to visit John and Lloyd at school, to enjoy Lloyd Jones family affairs, or to vacation. Wright's sister Jennie (Mary Jane) married Andrew T. Porter and went to live in Toronto but, like her mother before her, persuaded him to relocate near her family. By September 1907, her brother had designed "Tanyderi," the Porter house just over the hill from the School in the shadow of the Romeo and Juliet windmill he had built ten years before.[27] The family migration was often reversed, as in September 1908 when Catherine Wright gave one of her "informal musicales" for Jennie Lloyd

Porter, some sixty friends, and Lloyd Jones relatives.[28] Wright was never very far from his "clan."

According to their passports, issued February 5, 1905, Catherine Wright was thirty-four years old, five feet eight inches tall, with a high forehead, blue eyes, light auburn hair, and a fair complexion. Her husband was listed as thirty-seven, five feet eight and one half inches, with a sloping forehead, brown eyes, dark hair and complexion, and smooth-shaven features. His chin was considered regular, his nose large, and his mouth "not large."[29] In photographs of the period, he is a handsome man with deep penetrating eyes and a confident carriage. Not a few women found him attractive. More than once he was seen driving around town in the company of unidentified female companions, prospective clients, he said.[30]

With parties at Hillside and more parties in Oak Park, speaking engagments, newspaper articles, and local recognition, Wright was socially prominent and seemingly very happy. His neighbors liked him, clients flocked to his office, his children popped in at work, fellow members at Unity Temple admired him, other architects followed his lead, and much of the profession respected him. To most observers in 1909 there was nothing on the horizon, not even a tiny cloud, to suggest that his fortunes might change.

NOTES

1 Florence Fifer Bohrer, "The Unitarian Hillside Home School," *The Wisconsin Magazine of History*, 38 (Spring 1955), 151–155. Construction can be followed in *The Weekly Home News*, October 17, 31, November 28, December 12, 19, 1901; January 30, April 24, May 8, August 21, December 18, 1902; January 22, February 19, April 9, December 3, 1903.

2 *The Weekly Home News*, November 6, 1902.

3 Frank Lloyd Wright, "The New Larkin Administration Building," *The Larkin Idea* (November 1906), reprinted in *The Prairie School Review*, 7 (First Quarter 1970), 15–19.

4 Russell Sturgis, "The Larkin Building in Buffalo," *The Architectural Record*, 23 (April 1908); Charles E. Illsley, "The Larkin Administration Building, Buffalo," *The Inland Architect*, 50 (July 1907), 4; "Current Periodicals," *The Architectural Review*, 14 (July 1907), 184. Also Frank Lloyd Wright, *An Autobiography* (New York: Duell, Sloan and Pearce, 1943 ed.), 150–152.

5 F. L. Wright, *An Autobiography*, 153–160; *Oak Leaves*, November 21, 1908. Old Unity was burned June 4, 1905. Wright received the commission for its replacement in September and completed the plans by February, 1906. Ground was broken in May, and Unity House, the smaller cube, opened

in September 1907. Construction halted for lack of funds from December
to April 1908. The church proper held its first services October 25, 1908.
See *ibid.*, September 16, December 9, 1905; February 24, 1906; October
24, November 21, 1908; November 12, 1910; *The Oak Park Argus,* September 16, 1905.

6   See the bibliography in Robert C. Twombly, *Frank Lloyd Wright: An Interpretive Biography* (New York: Harper & Row, 1973), for a list of Wright
illustrations in *Inland Architect.*

7   F. W. Fitzpatrick, "Style," *The Western Architect,* 14 (October 1909), 32;
"Chicago," *The Inland Architect,* 45 (June 1905), 46–47; *ibid.*, 52 (December 1908), 77.

8   *American Architect and Building News,* 76 (April 26, 1902), 29; 92 (November 30, 1907), 181.

9   Robert C. Spencer, Jr., "Brick Architecture in and around Chicago," *The
Brickbuilder,* 12 (September 1903), 187; "Art Gallery Designed by Frank
Lloyd Wright," *The International Studio,* 39 (December 1909), xcvi; Harriet
Monroe in the *Chicago Examiner,* April 13, 1907.

10   *The Architectural Review,* 10 (May 1903), 152; 14 (July 1907), 184; 15 (April
1908), 74, 78; *The Architectural Record,* 18 (July 1905), 63–65.

11   See the Chicago Architectural Club catalogs from 1902 and 1907; *Chicago
Examiner,* April 13, 1907.

12   *American Architect and Building News,* 76 (April 26, 1902), 29.

13   *The Western Architect,* 13 (May 1909), 54; "Architectural Students Visit
Chicago," *The Inland Architect,* 51 (May 1908), 46.

14   F. L. Wright, "In the Cause of Architecture," *The Architectural Record,* 23
(March 1908), 155–222, punctuation slightly altered here.

15   F. L. Wright, "In the Cause of Architecture," 1908, 164; Don L. Morgan,
"A Wright House on the Prairie," *The Prairie School Review,* 2 (Third
Quarter 1965), 5–19. Also see Nancy K. Morris Smith, Ed., "Letters, 1903–
1906, by Charles E. White, Jr., from the Studio of Frank Lloyd Wright,"
Journal of Architectural Education, 25 (Fall 1971).

16   H. Allen Brooks, "The Studio," *The Prairie School,* 78–87, the source of
this quotation (page 83), is the best discussion of the Oak Park group.

17   Quoted in Mark L. Peisch, *The Chicago School of Architecture: Early
Followers of Sullivan and Wright* (New York: Random House, 1964), 45.
This book also contains valuable material on the studio (pages 39–52).

18   H. Allen Brooks, *The Prairie School: Frank Lloyd Wright and His Midwest
Contemporaries* (Toronto: University of Toronto Press, 1972), 79, 85 (to
which I am indebted for this section), also discusses the demise of the
Prairie Movement. Also see Susana Torre, "A Feminist Monument (for
Marion Mahony)," *Heresies,* 1 (May 1977), 107.

19   M. L. Peisch, *The Chicago School,* 39.

20   David Gebhard and Harriette Von Breton, *Lloyd Wright, Architect* (Santa

Barbara: University of California Press, 1971), 97; *The Weekly Home News,* December 17, 1908; F. L. Wright, *An Autobiography,* 109–110.

21 *Oak Leaves,* September 21, November 2, 1907; April 10, 1909; *The Weekly Home News,* February 25, 1909; *The Chicago Tribune,* November 8, 1909.

22 "Tribute" to Donald Robertson, *Oak Leaves,* December 14, 1907.

23 *Oak Leaves,* April 29, 1906.

24 On the Wrights' Japanese activities see *Oak Leaves,* February 25, 1905; February 10, March 24, April 29, 1906; F. L. Wright, *Hiroshige: An Exhibition of Colour Prints from the Collection of Frank Lloyd Wright* (Chicago: The Art Institute, March 29, 1906), a catalog for which the architect wrote a foreword, copy in possession of the Burnham Library, the Art Institute, Chicago.

   The Chicago Tribune reported on November 8, 1909 that Catherine Wright worshipped her husband, let him design all her gowns, and dictate where and when she should appear. This seems to be verified by other evidence, discussed in Chapter Five.

25 F. L. Wright, *An Autobiography,* 114–117.

26 *Chicago Blue Book, 1911,* page 759, and *Chicago Blue Book, 1916,* page 505; *Annual Report Abraham Lincoln Center and All Souls Church, 1911* and *1913* list Anna and her daughters by address, as does the *Fifteenth Annual Report of All Souls Church, 1898.*

27 On Wright family affairs at Hillside see *The Weekly Home News,* June 26, December 4, 1902; May 19, November 9, 1904; April 4, 11, 30, May 7, June 13, 1907; October 8, 1908; March 18, May 20, June 10, 1909. On "Tanyderi" see *ibid.,* September 26, 1907; January 23, 1908.

28 *Oak Leaves,* September 26, 1908.

29 In the FLW Collection, Avery Library, Columbia University.

30 *The Chicago Tribune,* November 8, 1909; Otto McFeely, Oak Park, to Bruce Barton, New York, February 6, 1956, Barton Collection, SHSW.

1907–1912

CHAPTER FIVE

Affinity Tangle

And then something went wrong. There came a time for Frank Lloyd Wright when architecture lost its adventure and family life its joy. Believing that marriage, suburban, and professional pressures were conspiring to destroy him, he suddenly threw them off in a desparate act that perilously threatened his career. After a European interlude with a client's wife, he retreated to a rural enclave to take up the artist's life. The ensuing social ostracism, together with an unshakable conviction of the wisdom in his moral and architectural positions, intensified his iconoclasm and his disdain for conventional behavior. In 1912, at age 44, Wright's prospects were uncertain. He found himself on the razor's edge between past glories and future oblivion.

□ □ □

"In the Cause of Architecture" was only one indication of Frank Lloyd Wright's growing stature. His third article for *The Ladies Home Journal* appeared in April 1907, the same month he was featured so conspicuously at the Chicago Architectural Club's exhibition in the Art Institute. His influence extended to New York and Boston through the pages of *The Record* and *The Review*. In 1905 he received seventeen commissions, in 1906, 1907, and 1908, sixteen annually, and in 1909, nineteen, the most in any single year of his practice. The Larkin Building and Unity Temple established his reputation in nondomestic work, like the Coonley and Robie Houses in the residential field, and in 1908 he completed presentation drawings for the magnificent Harold F. McCormick estate in Lake Forest, Illinois, an apparent entree into the highest levels of Chicago's industrial aristocracy. In 1909 he showed at the Architectural Clubs in Pittsburgh and Minneapolis. Everything was going very well indeed.

Then without warning, seemingly without cause, he threw it all over. Leaving his wife and six children, entrusting his uncompleted work to an assistant and a hastily selected colleague, he eloped to Europe with the wife of a client, creating a local sensation. The "prominent Oak Park architect," *The Chicago Tribune* intoned, was responsible for "an affinity tangle. . .unparalleled even in the checkered history of soul mating."[1]

In September 1909, Wright went to New York to meet Mamah Borthwick Cheney (Fig. 5.1) who had left her children with a friend in Colorado where she had spent the summer. The Wrights and the Cheneys had been a familiar foursome in Oak Park, attending concerts and other social functions together after 1904 when the architect designed the Cheneys' house a few blocks from his own. The women were members of the same civic organizations and in 1907 collaborated on a paper on Goethe given to a local literary club. It was during this three-year period when Mamah Cheney saw quite a bit of Wright, that "the thing happened," as the architect put it, "that has happened to men and women since time began—the inevitable."[2] The love affair had been discussed in Oak Park where the couple made no attempt to disguise their feelings, even from their spouses; but in November 1909, when the urban dailies discovered the elopement, an open secret turned into a press scandal.

When he left Oak Park on September 20, Wright told a local reporter he would be in Germany at least a year to work on a book. He neglected to say, of course, that Mamah Cheney would accompany him, although his family and friends knew his plans. The story came to light only when an enterprising Chicago newsman, aware that Catherine Wright was at home, saw the entry "Frank Lloyd Wright, and wife" in the register of Berlin's Hotel Adlon. Subsequent press accounts, including interviews with Catherine, established that the architect's "strange infatuation" with Mrs. Cheney over a period of years had almost caused the Wrights to separate before. Calling her rival "a vampire" and denouncing her for all the troubles, Catherine admitted that her husband was "a strange man. Only a few of his friends are able to understand him. E. C. Waller, Arthur Heurtley, and Hamlin Garland," she said, "these are the men who are his friends. They know. . .what he has had to contend with." He had fought great battles in the world of architecture, Catherine continued. "He is fighting one now, and I know he will win. This is a struggle that he has fought out before."[3]

Figure 5.1 Mamah Borthwick Cheney, date unknown. A *Chicago Tribune* photo.

The activities of the "soul mates" during their year in Europe are known only in broad outline. First they went to Berlin where the architect made preparations for the folio of drawings, *Ausgeführte Bauten und Entwürfe von Frank Lloyd Wright,* a retrospective on his work since 1900, and for a smaller book of photographs, *Frank Lloyd Wright Ausgeführte Bauten,* published by Ernst Wasmuth in 1910 and 1911, respectively. Then he rented a small villa overlooking the plaza Michelangelo and the David statue in Florence where he, an assistant, and his eldest son Lloyd, who came to help him, assembled and revised the drawings. Mrs. Cheney remained in a Berlin apartment, seeing Wright for several days at a time when he came periodically to consult his publisher. After he finished assembling the illustrations sometime during the first half of 1910, Mrs. Cheney joined him at a villa in Fiesole, Italy, where Wright wrote an introduction to the folio. Although they may have planned to settle there—he sketched a home and studio for the place—they spent several months inspecting Italian art, sculpture, and architecture, reading a great deal, translating Goethe (the architect's favorite), and preparing for publication English editions of the work of Ellen Key (a Swedish advocate of motherhood without marriage), in short, living the life of wealthy American expatriates.[4] They were very happy together.

But Wright was still reluctant to break his ties with home, as Catherine had told *The Tribune* reporter, appearing unable to make up his mind about the future. His love and attraction for Mamah Cheney competed with his strong feelings, perhaps even his guilt, about Catherine and the children. "I am going back to Oak Park," he wrote his London friend Charles R. Ashbee in July 1910, "to pick up the thread of my work and in some degree of my life. . . ."[5] Mamah returned to Oak Park in July, but not to her husband. Edwin Cheney reported that in June 1909 Mamah had told him she was leaving for good, and this turned out to be correct. In August 1910 she took her children on vacation and later, after her husband moved out, returned with her son to their home at 520 North East Avenue, never to live with Edwin again. Wright remained in Europe until about September 20 when he sailed from Germany, arriving in Oak Park on October 8 for an apparent reconciliation with Catherine and his family, just as she had predicted. "The infatuation of the two Oak Park soul mates," *The Chicago Tribune* said, "has ended."[6]

After October 1910, things seemed back to normal. *The Weekly Home News* in Spring Green, Wisconsin, reported in May 1911 that Anna Wright was "building her a home in Hillside valley, . . . a little north and west of the old millsite," but no one connected this with her son. In August, Edwin Cheney won an uncontested divorce and custody of the children without mentioning Wright at the hearing. Had they known about construction at Hillside, perceptive observers might have wondered why Wright built a brick wall between his house and studio at Oak Park, put his family into the Chicago Avenue side, now a second residence, and moved into the Forest Avenue home by himself. Only his family knew that he had escorted Mamah Borthwick (now using her maiden name) to Wisconsin after her divorce in August, then retreated into his bachelor quarters in Oak Park to work furiously on his architecture. But on December 24, 1911, his double life ended, and his secrets were revealed. The Chicago papers reported he had returned to Hillside on December 21, putting his Forest Avenue property up for rent. At first denying Mamah was with him or that he had left Catherine a second time, he finally decided he could hide the truth no longer. At a press conference in Spring Green on Christmas Day, Wright announced the Mamah Borthwick and he would live permanently at "Taliesin," the home he had been building for her, not his mother, since May.[7]

Historians have offered several explanations for Wright's desertion of family and clientele. One the architect put forward himself has been readily accepted: he was tired of his domestic situation and in love with another woman. Personal considerations were obviously crucial, but they do not take into account his persistent assertion, stated in various ways, that "I found my life in my work."[8] If he was as consumed by architecture as he maintained, and there is no reason to think otherwise, then why did he close his studio and abandon his thriving practice? On this issue the historical consensus has been that Wright was "a hurt and sensitive genius, driven by the indifference of his countrymen into the arms of appreciative foreigners."[9] But the legend that he had taken a stand "alone in my field," designing buildings "unhonored and ridiculed" by "abuses seldom described" has been uncritically accepted too long. The related assertion that Wright left because in 1908 Harold F. McCormick rejected his drawings in favor of an estate designed along traditional lines depends on the untenable assumption that the loss of a single commission—however magnificent—could undermine the work of a decade.[10] Wright's decision to leave involved both personal and architectural considerations woven into a matrix more complicated than all these suggestions combined.

By no stretch of the imagination was Wright's work abused or rejected during his Oak Park years, and he knew that very well. What bothered him most by 1907 was precisely the opposite: uncritical acceptance and unthinking praise. Perhaps his view of professional criticism was naive. He expected searching analysis from which he could learn, a kind of Socratic dialogue that would help his ideas develop. What he got even from admiring critics, he complained, were superficial responses to the obvious features of his work—uninformed reactions to his aesthetic and functional innovations. Wright revealed his disappointment quite eloquently in a long letter to Harriet Monroe after her friendly review in the *Chicago Examiner* of his April 1907 exhibition at the Art Institute. Although she liked his "most interesting experiment," comparing it favorably with the great historic styles, she nevertheless derided its "unusual, at times ever bizarre" appearance. Apparently believing that Monroe of all the critics should have been more supportive, Wright accused her of shallow judgment, of not accepting his work on its own terms, and of failing to probe its underlying philosophy and its fundamental objectives. His letter expressed a pent-up dissatisfaction with the way in which his buildings had generally been discussed.[11]

"I am hungry," he told her, "for the honest, genuine criticism that searches the soul of the thing and sifts its form. Praise isn't needed especially. There is enough of that, such as it is, but we all need intelligent painstaking inquiry. . .into the nature of the proposition." Without that kind of discussion, he insisted, his architecture would only be "lightly touched up with House Beautiful English for the mob," that is, with flattering oversimplifications for mass consumption. The struggle to create a work of art was difficult enough, he wrote, without prominent voices making it "unnecessarily grim and temporarily thankless" by labeling it a certain "type," thereby diminishing its uniqueness. Shortsighted analysis would not "harm the inherent virtue of good work," but it could mislead the public and discourage the artist. "When an individual effort to be true to a worthy ideal has the courage to lift its head, it deserves something better than the capricious slapstick of 'the type,'" he chided Monroe, "even if the slap appeals to the gallery, in other words 'to our very best people.'" His own architecture, he claimed, had "met little more than the superficial snap-judgment of the 'artistically informed.' I am quite used to it, glad to owe it nothing. . . . But meanwhile the *Cause* suffers delay! That is the price the public pays for 'the type' and it is the serious side of the matter."

The objectives of his work and the "cause" for which he fought, as he elaborated in *The Architectural Record* the next year, were the rejuvination of architecture, the creation of indigenous forms to express and suit life in the United States, and the destruction of "Fakery and Sham [that] rule the day." An American architecture is a possibility and will be a definite probability when it is conceived and executed with "*organic consistency* and such individuality" as his own work revealed. But "conscientious efforts of this nature" will founder and die unless they "receive the encouragement on their native hearth that they already have in conservative England or in France. . . ." There, he noted, but not in the United States, his designs were "accorded the rare virtue of originality without eccentricity." He did not want to be remembered as the creator of an exotic new style, indeed, of any style, but simply hoped critics would understand that his architecture was first of all concerned with fundamental social and cultural questions. Any analysis, like Harriet Monroe's, that did not discuss him on these terms, he contended, missed the point entirely.

As this letter makes clear, it was not lack of building opportunity or adverse public opinion or even negative comments in the architectural press that bothered Wright. Rather, it was the shallow level of analysis among critical supporters who failed to grasp the broader implications of his work. But if praise as a substitute for scrutiny was useless, it was positively destructive when it subverted his identity by forcing him into a group, by plugging him into a style. As the Prairie School became popular and influential across the Middle West, many critics lumped Wright with a dozen or more practitioners working in his manner, unaware that the distinguishing characteristics of their work had originated with him and him alone. Some of the others, such as Walter Burley Griffin and William Drummond, good architects in their own right, had once been his employees, and none was his equal, although George Maher and possibly Robert C. Spencer, Jr., had momentarily achieved greater popularity. The problem as Wright saw it was not the success of "The New School of the Middle West," which he was perfectly pleased to endorse in his 1908 "In the Cause" essay. The problem had to do with his own very rapid ego development forcing him to assert his primacy in Prairie School ranks. He strongly objected to being reduced to just another member of just another movement, especially one that depended so heavily on his own pioneering efforts. He rebelled against being grouped with traditionalists like James Gamble Rogers and Howard Van Doren Shaw who violated his most fundamental principles but were said to have the same philosophy—perhaps because they had once been members of "The Eighteen"—or with opportunists like George Maher who designed prairie-ish houses when clients wanted them but had no real commitment to the style or to the cause. Wright was annoyed and upset when his leadership role was slighted and his obviously superior talent demeaned by glib categorizing. Somehow he had been swamped by the dimensions of his own succes, overrun by a bandwagon he had not intended to create.[12]

Another irony had arisen to plague him. Years after the fact, observers repeatedly called him "a follower" or "a pupil" of Louis Sullivan. It was almost a convention to open a description of prairie architecture by mentioning Sullivan who, as one critic claimed, created a new style, then passed it on to Maher, Drummond, Wright, and other "disciples." Analysis like this overlooked some rather obvious facts. One was that Wright had never really been Sullivan's "pupil." He had learned a great deal from his Master, and was the first to admit it; but in his residential work for Sullivan, Wright was his own teacher. Critics also failed to mention that after the dissolution of his partnership with Dankmar Adler in 1895, Sullivan's output had dropped precipitously; that most prairie school architects had never worked with him; that his influence came from past performance, not continuing effort; and that Wright, not Sullivan, had revolutionized the house. Sullivan would never have claimed that he taught Wright enough about residential architecture to account for so great an accomplishment. It had almost been the opposite, in fact: the only two homes Sullivan designed between 1892 and the end of his career in 1922 (see Chapter Two) were heavily indebted to Wright. So to be constantly described as Sullivan's "pupil" only reinforced Wright's belief that he was not being judged on his own merits.[13]

There was yet another important source of Wright's dissatisfaction, having to do with his own feeling about himself. The "absorbing, consuming phase of my experience as an architect ended about 1909," he recorded in his autobiography. "I was losing my grip on my work and even my interest in it. . . . [It] seemed to leave me up against a dead wall. I could see no way out. Because I did not know what I wanted I wanted to go away."[14] By 1907–1908, he had completed the Coonley and Robie Houses, had supervised the opening of Unity Temple, had finished the McCormick project, and had produced such other notable homes as those for E. E. Boynton in Rochester, New York, Isabel Roberts in River Forest, Illinois, and E. A. Gilmore in Madison, Wisconsin. With the exception of the Frank J. Baker and Elizabeth Gale Houses in Wilmette and Oak Park, his 1909 ventures lacked the resourcefulness, the drama, and the excitement of the preceding four or five years. It was as if he sensed the prairie genre had reached its limits, that he had explored all its possibilities, that he had reached a logical and successful conclusion, and that nothing was to be gained from further effort. He needed rejuvenation, which he soon found in Italian architecture.

The great achievement of 1907—the Robie, Coonley, and McCormick projects—was the climax of his prairie adventure. Their success was partly due to challenging sites, unusually generous budgets, or supportive clients, a rare combination of factors that may have stimulated Wright to exceptional effort. The two additional years he remained in Oak Park were by contrast something like the denouement of a play, when he sensed that the satisfaction of creativity had ended and that the curtain was falling on his great performance. With every building he produced, the "style" gained further popularity and the "school" new adherents who imitated his "manner, rather than the substantial value of his work," as one journal put it.[15] The longer he remained in his studio, the more of his identity he lost. He felt, it seems, that the introspection of compiling a portfolio might give him a clearer perspective on what he had already accomplished and that the architectural treasures of the Continent might inspire him in new ways and new directions.

□ □ □

Whatever anyone else may have thought, Wright knew the value of his own work. As he gained knowledge and experience and as he came to believe in himself without serious reservation, his self-image began to change, making him increasingly jealous of his individuality. He learned to see himself as a free spirit, as a creative person who had earned the right to take liberties with social rules and customs. Gradually he realized that his suburban as well as his professional situation was too confining. He could never be a truly free and independent man, nor could he be happy in any fundamental way, until he broke certain patterns and boundaries defining his life. The same storm clouds were gathering at home as at work; community and family also took him for granted, threatening his freedom of expression by forcing him into roles and categories that negated his individuality. Happy home and quiet suburb, once ideals to be achieved, were now burdens to be shed.

Early in his career, when he considered it a marked improvement over his small-town background, Wright had adopted suburban life with abandon. Under the tutelage of Cecil Corwin, J. L. Silsbee's head draughtsman who befriended him upon his arrival in Chicago, Wright had acquired a taste for the good life. Silsbee, Sullivan, and their clients, the parishioners at All Souls Church where Wright met Catherine, and his own associates were more or less of a type, a reference group he admired and patterned himself after for several years. But as he learned to rely on his own judgment and to make his own choices, he grew less enamored with upper middle class conventions. As his inclinations and his preferences changed, suburban life became too ritualized, too predictable, and too stifling. He kept up many appearances—at dinner parties and speaking engagements, for example, where he could perform—but his behavior grew steadily more unorthodox.

Caring less for community opinion as the years passed, his personal style became more his own. He let his hair grow longer, down over his collar; his expensive clothes were unusually casual: flowing neckties and smocks, Norfolk jackets, riding breeches, and high-laced boots hardly met suburban expectations. He was nominally Unitarian, which itself was somewhat suspect among many at the turn of the century, but he rarely attended services. Sunday mornings sometimes found him playing with his children in the front yard while his neighbors on their way to worship looked on disapprovingly. He was regularly ticketed for driving his custom-equipped automobiles over the speed limit. He laughed too loudly at the theatre, boycotted Fourth of July celebrations (still considered a necessary demonstration of patriotism), steered away from politics, never locked his house, and kept late hours. Worst of all were his relationships with married women; his most flagrant violation of social propriety was to drive them around town in his open car. "He was not a mere Lothario," a friend later wrote. "He was a victim of women. They took up more of his time than really was necessary."[16] After 1904, when he designed her home, and certainly after 1907, Wright devoted a great deal of his time to Mamah Cheney.

Suburban life was made even more tedious by the shortcomings (from Wright's point of view) of his wife Catherine, the socially conscious young woman he had courted so eagerly two decades before. Catherine became pregnant immediately after marriage, and when six children came along in the next fourteen years she gave them most of her time. Wright said she paid scant attention to his architecture; she "knew only a few of her husband's clients' names," he wrote, "or what buildings he was building." She, too, had her complaints. He was more interested in his house and studio, Catherine claimed, than in his bride. "Architecture was my profession. Motherhood became hers," he wrote. "Fair enough, but it was division."[17] It was easy enough in retrospect for Wright to see a pattern of separateness from the very start of their marriage as he ruminated years later in the pages of his autobiography, but it does seem from contemporary evidence that Catherine—from lack of exposure, arduous family responsibilities, or for other reasons—did not keep pace with Wright's artistic and intellectual maturation. She tried to, as her prominence in local literary and cultural circles attests, but usually by following his lead. Her neighbors, although siding with her during Wright's absence late in 1909, told *The Chicago Tribune* that she appeared in public only with her husband's permission.[18] Catherine had apparently grown overly dependent and subordinate, even by standards of the day. Wright may have engineered it, but he came to dislike it.

During the lengthy publicity surrounding her marriage, from September 1909 until December 1911, Catherine never publicly criticized her husband, in the process denying her own womanliness. Despite the pain he caused her, she offered only excuses. What about those auto trips with married women? reporters asked. "Purely business," she said. And the talk of previous affairs? "Totally untrue." But what about his relationship with Mamah Cheney? Surely he must share responsibility for that? All her fault, Catherine insisted. She was the villian, the "vampire," and poor Frank was the innocent victim in a strange infatuation he had battled for years. When will he return? they asked. "As soon as business permits. He wants to come home and he will leave Mrs. Cheney behind." And who is to blame for all this? Edwin Cheney, Catherine replied, because he could not keep his wife away from her husband, and Mrs. Cheney, of course, but "Frank Lloyd Wright is as clean as my baby!"[19]

As her life with Wright continued to deteriorate through 1911, Catherine became even more obsequious and cloying. Why the dividing wall between the house and studio? Because with the two oldest boys grown and living elsewhere, her husband thought the place too large and wanted to sell the Forest Avenue half. What was Wright doing in Wisconsin with Mamah Borthwick? There was no truth to the rumor he had eloped again, Catherine insisted stoutly. He had built a new house for his mother, and if there was a woman in it, it was probably she.[20] Her husband had fought his whole life for what he believed, and that is what he is doing now. "I have fought beside him, and the struggle has made me," she claimed resolutely, relying on her bottomless well of self-efacement and self-denial to ignore the fact that Wright was in another woman's arms. "Whatever I am as a woman, aside from my good birth, I owe to the example of my husband. I owe myself to him and I do not hesitate to confess it."[21] Catherine continued to worship Wright for years, believing in his eventual return so strongly that she refused to grant him a divorce until 1922, when legally she had no choice.

Fortunately for Wright, Mamah Borthwick offered a more stimulating alternative than Catherine. Mamah more closely resembled the two women the architect would later marry than she did his first wife. Like Miriam Noel and Olgivanna Milanoff, the thirty-year old Mamah (in 1909) was artistic, independent, strong-willed, and more unconventional than her predecessor. Like other "liberated" upper middle class women of the period, all three were uncomfortable with the roles of wife and mother that social custom assigned and looked outside the family for release of energy and talent. They were well read, sophisticated, and cosmopolitan, and each had had children by a previous marriage. Mamah Borthwick and Miriam Noel did not seem to bend to Wright's will. Although Olgivanna Milanoff did, she found aspects of their life she could control despite him.

Mamah Borthwick had been restless as Mrs. Cheney, the suburban housewife. After graduating from the State University, she became head librarian in Port Huron, Michigan. Presumably reluctant to give up her career, she rebuffed Edwin Cheney's proposals several times before finally consenting to marry, and she continued to take more pleasure in art, literature, and women's movements than in the daily household routine. Unlike Catherine, who supervised her own kindergarten and was a doting mother, Mamah left her children in the hands of a governess and at boarding school. With Wright, the artist, she could more fully explore her talents and express herself than with her husband, the manufacturer. She was actively interested in Wright's work—Oak Park rumor had it that Edwin Cheney took no part planning their home, leaving it entirely to Mamah and her architect—and shared some of his literary interests; but she had her own activities, for example, translating the work of the Swedish feminist Ellen Key and other French and German women writers. According to *The Chicago Tribune*, Mamah was locally known as capricious and temperamental, manifestations perhaps of domestic unhappiness. But she was certainly strong enough to cope with Frank Lloyd Wright, to leave her settled existence in the suburbs, and to live a highly individualistic life of social ostracism in Europe and in rural Wisconsin.[22]

Wright was also attracted to Mamah because she had freed herself from her children, a second source of domestic discomfort. In an effort to establish a community of kindred spirits at 428 Forest Avenue, the Wrights permitted their offspring considerable independence, which turned out to have its disadvantages. When the architect moved his draughting table to Oak Park from his downtown office in 1893, he did so, he announced, "to secure the quiet concentration of effort" possible only outside the "distractions of the busy city."[23] But different disturbances arose, and two years later he moved again, this time into a studio in a separate building attached to his house, difficult for the children to get to. But as his second son John remembered, "I was able to discover and find my way. . . .I could get to the balcony from a hidden stairway. . .[and] throw things over the railing on the. . .tables and the heads of the. . .men." The children gave their father no peace. According to John, they listened on the telephone extension, interrupting conversations with clients. They broke Wright's custom-designed decorations and furniture, squirted him with the hose, sat on his dress hat, and were generally unresponsive to discipline. "Things began to smash," the architect himself recalled. "Cries to resound. Shrieks. Quarrels and laughter. . . .Destruction of something or other every minute." "I often wonder now," John wrote in 1946, "why he didn't leave sooner."[24]

He did not leave because "he was preeminently a lover of home and family." He invested considerable money, time, and energy re-creating for himself the atmosphere he remembered from the Lloyd Joneses. Twenty years of married life and the dominant motifs of his residence confirm that. "He loved fatherhood," John insisted, "he just didn't like. . .everything that goes with it." More than two decades after his departure, Wright remembered that "everything, personal and otherwise, bore down heavily upon me. Domesticity most of all. . . .A true home is the finest ideal of man, and yet—well to gain freedom I asked for a divorce." Home versus freedom: the two were no longer compatible. By 1909 personal independence beckoned Wright more alluringly than the security of family and suburb, and the dictates of his artistic temperment pulled more compellingly than parental attractions. "The architect absorbed the father in me," he confessed, mindful of distateful suburban mores, perhaps "because I never got used to. . .being one as I saw them all around the block and met them among my friends. I hated the sound of the word papa."[25] His success in forming a close-knit family had unexpectedly stifled his individuality. William C. Wright left home after failing to cement strong group ties; his son fled to escape them.

Dichotomies between the artist on the one hand and family man and suburbanite on the other had appeared in the architecture Wright designed for himself as early as the 1890s when he asserted that his professional aspirations were more unorthodox than his domestic ide-als, hoping to maintain a balance between the two by separating them from each other. His 1895 studio addition to his 1889 home was partly to accommodate a larger family and work load but was also a retreat from rambunctious children. The house façade facing the street is formal and symmetrical (see Fig. 2.6), well within the familiar "shingle style" defined by Vincent Scully, suggesting orthodox family behavior and adherence to community expectation. But the interior is another matter (see Fig. 2.2), with open circulating spaces, unusual vistas, and playful events implying an individualistic, somewhat freewheeling life style. By contrast, the studio is unmistakably esoteric (Fig. 5.2). Its intricate and complex facades, numerous windows, broad planes and

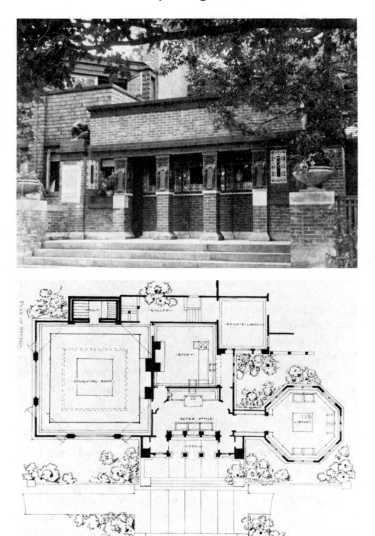

Figure 5.2 Chicago Avenue entrance and plan to Frank Lloyd Wright's Studio (1895), Oak Park. From *The Chicago Architectural Annual (1902) by the Chicago Architectural Club, 15th Exhibition.*

interwoven lines, its varying materials, abstract ornament, and its multifold but carefully related contrasts all suggest experiment and change. If the façade of the house hinted to neighbors that family life should be orderly and simple, and if its interior suggested to guests that domesticity was more complicated than they might have expected, the studio shouted to clients that Wright's architectural work was not governed by the usual rules and formulae.

The studio undoubtedly reflects the rapid evolution of Wright's design abilities between 1889 and 1895, but it is also a statement about social organization. Wright chose to segregate his family from his work by erecting separate buildings (he might have expanded the house), making little attempt to harmonize the two styles, so that the studio clearly rejected the middle class conventions the residence so obviously embraced. Whereas the house fronted on quiet residential Forest Avenue, soon to have six more of his designs, the studio faced busy Chicago Avenue, a main thoroughfare leading directly downtown. Set further back from the street then its neighbors, the house cherished its tranquility, while with precisely the opposite gesture the studio's steps opened directly to the sidewalk (Fig. 5.3). Anyone could see that the buildings had entirely different purposes. Wright had concluded in 1895 that to avoid conflict his professional affairs should be separate from family obligations: "I didn't see much of him except at meal time," one of his sons recalled.[26] But this solution failed: the family continued to intrude. If Wright could not prevent his private life from interfering with his work, perhaps outside the suburbs and with different living arrangements the two might merge in happier union.

Wright built Taliesin at Spring Green[27] specifically with Mamah Borthwick in mind, and as an architectural metaphor it reveals more about him than anything he wrote. Wright's work and his relationship with Mamah needed a quiet isolation, and in his precarious situation Taliesin was an optimistic attempt to solve the architectural and per-

Figure 5.3 Frank Lloyd Wright Studio (1895), Oak Park, with his 1889 residence in the rear. From *Annual of the Chicago Architectural Club Being the Book of the Thirteenth Annual Exhibition* (1900).

sonal problems that had finally made life in Oak Park impossible. But at first glance Spring Green seems an unlikely retreat: Wright could not escape publicity where everyone knew him, within the orbit of the Chicago papers that had made him front-page news. Nor did the disapproval of relatives and friends lend hospitality to the place. Nevertheless, there were compelling reasons to choose the family seat. Since he expected to lose commissions, building on his mother's land (probably gotten by inheritance) would reduce expenses, while the local abundance of fieldstone meant cheap materials. He also looked for inspiration from the environment he had loved as a boy. By leaving Oak Park he had rejected marital responsibility and violated social norms; the return to Spring Green was a pilgrimage to the safety of childhood familiarities.

At Taliesin Wright made provision for all his needs. Intended to be as self-sufficient as possible, in addition to living and draughting quarters it included an icehouse, recreational facilities, stables, a granary, a power plant, and its own water supply.[28] Unlike the architecturally simpler studio-home in Oak Park, it was much more functionally diverse although consistent in style, materials, and mode of expression. In the earlier buildings Wright had declared his work more unconventional than his family, but he found that the separation of the two preserved the integrity of neither. Placing his faith in new surroundings and different personal relationships, he now reunited his roles under one roof. Taliesin elaborated a dominant theme of the Oak Park studio by stating unequivocally that Wright alone would define the rules governing his personal as well as his professional life. It was clearly the home of an unusual and self-confident person. As much a declaration of independence as his recent actions, as much an autobiography as the book he later published, Taliesin is a key to Wright's psychological and intellectual profile in 1911.

There are several ways to analyze the meaning of this famous building. First of all, it was environment embracing, nestled into and around a hilltop but not on it (Fig. 5.4); hence its name, which is Welsh for "shining brow," since it was built into the brow of the hill, not placed on top of it. It was often difficult to determine where the building ended and the landscape began. Vaguely L-shaped with appendages, including walled gardens that rooted it to site, its long window series and overhanging eaves brought the outside in, while its layers of fieldstone symbolically reiterated a prominent natural feature of its surroundings (Fig. 5.5). There were courtyards, terraces, pools, trees, and plantings everywhere, firmly establishing an intimate relationship with the outdoors, not *any* outdoors, be it noted, but one he partic-

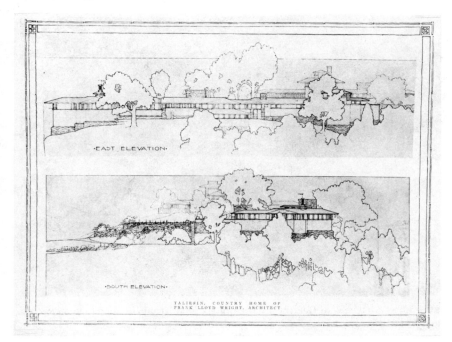

Figure 5.4 Elevations of Taliesin (1911), Spring Green. From *The Western Architect,* February 1913.

ularly loved. If Wright attempted to maximize contact with nature—to him benign and inspirational—he was also looking to minimize contact with a suspicious and critical world.

From another point of view, Taliesin is a kind of stone fortress, overlooking the countryside from its commanding position (Fig. 5.6). Its floor plan and enclosed hill made it accessible only by exposed routes. Taliesin's ground-hugging arrangement, its low eaves, sheltered windows, and hidden courtyards rendered it secure, from both climate and unwanted visitors. Its remote rooms and numerous gardens, where privacy was augmented by strategically placed shrubbery, contributed to a retreatlike atmosphere. Taliesin's very complexity was itself a protective measure, understood by inhabitants but disconcerting to outsiders. Many of these motifs had been features of the prairie house (of which Taliesin was perhaps the greatest example), but Wright developed them further here. It is not insignificant, of course, that with all the available sites on his mother's two hundred-acre tract, Wright built on the hill rather than in the valley, a decision enhancing Taliesin's psychological strategy as well as its aesthetic success.

Figure 5.5 Partial view of Taliesin (1911), Spring Green. From *The Architectural Record,* June 1913.

There is yet a third way, possibly the most important, to interpret this building. Wright had tried, he wrote, to "marry" his buildings "to the ground" so that they could not "be intelligently studied apart from their environment," the implication being that no one of them could have been built anywhere else. Taliesin performed such a marriage. It was designed for its spot and could not have been erected elsewhere. But that spot was also a social as well as a physical place, and if Taliesin was successfully married to site, it also made overtures to Spring Green, Wright's new community. Unlike most of the houses he would build during the 1920s, Taliesin did not throw up intimidating barriers between itself and outsiders. Despite its obvious protective measures it was a defensive, not an aggressive, building. An optimistic prophecy in stone of the social relationship he hoped to establish, it was an attempt to link Wright's private domain with his boyhood community, in 1911 some 730 people, many of them relatives, he had known over thirty years. Later on he wrote: "There was a house that hill might marry and live happily with ever after."[29] He might also have written: "There was a town that I might marry. . . ." Although Taliesin's controlled access indicated contact would be initiated by the architect and on his terms, Wright wanted to build bridges to his neighbors.

Figure 5.6 View of Taliesin (1911), ca. 1913, with Spring Green in the background. From John Lloyd Wright Collection, courtesy Avery Library, Columbia University.

□ □ □

Wright's desire—his need, in fact—to convince Spring Green that his actions were well intentioned and that his presence was not threatening led him on Christmas 1911 to call a press conference and on several subsequent days to issue clarifying statements. Another motive behind his outspoken self-revelations was a kind of missionary zeal about his firmly held but unpopular ideas on marriage. Silence about his love life would have probably been the wiser course, but instead of letting the affair blow over he courted a confrontation. His insistence that people listen exposed a peculiar symbiotic relationship with public opinion. Every time he spoke out, he further alienated a society unable to tolerate such flagrant violations of its mores; fully intending to go his own way, Wright seemed not to care. But on the other hand, he explained himself so often and at such length that he obviously wanted to convince people, to make them see things his way, for he cared what they thought. Had he been completely iconoclastic, he would have said nothing, let alone make conciliatory gestures. But while he extended his hand, he also thumbed his nose by his behavior, at least so people thought. His new role as a moral critic obliged him to speak his mind, but it also put him on the defensive.

His Christmas message was his most contemporary interpretation of the events leading to his flight from Oak Park. He and Catherine had grown apart, he said, primarily because she had devoted herself to her children while he became absorbed in his work. Neither was particularly to blame. Far from harming his family by leaving it, he claimed, he had actually acted in its best interests. Not only had he left it financially secure, but the new arrangement would in the long run be beneficial: living with his true love would be an example of integrity to his children, whereas to have lived a lie in their presence would only have warped their character. His basic conflict was between professional and domestic obligations; he could not simultaneously be an architect and a parent. There had come a point when giving "expression to certain ideals in architecture" was more important than fatherhood, and since he was essentially an artist, he had discovered that his buildings were his truest children. More than anything else he had wanted to develop an organic architecture, "American in spirit . . . . I feel I have succeeded in that," he said, and if the world rejected his work because of his private life, "it will be a misfortune."

Wright disclosed what was really on his mind in the last section of his statement. He admitted violating social mores, but he claimed to have been loyal to a "higher law." Prohibitions and restraints "are made for the average," he declared. "The ordinary man cannot live without rules to guide his conduct. It is infinitely more difficult to live without [them] but that is what a really honest, sincere, thinking man is compelled to do. And I think," said Wright, now speaking more autobiographically, "that when he has displayed some spiritual power, has given some concrete evidence of his ability to see and to feel the higher and better things of life, we ought to go slow in deciding he has acted badly." Since he had contributed personally to society's improvement, Wright was arguing, people ought to trust his judgment in moral matters and absolve him from their petty obligations. Wright had formulated an artist's credo.[30]

Since neither he nor the reporters were satisfied with the Christmas message, he decided to prepare another, in the meantime issuing a short statement every day between December 27 and 31. Influenced by Ellen Key, he criticized the institutions of marriage and the family for turning people into property. No person should "own" someone else, he said, as wives and husbands now legally "own" each other. He also assured the townspeople that he had not arrived among them to defy convention but to get back to work. "The fact that I am here in the 'front yard' of my family is sufficient proof. . .I have come to mind my own business in my own way. . . ."[31]

But his relatives were hardly sympathetic, at least Jenkin Lloyd Jones was not. Convinced that sudden financial troubles at the Hillside School were the result of Wright's presence in the vicinity, he wrote his sister Jane on December 28 that "we as a family and as neighbors out [sic] to do something to set ourselves right with the country, the world and [to prevent the destruction] of the school which now as I predicted last summer has received the deadliest blow of all." But what can we do, he wailed, to save ourselves from "that blinded egotist in the 'Haven of Pleasure,'" that "Palace of Folly?" The school would never recover, he added in January 1912, "until the Wright scandal blows over if it ever will." And Uncle Richard, speaking for the family to the papers, said that "we certainly do not approve of his actions." Pressure from the Lloyd Jones forced Wright to issue a notarized statement reiterating "the fact that my aunts are in no way connected with me socially or financially. . . . I am not even a neighbor. There could be no less intercourse between us were I in another world and. . .this will remain so."[32]

On December 30, 1911, Wright gave his "last word" on the subject (although it was not), a completely accurate assessment, he insisted, from his point of view. Reading his statement in the third person, he referred to "four people, a wife and a man and a husband and a woman." He described the affair as if it had happened to someone else, as if it were a hypothetical situation from which he was extracting important lessons for society's benefit. He told how a man and a woman had fallen in love, how they had waited a year to be sure, and how they had gone to Europe openly with the knowledge of all concerned. The husband and the wife, of course, tried to separate the lovers without understanding that the bond uniting them was far stronger than mere infatuation.

During the year they waited with their families "to make certain that love was love," "all was wretched, all false, all wasted." But they learned they could live honestly and happily only with each other regardless of social consequences. To abide by society's dictates and stay with their legal mates was a mockery, and by 1909 their lives had become a lie. By the time the man returned to his family after a year with the woman in Europe, he had concluded there was no recourse but to make the ultimate break. "Thus may be written the drama that is played now in countless cases behind the curtain," Wright remarked bluntly, "so that honest souls may profit. And most will call it the triumph of 'selfishness.' I cannot care. . . ." Perhaps the truth is but "the 'selfishness' of nature." He had described his and Mamah's leap of faith, he implied, so that others in similar situations might take courage and follow their example, because integrity and happiness were far more important than legality. Such sensational views were eagerly received by the press, of course, but not by Spring Green.[33]

Speaking for the community, *The Weekly Home News* saw great danger in Wright's behavior. Holding fast to traditional and provincial values, editor W. R. Purdy believed that "no man and no woman can live in the relation which these two brazenly flaunt and explain it to law-abiding, God-fearing people" without "insult[ing] decency." The couple was "a menace to the morals of the community and an insult to every family therein." Their former spouses were better off without them, Purdy contended, since Wright and his companion were "either insane or degenerate." Far from being Mamah Borthwick's "soul-mate" as the metropolitan press said, Wright was merely engaging in a publicity stunt designed to bring even "more advertising than his knee-panties, long hair and other funny ways. . . ." The most tragic aspect of this affair, the editor thought, was its impact on the Lloyd Joneses. As teachers and ministers, doing "all in their power to discourage vice and immorality," they were "disgusted, humiliated, and chagrined" by Wright's actions.[34]

The architect replied to Purdy's blast shortly after the New Year. He denied any intention of dragging scandal to the community, and said his behavior was not prompted by immorality or bravado. Praising Spring Green's "consideration and courtesy," he expressed his "admiration for the dignity [it] has maintained in this onslaught of slanderous intent." Someday, he promised, he would be "valuable and helpful to the people here. . . . Give me," he asked, "the benefit of the doubt."[35] Some did, but others did not. One man recounted how he had met Wright on a road shortly before Christmas and had a nice talk about horses. "But this love affair of his is beyond me," he added rather reluctantly. "I've only had a common school education and when he explains why he left his wife and children. . .he gets beyond my depth." Most local people had known Wright long enough not to be surprised by anything he does, *The Chicago Tribune* reported. "They are interested in his eccentricities, but his wide reaching family connections in the community and his reputed wealth seem to restrain public condemnation of him." Not for everyone, of course. A group of neighbors asked the Iowa County Sheriff to investigate Wright, but he would act only if someone swore out an arrest warrant and was not even sure if the architect had broken the law. Two people living under the same roof, the sheriff said, even at a "Crazy House" as Taliesin was dubbed, was not a criminal act. The Ladies Aid of the Spring Green Congregational Church, where Wright's father had once lectured, forwarded a resolution of disapproval to Mamah Borthwick and her architect, but aside from that nothing overtly hostile happened.[36] The community slowly resigned itself to its new arrivals.

Wright needed Spring Green in 1912 more than it needed him; but reluctant to compromise, he put severe strains on its generosity. Promising nothing more than to be good and to be helpful and valuable "in time," he asked his neighbors to ignore the past and present irregularities that offended them so deeply. Wright made equally difficult demands on his predominantly urban clientele. In Oak Park he had been minutes away from the Loop where he maintainted a business office. Now, his remote location forced clients to write or make an arduous journey to Taliesin. Hiring Frank Lloyd Wright after he moved to Wisconsin involved a demonstration of how much he was needed, which is exactly what he wanted to know.

NOTES

1 *The Chicago Tribune*, November 7, 1909.

2 *The Chicago Tribune*, December 31, 1911.

3 The events of late 1909 were reported in *The Chicago Tribune*, November 7–9, 1909; *Oak Leaves*, September 25, 1909 (last page).

4 Lloyd Wright to Linn Cowles, February 2, 1966, FLW Collection, Avery Library, Columbia University; letters from Wright to Ashbee, July 8, 24, 1910, in Allan Crawford, "Ten Letters from Frank Lloyd Wright to Charles Robert Ashbee," *Architectural History*, 13 (1970), 66–69.

5 Wright to Ashbee, July 8, 1910, in Crawford, "Ten Letters from Frank Lloyd Wright," 66.

6 Wright to Ashbee, July 24 and September 26, 1910, in Crawford, "Ten Letters from Frank Lloyd Wright," 68–69; *The Chicago Tribune*, August 3, October 9, 1910; August 6, 1911.

7 *The Chicago Tribune*, August 6, December 24, 26, 1911; *The Chicago Record-Herald*, December 24, 1911; *The Weekly Home News*, May 25, 1911.

8 *The Chicago Tribune*, December 26, 1911.

9 Concisely stated but not accepted by Norris Kelly Smith, *Frank Lloyd Wright: A Study in Architectural Content* (Englewood Cliffs, N.J.: Prentice-Hall, 1966), 83.

10 Wright developed the "unhonored and ridiculed" legend in "In the Cause of Architecture: Second Paper," *The Architectural Record*, 34 (May 1914), 405–406 ff., to be discussed in Chapter Six. Neither Henry-Russell Hitchcock, *In The Mature of Materials: The Buildings of Frank Lloyd Wright, 1887–1941* (New York: Duell, Sloan and Pearce, 1942), 59–60, nor Grant C.

Manson, *Frank Lloyd Wright to 1910: The First Golden Age* (New York: Reinhold Pub. Corp., 1958), 211–213, could decide whether personal or professional considerations were of greater importance in Wright's departure, although Manson (pages 202, 211) weights the "McCormick fiasco" heavily.

11 The review appeared April 13, Wright's letter followed ca. April 18. Both are in the Monroe Poetry Collection, University of Chicago Library.

12 See, for example, *The Brickbuilder,* 12 (September 1903), 187; *The Architectural Review,* 10 (May 1903), 152; *ibid.,* 15 (April 1908), 69–74; *The Inland Architect,* 45 (June 1905), 46–47; *The Western Architect,* 14 (October 1909), 32. Many of the articles that grouped Wright also praised him.

13 The same articles that discussed the Prairie School usually cited Sullivan's leadership. The comparison continued, becoming even more pointed by 1911. See "A Departure from Classic Tradition: Two Unusual Houses by Louis Sullivan and Frank Lloyd Wright, Architects," *The Architectural Record,* 30 (October 1911), 327–338, and "Comparison of Master and Pupil Seen in Two Houses," *The Western Architect,* 17 (November 1911), 95.

14 Frank Lloyd Wright, *An Autobiography* (New York: Duell, Sloan and Pearce, 1943 ed.), 162.

15 "Work of Frank Lloyd Wright—Its Influence," *The Architectural Record,* 18 (July 1905), 61.

16 Otto McFeeley to Bruce Barton, February 6, 1956, Barton Collection, State Historical Society of Wisconsin (SHSW). On life in Oak Park see F. L. Wright, *An Autobiography,* 109–120; John Lloyd Wright, *My Father Who Is on Earth* (New York: G. P. Putnam's Sons, 1946), 15–17 and *passim;* Maginel Wright Barney, *The Valley of the God-Almighty Joneses* (New York: Appleton-Century, 1965), 133–134; *The Chicago Tribune,* November 8, 1909; September 24, October 10, 1910; *Baraboo Weekly News* (Baraboo, Wis.), January 18, 1912.

17 F. L. Wright, *An Autobiography,* 109–111.

18 *The Chicago Tribune,* November 8, 1909.

19 *The Chicago Tribune,* November 7, 9, 1909.

20 *The Chicago Tribune,* December 24, 1911; *The Chicago Record-Herald,* December 24, 1911.

21 *The Chicago Tribune,* November 7, 1909. Catherine also continued her civic activities as if nothing had happened: *Oak Leaves,* November 12, 1910; December 16, 1911.

22 *The Chicago Tribune,* November 8, 9, 1909; August 16, 1914; *The Chicago Record-Herald,* December 28, 1911.

23 1893 Brochure announcing his practice reproduced in J. L. Wright, *My Father,* 22.

24 J. L. Wright, *My Father,* 27, 53, 54; F. L. Wright, *An Autobiography,* 111.

25 F. L. Wright, *An Autobiography,* 113, 163; J. L. Wright, *My Father,* 55.

26 J. L. Wright, *My Father,* 27.

27 Taliesin is actually located about three quarters of a mile northeast of the Home School off State Highway 23 in what was the tiny hamlet of Hillside, Iowa County, across the Wisconsin River from Spring Green, Sauk County. Since Taliesin is popularly thought to be in Spring Green, to assign it otherwise would only cause confusion.

28 Wright published the plan and elevations in *The Western Architect,* 19 (February 1913), n.p. Also see F. L. Wright, *An Autobiography,* 171.

29 Introduction to *Ausgeführte Bauten und Entwürfe von Frank Lloyd Wright* (Berlin: Ernst Wasmuth, 1910); F. L. Wright, *An Autobiography,* 168–169.

30 *The Chicago Tribune,* December 26, 1911.

31 *The Chicago Tribune,* December 28, 29, 30, 31, 1911; January 1, 1912; *Chicago Record-Herald,* December 29, 31, 1911; *Wisconsin State Journal,* December 30, 1911.

32 Jenkin Lloyd Jones to Jane Lloyd Jones, December 28, 1911, January 4, 1912; notarized statement, February 3, 1912, all in Jane Lloyd Jones Collection, SHSW; Richard Lloyd Jones in *The Chicago Record-Herald,* December 28, 1911.

33 *The Chicago Tribune,* December 31, 1911.

34 W. R. Purdy, "A Prophet is not without Honor Save in His Own Country," *The Weekly Home News,* December 28, 1911.

35 Letter to the editor of *The Weekly Home News,* January 4, 1912.

36 *The Chicago Tribune,* December 27, 30, 1911; *Baraboo Weekly News,* January 4, 1912.

1910-1914

CHAPTER SIX

Spiritual Hegira

During his years with Mamah Borthwick, Frank Lloyd Wright designed three architectural landmarks and wrote three important essays. A major exhibition in Chicago enhanced his national stature and his German publications made him influential on the Continent. But despite his great accomplishments, he seemed preoccupied. Some of his projects were mechanical adaptations of earlier prairie houses, uninspired replicas of aging ideas. Occasionally, in the Midway Gardens, the Imperial Hotel, at his own Taliesin, and with other exceptional opportunities, his imagination was stimulated and he rose to the challenge. But he seemed to be less interested in more commonplace residential work. These were years of reflection and self-evaluation as he elaborated his socioarchitectural philosophy. These were the first of many inbetween years, the beginning of a quarter-century hiatus separating periods of staggering achievement. And these were years that ended in tragedy.

□ □ □

Frank Lloyd Wright designed twenty-two buildings in 1911, three more than in 1909, leading some observers to believe that he had weathered the storm of 1910 quite handily. But a broader perspective shows 1911 to have been an aberration, for outspokenness and scandal had indeed tarnished his reputation. His twenty-one executions out of fifty-three commissions from 1910 to 1914 were notably fewer than fifty-seven of eighty-four in the preceding half-decade. Wright built only thirteen of thirty-one designs during the four years he actually lived with Mamah Borthwick (1910, 1912–1914), and of these, two were

144

alterations of existing structures while another was an addition to Avery Coonley's estate. The most graphic measure of Wright's plummeting fortunes was that in 1912, 1913, and 1914, his years in Spring Green with Mamah, he saw only seven designs reach completion for paying customers. Several of his clients had known him before 1910, so it appears that his two highly publicized "spiritual hegiras"[1]—to Europe and to Wisconsin—kept almost everyone but a few old friends from making the pilgrimage to Taliesin.

With his building opportunities reduced, he devoted more attention to his writing, in 1910 and 1912 publishing important essays that further illuminated his concept of "organic architecture." Together they constitute his most lucid and comprehensive philosophical statement before his torrent of books, articles, and lectures in the 1930s. In his 1910 essay, the introduction to *Ausgeführte Bauten und Entwürfe von Frank Lloyd Wright*, written in Italy during his elopement with Mamah Borthwick, he placed himself firmly in a specific architectural tradition. Second was the short but incisive text of *The Japanese Print: An Interpretation* (1912), a highly autobiographical theory of the artist's methodology and social function that has generally been neglected because it was not directly concerned with buildings. His third noteworthy essay in these years, "In the Cause of Architecture: Second Paper," added little to his philosophy but is important as self-evaluation and as a critique of the profession.

Wright opened his introduction to the 1910 German folio (Fig. 6.1) by remarking that his recent tour of Florentine art and buildings had verified two things he already knew: while the "false ideals" of the Renaissance negated organic architecture, the "Gothic spirit" encouraged it. Like folklore and folk song, organic architecture was indigenous, "intimately interrelated with environment and with the habits of life of the people." Unlike other styles, Gothic architecture responded to actual needs, had been built by methods and tools appropriate to its time and place, and had looked to "natural law" for its structural principles and expressive forms. Renaissance or "inorganic" architecture, on the other hand, had pasted imitations of older styles over outmoded construction techniques, had ignored nature to eulogize historical curiosities in building form, had disregarded contemporary needs and living habits, and had failed to develop its own standard of beauty. By copying classical antiquity, the Renaissance had perpetuated tired concepts, dead forms, and was, architecturally, the antithesis of creativity.

Wright did not mean to advocate a Gothic revival—"the conditions and ideals that fixed the forms of the twelfth are not [those] that can

"Ausgeführte Bauten und Entwürfe von Frank Lloyd Wright"

Two portfolios 17½" x 25½" in size; of lithographed plates showing plans, elevations, and perspectives of seventy buildings by this architect. Published by Ernst Wasmuth, of Berlin. Special arrangements have been made for selling this work direct to the purchaser. Write for descriptive circular to

FRANK LLOYD WRIGHT, 605 Orchestra Hall, Chicago

Figure 6.1 Advertisement for the Wasmuth portfolio (1910) in *The Architectural Record*, January 1913, showing the Avery Coonley living room (1907), Riverside, Illinois.

truthfully fix the forms of the twentieth century"—but to reinvigorate the Gothic *spirit*. An interpretation of the best traditions using contemporary architectural language, the "spirit" of which he wrote was "not a stupid attempt to fasten [ancient] forms upon a life that has outgrown them." On the contrary, if modern architecture embraced the Gothic attitude it would necessarily acknowledge modern circumstances: democratic institutions, personal liberty, and technological change. With machinery dictating the way it was built, and democratic individualism shaping its organization and appearance, organic design would be an "outgrowth. . .of conditions of life and work [it] arose to express." Anything else would deny the character of twentieth century America and, like the inorganic creations of the Renaissance, be absolutely removed from time, place, and people—"borrowed finery put on hastily," not developed "from within" life as lived.

With the exception of Louis Sullivan's work, Wright claimed, his own was the first consistent protest—in five hundred years, be it noted—against the "pitiful waste" of Renaissance imitation. His was a serious attempt to formulate industrial and aesthetic ideals based on native tools and living conditions for American residential design.

Since the admirable national characteristics of broadmindedness, independent thought and judgment, and common sense were primarily Western and Midwestern, the Gothic spirit would most likely take root there, he claimed, in an architectural adaptation of Frederick Jackson Turner's famous "frontier thesis." Although Eastern fashion setters still preferred outmoded Old World styles, the public would eventually rebel against their artistic tyranny to heed the Midwestern businessman, that repository of clear thinking, whose instincts were much sounder in architectural matters. Standing ahead of public opinion, many no-nonsense, hardheaded, practical-minded business leaders— the best and most representative Americans, Wright thought—had already recognized the advantages (but not the cultural import) of his own designs. These men were "part and parcel and helpful in producing the organic thing. They can comprehend it. . . . It is thus the only form of art expression. . .for a democracy, and, I will go so far as to say, the truest of all forms." Wright did not add, for he rarely thought in such terms, that the prairie house was as much a class statement as a democratic manifesto.

The concept of organic architecture was based on several as yet unstated assumptions. Implicit was Wright's belief that truth and beauty were not relative but absolute, waiting for discovery and expression by the artist who probed the fundamental law and order in every existing thing. Wright believed that everything, every tool, client, rock, building, or flower, had its own truth, its defining essence, its absolutely unique "nature." Once the "nature" of a *problem*, for example, was understood, its solution became obvious. Since any given building project was at bottom a response to a specific human and architectural problem, an organic design would be the *only, inevitable* solution. It would express the conditions that called it into being, conditions the architect could discover since his primary obligation was to explore the "nature" of everything involved in the work. Thus, a person disciplined by organic principles, knowing the properties of his tools and the ramifications of the opportunity, "working out his problems with what sense of beauty the gods gave him," is governed by the very nature of the undertaking. Clients could trust that architect implicity because, limited by organic method, he was "the only safe man."

The goal toward which he struggled, he declared, was unity. Every aspect of a building—the furniture, light fixtures, rugs, heating vents, pictures, and downspouts—everything should be harmonious. If the architect would think of appurtenances as solutions for subproblems within a larger organic entity, each aspect of the project would assume its inevitable place and form, as leaves and branches on a tree. The same dynamic, he said, applied to groups of buildings. Given similar tools and social conditions, and a proper regard for organic principle, Wright believed that architects would arrive at mutually harmonious conclusions. If all the organic buildings in the world—Gothic and prairie, tall and short, pointed and square, wood and stone, in all their "bewildering variety"—were put in one place, "harmony in the general ensemble [would] inevitably result; the common chord. . . being sufficient to bring them all unconsiously into harmonious relation." Far from contradicting each other, the combined efforts of all the American architects committed to organic principles would ultimately constitute an authentic native genre for the first time in national history.

The self-consciously American architect closed his German essay by admitting his "debt to Japanese ideals," his most explicit reference yet to that source of inspiration. It was therefore appropriate that his next important statement of aesthetic and philosophical principles was *The Japanese Print* (1912), a thirty-five-page book that was not directly concerned with architecture. Several scholars trace Wright's interest in Japan to exhibitions at the 1893 World Columbian Exposition which he saw in Chicago. However influential that event may have been, he made but one brief reference to Japan before his 1905 visit, in the 1901 Hull House lecture. But he returned with enough prints and with sufficient expertise to lecture on Japan and to stage an exhibition in 1906 at the Art Institute, the catalog from which was published as *Hiroshige* with his own introduction. By 1912 he was a nationally known expert on Japanese printmaking, on his way to assembling "one of the most important collections. . .in the world," a fact not generally appreciated by Wright admirers.[2] Had he not succeeded at architecture, he might conceivably have devoted a career to the study of Eastern art.

In *The Japanese Print*, Wright turned several of his 1910 assumptions into explicit statements. He took as his own the platonic notion that "the laws of the beautiful are like the laws of physics. . . . They pre-exist any perception of them." A thing was beautiful because it was an embodiment and an expression "of that precious something in ourselves which we instinctively know to be Life. . . . And when we say, 'It is beautiful,' we mean that the quality in us which is our very life recognizes itself" in the object. Thus, organic art, the only true art, derived its beauty from an honest creative process, and from its structure, which was form arranged or fashioned to build an Idea, "a larger unity,—a vital whole. . .which must always persuade us of its reasonableness." Geometry was the grammar of structure, and Wright believed that certain shapes were endowed with "spell power," or symbolic properties, which gave meaning to the Idea. The circle, for example, indicated infinity; the spire, aspiration; the triangle, structural unity; the spiral, organic process; and the square, integrity. The artist could express the Idea of beauty and find the hidden core of reality by knowing the value-laden nature of these shapes which were "fundamental verities of structure, pre-existing and surviving particular embodiments in [the] material world."

Of all artists, Wright maintained, the Japanese printmaker was best at capturing Idea in geometric form. After studying a pine tree, for example, he would attempt to express not its literal appearance but its very nature, those essentials making it a pine and not an oak or a maple. If the species disappeared from the earth, he would be able to preserve it for all time with a few lines and simple shapes because he had mastered its specific and distinguishing characteristics—its "nature." By this Wright meant neither the great outdoors of plants and animals nor "that outward aspect that strikes the eye as a visual image." By nature he meant that "inner harmony which permeates the outward form. . .and is its determining character; that quality in the thing. . .that is its significance and it's [sic] Life for us,—what Plato called. . .the 'eternal Idea of the thing,'" knowable only by patient sympathetic study.

The central problem for an architect was how to put "the Idea of the thing"—a building—into appropriate form. Since ideas existed for humanity only by virtue of their forms, Wright insisted in the best Socratic manner that there could inevitably be but *one* way for a particular artist to express anything, be it flower, emotion, or dwelling place. And this expression could include only what was absolutely necessary to convey the essential meaning. The Japanese had perfected the technique of stringent simplification, and this is what attracted Wright most strongly to their art, that is, "elimination of the insignificant and consequent emphasis on reality." By stripping away nonessentials they arrived at the nature of the object—its geometry, its pure form, its fundamental irreducible essence. The trick, of course, was to know when to stop simplifying. While "more would have been profane," Wright explained, "less would have failed of the intended effect." Like Japanese prints, organic architecture occupied a tenuous position somewhere between profanity and failure.

To simplify, Wright continued, was in a sense to dramatize, and to dramatize was to "conventionalize," a concept since dropped from artistic vocabularies. Conventionalization was the process of capturing essence, of reducing a subject to its fundamentals, for the purpose of eternal preservation. Western art was based on antithetical tendencies, Wright claimed, upon imitation, literal reproduction, and realism. It functioned on the surface, unconcerned with interpretation or with searching for the living concept that defined the subject. Ancient Egypt had understood conventionalization, and its art was everything Western art was not. Egypt, for example, knew the lotus, "and translated the flower to the dignified forms of her architecture. Such was the lotus conventionalized. [If Egypt] had plucked the flowers as they grew, and given us a mere imitation of them in stone, the stone forms would have died with the original." But its artists passed the very principles of "lotusness" through a spiritual process whereby its nature was intensified and adapted to practical use. Thus the lotus gained everlasting life.

The process of conventionalization held crucial implications not only for organic architecture but also for humanity itself. The main problem in any society, Wright believed, was its continuing struggle to domesticate or civilize itself. In its search for the proper ordering of human life, society more often than not made unintentional policy errors, resulting in friction and discord. Real civilization, the true goal of social organization, would be

a right conventionalizing of our original state of nature, just such a conventionalizing as the true artist imposes on natural forms. The law-giver and reformer of social customs, must have, however, the artist's soul. . .if the light of the race is not to go out. So, art is not alone the expression, but in turn the great conservator and transmitter of the finer sensibilities of a people. More still, it is to show. . .just where and how we shall bring coercion to bear upon the material of human conduct. So the indigenous art of a people is their only prophecy and their school of annointed prophets and kings. Our own art is the only light by which. . ."civilization" may eventually make its institutions harmonious with the fairest conditions of our individual and social life.[3]

So if civilization was obliged to fit the natural man into "this great piece of architecture we call the social state," it must rely on its artists, not its scientists, clergymen, or politicians, to reconcile society harmoniously with individual life principles. Behind social institutions, Wright insisted, was the artist's vision, for he alone could translate into structure and form the essence of what it meant to be human and to live happily with others.

Wright had stated these ideas somewhat primitively at his Taliesin press conference on Christmas Day, 1911. Then he had argued that society should recognize the artist's unique social function, his special ability to understand human nature and, because of his contribution to the general welfare, should absolve him from tedious responsibilities. Having demonstrated his allegiance to a "higher law," he ought to be exempted from rules and regulations governing "the average" (see Chapter Five). Now Wright was urging the artist to take an active leadership role, to bait the hook rather than get off it. Since social peace required a harmonious interrelationship of civic parts similar to organic architecture, who better to give laws and administer state than the architect himself. Wright did not insist upon these views again until the 1930s, when his Broadacre City scheme for a replanned America included an architect with sweeping regulatory powers as head of government. (Always a staunch opponent of political fascism and any kind of official tyranny, Wright may not have realized the authoritarian implications of this idea.)

The Japanese Print was an extended metaphor to some extent for political, but more immediately for architectural, activity. It was clear that in analyzing printmakers Wright was actually describing his own methods of work and his own architectural objectives. *The Japanese Print* revealed the many affinities between that art form and his designs, not so much in visual similarities of expression and form but in philosophy and technique. His often-stated goal was to rethink the nature of the residence, to simplify or reduce it to essentials, and to translate the Idea of it into indigenous forms using materials and methods appropriate to time, place, culture, and the state of the art, in short, to "conventionalize" the family living place. That was how Wright would have defined "organic architecture." This short but neglected book was one of his most coherent statements of the function of art and of the principles upon which his own work was based. It has unfortunately been buried under the mountain of his later writings, its importance reduced by the imprecision of his later prose.

Wright's sympathy for Japanese art may have helped land the commission for the massive Imperial Hotel (1913–1922) in Tokyo (to be discussed in Chapter Seven). Since the emperor intended to build a reception center for Japan's increasing number of North American and European visitors, he wanted a Western architect, and none was more attentive to the East than Wright. His own version of how he received the commission does not coincide with facts since come to light. A commission of prominent Japanese had been touring the world in search of the proper architect, Wright claimed in his autobiography, when they came upon several of his prairie buildings near Chicago. Immensely impressed with the similarities between his art and theirs, they offered him the job during their week-long stay at Taliesin sometime early in 1915. Actually, the circumstances were a bit different. It is now known that Wright secured the commission as well as approval for a preliminary plan during his second visit to Japan with Mamah Borthwick, at the emperor's invitation, from January to May 1913. So if a commission reached Spring Green, it must have been in 1912, although it was not mentioned in contemporary records, particularly *The Weekly Home News,* which would have featured it prominently. For several months after he returned to the United States in May, Wright labored over the final drawings, which were ultimately put off until 1915 or 1916, interrupted among other things by his rush to design and complete the spectacular but short-lived Midway Gardens in Chicago.[4]

The block-long pleasure palace on the Midway Plaissance at Cottage Grove Avenue (Fig. 6.2) was demolished in 1929, but for a year or two before World War One it was a unique experiment in American entertainment.[5] The idea was to create a Continental *garten* with facilities for operatic, symphonic, and popular music, indoor and outdoor dining and dancing, private banquets, and alcoholic refreshment. Conceived in the fall of 1913 by Edward C. Waller, Jr., whose father had commissioned Francisco Terrace in 1895, the $350,000 edifice was designed and erected with breath-taking speed. Ground was broken in February 1914, followed by frenzied construction until August, when the Gardens opened with its decorations still unfinished. Despite initial fanfare and popularity, the owners faced bankruptcy as early as

Figure 6.2 The Midway Gardens (1913–1914), Chicago, view across outdoor restaurant. Courtesy Museum of Modern Art, New York.

October but avoided financial disaster until 1916, when they sold the structure to the Edelweiss Brewing Company.

The failure was not architectural. Most observers were awe-struck by its immensity, beauty, and grandeur. Failure can be traced to the war's inhibiting impact on night life by 1916, to the Garden's untimely association in the public mind with Germany, to Chicago's reluctance to experiment with unfamiliar styles of recreation, and to Midway's location in an ethnically changing, essentially residential neighborhood some distance from The Loop. Edelweiss turned the place into a huge beer garden, catering to working class patrons whose recreational tastes did not include the original activites. After Prohibition, it changed hands several times, serving as a garage and a car wash before its destruction—along with that of the stock market—in October 1929. By this time Wright had reluctantly dissociated himself from Midway but derived a certain satisfaction when its sturdy construction raised costs high enough to put the demolition contractor out of business.

Despite its short life, Midway Gardens was a brilliant achievement, Wright's conscious attempt to reestablish a pre-Renaissance situation when, he had argued, "all other arts simply obeyed and placed themselves under the discipline of architecture.[6] Midway was his Gothic cathedral in which music, painting, and sculpture were conceived as artistic embellishments to the master plan, bringing him into conflict with chief sculptor Alfonso Iannelli, among others, who was repeatedly forced to subordinate his imaginative ideas to Wright's wishes. Whether the architect actually solved sound problems in the concert hall himself, as he claimed, is unknown, although he once had Dankmar Adler, the accoustical engineering genius of the Chicago Auditorium, as his mentor. His work in the "allied arts," however, was impressive. Even though he employed sculptors Iannelli and Richard Bock (his colleague at the Oak Park studio) and several painters from the Chicago Art Institute School, the architect himself sketched the murals, windows, statuary, and virtually every decoration for others to develop and execute, subject to his approval. "The remarkable thing," one scholar writes, is that his nonobjective creations in several art forms were entirely his own inventions, even though they "were almost exactly contemporary parallels to the work of the most advanced French and German painters and sculptors."[7] Midway's cubist, abstract, and futurist art were certainly as revolutionary, if not as important for the unfolding of the modernist movement in America, as the famous Armory Show in 1913. Since Wright was in Tokyo during the show's Chicago engagement from March 24 to April 16, he could not have seen it but may have had access to reproductions. Whether it influenced his ideas or not, both the Armory Show and Midway Gardens helped move graphic and sculptural art into the twentieth century.

As architecture, the Gardens was a massive, exceptionally complicated brick and concrete edifice with a myriad of strong elements, so visually stimulating as to be almost distracting but somehow harmoniously resolved. At the same time playful and dignified, spacious and intimate, expansive and intricate, Midway's union of opposites and its orderly arrangement of disparate pieces gave functional and aesthetic coherence to the bewildering complexities of an urban experience. Its demolition after two years of intended use and more than a decade of unintended abuse was itself symbolic of urban unpredictability (some might say decay), and was a tragic loss to American architecture. It was stimulating, adventuresome, and staggering, a recreational and architectural *tour de force* the like of which was never again seen in America. As one happy Chicagoan remarked, after praising its beauty and practicality in 1914, it is "the finest thing of the kind in this country at least, if not in Europe, to boot."[8]

Taliesin, Midway Gardens, and the early drawings for the Imperial Hotel were Wright's best, indeed, outstanding work during his years with Mamah Borthwick. Measured against the earlier prairie houses, however, his residential output from 1910 to 1914 was comparatively unspectacular. The House for Harry S. Adams (1912) in Oak Park bears a close resemblance to the one for Frank Thomas down the street, although the materials are different and the Adams porte-cochere relates it more harmoniously to the ground. With a few variations, the exterior of the William B. Green House (1912) as built in Aurora, Illinois (Fig. 6.3), would have looked like the E. A. Gilmore residence (1908) in Madison, Wisconsin. Both these 1912 buildings lack the flair and drama of Wright's late Oak Park work. They are somewhat blocklike and stubby, not nearly as well terminated as many of their predecessors. Even elaborate "Northome" for Francis Little in Wayzata, Minnesota, executed in 1912 and 1913 from plans probably drawn earlier, lacked a sense of repose. For all its careful supervision, exquisite detailing, and exciting site features, Northome's living room was too cavernous, parts of the interior too impersonal, and the façade (especially in back) too banal. It failed to take full advantage of its Lake Minnetonka setting, nestling into its hilltop only through the obvious device of a partial excavation. The Adams and Green residences, even Northome to an extent, looked as though the architect had been willing to settle for less. Northome should have been more exciting

Figure 6.3 William B. Green House (1912), Aurora, Illinois. Photo by author.

and better situated than it was; the two smaller homes looked like mechanical reproductions of old ideas, tired variations on familiar themes.

Yet Wright was not incapable of designing residences that took some of those old ideas a bit further. A number of unbuilt and partially built structures evoked memories of earlier high standards perhaps because of unusual sites, large budgets, and close friendships with clients. Wright had known Francis Little, for example, since he designed his Peoria house in 1902. In 1910, Little helped finance his architect's German publication. Northome was not his best effort, but Wright put special care into this expensive project for "my client-friend and friend-client."[9] The 1911 design for his attorney Sherman Booth was much more exciting although, as built, it is a considerably diminished version of the original. Perched on the edge of a ravine with a wing and entrance bridge flung to the opposite ridge, the Booth House would have been as closely identified with site as Taliesin. When it was finally erected on a reduced scale in 1915 without the architect's supervision, it was a pale replica, but its excellent living room and uncanny exterior resemblance to Piet Mondriaan's "neo-plasticist" paintings make it particularly noteworthy (see Fig. 7.9).

The Booth House, Taliesin, and the project for A. W. Cutten (1911) in Downer's Grove, Illinois, signaled a new emphasis in Wright's residential genre. Each begins in a massive central core, either a rectangle with a slightly pitched roof or, in the Booth House, a cube with a slab roof. From the core several wings, pergolas, bridges, or other extensions shoot out on more than one level in more than one direction. (The earlier prairie houses had been linear or cruciform.) These extensions crossed others at right angles parallel to the central mass, forming courtyards or compounds enclosed on three or four sides. Although each portion of the residence was connected to the rest, the whole was divided into semidetached units housing different functions. Wright first developed this "zoned" arrangement in 1907 for Avery Coonley's estate, reemploying it thirty years later at Herbert Johnson's "Wingspread" in Racine, Wisconsin. The monumental McCormick project (1907) was based upon this idea, as was the Edward Schroeder project (1911 or 1912) in Milwaukee, though on a reduced scale.

Henry-Russell Hitchcock noted that in the Booth design the floor plan was more open and the central core more massive than in the prairie houses of the previous decade,[10] and the same could be said of its other "zoned" contemporaries. To reemphasize family mutuality was not much of a step forward for Wright. But to surround it with a kind of protected compound where porches were occasionally raised to the second level and in perspective sheltered by immense amounts of shrubbery further advanced the notion of group privacy in which he had placed such faith at Taliesin. The 1911 designs showed that Wright was taking the social reserve and physical detachment of the prairie house even further than he had before he was condemned for his involvement with Mamah Borthwick.

Like these late prairie houses, a number of slab-roofed designs were also related to earlier efforts, generally with good results. The Carnegie Library project (1913) in Ottawa was similar to the unexecuted Yahara Boat Club (1902) in Madison, while the design for a State Bank (1914) in Spring Green was a much-refined and much-developed version his earlier banks, beginning with the 1901 *Brickbuilder* plan. The O.P. Balch House (1911) in Oak Park, reminiscent of earlier slab projects, was pleasing but uninspiring. Of the two homes he designed for himself but never built, the 1911 Goethe Street residence in Chicago had exterior similarities to the Kehl Dance Academy project (1912) in Madison and was a trim, compact townhouse much superior to the dull and rather forbidding studio home (1910) for Fiesole, Italy. The best of the slab buildings was the Coonley kindergarten playhouse (1911) in River Forest, absolutely symmetrical in composition, but its far-overhanging eaves at different levels and distances from the street created the sensation of descending, intersecting planes. Openings through the eaves allowed light to play on the façade and to illuminate the abstract geometrical windows Wright designed in colored glass. Among the fascinating interior features were round table tops supported by octagonal storage spaces alternating between drawers and triangular open shelves. Playhouse window motifs reappeared two years later in murals for Midway Gardens.[11]

Partly because of his 1910 trip to Europe, his social standing in 1912, and his efforts on the Imperial Hotel and Midway Gardens in 1913 and 1914, the residential proportion of Wright's work dropped from two thirds during the first decade of the twentieth century to slightly less than one half of his output from 1910 to 1914. It seemed as if his marital situation would no longer allow clients to entrust him with their family needs even though they continued to hire him for business purposes: from 1910 to 1914 he designed nineteen fewer houses than in the preceding half-decade but only two fewer nonresidential buildings. By 1914 Wright was as much a commercial as a domestic architect.

Three additional nonresidential buildings therefore deserve brief mention. The hotel at Lake Geneva, Wisconsin (Fig. 6.4), designed in the summer and fall of 1911, was a block-long, two-story rectangle, to have been intersected twice by cross axes of porches, public rooms, and patios. Its gently sloping site was intended to be a landscaped garden, culminating in a pavilion–boathouse at the lake shore. Much of this was never built, and the finished product looked a great deal like Wright's National Park recreation building (1912) in Banff, Alberta. Both illustrate how closely his public and private structures resembled each other, how easily he could adapt his architectural system to various kinds of problems. In this respect the unexecuted twenty-six-story tower (1912) for the *San Francisco Call* is also noteworthy. Its emphatic vertical articulation had its origin in the best of Louis Sullivan's commercial work, but its concrete slab construction made for a heavier more textured surface than most skyscrapers. Its far-projecting roof ended in pergola slabs like the Coonley playhouse, and its ornate lower façade—with recessed entry, greenery-dripping urns, spandrel friezes, and elaborate trim—resembled the Goethe Street and Kehl Academy projects.[12]

Wright's most successful buildings during his interlude with Mamah Borthwick were called up by special circumstances. Confronted with exceptional challenges like the Midway Gardens and the Imperial Hotel, he produced exceptional designs. He performed equally well when he was personally involved, at Taliesin, for Sherman Booth, and for his friend Avery Coonley. Wright also seemed to be stimulated by

Figure 6.4　Lake Geneva (Wisconsin) Hotel (1911). Source unattributable.

the possibilities of concrete, slab-roofed buildings to which he was no stranger and which he would explore further in the 1920s. He also did well with ample budgets. But when it came to ordinary prairie houses—insofar as they can be called ordinary—for the usual sort of client with normal financial capacities, Wright did not seem terribly interested. If he had lost touch with the genre before 1909, he had certainly not regained it by 1914.

☐ ☐ ☐

Perhaps his feelings about the Prairie School had something to do with his disinterest. After 1911 he grew so disenchanted with his former associates that he attacked them publicly in the May 1914 *Architectural Record*, strongly enough, in fact, to sever all ties. Claiming sole responsibility for every distinguishing characteristic of the prairie movement, "In the Cause of Architecture: Second Paper" insisted that he "alone, absolutely alone," had developed the new residence. The essay added little to his design philosophy, but it was important because it marked a formal break with professional groups and his assumption of an independent ideological posture. It was also his first proclamation of the "persecuted genius" legend, an interpretation of his life as a continous battle against overwhelming odds, as a struggle for principle despite social ostracism, professional indifference, financial hardship, public ridicule, and personal rejection. (He had held this view privately for some time, since in 1909 Catherine Wright told

reporters essentially the same story.)[13] Having hewn his personal independence and uncompromising architecture out of the rock of
skepticism and hostility, so the story goes, he was proved correct over
and over again. Publicly begun by Wright in 1914 and perpetuated by
his closest admirers until the present day, the "persecuted genius"
legend become a major component of his self-image.

In 1893, Wright contended in the *Record*, "I took my stand, alone
in my field [when] the cause was unprofitable, seemingly impossible,
almost unknown, or. . .as a rule, unhonored and ridiculed." Distinguishing between the considerable attention given his work—including more than its share of "abuses seldom described (never openly
attacked)"—and the lack of recognition given the "cause," Wright
claimed that the appearance of his buildings had been widely copied
but that his fundamental principles had been ignored. His goal had
never been novelty for its own sake or to achieve success in any
regularly accepted sense but to develop an organic architecture whose
principles "are common to all work that ever rang true in the architecture of the world." The "cause" was professional revitalization
through the ideals and methods of organic design, and for its sake he
"deliberately chose to break with traditions in order to be more true
to tradition than current conventions. . .would permit." Since the first
day of his independent practice, he insisted, he had struggled for this
objective.

Although Wright did not specifically say so, organic architecture was
as much a process as a finished product. *How* the architect arrived at
his ideas and developed his plans was as important as the building
itself, a factor lost on many of his followers. Copying appearances
only, he wrote, they had pretentiously put forward "half-baked, imitative designs (fictitious semblances). . .in the name of a
movement. . .particularly while novelty is the chief popular standard."
His own buildings had created a market for "something different" in
a period clamoring for reform. But the prairie architects who popped
up in response, he believed, had sold his ideas as theirs, changing a
detail here, adding a touch there. Without original thinking or creative
struggle, ignorant of the *substance* of his work, they were actually
new kinds of eclectics, direct descendants of the Victorian Revivalists
he had battled in the 1890s. Although he would be accused of selfish
motives, he felt obliged to tell the truth for the sake of the cause, he
said: "The New School of the Middle West" had gone sour, "a promising garden seems to have been overcome with weeds." The movement had degenerated into just another style, offered for sale to the
aesthetically progressive, like colonial, classic, and French provincial

to the more conservative. In pursuit of the almighty dollar, prairie architects were now "prostitutes," pandering anything, even his own unconventional ideas, as long as it sold.

The 1914 "In the Cause of Architecture" paper was Wright's literary counterpart of his move to rural Wisconsin. By dissociating himself from the very group of architects he had publicly embraced in his 1908 "In the Cause" essay—some of whom had been his friends for twenty years—he extended his iconoclasm into professional circles. The 1914 article introduced his legendary irascibility, his overblown ego, his unwillingness to say anything good about colleagues or their work. In 1908 he had prophesied that the Prairie School would someday be a significant force in American life and had affectionately noted his warm "comradeship" with Robert Spencer, Dwight Perkins, Myron Hunt, and other fellow pioneers on the architectural frontier. But in 1914 he implied that their only accomplishment had been to follow his lead and that they had no worthy ideas of their own. His words recalled "The Architect" speech of 1900, except that the neophyte's scattergun criticism of his elders devolved into an elder's bitter attack on a particularly close group of associates and friends. What irked them most was not Wright's claim to unrivaled greatness, to sole responsibility for the new residence, or even that to plagiarize him was better than plagiarizing the Renaissance. What irritated them most was his contention that all their work was derivative, that no one else was any good at all.

There were several reasons for Wright's inflamed rhetoric and passionate accusations. One was a belief that several of his commissions had been stolen while he was away in 1910. The promoters of Wright's City National Bank and Hotel (1909) in Mason City, Iowa, for example, planned to finance two residential communities—Rock Glen and Rock Crest—involving a sizable number of private and public buildings. Wright expected to get the commission but it went instead to former employee Walter Burley Griffin, who with his wife Marion Mahony designed it between 1910 and 1916. Although Mahony had been a valuable member of the Oak Park staff for more than a decade, Wright spoke bitterly about them both. The Mason City project, one scholar says, "created an unalterable breach between the Griffins and Frank Lloyd Wright."[14]

He was even more suspicious of Mahony in her role as assistant to Herman V. von Holst, whom Wright had left in charge of six uncompleted or still-to-be-designed commissions in September 1909. Before he fled Oak Park, he had finished the plans for the E. P. Irving House (Fig. 6.5) in Decatur, Illinois; but when it was published in 1913, von

Figure 6.5 E. P. Irving House (1909), Decatur, Illinois. From *The Western Architect,* April 1913.

Holst claimed coresponsibility, presumably because its surface materials were changed during construction. In this case Wright had reason for anger. But not so with the other five commissions he had left with von Holst who in turn assigned them to Mahony. Wright had drawn only the exterior of the Robert Mueller House (1909–1911) in Decatur and may have left preliminary sketches for the David M. Amberg residence (1909 and after) in Grand Rapids (Fig. 6.6), but Mahony

Figure 6.6 David M. Amberg House (ca. 1909), Grand Rapids, Michigan, principally the work of Marion Mahony. From *The Western Architect,* October 1913.

actually designed them. The remaining three—for Adolph Mueller (1910) on the same street as the other Decatur homes, and for C. H. Wills (1909) and the project for automobile magnate Henry Ford (1912), both in Detroit—were entirely Mahony's work. (Griffin planned the landscaping for the Mueller and Irving homes.)[15] In December 1911, Wright stated "that the work he had left. . .had been unscrupulously taken from him,"[16] believing he had not received sufficient credit for the little he did do, and that von Holtz, Mahony, and Griffin had capitalized on his absence to trade on his name.

Equally infuriating were real and imagined slights from his colleagues, some of which he exaggerated, although it was clear by a year or so after his return from Europe that his ideas were so widely accepted that his innovative role was being forgotten. In 1912, for example, Hugh M. Garden, briefly a draughtsman at the Oak Park studio, published "A Style for the Western Plains" as a chapter in a book entitled *Architectural Styles for Country Houses*, describing Wright merely as one of many prairie architects. The caption on an unidentified illustration of the Coonley House, next to photographs of several quite inferior buildings, read only, "a house at Riverside, Illinois, that is typical of the so-called 'Chicago School.'" Garden also implied that Sullivan, not Wright, had founded the "western" style of *residential* architecture. Charles E. White, Jr., Wright's collaborator on the River Forest Tennis Club (1906) and a former employee, extolled the virtues of casement windows, overhanging eaves, natural wood finish, and harmony between house and site in an article for *Country Life in America* but failed even to mention their foremost advocate. Writing in *Suburban Life Magazine*, William H. Symonds praised the eighteen-year-old Winslow residence, called it a "charming. . .country house at River Forest," captioned its picture "typical of much of recent Western architecture," but did not mention the architect. Three pieces like this in a single year undoubtedly demonstrated the extent to which the prairie house had become "a standardized commodity," as one historian writes; but this very fact, as well as the omission of Wright' name from the texts, could not have failed to enrage him.[17]

Developments in 1913 probably upset him even more. The photographs in feature-length articles by partners William Purcell and George Elmslie, who were currently receiving more attention that he was even though they had both in some sense been his "pupils," revealed how heavily their work depended upon his; but the texts said nothing at all about his influence or their indebtedness.[18] The American Institute of Architects seems to have insulted Wright intentionally in 1913 when it chose George Maher, only on occasion a prairie practitioner, and Dwight Perkins, Wright's 1898 associate on the All Souls project, to define and explain midwestern "progressive architecture." Their instructions were to analyze their own work, that of Sullivan who had "founded" the genre, of Irving K. Pond, and of others "whose names do not readily come to mind." Wright was not mentioned; indeed, he appears to have been specifically unmentioned.[19] Two things seemed to be happening with the prairie bandwagon between 1912 and 1914; everyone was climbing on board but few recognized Wright as the driver. This was partly his fault, of course, for he had left the country just as his ideas were gaining wide currency. This benefited his followers who were no longer forced to work in his shadow, especially after his self-imposed exile at Spring Green. But Wright did not see it that way. Believing the same factors that had caused him to close his office in 1909 were still operating in 1914, he demanded professional fealty while insisting on his iconoclasm. It was many years before he could get away with both.

By themselves these real and imagined slights do not explain Wright's vehemence in 1914, let alone the forty-five-year antiprofessionalism crusade to follow. There seem to have been more fundamental factors at work. His belief in the existence of a conspiracy to exploit and discredit him may have been a manifestation of mild paranoia. Certainly he displayed suspicious symptoms. In his essay, for example, he claimed that his buildings had often been attacked, but "never openly." Describing his departure from architectural tradition as a "dangerous" course full of "sacrifice" and "severe punishment," he expected it to be "fatal," since only one in a thousand dissenters survived. In private, he was just as beleaguered: "I seem to be be-set on all sides," he wrote to Harriet Monroe in 1914, "with prejudiced and sometimes evil intent."[20] This is the language of suspicion and fear, evidence of a mental attitude that transformed mundane affairs into cosmic events. Unable to distinguish between premeditated attack on the one hand and normal professional rivalry and ego gratification on the other, he interpreted imitation as robbery, ignorance as insult, and competition as open warfare. Expecting his colleagues to be grateful, he did not understand that borrowed ideas, pettiness, and envy were the inevitable concomitants of success. Having experienced social ostracism, it was easy for Wright to imagine the profession mustering its forces for a similar assault.

But his perceptions were not entirely accurate. During his years with Mamah Borthwick he continued to receive interested and complimentary treatment in the architectural press. *The International Studio* gave excellent coverage to the W. Scott Thurber Galleries (1909) in Chicago,

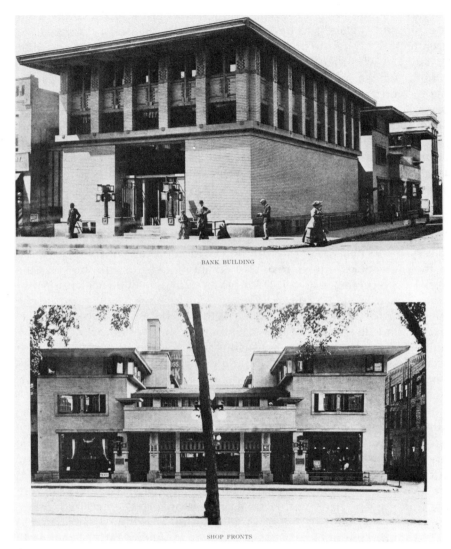

BANK BUILDING

SHOP FRONTS

Figure 6.7 City National Bank (1909), Mason City, Iowa. From *The Western Architect,* December 1911.

while *The Western Architect, The Architectural Review,* and the *American Architect* all featured the City National Bank (1909) in Mason City, Iowa (Fig. 6.7).[21] In 1911, *The Architectural Record* found Louis Sullivan's Babson House (1907) superior to Wright's Coonley Estate (1907) and thought Sullivan would in the end have a more positive impact on the profession than Wright, but it concluded that the younger man's work will also "obtain a place in the history of modern American domestic architecture," an overall assessment seconded by *The Western Architect.*[22] Both journals ran flattering pieces on Taliesin early in 1913, the latter reprinting portions of C. R. Ashbee's introduction to the 1911 *Frank Lloyd Wright Ausgeführte Bauten.* Montgomery Schuyler, perhaps the most influential critic of the day, expressed reservations about Wright's theories when he reviewed the German publications in 1912, but also pointed to the "real impressiveness of these designs," said that Sullivan and Wright "have the root of the matter and that their works are of good hope" for the future of American design, and called Wright "an architectural pioneer."[24]

His exhibitions were also well received. He showed two hotel projects at the Chicago Architectural Club's 26th annual in 1913. In *The Record,* Roy Lippincott said they were "typical of his peculiar genius." The next year, Harriet Monroe reviewed the 27th exhibition for the *Chicago Tribune,* noting this was the third time the Club had given Wright his own gallery. After Sullivan, she wrote, he is "the most important of American secessionists in architecture, and is so recognized by the leading secessionists abroad" for heading the rebellion against historic styles.[25] *The Sunday Record-Herald* complimented Wright's houses as exotic and brilliant but said his broad eaves shut out the sun, "carrying aestheticism too far." This sort of incomprehension showed only that the reviewer had never been inside one. On the other hand, Wright must have been pleased by the friendly interviews and commentaries run by *International Studio,* a prominent art magazine that began to give him space around the time he left Oak Park. Even his unsparing "In the Cause" essay drew praise from the editors at *Western Architect,* who admired his courage and integrity.[26] But the evidence suggests that unless Wright received unqualified praise and total credit for the prairie movement, he suspected treachery and evil intent.

The daily press gradually moved his private life from the headlines to the second section, then dropped him altogether. With the exception of a blast by the *Record-Herald* late in January 1912, the papers found little to print, leaving the Spring Green "soul-mates" to their life of quiet, almost remote, seclusion. Safe within Taliesin's walls, Wright made few compromises with his self-image: true to the artist stereotype, he paid bills reluctantly, with small regard for financial niceties. "As is his custom," a local newspaper reported in 1912, "he wore. . .riding breeches, high laced shoes, a Norfolk jacket, an auto cap with goggles, and a flowing tie." Whenever he went out "he attracted a great deal of attention." The metropolitan dailes recalled their stringers from Spring Green, but the small-town weeklies were ever vigilant, one eager editor noting Wright's "several mysterious trips" to Madison.[27] Since his life style and living arrangements were by popular standards unconventional, his every move was closely watched. He therefore tried to make as few as possible.

This suited Wright, for his life with Mamah Borthwick was intensely private. Therefore not much is known about it, although the weekly papers contain several clues. The couple kept to themselves but, not wishing to spurn their neighbors, attempted to establish friendly relations. The architect employed local craftsmen to build and maintain Taliesin and purchased many of his supplies in town, no small economic benefit to the tiny farming village. He had taken great care to explain himself to Green Spring, and there is no indication he ever replied in kind to hostility like W. R. Purdy's editorial in December 1911. Mamah Borthwick was equally gracious in her limited social contacts, a fact appreciated and publicly commented upon. She, too, shopped in town: despite the heads that turned whenever she appeared, she never lost her poise. Much of her time was devoted to Ellen Key. Mamah's translation of *The Morality of Women, and Other Essays* appeared in 1911, followed by *The Woman Movement* in 1912, the same year she and Wright jointly published Key's *Love and Ethics*. In 1913 and 1914, the architect contributed to the art exhibit at the intercounty fair, loaning numerous Japanese prints and vases to help make the event a success. Aware of constant scrutiny, the couple kept a discreet distance, but they remained cordial, never totally removed from the fringes of community participation.[28]

By the summer of 1914 the worst seemed to be over for Wright. The threat of police investigations and legal actions against Taliesin's inhabitants never materialized. The hostile social climate had been considerably reduced by Mamah's personality and Wright's straightforward relationships with his neighbors. As architecture, Taliesin was equally admired by local farmers and New York art critics. The exhibition with the Architectural Club in Chicago indicated continuing respect for his work, even if it did not immediately generate clients. During early August, Wright worked feverishly to complete Midway Gardens for a tidy fee with the knowledge that his next project would be the even more spectacular Imperial Hotel in Tokyo. Having achieved a *modus vivendi* with his neighbors and a settled life at home, Wright looked forward to more commissions. Even if they were slow in coming, he was happy with Mamah, happier than he had been in years.

Then came the most devastating blow of his life, shattering his dreams and all he had worked for. At noontime on August 14, 1914, while Wright was in Chicago at the Midway site, Mamah was presiding at lunch with her two visiting children, their young friend, and five Taliesin workmen. Unknown to them, the recently hired chef, Julian Carlston, surreptitiously locked the dining room door, set gasoline fires under the windows, and stationing himself at the single exit murdered with a hatchet those who tried to force their way out. Learning by phone only that Taliesin was in flames, Wright rushed back on the first train to find his worst fears confirmed, for amidst the ashes of his home Mamah and six others lay dead. Emotionally shattered and physically sick, he was in part sustained by Mamah's former husband, Edwin Cheney, who accompanied him to Spring Green, and by the very relatives and neighbors who had once condemned him. Working through the night without sleep, they helped extinguish the blaze, salvage some of Wright's possessions, and save one portion of Taliesin. Carlston was found the next morning, hiding with his wife.

The murderer's foul deed was never satisfactorily explained. Wright and his son John believed simply that he had gone mad, an adequate interpretation at the time, perhaps, for the tortured architect. Carlston's own story—he was seeking revenge against a fellow employee who had insulted him and was having lunch with the others—does not account for the brutality of a multiple killing. And the rumor that the superstitious Barbadian emigré had taken it upon himself to punish Wright's "immorality," prodded by vindictive preaching at a local evangelical church, does not explain why he acted in the architect's absence. A few days after he was jailed, Carlston committed suicide by poison, and with him died his secret. After Wright buried Mamah in a flower-filled grave next to Unity Chapel, he secluded himself in the remaining portion of Taliesin (Fig. 6.8) on the verge of breakdown, while outside the sheriff posted six armed guards to fend off "a crowd of morbidly curious" souvenir gatherers attempting to trample the grounds.[29]

Still in seclusion a few days later, Wright's first act was to thank Spring Green through the pages of *The Weekly Home News*.[30] "To you who have been so invariably kind to us all," be began his eulogy to Mamah, "I would say something to defend a brave and lovely woman" from those who still attack in her death as viciously as they did in life. "I am thankful to all who showed her kindness. . . . No

Figure 6.8 A portion of Taliesin (1911) not destroyed in 1914. Photo by author.

community anywhere could have received the trying circumstances of her life. . .in a more high-minded way." Spring Green had treated her courteously, he wrote, but "this she won for herself by her innate dignity and gentleness of character." Although their life together had been misrepresented, and Mamah was even now referred to as "another man's wife," she was a noble woman who valued her freedom more than motherhood, wifehood, or chastity, and who had the courage to live by her convictions.

"We lived frankly and sincerely," without secrecy or pretense, Wright insisted, "and we have tried to help others live. . .according to their ideals." Mamah was not a slave to theory: her unorthodox existence was not intended as a demonstration of Ellen Key's principles and had nothing to do with so-called free love. "The 'freedom' in which we joined," he said, "was infinitely more difficult than any conformity with customs. . . . Few will ever venture it." Such lives do not threaten society but "can only serve to ennoble it."

There were lessons to be learned from Mamah's example, Wright informed his readers: "You wives with certificates for loving—pray that you may love as much and be loved as well as was Mamah Borthwick! You mothers and fathers with daughters—be satisfied if what life you have invested in them works itself out upon as high a plane as it has done in the life of this lovely woman." There is no past, Wright exclaimed, and there is no future, so unless we realize that Now is Eternity—a thoroughly existentialist notion—"there will come a bitter time when the thought of how much more potent with love and affection that precious 'Present' might have been, will desolate our hearts."

"She is dead. I have buried her in the little Chapel burying ground of my people. . . . The place where she lived with me is a charred and blackened ruin, . . .[but] I shall replace it. . .as nearly as it may be done. I shall set it all up again for the spirit of the mortal that lived in it and loved it—and will live in it still. My home will still be there."

Wright closed his eulogy by reproducing a section of Goethe's "Hymn to Nature," which he and Mamah had found in a Berlin bookshop and translated together. It had comforted him once. He hoped it would again.

NOTES

1 Wright's phrase, "spiritual hegira," was quickly appropriated by The Chicago Tribune, November 8, 1909; December 25, 1911.

2 Frederick Gutheim, Ed., Frank Lloyd Wright on Architecture: Selected Writings, 1894–1940 (New York: Duell, Sloan and Pearce, 1941), 21; Clay Lancaster, The Japanese Influence in America (New York: Walton H. Rawls, 1963), 85–89, 220.

3 For the quotes in the preceding pages see The Japanese Print: An Interpretation (Chicago: The Ralph Fletcher Seymour Co., 1912), long quotation from pages 32–33.

4 Wright said he received the Imperial commission after rebuilding Taliesin, or sometime in 1915: Frank Lloyd Wright, An Autobiography (New York: Duell, Sloan and Pearce, 1943 ed.), 193. On the 1913 trip see The Sauk City Democrat (Baraboo, Wis.), January 16; The Weekly Home News, May 8; and the Baraboo Weekly News, June 19, 1913.

5 On Midway see F. L. Wright, An Autobiography, 175–184; Alan M. Fern, "The Midway Gardens," with contributions by Alfonso Iannelli, the sculptor, and John Lloyd Wright, who assisted his father on the project, in the Lexington Gallery Brochure on Wright and Iannelli (Chicago 1961); Alan M. Fern, "The Midway Gardens of Frank Lloyd Wright," The Architectural Review, 134 (August 1963), 113–116; The Sunday Record-Herald (Chicago), February 2, 1914, and The Chicago Tribune, October 4, 1914. Also see the letter from Barry Byrne to The Architectural Record, 129 (January 1961), 242, 246, saying that Iannelli, not Wright, was the sculptor.

  6 F. L. Wright, "The Art and Craft of the Machine," *Chicago Architectural Club Catalogue of the 14th Annual Exhibition* (1901).

  7 Henry-Russell Hitchcock, *In the Nature of Materials: The Buildings of Frank Lloyd Wright, 1887–1941* (New York: Duell, Sloan and Pearce, 1942), 63.

  8 Karleton Hackett in the *Chicago Evening Post,* quoted in *The Weekly Home News,* July 9, 1914.

  9 "Northome" has been well documented in Morrison Heckscher and Elizabeth Miller, *An Architect and His Client; Frank Lloyd Wright and Francis W. Little* (New York: Metropolitan Museum of Art pamphlet, May 2, 1973).

  10 H.-R. Hitchcock, *In the Nature of Materials,* 66–67.

  11 The buildings in this and preceding paragraphs are reproduced in Arthur Drexler, Ed., *The Drawings of Frank Lloyd Wright* (New York: Horizon Press, 1962), plates 38, 39, 43, 46; and in H. Th. Wijdeveld, *The Life-Work of the American Architect, Frank Lloyd Wright* (Sanspoort, Holl.: C. A. Mees, 1925), 28–33, 54, 82–83, 98–99.

  12 H. Th. Wijdeveld, *Life-Work,* 80–81; Drexler, *Drawings,* plates 42, 45, 47. The design and construction of the Lake Geneva Hotel may be followed in great detail in *Lake Geneva News,* November 9 (with perspective drawing), 16, 23, 30, December 28, 1911; April 4, May 2 (with illustration), 9, 16, June 27, July 4 (with illustration), 18, 25, August 1 (with photo), 15, 22, 29, September 5, 1912; *The Herald* (Lake Geneva), November 10 (with perspective drawing), 24, December 8, 1911; August 2, 1912.

  13 *The Chicago Tribune,* November 7, 1909. "Persecuted genius" in this author's term.

  14 Mark L. Peisch, *The Chicago School of Architecture: Early Followers of Sullivan and Wright* (New York: Random House, 1964), 98.

  15 By far the best source on von Holst, Mahoney, and Wright is H. Allen Brooks, *The Prairie School: Frank Lloyd Wright and His Midwest Contemporaries* (Toronto: University of Toronto Press, 1972), 148–164.

  16 *The Chicago Tribune,* December 31, 1911.

  17 M. L. Peisch, *The Chicago School,* 65, 154 note 25; Charles E. White, Jr., "Insurgent Architecture in the Middle West," *Country Life in America,* 22 (September 15, 1912), 16–17; William H. Symonds, "Rectangular Homes Beautiful and Practical," *Suburban Life Magazine,* 15 (September 1912), 119.

  18 Purcell and Elmslie, "The Statics and Dynamics of Architecture," *The Western Architect,* 19 (January 1913); Walter Burley Griffin, "Trier Center Neighborhood, Winnetka, Illinois," *ibid.,* 20 (August 1913). *The Architectural Record* had acknowledged Wright's preeminence three years earlier. "The obvious and inevitable comment upon the houses illustrated herewith and designed by Mr. Walter Burley Griffin is that they are strongly influenced by the success of Mr. Frank Lloyd Wright": "Some Houses by Walter Burley Griffin," *The Architectural Record,* 28 (October 1910), 307–310. *American Architect* agreed: 98 (October 19, 1910), 134.

19 *The Western Architect,* 19 (February 1913), 12, 15, quoting *Construction News.*

20 Wright to Monroe, April 13 and 20, 1914, Monroe Poetry Collection, University of Chicago Library.

21 "Art Gallery Designed by Frank Lloyd Wright, Architect," *The International Studio,* 39 (December 1909), xcv–vcvi; "City National Bank of Mason City, Iowa," *The Western Architect,* 17 (December 1911), 105; *The Architectural Review,* 18 (January 1912), 11; *American Architect & Building News,* 100 (December 27, 1911), 273–274.

22 "A Departure from Classic Tradition: Two Unusual Houses by Louis Sullivan and Frank Lloyd Wright, Architects," *The Architectural Record,* 30 (October 1911), 327–338; *The Western Architect,* 17 (November 1911), 95.

23 "The Studio Home of Frank Lloyd Wright," *The Architectural Record,* 33 (January 1913); "Taliesin, The Home of Frank Lloyd Wright and a Study of the Owner," *The Western Architect,* 19 (February 1913). Even Taliesin was later cited as an example of "what might be called the Sullivan school of design" by Peter B. Wright in "Country House Architecture in the Middle West," *The Architectural Record,* 38 (October 1915), 385–421.

24 "An Architectural Pioneer: Review of the Portfolios containing the works of Frank Lloyd Wright," *The Architectural Record,* 31 (April 1912), 427–436.

25 Roy A. Lippincott, "The Chicago Architectural Club; Notes on the 26th Annual Exhibition," *The Architectural Record,* 33 (June 1913), 567–573; Harriet Monroe, "The Orient an Influence on the Architecture of Wright," *The Chicago Sunday Tribune,* April 12, 1914. Also see *ibid.,* April 9, 1914. The two hotels in 1913 were at Lake Geneva and at Madison, Wisconsin. For a detailed description and a perspective drawing of the latter see *Sauk City Democrat,* March 14, 1912.

26 *Sunday Record-Herald,* second section, April 19, 1914; C. Matlack Price, "Architecture and Imagination; A Critical Note," *The International Studio,* 53 (September 1914); Henry Blackman Sell, "Interpretation not Imitation: The Work of Frank Lloyd Wright," *ibid.,* 55 (May 1915), quoting a Chicago paper, Spring 1914; *The Western Architect,* 20 (June 1914), 58.

Wright also received publicity from advertisements featuring his work. The Neponset Black Waterproof Building Paper Company used the Meyer May House (1908), Grand Rapids, and Wright's name in ads in *American Architect,* 99 (March 1, 1911), adv. page 36, in *The Western Architect,* 17 (March 1911), xiii, and probably in other places. The Atlas Portland Cement Company did the same with the Willitts House (1902) in *The Architectural Record,* 36 (November 1914), adv. page 69.

Wright advertised his own *Ausgeführte Bauten und Entwürfe von Frank Lloyd Wright* in *ibid.,* 33 (January 1913), adv. page 32, in the February (page 89) and March (page 102) issues, and again in October 1914 (adv. page 102).

27 *Baraboo Weekly News,* January 18, 1912. Also see the scathing indictment of Wright in the *Chicago Record-Herald,* January 26, 1912.

28 *Chicago Record-Herald,* February 21, 1912; *The Weekly Home News,* June 19, August 14, 1913; August 27, September 10, 1914. *Love and Ethics* and *The Morality of Women* were published by the Ralph Fletcher Seymour Company in Chicago, *The Woman Movement* by G. P. Putnam's in New York.

29 Wright recorded his reaction to the tragedy in F. L. Wright, *An Autobiography,* 184–190. Contemporary accounts are in *Sauk City Democrat, Iowa County Democrat* (Mineral Point), *Baraboo Weekly News,* and *Republican Observer* (Richland Center), August 20, 1914; *The Chicago Tribune* and *The New York Times,* August 16, 1914. *Oak Leaves* in Oak Park was forced to "bow its head in silence," August 22, 1914.

In the course of its story *The Weekly Home News,* August 20, 1914, included one of the best contemporary descriptions of Taliesin:

"It is a long, low structure, carved into the brow of the hill. On three sides the building bounds an oblong court. The fourth side is a terrace joining the bungalow to the hill upon the side of which it clings. At one end of another adjoining court are the granary, stables, and men's sleeping rooms; then, at right angles and connecting the two ends, is that part which contained offices, studio and an open loggia. Then comes the portion, near the entrance to the court, built for Mr. Wright's mother, which was being temporarily used as a dining room by the workmen and draftsmen. Adjoining this dwelling, Mr. Wright himself lived. All this portion [the south wing—two thirds of the entire complex] is completely burned. Mr. Wright will start at once to rebuild."

Murdered were Mamah Borthwick, age 35; her children John and Martha, 11 and 9, respectively; Emil Brodelle, draughtsman; Thomas Bunker, hostler: David Lindblom, gardener; Ernest Weston, 13. Escaping were his father William Weston, foreman of Taliesin's employees, and Herbert Fritz of Chicago, later a Madison, Wisconsin, architect.

30 "To My Neighbors," *The Weekly Home News,* August 20, 1914.

1914–1932

CHAPTER SEVEN

A Regular Life
Is Cunningly Ambushed

The affirmation of life in Frank Lloyd Wright's eulogy to Mamah Borthwick did not impress the forces governing his fate, for the next two decades were filled with personal disaster and professional disappointment. The Imperial Hotel kept him occupied during World War One and the subsequent recession, but extended marital difficulties in the 1920s contributed to his own architectural doldrums long before the stock market crash affected the rest of the nation. Just as he successfully resolved the problems that had denied him a share of the Great Prosperity, the Depression intervened, and he lost many opportunities to execute impressive designs. Without work, he turned to writing and lecturing. Considered an elder statesman whose career had passed its peak, Wright was known by 1932 as a cranky, unpredictable eccentric who criticized others vociferously but produced little himself.

□ □ □

"Something in him died with her," John Lloyd Wright remembered sadly, "something loveable and gentle. . . in my father" that Mamah Borthwick had nurtured.[1] To escape his sorrow Wright forced himself to work, deriving more satisfaction from it—perhaps sustenance is a more accurate word—than he had for several years. While seeing to details on the Midway Gardens in the fall of 1914, he began to rebuild Taliesin (Taliesin II, he called it), completing it about a year later. Shortly thereafter he published his first planned community, in the form of an outline for a suburban quarter section, and made preparations for the commercial distribution of his "American System Ready-Cut" standardized homes, a scheme for low-cost apartment units, some of which were erected in Milwaukee (Fig. 7.1) in 1916.[2] By March he completed preliminary drawings for the Imperial, and late in December 1916, after a farewell banquet given by Chicago friends, he sailed from Seattle to Tokyo where he would live for much of the next six years.[3] His eagerness to tackle ambitious projects was in large part prompted by his need to regain control of his emotions for, as his son John recalled, "only architecturally was he able to hold his own."[4]

But Wright also leaned heavily, if at times uncertainly, on a new source of support, a woman entering his life shortly after Mamah's death who accompanied him to Japan. He had met Maud Miriam Noel (Fig. 7.2) in late 1914 or early 1915 when he invited her to his Chicago office, having been moved by her letter of condolence following the Taliesin tragedy. The daughter of a Kentucky physician, she had had three children by Thomas Noel, scion of a wealthy Tennessee family. After her divorce, Miriam had acquired further sophistication and social credentials among the Harry Payne Whitneys and Whitelaw Reids in Paris, where she lived for several years prior to World War One. Substantial alimony enabled her to sculpt, act, and associate with artistic and literary people even though her own talents were

Figure 7.1 "American System Ready-Cut" Apartments (1916) for Arthur L. Richards, Milwaukee. Photo by author.

Figure 7.2 Miriam Noel, date unknown. Courtesy State Historical Society of Wisconsin.

limited. She was, as one observer noted in 1915 when she was forty-three, "an extremely pretty woman. Her eyes are dark and luminous and her face is singularly mobile, expressive." In the parlance of the day she was "distinctly spirituelle," and Wright, fascinated by her elan, moved her into Taliesin with his mother shortly after they met.[5]

Miriam considered herself a liberated woman and, much more than Mamah Borthwick, was self-consciously artistic. Calling herself a "sculptress," she affected a lifestyle and a public posture similar to that of her famous contemporary Mabel Dodge Luhan. Mamah had been willing to live in Wright's limelight, but Miriam competed for it, which he found intriguing at first. In several press statements in 1915 she outlined a social philosophy quite close to his own. Contrary to popular belief, she said, there existed an aristocracy of artists performing socially uplifting work who should not be impeded by customs or institutions that might inhibit free expression. Responsible to higher laws than those society created, the artist was strictly disciplined nonetheless. "Frank Lloyd Wright and I," she insisted adamantly, "are as capable of making laws of our own as were the dead men who framed the laws by which they hoped to rule the generations that followed them." She and her lover were among the few who had achieved the true freedom possible "only through the illumination of the spiritual consciousness."[6] They lived, as she and many of her contemporaries liked to put it, only for art. Wright was undoubtedly attracted by Miriam's philosophy, to which he was already publicly committed.

Despite similar beliefs, their relationship was tempestuous. Wright could not give Miriam the total allegiance she demanded. She bristled at his occasional criticisms, at his preoccupation with work, but most of all at his continuing devotion to Mamah's memory. A very demanding woman, Miriam was frustrated by her inability to penetrate his innermost thoughts and feelings, particularly regarding "a dead woman whom you have tortured as you have tortured me," she claimed in a moment of anger, "and to whose memory you have given no real loyalty—merely a sentimental attempt to soothe your own conscience." There were those who thought Wright hypocritical for taking up with Miriam so soon after Mamah's death, especially when he had written so movingly of his love after the funeral in August 1914. Herein lay Miriam's dilemma and Wright's peculiar vulnerability. The fact seems to be that he could not function for long without "a sympathetic [female] comrade," as he put it.[7] After inviting Miriam to share herself with him, he continued to pine for Mamah. Forced to compete with her, Miriam sensed the architect did not love her as strongly as she loved him, or as completely as he had loved her predecessor. This made Miriam extremely aware of his every attention. Her rage at Wright's flirtation with a young woman at a party symbolized her own feelings of insecurity in the relationship as well as his insensitivity to her tenuous situation.

Difficulties like these—clashes of two strong and stubborn personalities—forced Miriam to leave Taliesin after nine months with Wright, in the late summer or early fall of 1915. The press did not discover the affair until shortly before November 7, the day *The Chicago Tribune* printed statements by Wright, his attorney Clarence Darrow, and by Miriam herself to explain the publication of her love letters, written from 19 Cedar Street, Wright's Chicago apartment to which she had moved. The letters were stolen from Taliesin by Nellie Breen, a housekeeper Wright had discharged because she disliked Miriam almost as much as working in a "love cote." Threatening a federal investigation for violation of the Mann Act, Mrs. Breen was stymied by Clarence Darrow who demonstrated the dubious nature of her allegation. The scandal received little attention outside Chicago, blowing over much more quickly than the "affinity tangles" of 1909 and 1911. Mutually under attack, Miriam and Wright resolved their differences to re-unite at Taliesin in November.[8]

This was not entirely to his family's liking. Although his mother Anna gave him moral support during the 1915 troubles, his other relatives found him increasingly difficult. Still smarting from the events of 1911, they were doubly upset when Wright reneged on an agreement with Ellen and Jane Lloyd Jones to purchase Hillside Home School. According to the provisions of a contract drawn in May 1915, Wright agreed for one dollar and "other considerations in hand paid" to take title to all Hillside property, except his aunts' furniture and personal apparel, and to acquire the entire capital stock of the school, a corporation organized under Wisconsin law, except for shares owned by early clients Susan Lawrence Dana of Springfield, Illinois, and Charles E. Roberts of Oak Park. Wright promised to reserve for his aunts during their lifetime three rooms with bath and board at the School, or at some other place, and to pay them each $250 annually, plus any medical expenses.[9]

In the summer of 1915, the sisters went to California, leaving school affairs and negotiations with their nephew in the hands of Jane Lloyd Porter, his sister. Although it was not in the contract, Wright agreed to send them each $50 a month for as long as their vacation lasted, but apparently failed to mail the October and November checks, ignoring their queries until the end of November when he claimed lack of money. "My aunts stood next to my mother and have given me voluntary early kindnesses," he wrote his sister Jane. "Because of this they are in California and because of this I have undertaken to save the school from bankruptcy. It can never mean anything but an expensive outlay for sentiment," he added rather bluntly. "I do not want you to feel that I owe you anything." When he finally sent the money, he told his aunts to consider it a loan and to mail him receipts. The sisters wrote to Jane saying that "developments of the summer and fall with regard to Mr. Wright's moral standing [meaning the Miriam affair] make him utterly powerless to project the interest of the school, hence his holding it robs it of 2/3 of its intrinsic value."

Largely because of their avowed disapproval of Miriam, and his own shortage of funds, Wright withdrew his promise of monthly stipends in January 1916, leaving his aunts stranded in California. Jane Porter's husband Andrew thereupon sold some Hillside livestock and wired the proceeds to the Coast. Claiming the contract had thus been violated, Wright canceled it with a minimum of tact: "There will be a swift conclusion of the whole matter in the courts," he threatened his aunts, "and this knocks you entirely out of a living for I am sure not a penny will reach you from the sale." Stockholder Charles Roberts complained to Jane Porter about "Frank's injustice," warning her "as a matter of policy" not to "antagonize him more than you have to." Jane Lloyd Jones wrote from Los Angeles that her nephew, of whom she was once so proud, was now "a *mad man*. . . . And *any* lady drawing him up without stint! He has caught a Tartar *this time*." When she discovered through a newspaper clipping that Wright would go to Japan on a reported $3,000,000 job, she reminded her niece that in her financial desperation she had had to borrow postage from sister Ellen, who was "almost broke too. I wonder now if Frank will not open his clutched hand toward you—as well as us."

But the clutched hand remained closed. Even though the "Tartar" had provided Wright with several thousand dollars to rebuild Taliesin, the magnitude of the task plus a lack of clients brought him close to bankruptcy. Legal episodes in mid-1916 illuminate both his financial difficulties and his deteriorating family situation. His brother-in-law, Andrew Porter, for whom he had designed "Tany-deri" near the Home School in 1907, sued Wright for $5000 worth of butter, milk, eggs, plowing, "and other articles and services" owed for over a year. A civil suit in the Lloyd Jones clan was unprecedented, but hostilities deepened even further when, with the approval of his wife Jane, Porter decided to seek reimbursement for medical expenses incurred in 1914 when the sick and the dead were brought to "Tany-deri" after the Taliesin fire. It is inconceivable that the Porters would have even contemplated such an action under normal circumstances. But mutual misunderstanding over moral and money matters had poisoned the atmosphere. The fact was that the architect simply could not meet his financial obligations, and was too proud to admit it. When Brentano's of New York sued him in 1916 for $29.10 worth of books he could not prove he paid for because the 1914 fire had destroyed both the merchandise and his records, he was certain that everyone was taking advantage. But his relatives, who knew about Miriam's money, about the cost of rebuilding Taliesin, and about the Imperial project, thought he was holding out. By 1916 he could add the Lloyd Joneses and at least one of his sisters to the list of people he had alienated. Anna Wright and Miriam Noel were almost the only ones he could trust.

□ □ □

Late in December 1916, Wright and Miriam embarked for Tokyo. For the next six years they lived together in Japan, California, and Wisconsin while Wright devoted most of his attention to the hotel and to a few other American and Japanese commissions. The story of the Imperial Hotel (Fig. 7.3) has been told and retold many times by Wright and others, making detailed repetition unnecessary. Suffice it to say that its location on the periphery of the shock, plus its flexible foundation cantilevered off deeply driven piles, enabled it to ride out with

Figure 7.3 The Imperial Hotel (1913–1922), Tokyo. Furnished by David Roessler.

a "small amount of damage," according to the insurance underwriters' report, the disasterous earthquake of September 1923 which destroyed large sections of Tokyo, killed at least 92,000 people, and injured many more. (Wright attributed his success solely to design, conveniently forgetting location.) The hotel was a massive 230-room edifice of brick and limestone (Fig. 7.4) with shops and a post office and a theatre seating 1000 below the Peacock Room, which could accommodate the same number at dinner. The hotel, which finally costed out around $4,680,000,[10] was exceptionally ornate, intricately detailed, and ex-

Figure 7.4   Lobby of the Imperial Hotel (1913–1922), Tokyo. Photo by David Roessler.

ceedingly complicated, combining Western construction principles with Eastern aesthetics in what must be described as a fussy manner. The Imperial is usually cited as one of Wright's greatest achievements, and there is little doubt it was an engineering triumph as well as a visual *tour de force* and a traveler's delight.[11] But it did not add to the overall development of his architectural philosophy or in any major way to the aesthetic or organizational properties of his later designs. It was an important learning experience for Wright, to be sure. Its sheer monumentality kept him busy during World War One and during a time of personal difficulty. But in a very real way it was an architectural *cul-de-sac,* a once-around, never-to-be-repeated exercise that did not inform either the kind or the flavor of his subsequent work.

During the six years (1917–1922) in which Wright worked on and off in Tokyo, he produced a total of thirty-one designs, twenty-two for United States clients, nine for Japanese. Of these nine, six were houses, of which three were built. And of the three nonresidences, only one—the 1921 School of the Free Spirit in Tokyo (Fig. 7.5)—was completed, making a total of five executed structures in Japan counting the Imperial. The houses recall late and post-Oak Park prairie work as well as the concrete homes he designed from 1920 to 1924 (see

Figure 7.5 Jiyu Gakuen Girls School of the Free Spirit (1921), Tokyo. Photo by Barry Bragg.

below). The twenty-two American projects included thirteen in California; of the ten actually built, at least six were in that state. The shift of Wright's work to the West Coast and to Japan was noted by Midwesterners. As early as 1917, reviewer–architect Thomas E. Tallmadge bemoaned the absence of Sullivan, Wright, Griffin, and the others from the 30th annual Chicago Architectural Club exhibition. Without specifically writing an obituary for the prairie movement, Tallmadge remarked that its omission "removed from the show the last vestige of local color. The exhibition would be just as appropriate in the halls of the Boston Museum of Fine Arts, as in our own Art Institute which stands for art ideals in the Middle West. . . . The only original note produced in our architecture in the past twenty-five years," Tallmadge declared, had been "expurgated."[12]

Wright returned from Japan for the last time in November 1922, leaving the Imperial unfinished in detail.[13] During his years abroad he had often been exhausted and sick, weakened by the climate, and quite lonely, despite Miriam's companionship. He had also been disturbed by international developments such as American entry into World War One, but was even more troubled by the growing enmity between this country and Japan. Near the end of 1922 he was quite happy to rest at Taliesin.[14] But the Imperial was not yet behind him. In April 1923, *The Western Architect* published his third "In the Cause of Architecture" essay, a lengthy description of the hotel illustrated with photos of recent and not-so-recent nonresidential work. When the Imperial survived the worst earthquake in Japanese memory, just as Wright said it would, he became something of an international celebrity. (Most people assumed the hotel was at the center of the shock, and he did nothing to dissuade them.) Taking advantage of his notoriety, he wrote *Experimenting with Human lives,* a pamphlet for the Los Angeles Fine Arts Society, and a two-part article for *Western Architect* explaining the hotel's construction principles. If his private affairs had been in order, according to prevailing standards, he might have attracted any number of clients, especially in the commercial field. But once again marital difficulties got in the way of professional accomplishment.

□ □ □

As soon as Wright returned to Taliesin in November 1922, he secured an uncontested divorce from Catherine Wright, thirteen years after their initial separation, on the grounds of voluntary estrangement for more than five years. He could have done this any time after 1916, but that he did not may indicate reluctance to wed Miriam, or simply the result of extended absences from home. It might have been at her insistence, therefore, that exactly one year after his divorce, in accordance with Wisconsin law, they were married in November 1923 in a secret midnight ceremony on a bridge over the Wisconsin River. After nine years of sharing him with the Imperial Hotel, with Mamah Borthwick, and with his mother Anna—who had moved to Taliesin in 1914 and who, at age seventy-eight, had traveled to Japan in 1920 when her son was dangerously ill—Miriam finally had him all to herself. But by the time of Anna's death in February 1923 it was too late.[15] Their relationship, highly unstable from the very beginning, doomed the marriage before it began.

Not all the blame for their inability to coexist happily should be placed on Wright's preoccupation with other people and other things. As her published letters and accounts of her behavior reveal, Miriam was a volatile, highly excitable, emotionally mercurial woman whose moods changed unpredictably and totally from day to day. She was given to exaggeration, indeed, to complete misrepresentation of facts to make them conform to her interpretations or her state of mind. Without offering any evidence, for example, she several times alleged that Taliesin, with Anna Wright living there, was a den of debauchery and claimed that Wright assaulted her repeatedly. After the wedding she became alarmingly erratic, completely eradicating what little was left of their mutual fascination. Wright married her to calm her, he said, but their visit to a psychiatrist may have only unsettled her further.[16]

The truth was that he married her out of a sense of protectiveness, obligation, and loneliness. Miriam had assisted him financially, had seen him through an emotionally difficult period, had committed herself to him and publically supported his socially unpopular views at a time when he was morally and professionally an outcast. He appreciated her loyalty during trying times. It was certainly an intentional overstatement to say, as his son did, that Wright was "wooed, grabbed and bagged. . .dominated, seduced, coerced, chastised, conscripted, overriden, and beshawed" by Miriam. Much of that could more accurately characterize Wright's behavior toward her. But it is certainly true that his need for female companionship worked to her advantage, and there is no doubt she wanted him very much. But theirs was not a marriage likely to last, so it came as no surprise when Miriam left Wright in April 1924, five months after the wedding.[17]

During the next year or so Wright seemed directionless, casting about to bring order and coherence into his life. Relaxing as often as possible at Taliesin (Figs. 7.6 and 7.7), he published two articles in commemoration of Louis Sullivan, whose death that April, fourteen months after his mother's death and coinciding with his separation, further saddened him. In November he announced that after January 1, 1925, he would make his home in Chicago, where he was preparing an office at 19 Cedar Street to accommodate twelve draughtsmen, to devote himself exclusively to commercial work.[18] Many of his designs in 1924 and 1925 also seemed to be experimental sallies at new frontiers. There was a tepee motif country club in Madison, Wisconsin; a concrete, metal, and glass skyscraper for Chicago; a spiral automobile objective wrapped around a planetarium for Sugar Loaf Mountain, Maryland; and a steel cathedral for New York City. But like his commercial practice, these visionary schemes never materialized, and beginning in April 1925, a series of misfortunes forshadowed further difficulties. Defective telephone wiring started a fire at Taliesin that caused between a quarter and a half million dollars' damage. With

Figure 7.6   Frank Lloyd Wright and Frank Neutra, architect Richard Neutra's eldest son, at Taliesin in 1924. Courtesy Dione Neutra.

Figure 7.7 Erich Mendelsohn, Frank Lloyd Wright, and Richard Neutra at Taliesin in 1924. Courtesy Dione Neutra.

only $30,000 insurance, Wright was forced to sell his old Oak Park home for $33,500 and go further into debt.[19]

In July 1925, he filed for divorce on the grounds of desertion but soon withdrew the suit when Miriam threatened to counter with a charge of physical cruelty. On Thanksgiving Day 1925, she announced to the press that she had opened her own divorce proceedings, accusing Wright of assault, specifically with beating her on two occasions. Miriam's accusation, which was not supported by documentaton, seemed to achieve its purpose, for Wright, eager to end the business, offered her a $10,000 lump sum payment plus $250 a month for the rest of her life, but refused to consider her demand for separate maintenance of his estate. Miriam's Thanksgiving press conference was the first public revelation of their separation, or of their marriage for that matter. So once again reporters in search of sensation flocked to Spring Green to receive an unexpected scoop (and to learn why Wright was eager for divorce) when they discovered that since February 1925 at the latest, Wright had been living with yet another woman, a Montenegrin divorcee Olga Milanoff. At this disclosure Miriam rejected his financial offer and withdrew her suit, presumably to consider new tactics, beginning a complicated legal (and extralegal) battle lasting until 1930. At the end of November, Wright renewed his desertion charge against Miriam, who responded by lodging a misconduct complaint against Olgivanna (as she was known) with the Bureau of Immigration. At first, Wright insisted she was merely his $100-a-month housekeeper, but when they were found registered in Chicago's Congress Hotel—in separate rooms, to be sure—he dropped all pretense. [20]

The granddaughter of a Montenegrin general and the daughter of a supreme court judge, Olgivanna was twenty-six and Wright fifty-seven when they met. She was born in 1898 in Cetinje, Yugoslavia, educated privately in Czarist Russia and Turkey, and while still in her teens married Vlademar Hinzenberg, an architect ten years her senior, by whom she gave birth to a daughter, Svetlana, in 1917. After the war she left her husband and moved to Paris where she pursued a life of art and mysticism. She came to Chicago from Paris via New York to discuss business matters with Hinzenberg who was also visiting this country, and was about to return home when she met Wright, apparently at a performance of the Petrograd Ballet on November 30, 1924. Olgivanna was noticeably beautiful—dark, aristocratic, and mysterious, according to Wright—and he was immediately captivated. He invited her to Spring Green, then followed her to New York, all the while wooing her vigorously until, in a matter of weeks, "Olgivanna was mine." By February 1925, she moved into Taliesin, secured a divorce two months later, and before the year was out gave birth to Wright's daughter Iovanna, his seventh child. [21]

Younger when she moved in with Wright than all the other women in his life except Catherine Tobin, Olgivanna represented the culmination of a logical progression in his love objects—from socially conscious suburbanite to self-conscious feminist to expatriate artist to foreign-born mystic. As Wright removed himself further from professional and moral conventions, he attracted companions each of whom, more dramatically than her predecessor, was unwilling to accept the roles or perform the functions society decreed for women. In France, Olgivanna had joined Georgi Gurdjieff's Institute for the Harmonious Development of Man (Fig. 7.8), one of the many "high thought colonies," in Sinclair Lewis' phrase, that grew up after World War One. Gurdjieff taught that western civilization had corrupted the original balance among the intellectual, emotional, and physical faculties or "centers" within individuals; his followers tried to restore their inner harmony through arduous labor, self-contemplation and analysis, dance-oriented programmed exercises, and other coordinated activities. Olgivanna spent four years at the Institute in Fontainebleau, and as an instructor of the exercises was fairly close to her enigmatic and remote teacher.[22] Wright was attracted to Olgivanna's youthful beauty, but even more to her quietly mysterious, even exotic, demeanor and to her mystical notions. As an aristocratic, foreign-born artiste, she was less committed to The American Way of Life than any of Wright's previous companions.

As late as June 1926, Miriam's strategy toward the architect and Olgivanna was still unclear. Delays and postponements in the divorce proceedings stimulated rumors that she would charge him with adultery or insist upon control of substantial portions of Taliesin. Using the press to dramatic advantage, she claimed to be penniless, sick,

Figure 7.8 Olgivanna Milanoff at far right, sewing at Georgi Gurdjieff's Institute for the Harmonious Development of Man, ca. 1923. From [C. S. Nott], *Teachings of Gurdjieff*, courtesy Samuel Weisser, Inc.

and alone, with no place to go. "I am still his wife and 'Taliesin' is still my home," she lamented. "If I can have just a corner of the bungalow to myself I will be satisfied." But it was more than a corner she wanted, for early in June she tried for three days to occupy Taliesin by force. Rebuffed on each attempt by Wright's employees, she succeeded only in destroying two signs reading "No visistors allowed," in detaining Wright briefly on a peace warrant, and in forcing Olgivanna into hiding.

Wright had already dropped his desertion charge against Miriam, but in view of her abortive siege of Taliesin, attempted to buy her off by offering $125 a month if she would leave him alone. And as on similar occasions, he decided to make a public explanation of his latest imbroglio.[23] In a letter "To the Countryside," published in the Spring Green *Weekly Home News*, June 10, 1926, he thanked the community for its patience, apologizing as he had several times before for causing scandal. He recognized that his home had been a storm center and that his "direct ways of meeting life" had embarrassed everyone. All he had ever wanted, he insisted, was a "quiet hearth" and "a sympathetic comrade," but his best intentions had a way of bringing odious notoriety, not to mention intolerable domestic situations. The present conflict had developed, he explained, because he really believed Miriam had left him forever. Thinking "no difficulty could arise to prevent me from making my life 'regular' here at last," he invited Olgivanna into his home. But he had misjudged Miriam, and found himself in "an ambush laid with a good deal of cunning. . . ."

"What I wanted to say to you," Wright emphasized, "was that I like you people. . . ." Noting that he was a third-generation Lloyd Jones, that he had invested heavily in the community, and that Spring Green was the one place on earth he felt genuinely happy, he told his neighbors that "I want to stay here with you, working until I die. I want to mind my own business and not be subject to public question if I can help it." (He hoped he would live long enough for that to happen.) Realizing that many readers would not believe a word he wrote, he insisted that his subsequent behavior would reassure friends and convince skeptics. "I think the countryside deserves the best of me," he concluded, "and if you. . .give me the benefit of the doubt. . .for a year or two I will come through right side up and you may yet take pride in Taliesin. . . . With affection," he signed his letter, "your—Frank Lloyd Wright."

His expiation did not forestall further misfortune, but his two-year estimate proved remarkably accurate. The next few weeks were the quiet before a storm. Although Miriam had accepted Wright's voluntary monthly payments of $125 without question or acknowledgement, on August 30 she suddenly filed a $100,000 alienation of affection suit against Olgivanna, who had not met Wright until seven months after Miriam left him. Events now began to break quite rapidly. Saying only that he was going abroad, Wright disappeared the next day to join Olgivanna in hiding. Two days later her former husband Vlademar Hinzenberg appeared on the scene to secure an injunction in Chicago preventing her from taking Svetlana, their nine-year-old daughter, out of the country. Claiming that the birth of Iovanna in December 1925 proved Olgivanna unfit to be the guardian of his child, Hinzenberg obtained a writ of habeus corpus in an effort to secure Svetlana's custody, immediately following this with warrants for the arrest of the fugitives for alleged violation of the Mann Act.[24]

Adversity began to pile up with the melodramatic rapidity of a soap opera. While the Sauk County, Wisconsin, sheriff circulated pictures and descriptions of Wright, Olgivanna, Svetlana, and the infant Iovanna, Hinzenberg telegraphed Seattle to prevent them from sailing for Japan where it was thought Wright had a standing invitation to practice. On September 6, 1926, the Bank of Wisconsin foreclosed on a $25,000 mortgage and, holding an additional $18,000 in liens and claims against Taliesin, took legal possession of the estate with the intention of auctioning Wright's personal property. Miram Noel got a court order granting her joint access with the bank, but before she could move in the bank secured an injunction preventing either Mr. or Mrs. Wright from entering the grounds lest they remove or damage anything to which it held a claim. Miriam initiated, then abandoned, an involuntary bankruptcy suit against Wright, and at the end of September, Hinzenberg offered a $500 reward for his arrest. Meanwhile, a Madison, Wisconsin, construction firm sued the architect for $4000 still outstanding on repairs to Taliesin after the 1925 fire. On October 9, Hinzenberg topped everyone else by suing Wright for $250,000 for alienating Olgivanna's and Svetlana's affections.[25]

Despite the persistent rumors that the Wright entourage had fled to Mexico, he and his companions were discovered on October 20 hiding in a cottage on Lake Minnetonka in Wildhurst, Minnesota, a few miles west of Minneapolis, where they had been living since September 7. (At the moment of his arrest, Wright was dictating the concluding pages of Book One of his autobiography.) After a night in the Hennepin County jail, he and Olgivanna were released when they posted $12,500 in bonds for allegedly violating the Mann Act, but were immediately taken from the county to a municipal court where Wright put up another $3000 to avoid detention on an adultery warrant secured by Hinzenberg. Legal wranglings kept them in Minneapolis until the middle of November when they were given permission to leave the state. Still barred from Taliesin, they traveled to California, hoping to enjoy a respite from a year of legal hassle and newspaper headlines.[26]

By October 1926 it was obvious that Miriam was as interested in punishing Wright for his romance with Olgivanna as in extracting his money. Insisting she would never agree to a divorce, she instructed her attorney to investigate the 1914 Taliesin murders and to inquire if Olgivanna had overstayed her visa. As her behavior became more erratic, opinion began to shift in Wright's favor. When Miriam claimed that the Bank of Wisconsin had conspired with Wright to deny her access to Taliesin, she was assessed $50 in court costs and her allegation was expunged from the records. The architect's son John and his former wife Catherine announced they were prepared to assist him in any way they could. Several prominent individuals, including poet Carl Sandberg, *New Republic* editor Robert Morse Lovett, and four Chicago academicians and publishers, petitioned the federal district attorney for southern Minnesota to drop the Mann Act indictments. Vlademar Hinzenberg withdrew his adultery and alienation suits after securing visitation rights with Svetlana.[27] Public sentiment coalesced even more strongly behind Wright when he and Olgivanna gave interviews to Madison's *Capital Times* describing Miriam's "tyrannies," including the story of how she had forced Olgivanna and her three-day-old baby out of a hospital into Chicago's streets. The Sauk County district attorney denounced Miriam's alienation of affection suit as a "black-mailing stunt" and withdrew his office from the case, while her counsel, noting her repeated rejections of the architect's financial offers, resigned. "I wanted to be a lawyer," he told the press, but "Mrs. Wright wanted me to be an avenging angel."[28]

The architect's fortunes improved somewhat in 1927 even though the year opened unpromisingly. Miriam followed him to California and tried to have him arrested for abandonment. A third fire at Taliesin in February destroyed $2500 worth of books, blueprints, and architectural drawings. Wright's Japanese print collection, valued at $100,000, was auctioned for less than $37,000 after a January and February exhibition at New York's Anderson Galleries. The proceeds were at first awarded to Miriam who had obtained a writ of attachment to recoup the money she had spent to rebuild Taliesin in 1915, but ultimately they were assigned to the gallery in payment for loans to Wright. In March, federal authorities in Minnesota dropped the Mann Act indictment for lack of evidence, but a month later the Bank of Wisconsin sold the livestock at Taliesin and renewed its efforts to take permanent title, which it had been unable to do when the February fire raised questions about actual property value.[29]   When Wright returned to Madison from California in May 1927, he was hit with a summons from Miriam to show why he should not continue her financial support. (He had suspended the voluntary $125 monthly payments when she sued for alienation of affection the previous August.) Still refusing a divorce, she insisted on separate maintenance of his estate. Despite her challenge to its claim, the bank won two settlements against Wright totaling $43,000 and gave him until May 1928 to pay before seizing his property. With Miriam enjoined from entering Taliesin while Wright had use of his studio to work off his debts, she apparently realized by the summer of 1927 that unless she came to terms she would have to accept even less alimony than he had offered in 1925. During June and July she pondered several offers, quibbling here with details, there with wording, until finally, after more than two years of unprofitable turmoil, they were divorced on August 25, 1927. Wright agreed to pay her $6000 in cash and to establish a $30,000 trust fund from which she could draw $250 a month for the rest of her life. Four days later several of the architect's friends organized "Wright, Incorporated," authorized by law to issue $75,000 in stock and to assume control of his estate and finances; with little money and few prospective clients, Wright was forced to sell shares in himself against his future earning power.[30]

After the divorce, Miriam's behavior became increasingly outrageous. In September she divulged plans to begin screen tests for a Hollywood career, after which she would study philosophy and sculpture in Paris. In October she threatened to renew morals charges against Olgivanna, announced she was going to have her face lifted, and claimed to have given birth to a baby daughter by an heir to a European crown whom she would soon marry, she said. Wright had her arrested for sending him a letter he claimed was so lewd, obscene, and indecent that it could not be admitted as evidence. After contracting to give a lecture in Milwaukee on "Morality and Art," Miriam tried to convince the Bureau of Immigration to deport Olgivanna. By the time she chased Wisconsin Governor Fred R. Zimmerman through the kitchen of a Chicago hotel to enlist him in her campaign to arrest Wright for violating an alleged divorce stipulation not to see Olgivanna for a year, and by the time she asked a United States senator to request the Justice Department to investigate why the Mann Act charges had been dropped, very little remained of her credibility. Her reward in July 1928 for breaking into Wright's rented home in La

Jolla, California, one night while he was away and smashing several hundred dollars worth of furniture was a thirty-day suspended sentence. This was her last contact with her former husband. Miriam Noel left Frank Lloyd Wright's life as she had married him—under cover of darkness.[31]

Unable to pay his $43,000 obligation to the Bank of Wisconsin by May 1928, Wright's personal effects, art pieces, and farm machinery were sold at public auction. By July, when the Bank took title to Taliesin in satisfaction of $25,000, he still owed over $10,000 more. But the news was not entirely discouraging. On August 25, 1928, a year to the day after his divorce, Wright married Olgivanna Milanoff in La Jolla, California. After an Arizona honeymoon, the newlyweds returned to Wisconsin in October. Taliesin, meanwhile, had been redeemed and the remainder of the architect's debts paid by the stockholders of Wright, Inc., among them critic Alexander Woollcott, playwright Charles MacArthur, Mrs. Avery Coonley, and another early client, Darwin C. Martin of Buffalo, the architect's sister Jane Porter, and his attorney Philip La Follette, later governor of the state. Legally, Wright, Inc., owned Taliesin and everything in it. Its hopes for financial return were based on the architect's ability to design buildings for profit, something he had been unable to do for several years.[32]

After his work on the Imperial Hotel, Wright's difficulties with Miriam Noel brought his practice to a virtual standstill. From 1915 to 1932 he executed only thirty-four commissions—two a year—of which twenty-nine were erected before 1925. And of the five buildings he completed from 1925 to 1932, two were for himself and a third was for a relative. World War One and his own absence from the country had reduced his opportunities, but not as much as his personal problems during the halcyon days of the Great Prosperity. Compared to the Oak Park years and even to his semiexile at Taliesin with Mamah Borthwick, the 1920s were a disaster for Wright who, long before the stock market crash, was quite familiar with lack of work. In the context of Miriam's antics, Wright appeared almost beatific, for a change, but he felt himself even more harrassed than between 1909 and 1911, or in 1915. The few designs he did manage to execute from 1915 through the 1920s reflected the suspicion, frustration, and need for privacy in his personal life. After 1914 he moved away from the prairie house genre, and his residences of the next decade offered little by way of a generally applicable theory of family living. Nor were they particularly influential for other architects, though they were interesting. They do, however, provide important clues to his own emotional and intellectual condition.

With Taliesin and his other "zoned" designs around 1911 (discussed in Chapter Six), Wright had stated that his own purposes could best be served by close contact with nature in a house ensuring privacy through controlled access and increased social withdrawal, making only limited gestures toward community involvement. Most of his residential work after 1914 revealed an even more socially tentative posture. Compared to the prairie house, his homes in 1915 and 1916 were boxy, self-contained, and inward, with inconspicuous entrances, smaller and fewer windows—at the street side most were on the second story—and greater areas of unbroken surface. A severe slab roof quite often replaced the gentle hip, sacrificing an easy horizontality for a tense, constrained solidity. Façades of the Sherman Booth House (Fig. 7.9) as built in Glencoe, Illinois, of most of the Ravine Bluffs Development homes of which it was part, and of the Emil Bach residence (Fig. 7.10) in Chicago (all 1915) were characterized by conspicuously heavy dark trim dividing lightly colored planes into geo-

Figure 7.9 Sherman Booth House (1915), part of the Ravine Bluffs Development at Glencoe, Illinois. Photo by author.

Figure 7.10   Emil Bach House (1915), Chicago. Photo by author.

metrical relationships, anticipating Piet Mondriaan's "neo-plasticism" even more than any of Wright's earlier buildings. In the F. C. Bogk House (1916) in Milwaukee (Fig. 7.11), windows of an exposed side were virtual slits; at first floor front they were deeply recessed across a walled terrace, while the main entrance on a side drive was removed from passers-by. In the project for an urban house (1916), the entrance was altogether hidden; the structure itself was a simple cube with exceptionally modest fenestration. The suburban homes tended to have more window space than the urban, but all the new houses were tightly organized, severely outlined bulwarks—with vigorously contrasting trim effectively defining their psychological as well as their physical limits—against a dialogue between inside and out. Unlike the somewhat tentative early prairie houses in the blocklike mode, these made no apology for their declaration of privacy, inwardness, and social retreat. And they tended toward even greater interior openness than his earlier efforts.

Seven of the nine buildings Wright executed in the United States from 1920 to 1924 were concrete California houses that carried the 1915–1916 tendencies further. At least four utilized the "textile block" system he developed during the winter of 1922–1923 for Mrs. George Millard's "La Miniatura" in Pasadena, that is, precast hollow blocks

Figure 7.11 F. C. Bogk House (1916), Milwaukee. Photo by author.

with geometrical patterns on the exposed sides, bound together at the site with steel tie rods and filled with poured concrete. The material was environmentally appropriate because of its ability to repel sun in summer and retain heat in winter; but these homes, particularly in block form, have metaphorical as well as practical significance. Most of their relatively few windows pierce the upper stories or face away from the street. With entrances to the side or screened from immediate view, and with real and symbolic barriers discouraging actual, as opposed to visual, contact between indoors and the land, the houses became secluded enclaves. Homes for John Storer, Samuel Freeman, and for Charles Ennis (all 1923 or 1924), suspended from Los Angeles hills and facing away from the street (unlike the prairie house) to take advantage of spectacular views, were seemingly impenetrable. Arranged in separately articulated units containing different household functions, they were terraced extensions and symbolic representations of the rugged hillsides. Wright achieved a close relationship between structure and site in this way, but one that dramatized topography at the expense of a human dialogue with nature.

With little to offer toward a theory of family structure and relationships, some of the concrete residences were hardly homes at all. The only California buildings he discussed (at great length!) in his autobiography were for two middle-aged women, Aline Barnsdall and the widowed Mrs. George Millard, who did not have families and who, like their architect (in his "Miriam years"), were socially vulnerable needing private retreats.[33] The Mayan "Hollyhock House" (1916–1920) in Los Angeles, a massive zoned complex of separate units, courtyards, gardens, pergolas, bridges, hidden recesses, quiet corners, and relatively few windows minimized by vast poured concrete planes (Fig. 7.12), was a thoroughly confusing maze to outsiders, protection in a way against those who harrassed Ms. Barnsdall for her Bolshevik soirees, but perfect for living, according to Wright, "like a princess in aristocractic seclusion." Ms. Millard's La Miniatura (Fig. 7.13), intended primarily as a library for her extensive book collection and a gallery for her art, was a fireproof vault in which casual movement and human clutter seemed disrespectful. The intricately patterned textile-block exteriors of the Ennis, Storer, and Freeman houses—their courtyards sunbaked plazas by day but ominous terrains at night—were playgrounds for the imagination, which could easily envision their interiors as silent mausoleums or places for eerie covens. Hollywood producer/director William Castle showed a certain perspicacity when he used the Ennis residence (Fig. 7.14) as a locale for *House on Haunted Hill* (1958), a horror movie starring Vincent Price. Obviously a monumental structure, it was, as Henry-Russell Hitchcock has understated it, "rather undomestic."[34]

Figure 7.12   Aline Barnsdall "Hollyhock" House (1916–1920), Pasadena. Photo by author.

Figure 7.13 Mrs. George M. Millard's "La Miniatura" (1922–1923), Los Angeles. From *The Architectural Record,* December 1927.

Although Wright's work in the 1920s may have drawn on the early stages of the International Style, on Mayan revival, or, as Vincent Scully has suggested, on Southwest native American architecture for inspiration, its overall character had a perculiar and direct relevance to his private life. The 1914 tragedy had made it painfully clear that removal to a rural setting did not increase personal security. Whereas some of the 1915–1916 houses were hasty, almost reflex responses to that event, hinting at increased detachment and retreat from social intercourse, the concrete homes of the 1920s, elevating detachment into seclusion and retreat into escape (including a kind of psycholog-

Figure 7.14   Charles Ennis House (1924), Los Angeles. Source unattributable.

ical escape into architectural fantasy land), were carefully thought-out, meticulously executed essays in solitude and isolation. Building with textile blocks, moreover, meant weaving together myriads of lines, designs, and individual pieces—solving a complicated architectural puzzle. The emphasis here was on parts and detail, on process, every bit as much as on total conception; putting and keeping something together was as crucial as what was kept together. Elaborating on the fortresslike, not the environment-embracing, qualities of Taliesin, the concrete block homes were less places to live than impregnable retreats from a hostile world, precisely constructed defense mechanisms suitable for a precarious existence with an erratic partner. The California houses—testaments to Wright's skills in architectural composition—were created when the fabric of his life was most directly threatened, when the dynamics of his interpersonal relationships were of utmost importance.[35]

His preoccupation with construction methods, heightened by working on the Imperial Hotel but later almost myopic under Miriam Noel's disruptive influence, was also reflected in his publications during the 1920s. Shortly after his final return from Japan, his article on the

Imperial Hotel for *The Western Architect* described its technology in greater detail than was usual for Wright. The two additional essays he wrote for the same journal after the September 1923 temblor—also called "In the Cause of Architecture" but subtitled "In the Wake of the Quake"—were his most technical yet. Denying the accusation that the hotel was a reactionary, "inorganic" building violating his oft-stated principles by ignoring modern technology and his own previous work, he admitted modestly that his intention had been "to assist Japan to its own architectural feet." Having therefore to remain within its national traditions and to rely upon its own construction methods, he encountered innumerable unforseen obstacles on the job which he described under the headings of "statement of the problem," "working out the plan," "the execution of the work," and "changes as the work proceeded." Unlike Wright's earlier publications, the articles were a kind of builder's minimanual.

His other major writings during the 1920s dealt with similar issues. In 1927 and 1928 he published two series of essays for *The Architectural Record* entitled (inevitably) "In the Cause of Architecture," for which he received a total fee of $7500 even though he never produced the fifteenth and final installment.[36] The first group of five articles treated such topics as machinery, standardization, steel, and prefabrication, while five of the second nine, subtitled "The Meaning of Materials," analyzed the characteristics and proper use of stone, glass, concrete, sheet metal, and terra cotta. Never before had Wright written so exclusively about architectural *process*, to the exclusion of theory, large objectives, and polemics. The spate of publications (seventeen in all) on method and technique coincided almost exactly with the nadir of his association with Miriam Noel—from 1923 to 1928 in the period between his second and third marriages—when he was preoccupied with restructuring his own life and with building viable social relationships. It might have been predicted, furthermore, that after he married Olgivanna and could settle into more normal habits, his attention would return to broader concepts. After 1928 until his death over thirty years later, his voluminous writings were by and large theoretical, abstract, and general, with very little of a technical or methodological nature. The 1920s were a literary and architectural aberration.

□ □ □

The *Record* series may have convinced Wright he could make money as an author, for during the years of scarce clients, his pen was mightier than his pencil. Whatever the motivation, these essays opened the floodgates of a speaking and writing deluge that never stopped. From 1929 to 1932 he published at least twenty speeches, articles, and reviews and was frequently interviewed in the mass and professional press. His 1930 lectures at Princeton University and at the Chicago Art Institute were released the next year in book form as *Modern Architecture* and *Two Lectures on Architecture*. He attracted considerable attention when in his fall 1931 informal talks at New York's New School for Social Research he called for improved skyscraper design, attacked urban planning, praised industrial architecture, and criticized the International Style.[37] All of this prepared the public for *The Disappearing City* (1932), a critique of urbanization and concentrated population, and for *An Autobiography* (also 1932), a difficult, revealing, inaccurate, but compelling book, which was widely reviewed and favorably received. His steady stream of publications and speaking engagements, in which he usually denounced conformity in American life and art, brought him the exposure he obviously enjoyed and cultivated. Wright had an uncanny ability to make news, to advertise himself, to capture the media's attention; and for the rest of his life he was constantly before the public, popping off on one or another issue whether or not he knew much about it. Since many observers thought his practicing days were over, they consigned him to the role of elder statesman, one he relished, but not as a companion to retirement.

His loss of several large and impressive commissions during the 1920s and early 1930s further confirmed the general impression that he was destined to build no more. Hopes for Edward L. Doheny's enormous ranch complex (1921), a multilevel concrete-block network of buildings, terraces, roadways, arches, and landscaping, resembling a surreal set of the futuristic film *Things to Come*, built up, into, and around the Sierra Madre Mountains in California with spectacular monumentality, were dashed when the oil speculator and political dabbler, who liked to hire front-page "names," got caught in the Harding scandals of 1924. A summer colony for Lake Tahoe (1922–1923) with wooden buildings and houseboats in awkward and rather fanciful tepee and leaf motifs (fortunately perhaps) never left the drawing boards. A thirty-two story skyscraper (1924–1925) for the National Life Insurance Company in Chicago (Fig. 7.15)—four fastidiously detailed towers set back against a main-axial spine with cantilevered floors and copper- and glass-hung walls—remained a vision only. There was also a planetarium (1925) with a spiral auto ramp on the exterior of Sugar Loaf Mountain, Maryland, and a fantastic steel cathedral (1925) for the Reverend William Norman Guthrie, with chapels for all denominations

Figure 7.15 Project for National Life Insurance Company (1924–1925), Chicago. Courtesy State Historical Society of Wisconsin.

that would have accommodated a million New Yorkers in the tallest building in the world. These elaborately detailed projects involved blending innumerable pieces and segments. Like the California textile blocks of which some were composed, they emphasized method and process, for their intricacies were as visually apparent as their scale.

Wright lost several more enviable opportunities after the 1929 stock market crash ended the speculative spirit. Plans for the San-Marcos-in-the-Desert winter resort at Chandler, Arizona, another massive concrete-block design in some ways reminiscent of the Doheny ranch, were first conceived in 1928 and completed in 1929 but never executed. One of his most interesting commissions, an adaptation of which was built in Bartlesville, Oklahoma, in 1952, was a skyscraper apartment block (1929) for William Norman Guthrie's St. Mark's-in-the-Bowery

Church in New York, three octagonal towers alternating vertical and horizontal façades, with cantilevered floors and hung exteriors of copper and glass.[38] Construction scheduled for 1930 was abandoned, as were the grouped apartment towers (1930) in Chicago based on the St. Mark's idea. Another unfortunate loss was the Elizabeth Noble apartment block (1930) in Los Angeles, a small, horizontally oriented structure of glass and concrete with wood-sheathed cantilevered balconies, very much related to the International Style. Although Wright secured fewer commissions during the 1920s than ever before, several would have brought large fees and considerable acclaim. The apartment buildings were particularly fresh, and their loss was felt by American architecture in general. But those who knew about them understood that Wright's creativity had by no means run out.

Precisely when his fortunes were lowest, he began to receive institutional honors and accolades, almost in inverse proportion to commissions. The Dutch architect H. Th. Widjeveld assembled *The Life-Work of the American Architect, Frank Lloyd Wright* in 1925, thereafter considered by its subject to be the best book about his designs. The plans, renderings, sections-through, and photographs were supplemented with articles by Wright and the editor, by critic Lewis Mumford, and by architects Louis Sullivan, Erich Mendelsohn, J. J. P. Oud, H. P. Berlage, and R. Mallet Stevens. In 1927 he was elected to the Royal Academy of Fine Art in Belgium, and five years later to similar institutions in Brazil and Berlin. While an exhibition of his work was touring Europe in 1931, he was invited to Rio de Janeiro as the guest of the Pan American Union to be the North American judge of competitive entries for a Christopher Columbus Memorial Lighthouse.[39] In 1930 the Architectural League of America fêted him at a dinner to open the first showing of his work ever staged in New York. In 1932 he was included in the now historic International Style Exhibition, organized by Philip Johnson and Henry-Russell Hitchcock at the Museum of Modern Art. Acting as something of a foil to the work of Walter Gropius, Mies van der Rohe, J. J. P. Oud, Corbusier, and thirty-five other Americans and Europeans, Wright was the only non-Internationalist invited. Whether he appreciated the distinction is uncertain—he said he did not, but it may have been a case of protesting too much—for he was already on record as a staunch opponent of the new European architecture.[40]

Published in an obscure denominational journal, *World Unity,* Wright's first important critique of the International Style has generally been overlooked. Reviewing Corbusier's *Towards a New Architecture* (1923, English translation 1927) in the September 1928 issue, he used the occasion to range far beyond its purpose. Later on, Wright would be friendly with van der Rohe, Gropius, Neutra, Mendlesohn, Schindler, and other "modernists," sometimes, at least, and jovially patronizing to "Little Philip" Johnson, even while he condemned their work, but he was absolutely relentless on the subject of Corbusier, his greatest rival for international acclaim. Corbusier was a tenacious defender and implacable publicist of his own position but, perhaps most importantly, was as egotistical as Wright himself. Everything good in Corbusier's work, Wright insisted in his review with characteristic modesty, had been developed twenty-five years earlier either by Louis Sullivan or Frank Lloyd Wright. Inspired by the look of machinery and by its products, the Swiss' architecture was "as stark as one of his gas-pipe railings," entirely without ornament, usually monomaterial, with an exaggerated emphasis on surface appearance. All this was a necessary "dressing down" to Beaux Arts, neoclassical, and Revivalist practitioners, Wright thought, but it still had momentous shortcomings.

Although Corbusier had been quite right to eliminate "ornamentia," he had achieved only the "semblance of simplicity." By stressing surface and mass, his severely plain "picture-buildings" ignored the "third dimension," namely depth, the external manifestation of interior space, which should be the essence of any structure. Surface, mass, and appearance were not the reality of architecture, Wright insisted, simply the expression of interior events, an idea about the organization of space. Corbusier conceived of buildings as pictures and designed them from the outside in; that is, he thought first of how they would look, then fit interiors to match. But if architecture was primarily the encasement and organization of humanly occupied spaces, then the proper method of design was Wright's own—from inside out, that is, visualizing the interior, then letting the idea dictate exterior expression. As far as the reviewer was concerned, the International Style was a new kind of imitation, not of historical forms the Victorians had copied, certainly, but of modern machinery. Thus it was a "new eclecticism," a cold, sterile euology to the latest technology. Whereas Wright claimed to harness machinery for human pleasure, Corbusier reproduced it to human detriment, appropriately calling his houses "machines for living." Despite its arrogance, Wright's review was a relatively calm, intelligent, and dispassionate, if pointed, critique of the new style. Had it been more prominently published and Wright not become so unreasonable on the subject later, this review might have begun a fruitful dialogue between International and organic architecture.

Wright's growing reluctance to compliment anything was rivaled only by his facility for unending criticism, one reason he was omitted from the planning committee of the 1933 Chicago World's Fair. At a protest meeting in New York's Town Hall Club in February 1931, Wright expressed indifference to the slight, compromised somewhat by his presence there, but feared, he said, that the nation would embrace the fair's "new eclecticism"—the International Style—as it had the classical revival of the 1893 Columbian Exposition, thereby retarding the development of an organic American architecture for another two generations.[41] The editors of *Outlook and Independent* approved his exclusion, correctly supposing that Wright's well-known irascibility would reduce to shambles any committee on which he served, but suggested that he design the next fair all by himself. Critic Douglas Haskell argued in *The Nation* that without Wright the event would be akin to a history of American literature without Ralph Waldo Emerson. Architect Henry S. Churchill wrote *The New Republic* that omitting Wright "was nothing less than a calamity"; the academicians had not ignored Sullivan in 1893, so why ignore his heir in the 1930s, especially when "he is the greatest living architect?" Reporting from the Continent to the same magazine, Catherine K. Bauer agreed with Haskell that Wright was the only American artist respected in Europe. His influence had stimulated its present architectural hegemony and, if Europe had moved beyond him lately, it was only because he had had so few building opportunities. "It was very difficult to break away from Wright," Bauer quoted a Dutch architect as saying. "For a while it looked as if the whole country were going American." Despite these testimonials and his suggestion of a fairgrounds floating in Lake Michigan, Wright remained on the sidelines, as he would in 1939 during New York's Century of Progress.[42]

By the early 1930s, Wright was capable of generating public controversy in any number of ways, leading observers to wonder how much of it was intentional, for he often seemed to be deliberately provocative. He acquired a reptuation, which he did nothing to discourage, for visiting a city and ridiculing its architecture. He narrowly avoided being subpoenaed by a local governmental agency in November 1930 after he called Milwaukee's new $10,000,000 County Building, of which city fathers were unduly proud, an "outrage" and a "pseudo-classic horror." Shortly thereafter he told a *New York Times* reporter there was "no excuse. . .whatever" for the proposed Radio City. "The space might better be cleared and given to the public for a park," he said, than to build that "crimes of crimes," that "monstrosity." (Later he would tell Los Angeles audiences their office buildings were "a dish of tripe" and Bostonians that their old structures were fire traps, vermin catchers, and the "pitiable remnant of a degenerate culture that was dead 500 years ago, before it left England," conveniently overlooking the work of Henry Richardson, whom he admired.)[43]

His image as a feisty iconoclast was considerably enhanced in 1932 after a street fight in Madison in which he suffered a broken nose from a man who knocked him into the gutter, claiming the architect owed him $282. "If you don't pay me," the assailant had shouted, "I'll take it out of your hide." After he did, five of Wright's apprentices bull-whipped the man, leading to short jail sentences and fines for all, including his future son-in-law and close associate, William Wesley Peters. Two weeks later an extortionist demanded money from Wright under threat of kidnapping. He turned the letter over to Madison police, hired a bodyguard, and ignored the offices of the Vigilantes of America, a national organization that had offered its assistance. These and similar flaps kept the architect's name before the public, but not as a great designer and certainly not with much dignity.[44]

By 1932 Wright was shrouded in a mantle of unpredictability. At sixty-five he was considered even by many of his admirers to be an eccentric, opinionated, flamboyant, arrogant, slightly screwy old man with strange ideas who talked too much. But the public seemed to like it. To those who considered him a master of modern design, others pointed out that he had built nothing significant in years. Henry-Russell Hitchcock and Philip Johnson listed him "among the architects of the older generation" in their 1932 book on the International Style, discussing his work in the past tense as if it were completed. "I have been reading my obituaries. . .the past year," he complained to Fiske Kimball, one of several architectural critics who had consigned him to retirement, but think with Mark Twain "the reports of my death greatly exaggerated."[45] As it turned out, he was very much alive, and in short order confounded layperson and expert alike with a flood of ideas and buildings that rivaled even the momentous achievement of the prairie years.

NOTES

1 John Lloyd Wright, *My Father Who is on Earth* (New York: G. P. Putnam's Sons, 1946), 86.

2 "Non-Competitive Plan for Development of a Quarter Section of Land" in Alfred B. Yeomans, Ed., *City Residential Land Development: Competitive Plans for Subdividing a Typical Quarter Section of Land in the Out-*

skirts of Chicago (Chicago: University of Chicago Press, 1916), reprinted in *The Western Architect,* 25 (January 1917); "The American System of House Building," *ibid.,* 24 (September 1916), 121–123; on the Milwaukee houses see Eileen Powell, "'Will What We Say Affect What is Done?'" *Wisconsin Architect* (July–August 1972), 7–10.

3　*Baraboo Weekly News,* March 30, December 28, 1916; *The Weekly Home News,* December 21, 1916; *The Western Architect,* 25 (January 1917), 4.

4　John Lloyd Wright, *My Father,* 86.

5　On Miriam Noel: John Lloyd Wright, *My Father,* 110–111; Frank Lloyd Wright, *An Autobiography,* (New York: Duell, Sloan and Pearce, 1943 ed.), 201–202, 204, 259; *The Chicago Tribune,* November 8, 1915; *The Capital Times,* September 1, 1926; March 11, 1933; *Baraboo Weekly News,* December 3, 1925.

6　*The Chicago Tribune,* November 7, 8, 14, 1915.

7　Noel to Wright, n.d., *The Chicago Tribune,* November 7, 1915; "To the Countryside," *The Weekly Home News,* June 10, 1926.

8　For the "Miriam Letters," Wright's statements, and the events surrounding the entire episode, see *The Chicago Tribune,* November 7, 8, 14, 1915; *Chicago Herald,* November 11, 1915; *Baraboo Weekly News,* November 11, 1915; *The Sauk County Democrat,* November 17, 1915.

9　For documentation of the episode discussed in this section see original copy of unexecuted contract, May 1915; "Statement with regard to the eighty dollars telegraphed to Los Angeles Citizens National Bank for the Lloyd Jones Sisters"; Jane Lloyd Jones to Jane (or Jennie) Porter, August 31, 1915; January 31, February 7, 1916; C. E. Roberts to Jane Porter, December 5, 1915; all in Jane Lloyd Jones Collection, State Historical Society of Wisconsin (SHSW). Also *Baraboo Weekly News,* April 20, October 5, 1916.

10　For basic information on the Imperial Hotel see Robert Kostka, "Frank Lloyd Wright in Japan," *The Prairie School Review,* 3 (Third Quarter 1966), 5–23. It is best illustrated in Cary James, *The Imperial Hotel: Frank Lloyd Wright and the Architecture of Unity* (Rutland, Vt. and Tokyo, Japan: Charles E. Tuttle Co., 1968). On the quake see Robert R. Bradshaw, a Van Nuys, California, structural engineer, to *The Architectural Record,* 129 (January 1961), 10, 242.

11　"The Imperial," James Weldon Johnson wrote in 1933, "is one of the great cosmopolitan hotels of the world. Everyone who stops there either achieves or has thrust upon him one of two divergent opinions as to its architecture and its plan. Americans, in particular, debate the question, because of the nationality of the architect. . . . I could see that the Imperial was not truly oriental or occidental. Nevertheless, I thought it a very skillful combination of Japanese beauty and American convenience. I admired greatly the low roofs, flowering courts, the tiled lobby and corridors; and I was thankful for my private bath and shower with running hot and cold water, the box spring in my mattress, and the easy chairs in my room:" *Along This Way* (New York: Viking Press, 1968 ed.), 395.

12 "The Thirtieth Annual Architectural Exhibit in Chicago," *The Western Architect*, 25 (April 1917), 27. For another strong endorsement of Wright during this period see Fiske Kimball, "The American Country House," *The Architectural Record*, 46 (October 1919), 341, 344.

13 It is almost impossible to reconstruct the chronology of his several trips to Japan. The following is known: He left Seattle December 28, 1916 (*Weekly Home News*, December 21; *Baraboo Weekly News*, December 28, 1916), and returned in May 1917 (*ibid.*, May 17, 1917). He went back to Japan late in 1918 staying for "almost a year" until October 1919 (*ibid.*, October 9, 1919; *Weekly Home News*, October 2, 1919). By February 1920 he had again been in Tokyo for "several weeks" (*ibid.*, February 19, 1920), arriving back at Taliesin in July (*Baraboo Weekly News*, July 15, 1920). His final return home "after a recent trip to the Orient" of indeterminable length was in November 1922 (*The Capital Times*, November 14, 1922).

14 *The Weekly Home News*, October 2, 1919; February 19, 1920; Wright to his daughter, Catherine Baxter, February 7, 1921, FLW Collection, Avery Library, Columbia University.

15 *The Capital Times*, November 14, 1922; September 1, 1926; *The Weekly Homes News*, February 9, 1920; February 15, 22, 1923; complaint filed by James J. Hill, attorney for Wright, July 10, 1925, Sauk County Circuit Court, Baraboo, Wisconsin.

16 Miriam's description of the relationship, a very revealing document, is an interview in the *Baraboo Weekly News*, December 3, 1925.

17 John Lloyd Wright, *My Father*, 111; *The New York Times*, October 29, 1926; *The Capital Times*, November 1, 1926.

18 *The Chicago Tribune*, November 27, 1924; *Baraboo Weekly News*, December 4, 1924.

19 *Baraboo Weekly News*, April 23, July 23, 1925; *The Capital Times*, April 21, 1925; *The New York Times*, April 22, 1925; *The Weekly Home News*, April 23, 1925.

20 *The Weekly Home News*, December 3, 10, 1925; *The Capital Times*, November 27, 28, 30, December 3, 1925; *The Milwaukee Journal*, November 29, 1925; *The New York Times*, November 27, 28, 1925.

21 Wright recalled meeting Olgivanna at a Sunday afternoon matinee of a Russian ballet; the Petrograd Company performed in Chicago on November 30: *The Chicago Tribune*, November 23, 1924. For information on Olgivanna see F. L. Wright, *An Autobiography*, 510–514; *The Capital Times*, November 28, 1925; September 2, 4, October 22, 1926; and Wright's article, November 1, 1926, wherein he candidly admitted Iovanna's birth out of wedlock, a fact known before that. Also see *Who's Who of American Women, 1970-1971* (Chicago: A. N. Marquis Co., 1969), 1365.

22 Sinclair Lewis' letter to his father, n. d., in Mark Shorer, *Sinclair Lewis: An American Life* (New York: McGraw-Hill, 1961), 378; Olgivanna (Mrs. Frank Lloyd Wright), "The Last Days of Katherine Mansfield," *The Bookman*, 73 (March 1931), 6–13; Robert C. Twombly, "Organic Living: Frank Lloyd Wright's Taliesin Fellowship and Georgi Gurdjieff's Institute for the Harmonious Development of Man," *The Wisconsin Magazine of History*, 58 (Winter 1974–1975), 126–139.

23 *Baraboo Weekly News*, March 4, 11, 25, May 27, June 10, 1926; *The New York Times*, January 17, June 4–6, 1926; F. L. Wright divorce files, Sauk County Court House, March 1, 5, 1926.

24 *Baraboo Weekly News*, September 2, 1926; *The New York Times*, September 4, 1926; *The Capital Times*, August 30–September 4, 1926.

25 *The Capital Times*, September 4, 7, 8, 10, 28, 1926; *Baraboo Weekly News*, September 9, 30, October 7, 1926; *The New York Times*, September 6, 8, October 10, 1926.

26 *The New York Times*, October 22, 31, November 2, 1926; *The Milwaukee Journal*, October 21, 1926; *Baraboo Weekly News*, October 28, 1926; *The Capital Times*, September 10, 23, October 1, 8, 21, 22, November 18, 1926.

27 *The Capital Times*, October 9, 13, 20, 28, 29, 1926; *The New York Times*, October 23, 29, 1926.

28 Olgivanna was interviewed by *The Capital Times*, October 22, 1926, followed on November 1 by "Frank Lloyd Wright Tells Story of Life; Years of Work, Love, and Despair." The other quotations are from *The Capital Times*, October 1, 25, 1926.

29 *The Capital Times*, February 1, 18, 23, March 1, 4, May 9, 1927; *The New York Times*, January 2, 7, February 8, 18, 20, March 5, 1927; *Baraboo Weekly News*, February 3, 24, April 18, 1927; *The Weekly Home News*, February 24, 1927.

30 *The Weekly Home News*, May 12, 1927; *Baraboo Weekly News*, June 23, 1927; *The New York Times*, July 3, August 27, 1927; *The Capital Times*, May 6, 10, 16, 19, 20, 25, 28, June 20, 21, 23, 27, 28, July 2, 20, August 26, 27, 29, 31, 1927. In 1930, the architect's former wife Catherine married Benjamin E. Page, Secretary of Frank Lloyd Wright, Inc.; they were divorced in 1937: *The Capital Times*, January 20, 1937.

31 *The Capital Times*, September 21, October 5–8, 10, 14, 19, 1927; July 14, 15, 17, 1928; *The New York Times*, July 15, 18, 20, 1928. There was one additional connection between them. In November 1929, Miriam won a $7000 judgment against Wright for dipping into the $30,000 trust fund. After her death in January 1930, attorneys for the estate secured Wright's arrest for having failed to keep the fund at maximum levels, although the case was ultimately dismissed: *The New York Times*, November 14, 1929; December 6, 19, 1930; February 18, 1932; *The Capital Times*, December 6, 19, 1930; March 11, 1933.

32 *The Capital Times,* July 30, August 27, October 8, 14, 1928; *The New York Times,* July 31, August 27, 1928; *Baraboo Weekly News,* May 31, October 11, 1928; *The Weekly Home News,* May 24, October 11, 1928.

33 F. L. Wright, *An Autobiography,* 224–233, 239–252.

34 Henry-Russell Hitchcock, *In the Nature of Materials: The Buildings of Frank Lloyd Wright, 1887–1941* (New York: Duell, Sloan and Pearce, 1942), 75–79; "'The House on Haunted Hill': Architectural Shrines Are Expensive Homes," *Los Angeles Times,* November, 1972: "I'll admit the exterior is forbidding," owner Gus Brown said in 1972, "but once [my friends] get inside, most of them like it."

35 For a flattering contemporary analysis see A. N. Rebori; "Frank Lloyd Wright's Textile-Block Slab Construction," *The Architectural Record,* 62 (December 1927), 448–456.

36 See the bibliography for a list of these articles. The fee is discussed in "Frank Lloyd Wright, 1869–1959," *The Architectural Record,* 125 (May 1959), 9.

37 *The New York Times,* September 17, 18, October 4, 1931.

38 St. Marks is described quite well in *The New York Times,* October 18, 19, 1929; and in *American Architect,* 136 (September 1929), 53–54. For beautiful color renderings, elevation, and plans see *The Architectural Record,* 67 (January 1930), 1–4. On the other unexecuted projects of the 1920s see Drexler, Ed., *Drawings,* plates 66–70, 97–103, 106–113, 114 for before the Crash, and plates 81–83, 122, 124–125 for after.

39 *The New York Times,* September 30, 1931; February 2, 1932; *Baraboo Weekly News,* April 23, 1931; *The Capital Times,* May 17, 1927.

40 *The New York Times,* May 29, 1930; *The Western Architect,* 29 (September 1930), 152. Wright's response to the International Style Exhibition was "Of Thee I Sing," *Shelter,* 2 (April 1932). Also see Catherine K. Bauer, "Exhibition of Modern Architecture: Museum of Modern Art," *Creative Art,* 10 (April 1932). Johnson and Hitchcock discussed Wright in their book—an outgrowth of the exhibition—*The International Style Since 1922* (New York: W. W. Norton & Co., 1932).

41 *The New York Times,* February 26, 1931; Wright, "Another Pseudo," *Architectural Forum,* 59 (July 1933), 25.

42 "American Architect," *Outlook and Independent,* 157 (March 11, 1931), 358; Douglas Haskell, "Frank Lloyd Wright and the Chicago Fair," *The Nation,* 131 (December 3, 1930), 605; Henry S. Churchill, "Wright and the Chicago Fair," *The New Republic,* 65 (February 4, 1931), 329; Catherine K. Bauer, "The Americanization of Europe," *ibid.,* 67 (June 24, 1931), 153–154.

43 *Baraboo Weekly News,* November 27, 1930; *The New York Times,* December 19, 1930; November 16, 1932; *The Capital Times,* January 23, 25, 1940. Wright's tribute to Richardson is in *ibid.,* August 9, 1935.

44 *The Capital Times,* November 1, 3, 4, 8, 30, 1932; *Baraboo Weekly News,* November 10, 1932; January 5, 1933.

45 Hitchcock and Johnson, *The International Style* (1966 ed.), 26; Wright to Fiske Kimball, April 30, 1928, in F. Kimball, "American Architecture," *The Architectural Record,* 65 (May 1929), 434.

1932–1938

CHAPTER EIGHT

Little Experiment Stations in Out of the Way Places

B ut the first order of business was not new houses. Although Frank Lloyd Wright is usually remembered as a residential architect and for his spectacular public buildings, he also devoted enormous energies to community planning. When introduced in 1901, in fact, the prairie house was part of a communal living arrangement later featured in Wright's 1913 suburban quarter section development. But his planning ideas did not reach maturity until his 1935 scale model of Broadacre City, the scheme for a decentralized America he advocated for the rest of his life. The model was constructed by the Taliesin Fellowship, a resident group of student apprentices Wright established in 1932, which in 1938 began to build Taliesin West, his winter headquarters. At the architect's disposal in his two isolated homes, the Fellowship was the first planned community he executed.

□ □ □

The architect had been toying with the idea of a Fellowship for several years. Always on guard against European cultural imperialism, in his 1930 Princeton lectures (published as *Modern Architecture*) he proposed corporation-subsidized "industrial style centers" to develop America's creative energies. At the direction of master craftspersons, forty students at each center would study glassmaking, pottery, textiles, sheet metal, woodworking, dance, music, or any of a host of other arts for seven hours a day, using the latest techniques and the most modern machinery. For another three hours they would till the

211

soil, learning to be self-sufficient in their "little experiment stations in out of the way places"[1] where, with the best teachers and equipment available, they would be completely free to create and to explore the possibilities of their crafts. Encouraged to write up ideas for publication, they would also advertise and market their products when sufficiently skilled, dividing profits with the sponsoring companies. There would be no examinations or graduations but, when the students were deemed ready, they would join university faculties or become high-level employees in the endowing corporations which would have first claim on their talents. The primary function of the centers would be to develop an indigenous cultural expression from a synthesis of artistic creativity and modern technology, beneficial to the individual, to industry, and to the nation.

Corporate America did not respond to Wright's idea, so in the summer of 1931 he moved to implement it himself by announcing that in the fall of 1932 he would open a "School of the Allied Arts" in the refurbished and expanded Hillside Building at Spring Green. (He had inherited the property in 1920 after his aunts Jane and Ellen Lloyd Jones died in May 1917 and November 1919, respectively.) For $650 each, seventy young people could study a variety of subjects under the tutelage of seven senior apprentices, three technical advisors, and the Master himself. Actually, Wright did not envision a school at all: instead of teachers, pupils, and pedagogy, there would be skilled craftspeople, novices, and physical labor. For three hours a day the apprentices would work in the fields, on Taliesin construction projects, in the kitchen, the laundry, or the barns, making the place as self-sufficient as possible. For another five hours they would study "organic" design or a related skill; everyone was expected to master Wright's teachings and to specialize in molding and casting, pottery, weaving, sculpture, drama and rhythm, "reproductive processes," or, of course, in architecture. Finished projects would be placed on sale as missionaries of modern art to help finance the operation. His purpose, he said, was "to make complete, well-rounded men, proficient in some special art or craft, and versed in all of them." Wright believed that education should be in the doing, not in the classroom.[2]

Critics speculated that the architect, short of capital for several years and with few clients in 1932, was assembling young people gullible enough to pay for the privilege of growing his food and repairing his estate. However truthful the allegation, it did not impede the growth of the Taliesin Fellowship as it was called when it opened in October 1932. Although tuition was soon raised to $1100 and enrollment lowered to thirty, Wright was forced to turn away nine Vassar coeds for lack of space, and before the year was out had a waiting list of twenty-seven. At first everyone lived in Taliesin proper, three quarters of a mile across Wright's land from the Home School where repairs, begun during the summer by local artisans, were taken over by apprentices in the fall. The building had suffered serious damage from vandalism and neglect after the school closed in 1917. But the old gymnasium was remodeled into a theatre and opened in November 1933, followed by a new draughting room–dormitory facility late in 1934 and by additional sleeping quarters, a dining room, a kitchen, and galleries until the complex was as completed as it would ever be in 1939. Wright supplemented tuition by opening the Playhouse, as the theatre was called, to the general public. Beginning in November 1933, guests could watch a foreign film for fifty cents on a Sunday afternoon, share doughnuts and a cup of tea with Olgivanna Wright, and chat with the man himself. After 1934 casual visitors were charged fifty cents for an apprentice-conducted tour of Hillside and Taliesin. Wright also solicited contributions from friends, former clients, and patrons of the arts.[3] He may have been exploiting every possible source of revenue, but he was hardly turning a large profit, even if he did live in the grand manner.

Although Walter Gropius and Mies van der Rohe were listed as sponsors[4] on Fellowship literature, Wright's establishment was quite different from the famous Bauhaus at Dessau in Germany.[5] Before it closed in 1933, the Bauhaus approximated a fellowship among equals, whereas Taliesin was not really a fellowship at all in that sense. The reputations of several Bauhaus teachers—Lyonel Feininger, Paul Klee, Wassily Kandinsky, and Marcel Breuer, for example—rivaled those of directors Gropius and van der Rohe. But at Taliesin no one, including senior fellows, dared to compete with Frank Lloyd Wright. Both institutions attempted to relate art to technology, but as time passed the Fellowship accentuated handicrafts, music, dance, even spiritualism. In Germany, on the other hand, teachers and students made significant innovations in machine-age aesthetics and major contributions to painting, sculpture, furniture design, and ceramics, as well as architecture. The Bauhaus curriculum was more formal, and, as an urban institution, it remained in contact with cultural and political currents. At Spring Green the students became ingrown, isolated, and provincial, neither criticizing their Master nor equaling his achievements.

Nor did the Fellowship closely resemble the old Oak Park Studio, which in many ways was more like the Bauhaus. Wright had certainly been the moving force at Oak Park, but he made excellent use of his talented assistants' inspiration, ideas, and advice (see Chapter Four).

As paid employees, not paying apprentices, they assumed important roles in the Studio's life, sometimes dealing directly with clients or even supervising entire design development and construction processes. He delegated major responsibility to Isabel Roberts, his secretary and office manager, to Marion Mahony in the areas of architectural sculpture and finished renderings, and to others whose skills he trusted.

At Taliesin, most apprentices had no significant responsibilities. After Wright's practice revived in 1936 (see Chapter Nine), he conceived the new plans himself, then turned them over for development to John Howe from Racine, Wisconsin, who had worked for him before the Fellowship opened. Howe delegated design details to various draughtspersons, subject to the architect's ongoing and final review which sometimes included last-minute changes in the client's presence. Wright's secretary Eugene Masselink took charge of Taliesin's many publications and also produced a number of decorative murals. William Wesley Peters, who became Wright's son-in-law in 1935, supervised outdoor work, including construction and farming, while his wife Svetlana, the architect's step-daughter, ran the kitchen, subject to the approval of her mother Olgivanna who hovered over the personal, social, and cultural activities of the Fellowship, later assisted by her younger daughter, Iovanna. Select senior apprentices received unparalleled architectural training during the late 1930s and early 1940s as on-site foremen on residential projects. This could necessitate innovative decision-making beyond the formulae specified in the detailed work sheet they took with them. But most Taliesin trainees never received the invaluable opportunity of working alone in the field. If they were not careful, they would find themselves exploited, like Mabel Morgan who, after five years of laboring every other week in the kitchen, was "very tired of it. . . . I'm getting too old," she complained to a friend, "not to worry about the future."[6] With senior fellows Howe, Masselink, Peters, and the architect's wife and daughters controlling room at the top, few apprentices could expect to climb the ladder to Wright's attention.

By the late 1930s, the Fellowship was undisguisedly hierarchical. Wright and his family in their "holy of holies" deep within the "Chinese box" of Taliesin's complicated architecture, as historian John Sergeant put it, dealt mostly with senior fellows who considered themselves on a higher echelon than apprentices. In October and November 1938, members of the rank-and-file produced an anonymous newssheet complaining about Wright's distance—"If you talked to us more often we would have more courage to tell our ideas"—and about their "supercillious" seniors living on "self-made pedestals" who looked arrogantly down their noses at the rest, preferring to ignore simple chores for the more cloistered and rarified draughting room. Social stratification encouraged some to leave, others to seek upward mobility by competing for the Master's attention through tireless labor or conspicuous cooperation. Architectural or personal individuality were not successful routes to the inner circle. As a result the "graduates" of Taliesin have not as a group equaled the achievements of their Oak Park predecessors.

Some, to be sure, made well-deserved names for themselves as historians, critics, and editors. Others, "unassuming architects," Sergeant calls them, are "working all over the United States [and in Europe] to realize their clients' needs," in the National Park Service, and in California and Midwestern cities particularly. But the Fellowship never produced a Walter Burley Griffin, a Marion Mahony, or a Barry Byrne. Independent spirits, like Paolo Soleri or Kevin Lynch, did not stay long. Wright's presence for them and for other truly creative people was too stifling and the rigidity of the place (see below) too confining. But for some this was the basis of the Fellowship's appeal. William Wesley Peters, one of the original 1932 apprentices, is even today a dedicated officer of the Frank Lloyd Wright Foundation after forty-six years. John Howe stayed for thirty-two, and Eugene Masselink died at Taliesin after thirty years or more. Before World War Two the average apprentice remained about three years. But after 1945, a higher percentage left after a few months; they could expect a letter of recommendation from Wright, but the Fellowship was not recognized by the American Institute of Architects, nor was work there applicable toward credit at professional schools. For those unwilling to spend their lives in subordination to Wright—either at Taliesin or in the outside world as self-appointed defenders of his name—it was better to study elsewhere.

Superficially, the Taliesin Fellowship seemed to be inspired by the old Hillside Home School, with its emphasis on close student–faculty relations, spontaneity, nature study, outdoor work, and individualized projects.[7] Certainly the legacy of Wright's aunts and the rehabilitated building itself invite the comparison, which may very well have occured to the architect. The most singular influence on the Fellowship, however, was not the Home School or the Bauhuas or the Oak Park Studio but a rather unlikely source, Georgi Gurdjieff's Institute for the Harmonious Development of Man at Fountainebleau near Paris where Olgivanna had resided from 1920 to 1924. The relationship between Gurdjieff and his Institute and Wright and his Fellowship has been examined in detail elsewhere.[8] It is enough to note here that the daily regimen, the master–student relationship, the importance of learning by doing, the general objectives, many of the basic principles, and several of the activities at the two establishments were quite similar. Neither relied on formal instruction; indeed, some observers felt they gave no instruction at all. Both Masters (as they were called) emphasized the value of physical labor as a necessary prerequisite to self-awareness and inner peace; both taught the importance of living naturally and of music and dance for achieving personal integration. Young people at the "schools" grew or prepared their own food, maintained the estates, and were expected to be obedient; they were isolated from, and considered themselves superior to, the outside world. Gathering en masse at least once a week at the Master's feet (literally the case at Taliesin where Wright sat on a raised platform, Fig. 8.1) for talk or a musicale, none could undertake any activity without specific permission or instruction. Olgivanna, who pretty much controlled the nonarchitectural aspects of Fellowship life, transmitted her Master's ideas to Wright, who institutionalized many of them at Taliesin before Gurdjieff himself came for his first visit in 1934.

The Wrights departed from Gurdjieff by regulating more closely the

Figure 8.1 The Taliesin Fellowship at a formal musicale in 1938. Courtesy State Historical Society of Wisconsin.

personal habits and attempting more determinedly to influence the thought processes of the apprentices. Smoking, drinking, late hours, sloppy posture, and untidy clothes were *verboten*. Wright initiated many of the rules, but Olgivanna enforced them relentlessly. When a colony of beards sprouted during the summer of 1934, for example, she "endured" this "unpleasant idiosyncrasy," this "harmful whim," for a while, she remembered, but then one day "laid down the law. Fourteen absurd beards were quickly shaven." One of the women remarked in defense of her hursuit colleagues that Smith College undergraduates had once engaged in a pipe-smoking fad which the administration ignored and the students soon abandoned. "I think it frightful that they let the young girls indulge in such a grotesque habit," Olgivanna remarked in alarm, with characteristic lack of humor. "They should have been disciplined instead." When another apprentice told her that young people should seek a wide variety of experiences as the basis of self-discovery, she replied: "You are preaching dangerous doctrine." One young Fellow from China, unfamiliar with American and Taliesin customs, rose to play his violin at a Sunday evening musicale wearing dirty, unlaced boots. Olgivanna flew into a rage: "You dare to come into our presence. . .in such deplorable attire!. . . . What right do you claim for such insolence in our house? Kindly leave this room." During the Fellowship's early years, she later explained, "I took it upon myself to exercise the utmost vigilance in order to preserve the cleanliness of spirit and the ideal we were serving."[9] Little wonder the more creative apprentices fled.

With its rigid hierarchical structure, individualism at the Fellowship was reserved for the Master's inner circle, social equality for the lesser apprentices. Tentatively accepted applicants were screened for thirty days, the architect reserving the right to dismiss them without explanation at any time, even after final admission. "The Fellowship. . .is not on trial," he explained, "the apprentice is." Therefore, "especial predilections or idiosyncrasies, although respected, will not be encouraged." There were fixed hours for work, recreation, relaxation, and sleep, and since the countryside was an unparalleled source of inspiration, for Wright at least, "daily life will be planned to benefit by its beauty." Although one young person was naive enough to write that "nothing in the life of the Fellowship is forced or artificial," that "the apprentice lives naturally and spontaneously, working at whatever tasks arise," Wright saw it somewhat differently. He once compared the Fellowship to "Robin Hood and his medieval band of freebooters." But the analogy was imprecise, implying a bit more equality than he was prepared to accept. He was somewhat more accurate on another occasion, though still retaining the entirely appropriate medieval metaphor, when he told a newspaper reporter that the Fellows cooperated with each other "like fingers on my hand. They are the fingers of the hands of Frank Lloyd Wright, and will carry on the principles I have enunciated." Apprenticeship, he continued, is "much like it was in feudal times. . .: an apprentice then was his master's slave; at Taliesin he is his master's comrade," but only, he added candidly, "to the extent he qualifies himself." Olgivanna noted that "discipline exercised over members of the Taliesin Fellowship grew stronger as the years went by. We had to show them the delicate line between self-expression and self-indulgence." It was therefore not surprising, as one reporter observed, that "Wright [and his wife, he should have added] dominated every minute of every apprentices's day."[10]

In keeping with Wright's proposals in the 1930 Princeton lectures, the Fellowship expanded its activities in 1934 to publishing. The first issue of *Taliesin*, a twenty-eight-page glossy magazine without advertising, rolled off the presses in December. Edited by Wright with articles from students and friends, it was scheduled to appear nine times a year but suffered the same fate as the Taliesin "quarterly" of 1940, which folded after two issues. Another publishing venture was longer-lived. Under a masthead silhouette of Wright's home, a column called "At Taliesin" appeared in both Madison newspapers—*The Capital Times* and the *Wisconsin State Journal*—in February 1934, later in two rural weeklies. Written to increase "understanding and appreciation of his work" and to give apprentices experiences in "articulation," Wright contributed occasionally but generally left it to underlings. Ostensibly a weekly column, it actually ran intermittently, often failing to meet its Friday deadline, sometimes not appearing for weeks at a time. Announcements of films at the Playhouse and of other Fellowship activities, summaries of Wright's or his guests' Sunday talks at Unity Chapel, and paeans of praise for "organic" living were its regular fare.

"At Taliesin" was intended to develop self-expression and literary ability among the apprentices, but it seems to have become, on occasion at least, a device for currying Wright's favor. Writer after writer extolled the glories of his philosophy and the benefits of his life style. We should be "forever grateful to Mr. Wright for the privilege of belonging to the Fellowship," Marybud Lautner wrote; she was happy to return from a visit home because "life at Taliesin is really life." "We bring the outside world to us," another fledgling journalist explained, "only when and where we need it." "Sunday evenings are always interesting," Bob Mosher remarked imperiously, "because we come in contact with the outside world and the degenerate city through the medium of the various guests that Taliesin attracts."[11] Whether the "various guests"—among them their *Captial Times* publisher—repented their degeneracy is unrecorded, but it mattered little to the young authors who, oblivious in their isolation to public sentiment and to their own pretentiousness, felt entirely compentent after a few brief weeks with Wright to pontificate on art, culture, and life.

Having learned his jargon and his phraseology, many pint-sized Frank Lloyd Wrights attempted to bandy about the Master's ideas without bothering to digest them. One anonymously written column exemplified a common practice of enlarging upon a cryptic passage from the architect's writings. "I sing an ode to manure," this one opened joyously. Once, like "you city-folks," I held my nose from "the odious cow-flop. . .but now I proudly stand on a six foot pile of it," having realized that "manure is an essential link in the great cycle of life." All civilizations were based upon it, and "when manure shall have vanished from. . .the earth," the author prophesied, "you can be sure that the end of man's existence is not far behind," hopefully with pun intended. Presumably not a scatologist, he or she had undoubtedly been impressed by page twenty-four of Wright's autobiography, where "dung" is described as the "indispensible wealth that goes to bring back the jaded soil to a greenness of the hills, bring fertility to life itself—for man!"[12] Wright, of course, was not the greatest literary model, and even if the ecological sentiments indicated that something was getting through to the apprentices, it is difficult to imagine such embarrassing prose at the Bauhaus or at Wright's old studio. It was not the worst moment for American letters when the rebirth of his practice put an end to the column in October 1937.

In 1936 the Fellowship organized a drama group, the Taliesin Players, followed two years later by a string quartet that gave summer concerts over Madison radio. A male chorus, a mixed choir, a recorder chorus, and a string ensemble began in 1940 and 1941, indicating the importance of music in Wright's educational theories, and in the 1950s the Fellowship organized a full orchestra and a dance company whose Gurdjieff-inspired works were choreographed by Olgivanna and Iovanna for public performances.[13] In the last decade or more of his life, when Wright's practice increased astronomically and when he took on enormous speaking and writing obligations, members of the Fellowship assumed greater design responsibility. By the mid-1950s, when he was physically unable to do much drawing, a handful of trusted assistants, but principally William Wesley Peters, worked out even his preliminary ideas on paper. One of the Fellowship's first important tasks, however, began early in 1934: to build under Wright's direction the twelve-by-twelve-foot model of Broadacre City, his scheme for a decentralized America. Completed in March 1935, it was first displayed the next month at the Industrial Arts Exposition at New York's Rockefeller Center, in the very heart of the urban civilization Wright hoped to abolish.[14]

The Fellowship worked on the model literally day and night from January 1935 until two weeks before the Exposition opened. Assembly took place in the Arizona desert near Chandler, at La Hacienda, a tourist hotel Wright rented every winter from 1935 until 1938 when Taliesin West, his new second home, was far enough along to be occupied. After his honeymoon in 1928, during which he served as consultant to former apprentice Albert C. McArthur who asked Wright to assist him with the use of textile blocks in the Biltmore Hotel in Phoenix, the architect's next venture to Arizona was in January 1929, when he built a canvass-roofed "Ocatilla Camp" to accommodate employees on the unrealized "San-Marcos-in-the-Desert" project. Near Ocatillo was an eight-mile-square ranch with a field of alfalfa running the entire length of one side—"a beautiful scene from the mountain top," a Wright workman wrote—named "Broad Acre."[15]

Wright had been arguing since the 1920s that modern cities were no longer habitable. Believing them too large, congested, frenetic, and physically and psychologically unhealthy to support life, he insisted that their only practical reasons to continue were as commercial centers and travel junctions. People, he thought, should resettle the countryside. Broadacre City, Wright's solution for urban problems, was first systematically outlined in 1932, in his book *The Disappearing City,* in a March 20 article for *The New York Times* magazine section, and in several speeches.[16] But his doubts about urban life can be traced all the way back to the 1890s when he opened a suburban design studio because he found Chicago too distracting. His first community plan, accompanying the prairie house in the February 1901 *Ladies Home Journal,* was tiny to be sure (only two residential blocks), but it began a life-long preoccupation. Despite his insistence during seventy-two years of designing private homes that no two buildings should be alike because no two clients were, his six decades of work on planned communities indicates that he was as absorbed by the possibilities of group harmony as he was dedicated to unfettered individualism. His own life style exemplified the one, while "the chief work of [his] mature life," as John Sergeant calls Broadacre City, was directed toward the other.

Unlike other visions of totally planned urban environments, Broadacres was not a city at all but a typical four-mile-square section of a decentralized and reorganized nation (Fig. 8.2). Wright did not think in terms of a rural–urban dichotomy or that cities should be entities discrete unto themselves. The Broadacre model was meant to be infinite or, as Sergeant says, "a continuum," without boundaries, limits, or borders. It was a vision of America itself; a synthesis of urban, rural, and suburban characteristics integrated on a national scale. Since the model seemed to be a small piece of the whole country but obviously included all Wright's specific proposals, its very completeness was partly responsible for misunderstanding. Many people did not comprehend that the model was holistic only by necessity, not in fact, and that the new America would not be an endless repetition of the four-mile-square depiction.

Broadacres provided for 1400 families in its sixteen square miles. "Entry," writes John Sergeant, the most recent and thorough student of the plan, "was by the main arterial road, or county highway, of ten car lanes above and two truck lanes and continuous warehousing below. Above the median ran a high-speed monorail. This bordered the west boundary of the model and attracted roadside businesses, markets, industry, and decentralized hotels (motels). . . . Next removed were owner-occupied light industrial units, workers' homes, and vineyards and orchards. The central area consisted of small homes, with three schools at its heart."[17] Based on an understanding that modern transportation and communication had conquered the time barrier, Wright did not see geographical dispersion as an obstacle to organized social life. He therefore adopted the county as the smallest official, administrative, and social unit. Linked directly to the national government, whose only functions were diplomacy, defense, and to regulate overseas trade, the county was large enough to be effective but small enough to permit meaningful citizen participation, thereby eliminating states and towns. All necessary services—schools, roads, commerce, recreation, police, the judiciary, and so on—would be operated from this level, where the highest official, the architect, would see that all structures were harmonious with each other and with their purposes and that everything affecting the public was effectively and humanely administered.

Broadacre City was reintegrated as well as decentralized, people

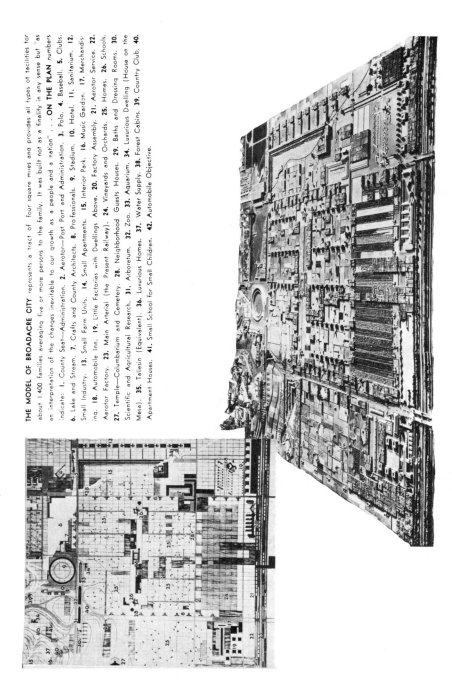

THE MODEL OF BROADACRE CITY represents a tract of four square miles and provides all types of facilities for about 1,400 families averaging five or more persons to the family. It was built not as a finality in any sense but "as an interpretation of the changes inevitable to our growth as a people and a nation". . . . ON THE PLAN numbers indicate: 1. County Seat—Administration. 2. Aerator—Post Port and Administration. 3. Polo. 4. Baseball. 5. Clubs. 6. Lake and Stream. 7. Crafts and County Architects. 8. Professionals. 9. Stadium. 10. Hotel. 11. Sanitarium. 12. Small Industry. 13. Small Farm Units. 14. Small Apartments. 15. Interior Park. 16. Music Garden. 17. Merchandising. 18. Automobile Inn. 19. Little Factories with Dwellings Above. 20. Factory Assembly. 21. Aerotor Service. 22. Aerotor Factory. 23. Main Arterial (the Present Railway). 24. Vineyards and Orchards. 25. Homes. 26. Schools. 27. Temple—Columbarium and Cemetery. 28. Neighborhood Guests Houses. 29. Baths and Dressing Rooms. 30. Scientific and Agricultural Research. 31. Arboretum. 32. Zoo. 33. Aquarium. 34. Luxurious Dwelling (House on the Mesa). 35. Taliesin (Equivalent). 36. Luxurious Homes. 37. Water Supply. 38. Forest Cabins. 39. Country Club. 40. Apartment Houses. 41. Small School for Small Children. 42. Automobile Objective.

Figure 8.2   Broadacre City model and key. From *American Architect*, May 1935.

222

might spread out to live, but the various ingredients of modern civilization would constitute a "diversity in unity," as Wright called it. Factories, for example, were located near their sources of supply, means of distribution, or their principal markets; with carefully regulated architecture and pollutant emission, they would not be isolated in separate industrial zones. Electrical power, oil, and gas fuel were received through underground conduits. Under the supervision of the county architect, all services—official, business, cultural, recreational—were clustered at half-mile intervals over the land, side by side with farm and home. Families controlled an acre of land for each member to be kept as long as it was productively used. Wright envisioned a food garden on every homesite and a dwelling that could in large measure be built by the family itself, using modern prefabrication. Although Broadacre City was superficially similar to back-to-the-farm movements and to other planned communities of the Depression, it was also the culmination of thirty years' evolution in Wright's thinking.

His first proposal for communal living had appeared in "A Home in a Prairie Town," the February 1901 *Ladies Home Journal* article announcing the prairie house. The "quadruple block" plan (Fig. 8.3), four suburban homes linked on each of two four-hundred-foot-square blocks by low walls enclosing common landscaping in the center, looked enticing but was quite unrealistic. Its half-acre per house made little sense to real estate agents eager to reduce lot size in rapidly expanding suburbs. The upper middle class that could afford the arrangement, furthermore, did not look favorably on communal land ownership and virtually indistinguishable houses. Norris Kelly Smith perceptively observed that only those with strong kinship or business ties would even consider the idea,[18] and as it turned out the closest Wright came to executing a quadruple block was the George Barton–Darwin D. Martin complex (1903–1904) in Buffalo, where Barton's wife was Martin's daughter and both men were executives for the Larkin Company. But the plan had at least one profound implication; if the beauty of a home depended in part upon its surroundings, the only way to guarantee aesthetic success was to design the entire neighborhood. In the strictest sense, the Quadruple Block was not a planned community, simply an architecturally harmonious residential cluster. But with its commonly owned and commonly used land and its design

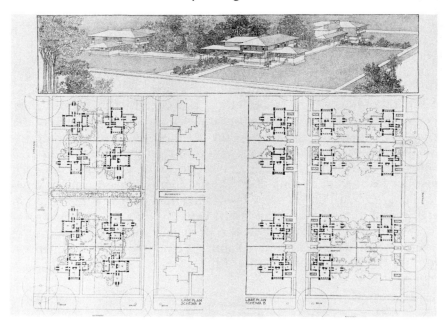

Figure 8.3 The Quadruple Block, first published in 1901. From *Ausgeführte Bauten und Entwürfe von Frank Lloyd Wright* (1910).

integration, it was philosophically alien to the normal arrangements of private enterprise.

The partially executed Como Orchard Summer Colony (1909–1910) at Darby, Montana, was a more complete community that also assumed and provided for closely linked interests among participants (Fig. 8.4). Conceived by a group of University of Chicago professors as a vacation retreat and a summer rental, Como Orchard consisted of fifty-three individual dwellings positioned around a recreation-dining hall. All the houses were variations on a basic architectural theme, grouped in clusters of two to six, themselves parts of larger formations. Wright made no attempt to scatter the homes casually in keeping with the rugged terrain or with vacation informality. Consequently, Como Orchard was peculiarly inappropriate to its purpose, unless for Wright it was communal living rather than summer relaxation. But even so he designed with a sociologically heavy hand. The dining hall, where all the households would eat communally like an extended family, governed the location of the dwellings, which were lined up like so many wooden soldiers on crossed and diagonal axes. The organization and atmosphere of the place emphasized the group, but in his attempt to

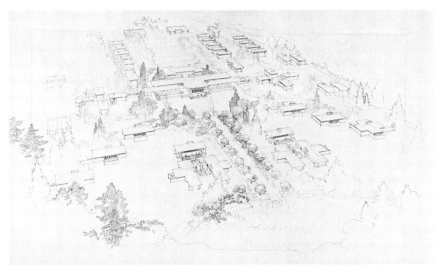

Figure 8.4 Como Orchard Summer Colony (1909–1910), Darby, Montana. From *Ausgeführte Bauten und Entwürfe von Frank Lloyd Wright* (1910).

provide for purposeful unity, Wright undermined individual variety, seemingly so appropriate in vacation spots. Overall, the plan is stiff and lifeless, with private cottages paying homage to the common hall. Even more than the Quadruple Block, Como Orchard emphasized the group by imposing an architectural and social conformity on its members.

Wright's first full-scale community was the 1913 "non-competitive plan" (Fig. 8.5) he sent to the National Conference on City Planning's contest for the development of a suburban quarter section (160 acres).[19] The scheme featured three variations on the quadruple block which, in the form of two-flat buildings and "better class" homes, accounted for two thirds of the land and nine tenths of the residential units in the quarter section, but for less than half the people. All the other housing—flats for working families and apartment buildings for single men and women segregated by sex—was scattered around the periphery in less desirable locations, revealing Wright's acceptance of conventional class prerogatives and sexual attitudes. There were other indications of his conservative social thinking. At the corner extremeties, the six apartment towers were as far removed as possible from upper income families. Two-family homes and "workmen's house groups" ran along the southernmost eight-block strip, fenced from the "better class" by a park and a lagoon. Blue-collar row houses were

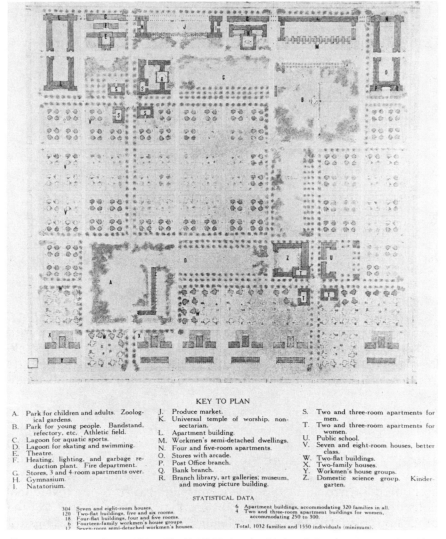

KEY TO PLAN

A. Park for children and adults. Zoolog-
    ical gardens.
B. Park for young people. Bandstand,
    refectory. etc. Athletic field.
C. Lagoon for aquatic sports.
D. Lagoon for skating and swimming.
E. Theatre.
F. Heating. lighting, and garbage re-
    duction plant. Fire department.
G. Stores, 3 and 4-room apartments over.
H. Gymnasium.
I. Natatorium.

J. Produce market.
K. Universal temple of worship. non-
    sectarian.
L. Apartment building.
M. Workmen's semi-detached dwellings.
N. Four and five-room apartments.
O. Stores with arcade.
P. Post Office branch.
Q. Bank branch.
R. Branch library, art galleries; museum,
    and moving picture building.

S. Two and three-room apartments for
    men.
T. Two and three-room apartments for
    women.
U. Public school.
V. Seven and eight-room houses, better
    class.
W. Two-flat buildings.
X. Two-family houses.
Y. Workmen's house groups.
Z. Domestic science group. Kinder-
    garten.

STATISTICAL DATA

304	Seven and eight-room houses.	6	Apartment buildings, accommodating 320 families in all.
120	Two-flat buildings, five and six rooms.	4	Two and three-room apartment buildings for women,
18	Four-flat buildings, four and five rooms.		accommodating 250 to 300.
6	Fourteen-family workmen's house groups.		
17	Seven-room semi-detached workmen's houses.		Total, 1032 families and 1550 individuals (minimum).

Figure 8.5 "Non-Competitive Plan" (1913) for the National Conference on City Planning. From Yeomans, Ed., *City Residential Land Development*.

placed nearest to the produce market, while apartments for single
men and women were tellingly separated from each other by "better
class" families, suggesting that Wright assumed a correlation between
high socioeconomic status and exemplary moral behavior. In general,
homes for the comfortable and affluent dominated the choice sites

near the parks and social and cultural services, while with a kind of grudging necessity the workers were farmed out to the periphery by themselves. That Wright designated housing by class is itself significant, but that he segregated it so neatly indicated his prejudices. The classes in their places were encouraged not to mix.

After the "better" dwellings, the most desirable areas in the 1913 plan were allotted to parks and recreation. Certain cultural and social services were also available: markets, schools, a library, power plant, garbage reduction plant, a fire department, and, despite the city's proximity, an art gallery and a museum. Some of this was included to satisfy the rules of competition, but since the architect was then free to organize the quarter section as he pleased, his omissions are quite revealing. For example, he made no provision for industry, professional or health facilities, public meetings, or mass transportation. He may have been counting on the availability of downtown services, but by excluding government buildings and a police department—found in any suburban community—he may have been suggesting that people could, or should, live in uncoerced harmony, a notion implicit in his handling of religion. Suburban America in 1913 was hardly clamoring for a nonsectarian "universal temple" of worship, but by offering it Wright gave notice that those he had segregated residentially should unite for spiritual purposes. Positing a community bound by common beliefs and assumptions (but presumably unaffected by class differences) and nurtured by a universal understanding of what was good and proper, the religious facility was the glue of social cohesion keeping people in preordained places more effectively, it seemed to Wright, than police or politicians. He recognized social distinctions in 1913, but not their capacity for tearing society apart.

Broadacre City revealed important changes in Wright's social attitudes. He seemed more favorably disposed toward social diversity in 1935, as if to acknowledge alterations in traditional civic bonds. The desirable center portion of the 1913 quarter section that had been the locale of "better class" dwellings with immediate access to spacious parks, for example, was in Broadacres entirely devoted to small farms and homes, schools, stores, professional facilities, and neighborhood garages (automobiles were banned from interior streets). Wright still recognized class distinctions but integrated income levels more thoroughly. Bathhouses and family farms were the nearest neighbors of the most affluent citizens, while apartment towers, grammar schools, and forest cabins were placed next to the upper middle class. (Prior residence patterns based on sex were also abandoned.) Wright's provision for religion typified his new attitude toward social diversity. The "universal worship" center remained from 1913, but grouped around it were nine sectarian temples, allowing for various modes of expression. In 1913 the religious edifice had rivaled the schools in size, but it was now overshadowed, indeed humbled, by a contiguous educational complex itself supplemented by neighborhood learning centers. Unlike the earlier scheme, Broadacres did not provide for segregated social classes, the superordinancy of religion, the old prerogatives of the rich, or mass acceptance of the "better" values.

Although Broadacre City was less obviously suburban than the 1913 plan, it was recognizably neither urban nor rural. It retained a basic gridiron arrangement but included enough winding streams and thoroughfares, circular buildings and landscaping, and dead-end streets to soften the rectilinear pattern of trans-Appalachian towns. Deriving much of its character from the small farms at the center, it was based on the concept of a sturdy modern yeomanry living close to the soil. But Wright also wove industry and government into the fabric of the countryside, with pollution-free factories in every county and public buildings, stripped of the usual architectural authority symbols, off in the corners. All the unsightly aspects of modern life, which in Wright's plan were not all unsightly—highways and telephone lines, railroads and the airport, maintenance buildings and the power plant—were buried or pushed to the periphery, screened from the general view but easily accessible. Utilities and consumer-oriented industries were locally controlled, publicly owned, and much reduced in scale; small businesses and professional services remained in private hands. Wright also proposed to abolish what he called "triple rent," a money economy with attendant interest rates, monopoly control of land, and private ownership of patents, and wanted to replace specie with some form of social credit as a direct medium of exchange.

Wright believed in capitalism but not in the way it was practiced. Influenced by the Greenbackers and the Populists from his youthful days in the Midwest, by Jane Addams and Florence Kelly in the settlements, by Robert M. La Follette's "Wisconsin Idea," by historian Charles A. Beard, economists Thorstein Veblen and the German Silvio Gesell, by Woodrow Wilson's theoretically antimonopolist "New Freedom," and by people like Thomas Jefferson, Ralph Waldo Emerson, Walt Whitman, Henry David Thoreau, Henry George, and some of the New Dealers, Frank Lloyd Wright rejected "the unacceptable face of capitalism." As a staunch opponent of private monopoly, he was much closer to the spirit of the International Workers of the World, as John

Sergeant has said, than to "Coolidge prosperity" or to traditional American conservative thought. Wright was not a socialist, although he knew Florence Kelly, the 1885 translator of Friedrich Engels' *The Condition of the Working-Class in England* (1845), and he was not an anarchist, even though he may have met Peter Kropotkin when he visited Hull House in April 1901.[20]

Wright believed that capital, like the populace, was too highly concentrated, that too few individuals controlled too much. By abolishing "triple rent," he maintained, the citizenry could regain control of the land, the means of production, and consequently of themselves. Broadacre City was essentially the blueprint for a postrevolutionary society based on

little farms, *little* homes for industry, *little* factories, *little* schools, a *little* university [and] *little* laboratories. . .for professional men. [It was based on] free use of the ground held only by use and improvement; public utilities and government itself owned by the people. . . ; privacy on one's own ground for all and fair means of subsistence for all by way of work on their own ground or in common offices serving the life of the whole.[21]

But aside from subsidized transportation for people to leave cities, Wright had no suggestions on how Broadacre City was to be realized, or how people were to get their land. That, of course, was a concrete political question, and Wright rarely talked concrete politics.

Broadacre City was therefore an improbable proposal because it included no means of achievement. The objective itself was humane, workable, common sensical and natural. It recalled the ways many Americans had once lived: on small farms close to the soil, in manageable communities, with local and regional economies, without residential segregation by class. Broadacre City was much more practical and in keeping with preferred human experience than Corbusier's "cities of tomorrow," his "Voison" plan for Paris or his "City of Three Million Inhabitants," for example, which housed people in mammoth high-rises plopped down in parks or in snakelike megastructures encasing open spaces reminiscent of huge prison yards. Corbusier's schemes denied the possibility of two fundamental human experiences: spontaneous street life on a human scale (that is, with a low-rise mix of architecturally diverse buildings) and close association with the land, in his plans kept at a distance for periodic recreation, not immediately available for everyday use.[22] But in Broadacres both were built in. Density was sufficient in the commercial clusters and in some residential neighborhoods for a vigorous street life, and everyone was able to live in close association with nature. Both architects' plans were utopian in the sense that their realization as conceived was highly unlikely. But Broadacre City was dismissed out of hand, while La Ville Radieuse became extremely influential, partly because Corbusier endorsed established economic and political arrangements. By contrast, Wright's attack on the "ultra-capitalist centers," as he called American cities, and on capitalism itself was fairly obvious.

Lacking a political strategy for implementation, Wright hoped Broadacre City would more or less evolve naturally ("organically"). And in part it has, not its economic or political features, for those were implicitly revolutionary, but in terms of land use, population movement, and corporate decentralization. According to the Census Bureau, America's eight largest metropolitan areas suffered a sharp population decline since 1970, wholly without precedent since the first census of 1790. Taken together, they lost 664,000 people between 1970 and 1973, the major victims being the cities and surrounding suburbs of New York, Chicago, Los Angeles, Philadelphia, and Detroit. The nation's growth since 1970 occurred in metropolitan areas of less than 1,000,000 and in nonmetropolitan counties smaller than 50,000 inhabitants.[23] America, in other words, has begun to decentralize, to spread out, in different and more fundamental ways than the familiar urban-to-suburban exodus, now itself slowing. Since Broadacre City was never intended to be suburban but spoke directly to this sort of phenomenon, it seems more relevant now than ever.

It was also prophetic in less sweeping ways. There is a growing recognition that removing main arteries and parking facilities to urban peripheries will benefit auto-choked central cities fighting last-ditch battles against expressways. In the 1950s, San Franciscans stopped the extension of an elevated freeway that would have destroyed the northern bay front, leaving a pedestaled connecting ramp soaring into empty space, much like the uncompleted four-level intersection at San Jose. Boston has decided to bury the horrendous Central Artery bisecting the city, and some New Yorkers opposed to Westway, the interstate threatening to cut off lower Manhattan from the Hudson River, have argued that even the old West Side Highway it is meant to replace should be torn down. By banning automobiles from interior roadways and providing ample public parking, Broadacres in effect embraced the notion of pedestrian streets, now popping up in Berkeley, California, in Madison, Wisconsin, and in several other places, along with mounting support for completely removing autos from substantial portions of the city.[24]

Broadacre clusters of commercial facilities antedated suburban shopping centers and interstate highway service areas, while pollution-free factories in the country foreshadowed "clean" industrial zones like expressway belts around Boston, Washington, and many other cities. Manufacturing and corporate headquarters have, of course, been moving to the suburbs and beyond for years, like apartment houses scattered among single-family dwellings or minority and low-income challenges to restrictive residential zones, calling into question the functional and class segregation that has long characterized metropolitan areas. Broadacre City included neighborhood schools and educational parks, both locally controlled. Wright understood the human need for light, space, and air, for living nearer to the land, and he knew the psychic damage caused by excessive noise, constant movement, and limited vistas. He hoped that Broadacre residents, as well as his actual clients, would construct their own homes, at least in part, and would band together when possible to achieve maintenance and purchasing economies (see Chapter Nine). He also designed with greater attention to ecological and environmental factors than has generally been recognized, and than most other architects even today. In these and several other ways, Broadacre City seems more up-to-date with every passing moment.

But the plan was hardly a back-to-nature crusade, not by incorporating as it did the latest labor-saving technologies. It was more comprehensive than New Deal Greenbelt towns which presumed the continuation of the central city, of speculation in land, and of restrictive zoning practices. Broadacres assumed a completely new social fabric, a radical reordering of life styles based on a rural–urban–suburban synthesis following a massive national retreat from the city. It assumed that capitalism and the modern state were inhumane, that people could live together peacefully without coercion on their own land if they shared in the means of production, that Art could improve Life through Architecture, and that a benevolent environment could remedy individual and collective maladies. But Broadacres had a serious flaw. It was well planned architecturally but so poorly thought out politically that it made little sense to even the most visionary reformers, urbanists (except Lewis Mumford and Paul and Percival Goodman), and political theorists.

There was another crucial shortcoming. No matter how Wright tried to disguise the fact with democratic rhetoric, the County Architect, even though popularly elected to abide by community decision, had unparalleled powers to influence every aspect of social life. In this respect Wright was not unlike many planners who assume they know what is best for people. Broadacres with County Architects would have been like the Taliesin Fellowship with Wright. But without him, or his surrogates, it was possibly the most humane scheme ever advanced by a major public figure and certainly one of the first to treat design problems as socioeconomic issues.

□ □ □

Within two or three years after finishing the Broadacre model, the Fellowship was hard at work on another important project. During a bout with pneumonia in 1936, Wright's doctor told him to spend his winters in a warmer climate. Since he was already in love with Arizona, he purchased 800 acres of public land in the Paradise Valley at Scottsdale near Phoenix, and within a year designed his second home, Taliesin West, for the Fellowship to construct. The first executed unit was the desert-stone, redwood-beam draughting room with a white canvas roof emitting soft diffused light and, with the help of side flaps open to the breezes, diminishing the intense heat. Built off an emphatically stated triangular plan, Taliesin West faced the looming Superstition Mountains on reflex axis, taking an ancient symbol of stability as a reference point in the desert's shifting sands. Multicolored stone and huge redwood trusses, later enhanced by green, irrigated gardens and deep, blue pools, combined to form a virtual rainbow of color, subtly augmented when shadows cast by stone pillar and overhanging beam played gaily with the sun. This oasis of beauty was another demonstration—the first in a long time, some thought—of Wright's exceptional versatility.[25]

Assuming that an architect will design the optimum house for himself and that it will reveal more about his domestic and social philosophy than client projects, it is useful to compare Wright's two Taliesins. Both were substantially altered over the years, so they stand significantly different from their original plans drawn in 1911 and 1938, respectively. But even as first conceived and published, they chronicle important developments in Wright's thinking. Like its predecessor, Taliesin West takes its cues from surroundings. Built from native materials and landscaped with local vegetation, its canvas and stone were appropriate in the hot climate. It integrated architecture and nature with consumate skill by nestling close to the ground (closer, in fact, than Wright's earlier work), by opening immediately to the outside through great stretches of movable façade and by incorporating pools, gardens, and plant life within its perimeter. Its local materials, far-flung terraces, open courts, and the edifice itself blended easily into the desert. Taliesin East (or North as it was now sometimes called), had merged into its hilltop so subtly at points that building and site were almost indistinguishable. The same was true in Arizona.

This intimate merging had contributed to a fortresslike atmosphere at Spring Green, but in the desert it worked in completely different ways. Alone with Mamah Borthwick in 1911, Wright had above all wanted privacy, protection from hostile outsiders, and a sense of shelter. Happily married for a decade by 1938, with commissions coming and new ideas developing rapidly (see Chapter Nine), he now faced the world confidently, without apprehension. Taliesin East achieved its security and its architectural success from a commanding hilltop position overlooking the valley, and by controlling its access routes like the castle of a feudal lord. But in a virtual reversal of site plan, Taliesin West sat alone and unprotected on the desert floor (Fig. 8.6), dominated by the mountains to which it paid tribute, exposed on all sides like the isolated home of a pioneer. Like the dispossessed agricultural migrants of the Great Depression who took their tents to California in search of fortune[26] and their Conastoga wagon predeces-

Figure 8.6 Taliesin West (1938), Scottsdale, Arizona. From *Arizona Highways*, February 1956.

sors the previous century, Wright's own canvas-roofed dwelling was an optimistic investment in the growth of the West. In 1911 he had been a wounded warrior inside enemy territory, licking his wounds in a stone retreat. Twenty-seven years later in Arizona, he used his solitude to map strategies for future campaigns, confident of ultimate victory. But the sand and the canvas and the water suggested a certain impermanence, as if Wright had learned that even the strongest fortress guaranteed nothing. Only the looming mountains were safe within themselves.

There were other important differences between the two homes. In the 1911 Taliesin, a central complex of courts, gardens, and terraces was ringed by the living, working, and service facilities (Fig. 8.7). Clockwise around the perimeter ran the draughtspersons' and gardener's quarters, the stables, assistants' rooms, Wright's own suite, the guest wing, and outstretching walls and gardens. Wright separated himself from employees on the longest possible diagonal through the building, in rooms pulling away from the house over the hill's slope. Flanking himself on one side with guests and the other with his private

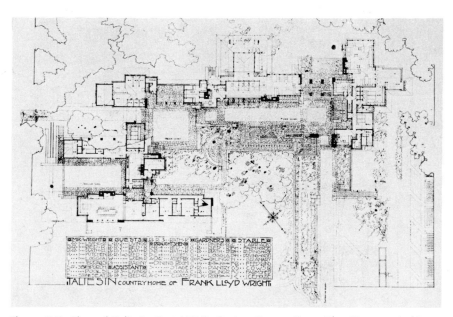

Figure 8.7 Plan of Taliesin East (1911), Spring Green. From *The Western Architect,* February 1913.

studio, he brought closest to him the things he trusted most: friends and work. Taliesin East was hardly gloomy, but for all its architectural progressivism, it endorsed the reserved, orderly, and dignified behavior of the times. Its inhabitants worked together but lived separate social lives. Architectural unity left sufficient room for personal withdrawal.

Taliesin West was almost the opposite (Fig. 8.8). Its center was devoted to living space, not courtyards, bringing residents together, not keeping them apart. It was a crossroads of cooking, dining, and guest facilities penetrated by gardens and terraces all flowing into the main draughting facilities in one direction, and in the other toward Wright's quarters at a far corner, separated from apprentice rooms only by a small common court. Taliesin West was more tightly organized and internally compact than Taliesin East. Reflecting the conservation of space and materials made necessary by modern social and economic requirements, it also affirmed close, almost familial, ties among inhabitants. Although some apprentices lived in tents and home-made structures scattered over the desert, Taliesin West was built for a Fellowship, a mutually united if hierarchical group, unlike its predecessor which was designed for two harrassed "soul-mates" alone in their seclusion except for paid employees. With bright colors and dancing, sunlit surfaces, breezy openings and cool passageways, light textiles and splashing water, Taliesin West was the spirit of youth

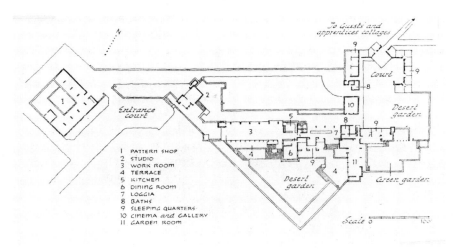

Figure 8.8 Plan of Taliesin West (1938), Scottsdale, Arizona. From *The Architect's Journal*, March 13, 1941.

and the exuberance of life itself, intangibles more characteristic of the seventy-one-year-old Master, ironically, than of the forty-four-year-old exile in 1911, or of the apprentices he controlled so thoroughly in 1938.

From then until Wright's death and even after, the Fellowship spent winters in Paradise Valley, the rest of the time at Spring Green. It traveled back and forth in auto caravans, sometimes varying the route from year to year, in the early days camping overnight at roadside near the Black Hills, the Grand Canyon, or some other natural wonder, or staying a few days with Wright's former clients so apprentices could see his work. The architect usually led these tours in his Buick, his Mercedes, or whatever he was driving at the time, top down unless it rained, a Fellow at the wheel, back seat loaded with rolled-up drawings, camping gear, and food. Each fall *The Weekly Home News* announced his departure for Arizona, and each spring his return to Wisconsin, describing the frenetic activity already underway to make Taliesin East presentable after its winter hibernation.[27]

In its two little experiment stations in out-of-the-way places, the Taliesin Fellowship was the first planned community Wright built. (His Usonia housing developments in Michigan and New York—not complete communities by any means—will be discussed in Chapter Nine.) Beginning in 1936 his rapidly increasing income made the Fellowship economically viable, strengthening the style of communalism he hoped to stimulate in his Usonian developments, in the nation as a whole, and in Broadacre City. Though he continued to promote it for the rest of his life—he devoted his last book to Broadacres in 1958— his final successes came from individual buildings, not community planning. Nevertheless, his residences and public structures after 1935 were designed in keeping with Broadacre themes of decentralization, self-sufficiency, and reverence for the land. As far as Wright was concerned each new commission was a missionary for the new America.

Taliesin West was one of many impressive designs returning him to the forefront of his profession. His renaissance might have been impossible without the Fellowship performing his labor, without the Broadacre model finally completed, and without his home life having settled into its own unique routine. Relieved of the old burdens, accompanied by a sympathetic comrade, he achieved an emotional equilibrium conducive to intellectual accomplishment. The next few years more than compensated for the tribulations of the past two decades.

NOTES

1 *Modern Architecture: Being the Kahn Lectures for 1930* (Princeton: Princeton University Press, 1931), reprinted in *The Future of Architecture* (New York: Horizon Press, 1953).

2 *Baraboo Weekly News,* July 15, 1920; "An Extension of the Work in Architecture at Taliesin to Include Apprentices in Residence," announcement brochure, reprinted in Frank Lloyd Wright, *An Autobiography* (New York: Duell, Sloan and Pearce, 1943 ed.), 390–394; *The Capital Times,* August 7, 1932; *The New York Times,* August 9, November 6, 1932. Also see Wright's pamphlet, *The Hillside School of the Allied Arts: Why We Want This School* (1931).

3 On the opening, building, and early activities of the Fellowship see *The Capital Times,* April 9, November 1, 3, 1933; May 18, 1934; November 13, 1936; *Baraboo Weekly News,* September 8, November 3, 1932; October 12, 19, 1933; March 8, June 7, 14, 1934; *The Weekly Home News,* April 13, 1933; January 4, May 24, July 12, 1934; May 11, October 5, 1939; *The Milwaukee Journal,* April 9, 1933, quoting *The Nation;* John Gloag, "Frank Lloyd Wright and the Significance of the Taliesin Fellowship," *The Architectural Record,* 77 (January 1935), 1–2; letter from James Watrous to *American Magazine of Art,* 26 (December 1933). Wright's elaborate plan for Fellowship facilities, only partially executed, is in *Architectural Forum,* 69 (January 1938).

4 "Friends of the Fellowship" were listed in *The Taliesin Fellowship* (Spring Green, Wis., 1933), a descriptive pamphlet including membership application. Many of the "friends" whose names were used were never asked permission.

5 The most comprehensive source on the Bauhaus is Hans M. Wingler, *The Bauhaus* (Cambridge, Mass.: The MIT Press, 1969 new ed.).

6 Letter to Helen Beal, quoted in John Sergeant, *Frank Lloyd Wright's Usonian Houses: The Case for Organic Architecture* (New York: Watson-Guptill, 1976), 100. Chapter Three of Sergeant's book, the source for much of the information in this section, is now the most comprehensive discussion of the Fellowship.

7 Mary Ellen Chase, who taught at Hillside from 1909 to 1912, creates a picture with many similarities to the Fellowship: *A Goodly Fellowship* (New York: The Macmillan Co., 1939), 87–121.

8 In R. C. Twombly, "Organic Living: Frank Lloyd Wright's Taliesin Fellowship and Georgi Gurdjieff's Institute for the Harmonious Development of Man," *The Wisconsin Magazine of History,* 58 (Winter 1974–75), 126–139.

9 Olgivanna (Mrs. Frank) Lloyd Wright, "Our House," *The Capital Times,* February 9, 1959; and her book, *The Shining Brow: Frank Lloyd Wright* (New York: Horizon Press, 1960), 85–86.

10 See "An Extension of the Work" and membership application cited in notes 2 and 4; Earl Friar, "At Taliesin," *The Capital Times*, April 24, 1936; Sterling Sorenson, "Wright's Taliesin is League of Nations in Miniature," *ibid.*, September 28, 1947; Bruce Bliven, Jr., "Frank Lloyd Wright," *The New Republic*, 103 (December 9, 1940).

11 *The Capital Times*, March 2, 1934; September 6, 1935; *The Weekly Home News*, March 29, 1934.

12 *The Capital Times*, May 4, 1935.

13 *The Capital Times*, November 11, 1936; August 17, 1938; July 19, 1939; October 19, 1940; October 30, 1950; November 7, 1951; *The Weekly Home News*, June 30, July 28, 1938; August 28, 1941.

14 *The New York Times*, March 27, 1935; *The Capital Times*, December 9, 1934; April 19, 1935; and the *Baraboo Weekly News*, March 20, 1935.

15 In *Frank Lloyd Wright: His Life, His Work, His Word* (New York: Horizon Press, 1967), 214, Olgivanna Wright mistakenly asserts that the Fellowship began its annual winter trips to Arizona in 1933, the year it started work, she writes, on the Broadacre Model. Preparation of the model actually got under way early in 1934 (*The Capital Times*, December 9, 1934), while the first Fellowship cross-country trek took place in January 1935 (*The Weekly Home News*, January 10, 1935; *Baraboo Weekly News*, January 24, February 28, March 28, 1935; and especially the *Wisconsin State Journal*, February 10, 1935).

   Both Olgivanna (*Frank Lloyd Wright*, 213) and Henry-Russell Hitchcock (*In the Nature of Materials: The Buildings of Frank Lloyd Wright, 1887–1941* [New York: Duell, Sloan and Pearce, 1942], 124, plates 276–280) give incorrect dates for the construction of Ocatilla Camp. Wright and his assistants left for the San Marcos Desert near Chandler in January 1929 and designed the camp when they got there: *Baraboo Weekly News*, January 17, 1929; *The Weekly Home News*, January 24, March 7, 1929.

   On "Broad Acre Ranch" see *The Weekly Home News*, April 18, 1929.

16 *The Capital Times*, February 18, 1932. My analysis of Broadacre City is based on these and other sources listed in the bibliography, and on J. Sergeant, *Usonian Houses*, Ch. 4, now the best discussion of Wright's decentralization plan. Some of the ideas in the following sections were developed at greater length in R. C. Twombly, "Undoing the City: Frank Lloyd Wright's Planned Communities," *American Quarterly*, 24 (October 1972), 538–549.

17 J. Sergeant, *Usonian Houses*, 125.

18 In my analysis of the quadruple block and of Como Orchard below, I have relied heavily on Norris Kelly Smith, *Frank Lloyd Wright: A Study in Architectural Content* (Englewood Cliffs, N.J.: Prentice-Hall, 1966), 87–90.

19 In Alfred B. Yeomans, Ed., *City Residential Land Development: Competitive Plans for Subdividing a Typical Quarter Section of Land in the Out-*

skirts of Chicago (Chicago: University of Chicago Press, 1916), reprinted in *The Western Architect,* 25 (January 1917).

20 Kropotkin did not visit Hull House "4 years after Wright's arrival in Chicago," or in 1891, as J. Sergeant says: *Usonian Houses,* 122. Verified by Rosemarie Scherman of Stony Point, N.Y., a biographer of Jane Addams.

21 Quoted in Stephen Alexander, "Frank Lloyd Wright's Utopia," *The New Masses,* 15 (June 18, 1935), 28.

22 Le Corbusier, *The City of Tomorrow* (1929), first published in Paris in 1924 by Editions Cres under the title *Urbanisme.*

23 *The New York Times,* June 16, 1975.

24 *The New York Times,* August 5, November 12, 1975; June 13, 1976; *Boston Sunday Globe,* November 28, 1976.

25 On the origins of Taliesin West see *The Capital Times,* December 26, 1937; *The Weekly Home News,* April 27, 1939; *Chillicothe* (Texas) *News Advertiser,* May 1, 1940; Vincent Scully, *Frank Lloyd Wright* (New York: George Braziller, 1960), 28–29.

26 For some curious parallels between Wright's yearly migrations to Arizona and the trek of the Oakies and Arkies see Eugene Masselink, "At Taliesin," *The Capital Times,* January 24, 1936.

27 See, for example, *The Capital Times,* October 24, 1934; January 24, 1936; *Wisconsin State Journal,* February 10, 1935; *Baraboo Weekly News,* February 28, 1935.

1936–1947

CHAPTER NINE

Usonia: Shelter in the Open

For another person, launching the Taliesin Fellowship, Broadacre City, and Taliesin West within six years might have been enough, an enviable swan song for someone turning seventy on June 8, 1937. But for Frank Lloyd Wright they marked a new beginning—"his second important creative career"—says architectural historian John Sergeant.[1] With Broadacres as his philosophical basis and social objective, with a corps of dedicated apprentices to help run his estate and his practice, and with new winter headquarters to sustain his health and his creativity, Wright returned to his first love: the private house. Actually, it was not a matter of returning, since he had never completely abandoned it. Since 1929 if not before, he had been rethinking the problem of the single-family residence and, as in 1901, after almost a decade of intellectual ferment, he produced an important new prototype in 1936. The Usonian house was as widely acclaimed and in several ways as radical as its prairie predecessor, moving Wright back to the center of public attention and into the profession's limelight. His surge of productivity after a quarter century of frustration was one of the dramatic resuscitations in American architectural history, made more impressive by his age and by the fact that most creative people, if they make major contributions at all, tend to do so within a single concentrated period, not two. Many of those who had written his professional obituaries were forced to admit that he was not only alive but very well indeed.

□ □ □

Frank Lloyd Wright's two periods of great achievement coincided with the Progressive Era and the New Deal, years of national reevaluation and reform. Perhaps intellectual and cultural upheaval or the questioning of economic and political institutions encouraged him to redefine the social purposes of his work, or perhaps the prevailing mood was unusually receptive to innovation. Wright's new architecture was popular because it addressed the real needs of large numbers of people in a straightforward way, without the eccentric and exotic overtones of the previous decade. During the prosperity of the early twentieth century, the prairie house had quieted the psychologically unsettling problems of metropolitan life experienced by well-to-do members of the upper middle class and had brought the single-family residence functionally and aesthetically up to date. But during the Great Depression, his Usonian clients were not so economically secure. It was not that they themselves had suffered financial loss, but that as younger people starting out in abnormally bad times they were uncertain about the future, meaning that Wright had to watch budgets closely. His problem—the one he most wanted to solve—was to design low-cost homes for middle-income families.

The first Usonian house he built but not the first he designed was for *Capital Times* reporter Herbert Jacobs in Westmoreland, now Madison, Wisconsin (Fig. 9.1). The origin of the name "Usonia" is still a mystery. It was *not* taken from Samuel Butler's novel *Erewhon* (1917) as is commonly thought; but whatever the source, it was undoubtedly a play on "USA."[2] Wright used it as a substitute for "America," not the nation he saw around him but that future America of Broadacre City. Designed in 1936 and built in 1937 for $5500 (about the price of a good-sized prairie house) including architect's fee, the Jacobs residence included several technological innovations that were both economical and humanly satisfying.

Its thin, concrete floor slab, for example, rested on a drained gravel bed in which wrought-iron steam or hot water pipes (longer-lasting copper was not yet readily available) produced radiant or "gravity" heat in the floor and up the walls, eliminating radiators, drafts, and temperature variations. Secondly, a two-by-four-foot horizontal module or grid governed the entire plan—in the architect's drawings and on the floor itself—enabling the contractor to locate doors and windows easily and to reduce labor and waste, since materials like plywood came in four-foot cuts. Walls, openings, shelves, built-in furniture, electrical switches and outlets, and other surface interruptions were simply centered on, aligned with, or related to the grid or its subdivisions, so that drawings could be rationalized, read, and executed with minimal misunderstanding. ("This is the most logical house I ever built," the carpenter on a 1940 Usonian said admiringly.) The

Figure 9.1 Herbert Jacobs House (1936), Madison, Wisconsin. Courtesy Burnham Architectural Library, The Art Institute of Chicago.

Jacobs residence also featured board-and-batten construction, that is, "ready made" wall units put up in one piece after assemblage at the site, serving as both interior and exterior finish. A core of plywood was covered on both sides by moisture-proof membranes to which were screwed narrow battens holding one-foot-wide boards (pine in the Jacobs House but grained cypress later). Erected in vertically shaped panels, the board and battens ran horizontally, reflecting the lines of the house. So determined was Wright to achieve horizontal consistency that he insisted each screw be left with its slot parallel to the floor. According to the University of Wisconsin's Forest Products Laboratory which followed construction closely, the "sandwich" walls were strong, well-insulated, cheaper, and more efficient than conventional alternatives.[3]

In addition to these three defining features—gravity heat, the geometrical grid, and sandwich walls—there were other ingenious innovations and economies in the Jacobs House. By using glass, waxed wood, and brick, Wright made paint, varnish, plaster, wallpaper, and wall decorations unnecessary. The slab roof contained twelve inches of insulation and air space, its long overhangs reduced maintenance on exterior surfaces, and it required no gutters or drainpipes. The concrete floormat, however, was drained at the rear of the house where it extended beyond the walls as a terrace. Believing the modern automobile was durable enough to withstand inclement weather, Wright replaced the garage with a carport adjacent to the front entry, sheltered by the house on two sides. He substituted open shelves for some of the kitchen cabinets, cleansing the air and ventilating the house by raising the clerestory windows in the kitchen a few feet above the roof line. In subsequent Usonians he did away with hanging fixtures, preferring to build in lights along with much of the furniture. Despite the absence of cellar and attic in the Jacobs House, storage space was more than adequate with large closets in each bedroom and partway down the exterior side of the bedroom hall. A fireplace near the center of the house in the living area gave supplemental heat if necessary, while the bathroom next to the kitchen saved on water piping. As the Usonian home matured from 1936 to 1941, Wright added imaginative touches and new wrinkles, but from the very beginning it was cost efficient, economical to maintain, and easy to run.

The spatial organization of the Jacobs House was as impressive as the technology (Fig. 9.2). Wright did away with the dining room in favor of a table connecting the kitchen and living areas, which were further separated by the large fireplace. The effect was to merge the three rooms into one, but always with a sense of functional diversity. For privacy, the house turned its back to the street, its only visible windows being a string of small clerestories running its length underneath the roof overhang. Facing into the lot, the Jacobs' eighteen-by-thirty-foot living area was lined with twenty-four feet of floor-to-ceiling windows and glazed double doors leading out to the terrace extension of the floor slab. Around the corner of the L, the glass continued as the inside wall of the bedroom wing, stopping short of the terminal room to prevent heat loss, while the overhead clerestories from the front reappeared along the wing's exterior. The house was sited in such a way that during the winter the sun passed across the expanse of glass providing enough light and heat to hold down utility costs, while in the summer it crossed overhead without shining directly in. The clerestories captured sun in the late afternoon to prolong the day, acted as vents for the living area, and threw decorative patterns of light on the plain concrete floor.

Herbert Jacobs was immensely pleased. Not only did he defend his

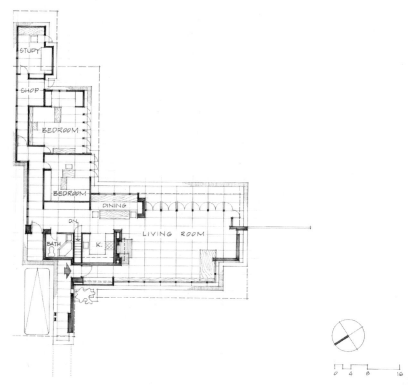

Figure 9.2   Herbert Jacobs House (1936), Madison, Wisconsin. Drawn by David Roessler and used with his permission.

home from skeptics but he also hired Wright in 1943 to design a second residence (built in 1948) when his family outgrew their original quarters.[4] Although no cheaper to construct than nearby houses of comparable size, the Jacobs residence was more practical and attractive, better organized, had more usable space, was easier to maintain, and was therefore economical. It was also a boon for Wright, whose professional resurgence was stimulated by a swell of clients after the Jacobs and other Usonian houses received national publicity between 1936 and 1938.[5] Although he built only twenty-five (but designed many more) through 1941 when World War Two stopped residential construction, the Usonians brought their greatest return after 1947 when Wright's practice began to surge spectacularly. But even more important, the small one-floor home with bedroom zone, patio, carport, open plan, gravity heat, and ample fenestration was an influential forerunner of postwar suburban housing. There were major differences, of course, between Usonian and conventional dwellings; picture windows overlooking postage-stamp lawns, for example, bore little relation to Wright's thoughts on privacy and land use. But as long as housing technology and middle class family life remained essentially unchanged from previous generations, the average postwar home did not appreciably improve upon the prototypical spatial and structural innovations Wright introduced during the late 1930s.

□ □ □

The new residence, of course, was not without precedent. Evolving from his own few designs between 1929 and 1936, and influenced by the International Style, it nevertheless owed its greatest debt to the prairie house which in many ways it updated. The open plan was the most obvious of the many similarities between them. Wright elaborated the concept during the 1930s, turning the main mass into a single functionally divided space, even more open than the prairie house, where kitchen, living, and dining spaces had still been separate rooms. If anything, the Usonian house accentuated its close relation to nature even more strongly than its predecessor by substantially increasing fenestration to facilitate real and visual contact with the outdoors. Like the prairie house it was uncompromisingly horizontal, usually rested on a cellarless slab, with casement windows only and regional materials frequently. Both house types had multilevel overlapping roof planes, modular construction systems, recessed entries, low ceilings, interpenetrating interior spaces, centralized fireplaces, and a number of other common features, although they were articulated differently. Furniture and accessories were often built in, along with flower boxes that in Usonians replaced the earlier concrete urn. There had been several slab-roofed prairie homes, and even a few confined to one floor.

But new technology and social habits made several prairie features obsolete. The porte-cochere, for instance, evolved into a carport. Dead air space under a pitched roof was now unnecessary for insulation, while new methods of waterproofing made slab roofs with their smaller surface areas practical. Open patios in the rear were becoming more popular than covered porches in the front, and servant quarters were no longer economically or socially desirable. Formal dining had lost its old prominence, and so a table in the living area next to the kitchen was more convenient than a separate room. Intricately stained and leaded glass had gone out of style and was financially prohibitive in the 1930s, while climbing stairs had come to be a burden, so Wright substituted plate glass and reduced the house from two or three stories to one or two. Gardening and lawn activities now had large followings: the Usonian house gave them ample space.

Usonian homes were lower and seemed longer than most prairie houses. With their flat roofs and lengthy overhangs, they did not need the vigorously contrasting trim Wright had used to indicate prairie house closeness to the land. Generally built of board and batten with brick sometimes replaced by stone, they were never cement-walled like several of their predecessors. Unlike the urban and suburban prairie houses—and partly because Wright actively solicited clients willing to build beyond areas of settlement—Usonians were more often on the outskirts of town (in today's terms "exurbia"), on the edge of small cities, or on large, wooded lots, taking advantage of irregular, occasionally spectacular, sites (hillsides, lake shores, and ravines). Since Wright's reputation was now national, the twenty-five new residences were geographically more dispersed than thirty years before, scattered in fourteen states from Massachusetts to California and Washington to Alabama. In the words of architectural critic Peter Blake, they were, "realistic and beautiful solutions to living in America."[6]

Perhaps influenced by the International Style, the Usonian house, Wright said, was made to "*look* more modern." Although he never admitted to contemporary influences on his work, especially from the younger Europeans, his new buildings were aesthetically in keeping with the latest trends. It is impossible to say of the Usonians as it is of the prairie house that Wright was almost solely responsible for the modern look, but it must be remembered that his work was different enough from the Internationalists to make its own impact. Although there are superficial similarities between his architecture and that of the younger generation, who found the appearance and workings of machinery an inspiration for their movement during the 1920s and 1930s, it is impossible to "prove" that Wright borrowed their ideas. He had ample opportunity to observe them closely during the 1932 International Style Exhibition at the Museum of Modern Art in New York in which he himself participated as a foil to the others, and he had been on record since his 1928 review of Corbusier's *Towards a New Architecture* as a staunch opponent of the new movement (see Chapter Seven), but his constant and spirited denunciations could easily have functioned to disguise his own indebtedness, especially from himself.

Nevertheless, the fact remains that the Usonian House resembled work by Mies van der Rohe particularly, whose project for a country home (1923), German Pavilion at the Barcelona Exposition in 1929, and Berlin Building Exposition House (1931), with their open plans, glass expanses, and their one (or mostly one) level formats foreshadowed Wright. Superficially, at least, a scattering of other homes paralleled those of Mies, among them Lois Welzenbacher's Schulz House (1928) at Westphalia, Germany; Karl Schneider's Werner House (1931) in Hamburg; and Hans Schmidt's Waldner House (1931) in Basle, Switzerland. And designs by Corbusier and Pierre Jeanneret, Otto Eisler, Walter Gropius, J. J. P. Oud, and by adopted Californians Richard Neutra and Rudolph Schindler, who had worked in Wright's office during the 1920s, must have caught his eye if not compelled his attention.[7]

The problem of the relationship between his work and theirs is a complicated one. All except Corbusier admitted having been profoundly influenced by the prairie buildings depicted in Wright's 1910 and 1911 Wasmuth publications, and even by some of the 1925 Dutch Wendingen designs. His 1922 project for G. P. Lowes at Eagle Rock, California, for example, and La Miniatura (1922–1923) for Mrs. George Millard in Pasadena (both shown in Wendingen) were not unlike several Corbusier residences of the late 1920s and early 1930s. La Miniatura also bears striking similarities to Gerrit Reitveld's Shroder House (1925) in Utrecht, Netherlands, which is more closely related, however, to Corbusier's 1922 Citrohan project, which may, in fact, have influenced both Rietveld *and* Wright. And therein lies the confusion. Although the Millard House seems in part derivative, Wright would never admit leaning on another architect, particularly a younger and equally arrogant Corbusier. The Europeans freely acknowledged their indebtedness to him, but never he to them. Even without Wright's polemics, the architectural causality is difficult to determine.

In several important respects the Usonian House departed significantly from the International Style. In their aesthetic theories the Europeans specifically embraced and attempted to widen a philosophical breach between nature and architecture. If Wright aimed to work with nature, they designed against it. Wright wanted to integrate building and site—to make indoors and out as unified as possible—but the Internationalists went the other way, for to them civilization was measured by its distance from the primitive. Many of their buildings were poured concrete painted white, unsoftened by wood, trim, or contrasting color. Regardless of nationality or environment, their work was pictorially similar, sometimes virtually interchangeable, holding no brief for regional, social, or cultural differences. Their houses, which Corbusier dubbed "machines for living," were rational, logical, and precise to be sure, the epitome of functionalism, in a very mechanistic way. But they were sometimes surprisingly inconvenient and energy inefficient and were often cold, sterile, and antiseptic, like plunked-down boxes no matter what their site. Wright claimed that each of his buildings was designed for a particular spot and could not be built elsewhere, meaning that setting was an integral part of his overall conception. He also relied on earth tones, wood grains, rich materials, the outside coming in, and anything else he could muster up to shape machine-made products into serene and intimately humane forms (without sacrificing convenience). By contrast, the Internationalists were proud of encasing their clients (and occasionally themselves) in fastidious, almost medicinal surroundings.

Nevertheless, two of Wright's own houses during his period of professional eclipse, namely for Richard Lloyd Jones (1929) in Tulsa and the Mesa project (1931) in Denver, were related to van der Rohe's scheme for a brick country home (1923), serving as transitions between the prairie and Usonian periods.[8] In Mies' project, an open-plan core built on one and two levels with a raised chimney stack was carried out horizontally in vigorously stated brick, contrasting vertical glass panels, and far-extended flanking walls. Wright's disastrously ugly Lloyd Jones House, with vertical tiers of plain concrete blocks alternating with similar tiers of windows the same width and height, was also on one and two levels with raised portions, large vertical expanses of glass, and modularly related rooms separately articulated on the horizontal exterior. The House on the Mesa was happier aesthetically and closer to the German's model. From a two-story living area above a billiard room, lower wings radiated out for services, the servants, guests, and a covered swimming pool. With concrete block and glass panels stretched along a low-slung but multilevel exterior, the House on the Mesa would have been an outstanding luxury home. The two designs were among the links between a one-floor building like the 1905 Glasner House (see Fig. 3.10) in Glencoe, Illinois, and the Usonian homes of the 1930s.

Other Wright designs in the early thirties reveal a developing interest in one-(or multi-)floor structures with open plans, although the Usonian resolution was still some distance away. In the Walter Davidson sheet metal farmhouses (1932), for example, the architect eliminated the dining room for the first time, replacing it with a table in a corner of the large kitchen, appropriate enough for the rural gemütlich he recalled so fondly from his own boyhood days (see page 89). In the unexecuted project for Malcolm Willey the same year, the dining table became an extension of the living room L. And in the Minneapolis home finally built for Willey in 1934 (Fig. 9.3), the kitchen and living spaces were essentially united, with only a dining table and a wall of open shelves between. The first Willey plan featured a horizontally sheathed upper floor deck, whereas the second was a single story of brick and wood, really a rectangle with embellishment. Then in 1935 Wright brought together most of the distinguishing Jacobs features—the one-floor plan with clerestories in a roof rising, overpowering horizontality, plate glass floor-to-ceiling doors and windows,

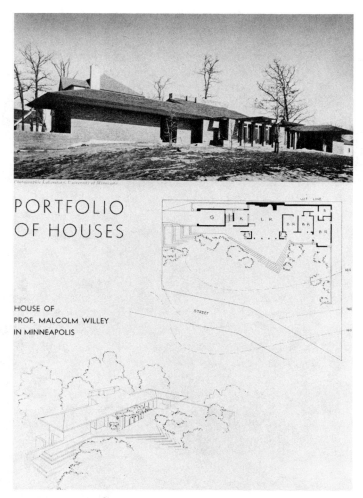

Figure 9.3   Malcolm Willey House (1934), Minneapolis. From *The Architectural Record*, July 1935.

roof and floor slabs, boards and battens, and the elaborated open plan—in the projects for Robert Lusk in Huron, South Dakota, and for H. C. Hoult in Wichita, Kansas, although the latter has not been published and cannot therefore be verified.[9] (Olgivanna Wright, senior fellow John Howe, and Taliesin archivist Bruce Pfeiffer, however, all say the Hoult project was the first Usonian.)[10] It is nevertheless clear that the Lusk and Hoult designs were very similar to the Herbert Jacobs House and that by 1935 the Usonian concept was essentially complete.

□ □ □

Having developed and built the Usonian house after a seven year or longer gestation period, Wright was not content simply to repeat the obvious and immediate success of the Jacobs format, but immediately began to explore new directions, searching as he always had for some elusive ultimate, some distant perfection, some new way to express his ideas. As early as 1936, he adapted Usonia to a hexagonal module, shown on the planning grid and in the shape of the house itself. Wright repeatedly asserted that the hexagon was more natural to human movement, allowing greater spatial freedom than the square. Thus, in the house for Stamford University professor Paul Hanna at Palo Alto, California (Fig. 9.4), axes and walls at 60- and 120-

Figure 9.4   Paul R. Hanna House (1936), Palo Alto, California. From *The Architectural Record*, July 1938.

degree angles produced an entirely different feeling than the rectangular arrangement. With implacable consistency, Wright began to push the sixty–one twenty format into every nook and cranny of the structure, including doors and jambs milled to close on angle in the Stuart Richardson House (1941) at Glen Ridge, New Jersey. Wrapped around the crown of a gently sloping hill, the Hanna's open V flanked a pool in a courtyard, while its guest wing, forming the third side of a hexagon, emphasized the house's impulse toward self-enclosure, making the circle the next logical step in Wright's exploration.[11]

The unexecuted project for movie assistant director Ralph Jester at Palos Verdes, California, was designed in 1938. All the rooms were round plywood drums, some of which protruded through the squarish slab roof as ventilator stacks. The roof and the floor mat extended into a huge, round fieldstone swimming pool as a canopy and a diving platform–patio area. The lounging space with its fireplace, the master bedroom–bath–breakfast nook complex, and the dining–kitchen–valet facilities were not attached to each other but stood separately on the glazed interior patio, making it necessary to go "outside" from room to room. But the house was laid out in such a way that the pool, the drums, and a walled exterior garden shielded the inside from prying eyes. When it rained the pool was designed to overflow into the ravine from which it rose; and had Jester built it, he could have swum to the edge for a magnificent view. (Almost twenty years later, Taliesin-trained architect John Lautner came up with a similar pool in the Los Angeles hills for a client who erected but never lived in his house.) Perhaps more than any other Wright residence, the Jester project brought "the outside in."[12]

As the Hanna and Jester designs reveal, Wright quickly moved beyond the Jacobs formulation. Historian John Sergeant, the most thorough student of this period in Wright's life, has identified five types of Usonian houses.[13] Certain features were common to all: gravity heat, the bedroom zone attached to the open plan, brick or stone and board-and-batten finish, the raised kitchen stack, one or another grid system, vast expanses of glass, the carport, and the façade closed to the public. But there were also important differences. The first and most common type was the "polliwog," as Wright called it, a T- or L-shaped plan like the Jacobs House (Fig. 9.2) with inline bedrooms in the "tail" at right angles to the public spaces in the main mass and utilities at the elbow. The second type was the "diagonal Usonian," in which a terrace, a wing, or just a single room jutted off at an oblique or acute angle with or without the hexagonal module. Third was the "in-line" plan (Figs. 9.5 and 9.6), similar to the polliwog but minus the

Figure 9.5   Alma Goetsch-Katherine Winkler House (1939), Okemos, Michigan. Photo by author.

tail, an elaborated block or rectangle with bedrooms clustered at one end or to one side. The fourth type was the "hexagonal" Usonian (Fig. 9.7), already discussed in connection with the Hanna house, which either grouped the bedrooms if the structure was essentially a solid mass or strung them along a wing if the hexagon was more complete.

Figure 9.6   George Sturges House (1939), Brentwood Heights, California. Photo by author.

Figure 9.7   Stuart Richardson House (1941; built 1951), Glen Ridge, New Jersey. Photo by author.

Last was the "raised Usonian," used for the edge of ravines or water. Here, part of the house was elevated on masonry piers, with three possibilities for public spaces. In the Lloyd Lewis residence (1940) for a publisher in Libertyville, Illinois (Fig. 9.8), they were raised to the second level with some bedrooms in a tail and other below. In research chemist Clarence Pew's House (1940) in Madison, Wisconsin, the bedrooms were placed on the upper story, enabling the living room and deck to take advantage of a spectacular view of Lake Mendota by dropping over and jutting out from a steep hillside. In the 1941 home for Gregor Affleck (Fig. 9.9), a Bloomfield Hills, Michigan, chemical engineer, Wright put everything on one floor, half of which was elevated, including sunken living and dining areas, where the site dropped off. Each type held many possibilities for design variation, which Wright in every case but the diagonal fully exploited, often with spectacular results.

No matter what the type, the social posture of the Usonian house, containing Wright's final thoughts on the family and its relation to the rest of society, struck a median between the prairie house and the textile-block designs of the 1920s. Prairie dwellings had looked toward the street with numerous windows, as if to address the community with a dignified reserve befitting their prosperous inhabitants. Set

Figure 9.8   Lloyd Lewis House (1940), Libertyville, Illinois. Photo by author.

Figure 9.9   Gregor Affleck House (1941), Bloomfield Hills, Michigan. Photo by author.

further back on their lots with doorways more sheltered than early nineteenth century New England Federalist homes, for example, built by a comparable socioeconomic class, they assumed a collective posture suitable for an urban gentry. The textile-block houses, on the other hand, faced away from the street and with their rugged materials, formidable sites, and apparently inapproachable façades seemed positively remote. Usonian homes did not shun social contact quite so obviously as the textile blocks, but they, too, guarded themselves well. Turning away from passers-by to face the interior of the lot, with minimal street-side window space and entries hidden under overhangs at the corner of the L or around the side, they were very private buildings (Fig. 9.10), even on large lots in the country where such precautions were hardly necessary. But with warm materials, close association with gentle land, and out-reaching features, Usonian homes did not, like their 1920s predecessors, give the impression of defensive retreats. After two decades of unhappy relations with the outside world, Wright could hardly return to the optimistic detachment of the prairie house, but neither could he safely withdraw into guarded isolation, as his own domestic and social experiences had shown. The Usonian house was a new social synthesis very similar in theme to Taliesin West (see Chapter Eight).

In its own quiet way, it assumed the family to be, in Wright's words, "a little private club." Combined with plantings and using its site

Figure 9.10 Herbert Jacobs House (1936), Madison, Wisconsin. Courtesy Burnham Architectural Library, The Art Institute of Chicago.

carefully, it formed a kind of enclosed compound, bordered on one, two, or even three sides by the structure itself and by trees, shrubbery, the terrain, or some other design device. The 1920s homes had been "rather undomestic" both inside and out. But the Jacobs House and its offspring made statements of detachment only to outsiders—the inside was certainly "domestic"—and then not so blatantly. A visitor approaching a Usonian home for the first time will almost certainly have trouble finding the entrance, but once inside is immediately drawn, seduced is not too strong a word, into the life of the household through a low reception area looking toward the glass walls of the living space. As he or she proceeds, subtly changing vistas and atmosphere offer an exciting architectural experience, "a continuing succession of mysteries," Loren Pope of Falls Church, Virginia, wrote about his 1940 residence, "leading you on beyond what your eyes can see," predisposing the visitor to appreciate the point of destination. United by its open plan but sheltered from the outside world as it looked into its private compound, the Usonian family had no need to "box up or hole in," according to Wright. Security "in every sense" was best found in "free wide spacing and integral construction. . . . Spaciousness is for safety as well as for beauty." No longer fortifications, he had stated in 1931, homes should be "shelter in the open." Or as Loren Pope added: "The house gives you a sense of protection, but never of being closed in. . . ."[14]

The Usonian home reflected changes in living habits since the 1900s. Born in the Progressive Era and come of age in the Roaring Twenties or the Great Depression, Wright's new clients were impatient with many of the old formalities and social customs. Something had happened to manners and mores by, during, or shortly after—historians are not sure—World War One. The Victorian Era had ended, the modern age begun. Greater informality and casualness was reflected in dress styles, popular art forms, recreational and sexual habits, and innumerable other activities. The pace of life had quickened, in part because of new kinds of transportation and mass communications. Tight budgets during the 1930s made many of the old conventions unfeasible, but some Americans had begun to abandon them even before the stock market crash because they seemed incompatible with a more streamlined postwar life style. As far as architectural planning was concerned, wasted time, motion, and space were both financially and socially frivolous. With radios, automobiles, moving pictures, and modern appliances it was easier, people thought, to get the housework done in order to have time for one's self.

The changing role and status of women undoubtedly influenced the internal reorganization of Wright's residences. No longer the fragile, subservient, headache-prone irrelevancy of popular fiction, the modern woman was competitive, outspoken, and self-assured. For some people Zelda Fitzgerald represented much of what was wrong with the postwar world, but perceptive observers understood, and social conservatives took heart from the fact, that the flapper was as much a media creation as a genuine social force. Closer to reality was James M. Cain's *Mildred Pierce*, the determined restaurant owner portrayed so effectively on the screen by (ex-movie flapper) Joan Crawford, whose reallife business acumen made the casting perfect, in retrospect at least. The proportion of all women holding jobs rose from twenty percent in 1900 to twenty-five in 1910, remaining about the same until it increased in 1940. But even more important, the percentage of *married* women working rose from five and one half in 1900 to fifteen percent in 1940, while the total number of female employees rose from fifteen percent of the workforce at the turn of the century to thirty percent on the eve of World War Two.[15] More and more married women preferred not to stay at home, but even the "housewives" who did were also beginning to think of themselves as having a career and were thus increasingly interested in labor-saving devices.

So, Wright later explained, "the housewife herself became the central figure" in his new home, a "hostess 'officio' [instead of]. . .a kitchen mechanic behind closed doors."[16] Since she wanted a compact, efficient home without servants, the architect moved the kitchen from the back of the house to the center, renaming it a "work-space" from which she could run the entire operation. From there she could supervise her children no matter where they were (except in the bedrooms), even outdoors. Without a dining room her steps were reduced, and when she entertained she could still participate in the general conversation (Fig. 9.11). Although he succeeded in making her life easier, Wright still assumed that the woman's place was in the kitchen, even with her husband at home. "Family processes are conveniently centralized," he stated in 1948 of a 1938 design, so "the mistress of the house can turn a pancake with one hand while chucking the baby into a bath with the other." And father? He is "meantime sitting at his dinner, lord of all."[17] The modern women's movement could rightfully object.

Nevertheless, the evolution of the dining room indicates important changes in Wright's thinking on family life since the 1890s. Once the most stately and formal room in his houses, it passed out of existence altogether, replaced by table and chairs strategically located en route from the living to the kitchen space. In some Usonian homes it was

Figure 9.11   From living area past dining table to kitchen in the Stuart Richardson House (1941; built 1951), Glen Ridge, New Jersey. Photo by author.

almost impossible to have an old-fashioned, big-family sit-down meal, for the table, permanently fixed in place and size, could accommodate only small gatherings. "Guests for any one dinner are limited to two or at most four," the former owner of a 1940 Wright house wrote, "because where can dishes for a proper dinner be put. . .?" The Usonian arrangement reflected a new informality in American domestic entertainment wherein the cocktail party, the leisurely evening, the buffet meal, and the backyard barbecue replaced elaborate occasions. The best way to handle a dinner, Marjorie Leighey continued, was to dispense with old customs: salad was served from a large bowl instead of on individual plates.[18] Or people might eat on small Wright-designed tables scattered about the living room. Dining was simply less socially important than once upon a time. In a cost-conscious, faster world, the formal dining room had become an anachronism.

The effect of all this was to increase family togetherness, in its separation from the outside world, even more than in the prairie house. If that building had weakened the identification of particular rooms with particular purposes, the Usonian house did away with certain rooms altogether, uniting more family activities in one place. The "living room" in a Wright house was apt to be used for eating, relaxation, cooking, play, entertainment, cultural enrichment, and, with patio appended, for virtually all other family functions. Of course, Usonian houses separated the bedroom zone from the living area, making adequate provision for personal privacy, according to Herbert Jacobs.[19] Even in the busy family space, concrete floors and brick walls absorbed childrens' noise, and there was usually a quiet corner tucked away under a light shelf, behind a room divider, or off in an alcove. The Usonian home was therefore not inhospitable to personal independence or individual retreat. Wright was no longer enamored with the potentially stifling group mutuality that had interfered with his own domestic situation in 1909. The Usonian house ensured the privacy of individual family members, but it also affirmed that the group should be a tightly knit unit, separate from but not completely rejecting the community in its compound close to nature.

The structure of this group might be egalitarian or authoritarian, depending on how vigorously parents chose to exercise control. At once old-fashioned and modern, the Usonian house could accommodate both traditional and progressive life styles. "Either the children get left or must get spanked into place," Wright remarked in reference to his homes, "else they have the whole house and the grown-ups do what they can do to make themselves as comfortable as [possible]"[20] (Fig. 9.12). The very choice, however, was a modern one. At least one

Figure 9.12 Children taking over living area in Stuart Richardson House (1941; built 1951), Glen Ridge, New Jersey. Photo by author.

father saw no dilemma: "The temptation is to be together much more," Herbert Jacobs recalled in 1956. "I think it does something to you subconsciously. I think it did something to my children. . . . Living in that house was fantastically wonderful."[21] Although another Usonian father admitted that family closeness could bring out the worst in him, Wright's clients from 1936 to 1941 were likely to adopt modern notions of progressive child rearing, that is, if educational level and occupation are any indication.

Most Usonian homeowners were college graduates; of the eighteen (of twenty-five) whose occupations are known, five worked in academic institutions, four were journalists or publishers, three were businessmen, three were chemists or engineers, two were civil servants, and one was a writer.[22] Several wives had out-of-the-house careers, and in at least two cases (Katherine Winkler and Alma Goetsch in Lansing, Michigan, and Rose Pauson in Scottsdale, Arizona) there were no children. Wright understood that youngsters constantly in the living room were apt to turn the house upside down in the process of taking it over. (Maybe that was one reason he made it so easy to get outside.) But he was really unopposed to that—for other people. So with the kitchen a part of the living area and bedrooms small enough to make children leave them, Wright encouraged intelligent modern families to confront their own interpersonal relations.

If the 1941 Arch Obeler gatehouse (the main residence was never executed) in Los Angeles is included, the architect built a total of 25 Usonian houses. As questionnaires and interviews establish again and again, his clients love their homes, indeed, are more than ordinarily enthusiastic, and leave, if they have to, with considerable reluctance. The Usonian residence was no exception. Its immediate popularity helped him secure nondomestic work (discussed in Chapter Ten) so that, from 1936 through 1941 until the war stopped it, his practice increased substantially. During the six years from 1930 to 1935, Wright had executed one building, the 1934 Willey House in Minneapolis, for a paying client. But during the six Usonian years he received thirty-three commissions that he ultimately built, five and one half annually on the average. In 1940 he completed twelve structures, eleven of them Usonians, his largest output since 1907. The walls of these homes were designed to be prefabricated (in the sense of being assembled at the site and erected in panels), and Wright encouraged his clients to do as much of their own construction as possible. Self-building and self-sufficiency were among his main objectives. But in fact most Usonians were not erected this way. After the Second World War, when his practice grew to unprecedented dimensions, more of his residences were large and luxurious (even though he continually experimented with cost reductions). The bedroom zone, open plan, carport, and other Usonian features remained, but as prices rose and he attracted affluent clients, it was increasingly difficult to provide middle-income people with low-cost housing. Nevertheless, the Usonian home was the model for his later work, the catalyst for his professional recovery.

□ □ □

"I don't build a house without predicting the end of the present social order," Wright told the Federal Architects' Association at Washington, D.C., in October 1938. "Every building is a missionary."[23] And his mission? The establishment of Broadacre City. The Usonian house and Broadacres, evolving together in Wright's mind during the 1930s, were mutually inseparable. Located on the outskirts of settlement, Usonian homes were intended to be advance agents of decentralization, examples of energy conservation and cost efficiency, and models of the kind of house people could expect in Broadacre City. Since they took up relatively small portions of their lots, Wright urged clients to grow their own food. One of the impulses behind easy-to-read grids and partial prefabrication, furthermore, was that owners might be able to do some construction themselves. Once in a while this happened—the Douglas Grant House (1945), built after 1951 in Cedar Rapids, Iowa, from fieldstone on the site, particularly excited Wright—but not as frequently as he hoped. He was hardly naive enough to believe that all his clients would have the time or develop the skills to put up a house, but he thought it might happen often enough to demonstrate the possibilities. Wright also advocated multifamily cooperation to achieve economies, to stimulate self-sufficiency, and to bring about "the end of the present social order." He therefore took advantage of several opportunities to extend Usonia from a single-family residence to collective building projects: transitions, he hoped, to Broadacre City.

In 1938 he designed the "Quadruple homes" (Fig. 9.13) at suburban Ardmore, Pennsylvania, near Philadelphia, built in 1939 for Otto Mallory of the Todd Company.[24] Also called "Suntop Homes," the scheme was an ingenious variation on a Broadacre City house type and on the quadruple block scheme of 1901 (see Chapter Eight). In each quadrant formed by crossing brick dividing walls, Wright placed a three-story apartment with six rooms, carport, penthouse, roof deck, and basement storage area. The thirteen-foot-high living space was overlooked

Figure 9.13   Suntop Quadruple Homes (1939), Ardmore, Pennsylvania. Photo by author.

by a mezzanine for dining, the kitchen, bath, and two bedrooms, with two more in the penthouse opening on the deck. While neighbors fearing compromise of their single-family enclave held up construction for almost a year, the $55-a-month rentals generated a long waiting list. The first four tenants were two museum assistant directors and two university professors. Like the single-family Usonian, quadruple homes enabled the housekeeper to supervise children in the living area, anywhere on the mezzanine, or in the private garden enclosed by a lapped board fence. Quadruple homes was an important innovation in land use, increasing normal half-acre density from eight or ten people to almost thirty. Wright built only one of the intended four units, for $16,000, or about $4000 per apartment. This economical idea was never taken up by the real estate industry, but it still holds potential for land-and energy-hungry cities.

By December 1941, Wright had developed the theme a bit further. Selected in August to design a 100-home project for defense workers at Pittsfield, Massachusetts, he inserted a sixteen-by-thirty-six-foot yard into each quadrant of the Suntop plan, pulling apartments away from the dividing walls. This increased lighting in the rear rooms and enabled him to enlarge the living area by twenty-seven square feet. Otherwise the interior remained pretty much the same. He had hardly completed the drawings, however, when Massachusetts architects successfully convinced House majority leader John McCormick to pressure the Division of Defense Housing, Federal Works Administration, to reassign the project to someone licensed in the state. Wright had already refused to sell the plans to the government, a condition of construction, since that would have meant foregoing control, so he would have lost the commission anyway. He was paid for preliminary sketches, but Washington refused to reimburse him for his trip to Massachusetts when he selected the site himself. The Pittsfield debacle was his last attempt at quadruple homes.[25]

The unexecuted "cooperative homesteads" of 1942 for auto workers near Detroit were also related to Broadacre City. On its acre of land, each low-cost house was to be sustained not only by the owner's industrial job but also by self-building and its own garden, so the architect put a storage area for vegetables and dry food plus a workshop next to the carport. This was the project in which Wright introduced the berm, a sloping, grassed-over bank of earth rammed against the outside walls to the window sills, deflecting winds with cheap but effective insulation. The floor plan was a variation on the "in-line" Usonian, a rectangle with living–dining–kitchen–bath facilities connected by a truncated hall to two bedrooms. The pitched roof was echoed in the living area but in the bedrooms was hidden by a dropped ceiling. With its workshop, garden, food storage, and earth walls, the homesteads would have contributed to the overall self-supporting objectives of the cooperative.[26] Although the project was never built, Wright used the berm when he executed the 1943 second Jacobs House (Fig. 9.14) at Middleton, Wisconsin, in 1948–1949 and again in 1951 in the Thomas F. Keyes residence at Rochester, Minnesota.

Another cooperative project from 1939 proved to be a model for three other Wright-designed communities after the war. During the late 1930s, eight Michigan State University professors at East Lansing formed a food co-op and later purchased a forty-acre tract of land. Katherine Winkler and Alma Goetsch of the art department approached Wright who in 1939 developed site drawings (Fig. 9.15) all the way through the working stage. The plan called for seven Usonian homes (Winkler and Goetsch would share one) plus a caretaker's cottage ringing a commonly owned farm including small fields, an orchard, and a fish pond. Access to houses was by a U-shaped road around the farm, with each residence set back across its own private garden up a long drive. Just as construction was about to begin, a source of private financing collapsed, and the group was unable to

Figure 9.14 Berm at rear of Herbert Jacobs House (1943), Middleton, Wisconsin. Photo by author.

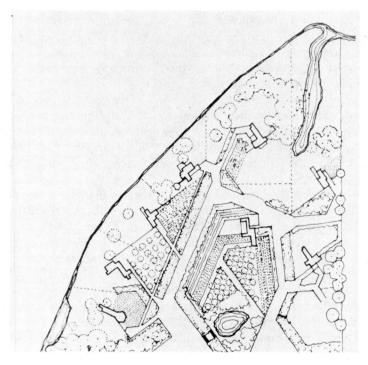

Figure 9.15 Usonian Cooperative (1939), Lansing, Michigan. Drawn by John Sergeant and used with his permission.

264

secure a bank loan. Wright was so enamored by the project that he appeared before the Federal Housing Authority in Washington himself, but to no avail. FHA claimed, among other things, that "the walls will not support the roof; floor heating is impractical; the unusual design makes subsequent sales a hazard." The scheme fell through, and only the Goetsch-Winkler House (1939) was built, on a different site in Okemos, Michigan. Although Wright designed homes for several of the other participants after the war, only Erling P. Brauner executed his in Okemos in 1946. Nevertheless, the Lansing Usonia, says John Sergeant, "may be regarded as the first practical demonstration of the principles of Broadacre City."[27]

After World War Two, Wright was more successful with his Usonian communities, two of which were realized in or near Kalamazoo, Michigan. The architect's four houses in Galesburg Village (Fig. 9.16), laid out with more than forty lots ten miles east of the city, used concrete blocks as a way of circumventing the postwar materials shortage. The cooperative was formed by a group of Upjohn Institute chemists who made the blocks themselves from a Taliesin mold, obtained materials in bulk, and built their own homes. Wright designed the overall plan in 1947, but the houses were not erected until 1951 and 1953. Parkwyn Village in Kalamazoo was also a nonprofit organization, but here members called in contractors to help with construction, although much of it was self-built. Wright designed the site plan in 1947 for almost forty homes, including five concrete-block residences executed between 1951 and 1955 (Figs. 9.17 to 9.19). Parkwyn admitted newcomers as the years passed, so most of the buildings were done by other architects. House lots in both villages were one-acre circles, the spaces between owned and maintained collectively. Access to Galesburg was by a bewildering maze of roads that ensured privacy for residents but could prevent callers from venturing in, especially at night. At Parkwyn, homes were grouped on both sides of an easily manageable loop.[28]

The most important, largest, and last of Wright's Usonias, as this one was called, was for Pleasantville, thirty miles north of New York City. The project grew from the inspiration of engineer David Henken who specifically wanted to build a portion of Broadacre City. He and his wife Priscilla Henken moved to Taliesin for two years as apprentices and then in 1944, with a group of interested families, incorporated under New York State law as a Rochdale cooperative. In 1947 they purchased a hilly, heavily wooded ninety-seven-acre tract and hired Wright, who designed three circular road systems governing the location of fifty round house lots. Each group of six one-acre sites

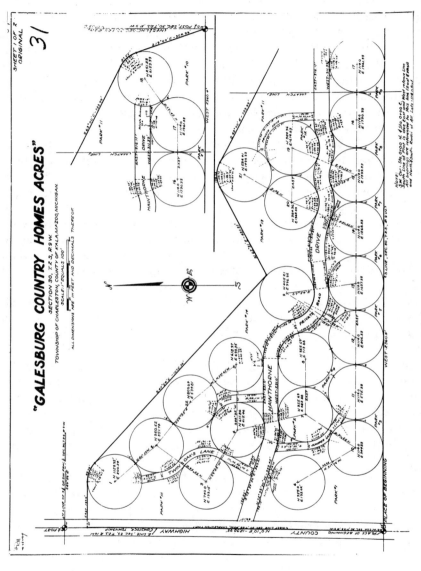

Figure 9.16 Galesburg Country Homes (1947–1949) near Kalamazoo, Michigan. From Kalamazoo County, Michigan, plat records.

Figure 9.17 Circular home built between 1951 and 1955 at Parkwyn Village, Kalamazoo, Michigan. Photo by author.

Figure 9.18 In-line home built between 1951 and 1955 at Parkwyn Village, Kalamazoo, Michigan. Photo by author.

Figure 9.19 Hexagonal home built between 1951 and 1955 at Parkwyn Village, Kalamazoo, Michigan. Photo by author.

encircled a seventh reserved for a park, the triangular spaces between remaining as buffer zones with greenery. Land not used for houses was allotted for playgrounds, gardens, a childrens' farm, a pool, a community building, guest cottages, and an athletic field.

The cooperative dug its own well, built a storage tank and a pump house, laid out the water and road systems, brought in electricity, and purchased fire-fighting equipment and heating pipes in bulk. Wright designed three model homes (Figs. 9.20 to 9.22) between 1950 and 1951 (Henken did his own), and by 1954 there were thirty-three houses built by a total of nine architects. Wright agreed to serve as consultant, helping to see that all the structures were properly oriented, incorporated built-ins, radiant heating, the open plan, and other Usonian features. Although he established standards for size, materials, and modules, which were by and large adhered to, the houses were all different, even though Wright's influence was apparent throughout. Residents came from a variety of occupational and religious backgrounds, ranging in age from their middle twenties to over sixty.

Members of the co-op paid a $100 entrance fee, bought a $5 share for each person in the household, and put $50 a month into a common fund, credited to individual accounts. When they were ready to purchase the $20,000 site, they had saved $40,000, or $1200 per family.

Figure 9.20 Sol Friedman House (1950), Pleasantville, New York. Photo by author.

Figure 9.21 Edward Serlin House (1950), Pleasantville, New York. Photo by author.

Figure 9.22 Rear and roof of Roland Reisley House (1951), Pleasantville, New York. Photo by author.

Before construction could begin, each home builder was required to raise forty percent of anticipated expenses in cash, including $3000 slated for architect's fees. At first, as might have been expected, the co-op could not get a mortgage, so in 1948 it built five demonstration homes on its own. Soon two more were underway, with another eight approved after builders agreed to raise the entire cost before construction. By early 1950, with fifteen owner-financed homes completed or in progress, the Knickerbocker Savings and Loan Association agreed to a four-and-three-quarter-percent, ten- to twenty-year group mortgage, using all the houses as security, including those already built and paid for. Members contributed monthly to a new sinking fund to reduce the mortgage and meet community expenses, in addition going on bond for their own ninety-nine-year leaseholds so that if Usonia defaulted they would be responsible for their own dwellings and land. If individuals met hard times, on the other hand, the co-op would carry them for at least six months. Usonia held title to the entire tract and all the houses.

If someone wished to withdraw from the co-op, (s)he turned the house over to Usonia for sale, taking away equity plus a share in the proceeds determined by a Bureau of Labor Statistics inflation index if there was a profit, but absorbing the difference if the residence sold at a loss. Some members, impatient with voting and discussing every issue, lobbied early for private ownership. By 1955, largely because of the inability of newcomers to get mortgages, cooperative home and land ownership was discontinued, although the roads, the water supply, electrical facilities, and the swimming hole are still maintained collectively. Wedge-shaped and circular pieces of land between the houses were divided among individuals, so that today each owns about an acre and a quarter lot. By the late 1960s the original fifty sites had all been purchased. Most of the newer dwellings were not gravity heated but in other ways were generally faithful to Wright's design philosophy. Although the cooperative conception has been seriously compromised—causing David Henken to withdraw from the little that is left of it—there is still a strong and congenial sense of community among Usonia residents.[29]

Between 1936 and 1947, Usonia evolved from a house type into a residential community. By the time Wright laid out his three master plans in 1947 he was no longer designing Usonian homes in the original meaning of the word. Materials had changed to concrete block in Michigan and to fieldstone at Pleasantville, where residences were notably larger and more luxurious than ten years before. As collectivities, the communities reflected the Usonian–Broadacre City self-build, self-help philosophy, even if individual Pleasantville homes did not. The irony was that by the time Wright saw his hopes for a new America partially realized, he was less committed to doing the kinds of plans middle-class people could readily afford. Not only were lending institutions, government agencies, and the American tradition of individualism in home building against him, not only did inflation make inexpensive construction more difficult, but Wright himself was increasingly susceptible to an egomania expressing itself in spectacular and monumental edifices. Not that he refused to accept small projects after 1947, but by age eighty, riding a wave of popularity and wealth, he lived and worked on a grand scale. The later residences developed from his 1930s ideas but were often built for affluent clients who hired Wright for his name. New variations, innovative touches, and dazzling projects flowed from his drawing board like a torrential river. But "shelter in the open" came to mean shelter for the well-to-do. Whatever he may have said about it, his late work did not threaten the "present social order." After the war he was just as concerned with

making money—and with having a good time at it—as with helping
people save it.

NOTES

1 John Sergeant, *Frank Lloyd Wright's Usonian Houses: The Case for Organic Architecture* (New York: Watson-Guptill, 1976), 9. I am heavily indebted to Sergeant's excellent book for much of the information and
several matters of interpretation in the first, but especially the third and
fifth sections of this chapter.

2 Sergeant, *Usonian Houses*, 16. On the Jacobs House see *ibid.*, Ch. 1,
especially 18–21; Frank Lloyd Wright, *The Natural House* (New York:
Horizon Press, 1954), 81–91; Wright's issue of *Architectural Forum*, 68
(January 1938); his lecture to the Fellowship in *The Capital Times*, November 30, 1936; and Herbert Jacobs to author, February 3, 1978.

3 *The Capital Times*, January 23, 1938; Loren Pope, "The Love Affair of a
Man and his House," *House Beautiful*, 90 (April 1948), 80.

4 *The New York Times*, December 8, 1940; Herbert Jacobs, *Frank Lloyd
Wright: America's Greatest Architect* (New York: Harcourt, Brace & World,
1965), 127–133. The design of the second Jacobs House is usually attributed to 1942, but Sergeant believes it to be 1943: *Usonian Houses*, 174,
footnote 74.

5 A column by Eugene Masselink in Madison's *Capital Times*, January 15,
1937, mentioned "a short notice regarding the low cost house we are
about to build in Madison [that] appeared in the newspapers of America"
and quoted several letters received in response. Wright's article entitled
"A Little Private Club" in the September 26, 1938 issue of *Life* magazine,
offered a 26 × 16 × 8 inch scale model of a home suitable for $5000–$6000
income, complete with floor plans and cut-out furniture for $1. The draw-
ings and text were reprinted in *Architectural Forum*, 69 (November 1938),
331–340.

6 Peter Blake, *Frank Lloyd Wright: Architecture and Space* (Baltimore: Penguin Books, 1964 ed.), 106.

7 For a brief survey of this work available to Wright see Hitchcock and
Johnson, *The International Style Since 1922* (New York: W. W. Norton &
Co., 1932).

8 For Mies' project see Arthur Drexler, *Ludwig Mies van der Rohe* (New
York: George Braziller, Inc., 1960), plates 6 and 7. Drawings for the Lloyd
Jones House and Mesa Project are in Arthur Drexler, Ed., *The Drawings
of Frank Lloyd Wright* (New York: Horizon Press, 1962), plates 91–92 and
126–131, respectively. To appreciate fully the unattractiveness of the Lloyd
Jones House see the photograph in Edgar Kaufmann, Ed., *An American
Architecture: Frank Lloyd Wright* (New York: Horizon Press, 1955), 236. Its

planning and construction may be dated from the *Baraboo Weekly News,* November 22, 1928; March 26 and August 6, 1931.

9 On the Willey schemes see Frank Lloyd Wright, *The Living City* (New York: Horizon Press, 1958), 62–63; *The Natural House* (New York: Horizon Press, 1954) 68–76; and *The Architectural Record,* 78 (November 1935), 313–315; as well as *The Weekly Home News,* May 3, 31, June 28, 1934, and *The Capital Times,* December 9, 1934. See J. Sergeant, *Usonian Houses,* 26, for a plan, *The Capital Times,* February 12, 1937, for a description, and A. Drexler, Ed., *Drawings,* plate 153, for a rendering of the Lusk project.

10 J. Sergeant, *Usonian Houses,* 23, and Olgivanna Wright, *Frank Lloyd Wright: His Life, His Work, His Word* (New York: Horizon Press, 1967), 214.

11 On the Hanna House see J. Sergeant, *Usonian Houses,* 32–35; "Honeycomb House," *Architectural Record,* 84 (July 1938), 58–74; *The Architect and Engineer,* 130 (August 1937), 3; and "A Great Frank Lloyd Wright House," *House Beautiful,* 105 (January, 1963), entire issue.

12 On the Jester project see J. Sergeant, *Usonian Houses,* 36–37; A. Drexler, Ed., *Drawings,* plates 162, 163; and E. Kaufmann, Ed., *An American Architecture,* 245.

13 J. Sergeant, *Usonian Houses,* 40–71.

14 F. L. Wright, "A Little Private Club," *Life,* 5 (September 26, 1938); *The Living City,* 96; *Two Lectures on Architecture* (Chicago: University of Chicago Press, 1931), reprinted in *The Future of Architecture* (New York: Horizon Press, 1953), 189; L. Pope, "Love Affair," 33.

15 William H. Chafe, *The American Woman: Her Changing Social, Economic, and Political Roles, 1920–1970* (New York: Oxford University Press, 1972), 55–56.

16 *Sixty Years of Living Architecture: The Work of Frank Lloyd Wright* (New York: Guggenheim Museum exhibition brochure, 1953).

17 *Architectural Forum,* 88 (January 1948), 80.

18 Marjorie F. Leighey, "A Testimony to Beauty" in Terry B. Morton, Ed., *The Pope-Leighey House* (Washington, D.C.: National Trust for Historic Preservation, 1969), 60. The original owner of this house wrote a virtually unqualified endorsement of its practicality, comfort, and beauty: Pope, "Love Affair."

19 *The New York Times,* December 8, 1940.

20 F. L. Wright, *The Natural House,* 168–169.

21 Transcript of "Frank Lloyd Wright" from *Biography in Sound,* National Broadcasting Company radio, August 7, 1956, page 31, in FLW Collection, Avery Library, Columbia University.

22 Computed from J. Sergeant, *Usonian Houses,* Ch. 2.

23 *The Washington Post,* Section Two, October 26, 1938.

24 "Usonia Comes to Ardmore," *Architectural Forum*, 71 (August 1939), 142–143; J. Sergeant, *Usonian Houses*, 72–73.

25 J. Sergeant, *Usonian Houses*, 74–75. *The Capital Times*, December 28, 1941, and Talbott Wegg, "FLlW *versus* the USA," *AIA Journal*, 52 (February 1970), 48–52, show that the Pittsfield project was designed in the fall of 1941, not in 1942, as Sergeant says. Also see *The Capital Times*, January 23, 1942; *The New York Times*, January 22, 1942; and Loren Pope's letter to *Weekly Bulletin, Michigan Society of Architects*, 18 (September 5, 1944), 3. Renderings appear in *Architectural Forum*, 88 (January 1948).

26 *Architectural Forum*, 88 (January 1948); A. Drexler, Ed., *Drawings*, plate 179; J. Sergeant, *Usonian Houses*, 76–77.

27 J. Sergeant, *Usonian Houses*, 78; "Rural Housing Project," *The Architect and Engineer*, 136 (January 1939), 58; *Architectural Forum*, 88 (January 1948).

28 *Architectural Forum*, 88 (January 1948); J. Sergeant, *Usonian Houses*, 79; "This New House by Frank Lloyd Wright is a Rich Textbook of the Principles He Pioneered," *House & Home*, 3 (March 1953), 106–113.

29 J. Sergeant, *Usonian Houses*, 79–80; Priscilla J. Henken, "A 'Broad-Acre' Project," *Town and Country Planning*, 23 (June 1954), 294–300; "Usonia Homes," *Journal of Housing*, 10 (October 1953), 319–320, 344–345; *House and Garden*, 99 (February 1951), 52–55; Frederick Gutheim, "Westchester Colony Uses Circular Lots," *The New York Herald Tribune*, October 10, 1948, Section VI; *The New York Times*, October 10, 1948, Section VIII; *ibid.*, May 27, 1949; interviews at Usonia, October 23, 1977.

1936–1945

CHAPTER TEN

Characteristically Modest Projects

As an attempt to ease financial burdens for middle class people, the Usonian House was not unrelated to the Great Depression. Wartime prosperity was still a distance away, however, when Frank Lloyd Wright built for clients like publisher Lloyd Lewis, considerably more affluent than journalist Loren Pope, earning barely $3000 a year in 1940, or English professor Paul Hanna who mortgaged himself to the hilt to pay for his home. Architectural idealism is one thing, professional opportunity quite another. So when a Pittsburgh department store magnate and a prominent Wisconsin manufacturer hired Wright to do a luxury weekend home and a new office building, he could hardly refuse, particularly since he had always been drawn to different kinds of architectural problems. In 1936, during a decade of heightened class consciousness, he tackled middle-income housing, the disposal of surplus wealth, and employment conditions of working people, but as design, not as political problems. Nevertheless, with the revival of his practice after 1936, he used his innumerable speaking and writing opportunities to advocate unpopular issues, among them the Soviet Union and opposition to American entry in World War Two. As he entered his eighth decade, he was as brash in word as he was in deed.

□ □ □

Had he not been sick last year, Wright told the readers of London's *Architectural Review* in February 1937, "I should show herewith seven

275

pieces of recent work from my own hand that, with the characteristic modesty which had endeared me to you all, I assume to be 'the trunk of the tree going on growing up,'" in other words, seven new buildings he thought were terrific.[1] And there was a certain justification for his immodesty, since one of them would have been "Fallingwater," the luxury vacation retreat he designed in 1936 for Bear Run, Pennsylvania, and Pittsburgh millionaire Edgar Kaufmann. Cantilevered over a waterfall (Fig. 10.1), this magnificent home has probably been photographed, written about, analyzed, and applauded more than any other Wright building. Not only did it win him enormous acclaim at the time but it is regarded as one of the finest structures ever built. One critic calls it "the most famous modern house in the world," while another says it is "one of the complete masterpieces of twentieth-century art."[2] Given a generous budget by an admiring client (who later became something of a patron since the house has been open to the public for several years), the architect exploited his op-

Figure 10.1   "Fallingwater" (1936), Bear Run, Pennsylvania. Photo by Woburn Studios, London.

portunity to the fullest, producing his most impressive residence ever, one that hundreds of thousands of people have gone out of their way to see and that almost everyone acknowledges to be virtually unsurpassed. At age sixty-nine, with a single stroke, Wright stood the profession on its ear.

The suggestion by one historian that the house on Bear Run is without precedent in Wright's or any other architect's work[3] may be an exaggeration, since it has elements—but only elements—of the International Style and the prairie house. Perched on the brink of a precipice, it vaguely resembles Richard Neutra's Lovell House (1929–1930) at Los Angeles in siting and in façade composition, but Wright's superior building is in concrete and cantilever construction, contrasting sharply with his former employee's steel frame. Fallingwater's horizontal terraces hinted at the raised ground level of Corbusier's Savoye Villa (1930) at Poissy-sur-Seine in France; but while Wright's house planted its roots firmly into the rocky hillside, Corbusier's sits gingerly on its pole supports, seemingly afraid to tickle its bottom on the flat, grassy site. Some of the architect's early residences also anticipated Fallingwater, for example, the crossed cantilevered porches of the 1909 Elizabeth Gale House (see Fig. 3.22) in Oak Park and the interpenetrating planes and soaring lines of the 1907 Robie House (Fig. 3.14) in Chicago. Fallingwater was not unprecedented, but as modern dwellings go it was virtually unmatched.

One of its most remarkable characteristics is its absolute refusal to be confined. Robie House cantilevers had shot off in two directions, but Fallingwater seems to take flight every way at once, making it exceptionally difficult to visualize or to describe to someone who has not seen it. (Most photographs do not completely capture it.) This, in fact, may have been one of Wright's objectives: to defy description, to destroy catagories. "It has no limitations as to form," he once remarked.[4] So difficult visually to comprehend—so impossible to harness, as it were—Fallingwater disrupted expectations about what a house should be or do. Visitors are surprised, for example, by its comparatively few rooms, assuming it to be much larger than it is. Most of its floor space, surface area, and expense were devoted to a massive living and dining room and to terraces and canopy slabs shooting out in several directions, while its three bedrooms and the usual services take up a small proportion of its three levels. Fallingwater was not so much a family residence as a weekend entertainment retreat and, like the Guggenheim Museum in New York, is partly an exercise in architectural sculpture. It should not be accused of "impracticality" or unnecessary expense; for as Henry-Russell Hitchcock has wisely stated, architecture lives not only "through the solution of generic problems [to which Wright devoted considerable attention] but quite as much by the thrill and acclaim of unique masterpieces."[5]

Like few other buildings before or since, Fallingwater exploited site to advantage. Two unbelievably cantilevered terraces, partially sheltered one by the other and by slab roof canopies, cross twelve feet above a waterfall in Bear Run which passes in front of the structure's main massing. Horizontal sweeps of reinforced concrete mirror the ledge on which it rests, while the vertical thrust of a stone fireplace and chimney stakes the house firmly in place, echoing the plunging stream, reaching for the sky. Its composition is an abstract reformulation of its natural site, a poetic but not a literal interpretation of the defining features of its locale. Without Fallingwater, Bear Run would have remained a beautiful forest stream, like thousands of others; but with it, the place became unique. Here was an unsurpassed example of humanity making the world a better place, of art working to improve nature. Fallingwater also supported Wright's contention that an organic building was appropriate only on its particular spot, and nowhere else.

But Fallingwater achieved its truest measure of greatness in the way it transcended site to speak to universal human concerns. In its startling departure from traditional modes of expression, it revealed an aspiration for freedom from imposed limitations; and in its successful partnership with the environment, it was a guidepost to humanity's proper relationship with nature. Fallingwater was also a resolution of dichotomies. At the same time strikingly substantial and dangerously ephemeral, it is securely anchored to rock and ledge, but seems to leap into space. It embodies change and changelessness simultaneously, for its imperishable stone and concrete elements form entirely new compositions as the angle of vision shifts (compare Fig. 10.1 with Fig. 10.2). Solid rock and rushing water reflect the permanence and impermanence of life itself. Fallingwater sinks its roots deeply into the ground to grow out of its site more like a plant than most other buildings, yet it is a masterpiece of sophisticated construction techniques. Composed of myriads of rectangles, it is never redundant; built of innumerable pieces of varying size and material, it nevertheless achieves a unity few structures approach. Fallingwater is a study in opposites—motion and stability, change and permanence, power and ephemeralness—that make the human condition a paradox of welcome adventure and anxious uncertainty. The philosophically ambiguous house at Bear Run may have been a comment on the social

Figure 10.2   "Fallingwater" (1936), Bear Run, Pennsylvania. Photo by author.

contradiction of a rich man's wealth in times of general depression, but it was also Wright's nature poem to modern humanity.[6]

□ □ □

With Taliesin West, the Usonian House, and Fallingwater, Wright's fourth major achievement during the late Depression was the Administration Building (1936) for the Johnson Wax Company in Racine, Wisconsin, a streamlined package with old-fashioned contents (Fig. 10.3). If the architect viewed the contemporary household as a little private club, he thought of the office force as a kind of extended family. The Administration Building, in keeping with the Johnson Company's philosophy, indeed, with that of many pre-World War Two employers, offered a humane though outmoded interpretation of working relationships. Johnson Wax was family-owned and family-managed, antiunion, and small town. The Johnsons were Racine itself, and as the largest local employer its attitude toward workers and community was almost feudal. Unlike the impersonal giant corporations that were tightening control over American industry, the Johnsons thought of their organization as a large, happy family. Taking

Figure 10.3 The Johnson Wax Company Administration Building (1936), right, and the Research Tower (1946–1947), left, Racine, Wisconsin. Courtesy Johnson Wax Company.

pride in their civic improvements and in their social and cultural contributions, they dealt with Racine as protectively as a father does with his children. Wright's design was therefore not simply a place to work in but a place "to live in" as well. Speaking only to the situation at Johnson Wax, it was a totally inappropriate model for labor–management relations elsewhere, except perhaps in paternalistic company towns.[7]

The Administration Building was a windowless brick rectangle lit by skylights and two strips of translucent Pyrex tubing encircling it just below the cornice line and a few feet above eye level. Like the 1904 Larkin Building in Buffalo (see Fig. 4.4), it sealed out the ugliness of its shabby industrial working class environment and, like its parent structure, had for its main office space a single large room (20 × 128 × 208 feet) ringed by a balcony. (Wright liked to say that the "masculine" Larkin Building "sired" the "more feminine" Johnson offices, where rounded corners and curving lines presumably carried sexual overtones.)[8] Indirect lighting, rich materials and ornamentation, custom-designed furniture, and a structurally unnecessary scattering of aesthetically pleasing, room-dividing pillars combined to create unusual warmth and quiet for such a large and busy space (Fig. 10.4).

Since the main entrance led to a roofed over parking area at the center of the lot, the entire composition was completely self-enclosed. Secure within its beautiful home, the Johnson "family" could ignore its gloomy surroundings and presumably be induced to forget the depressing social and economic conditions in the outside world. This may explain the architect's attempt to make the building "as beautiful to live in and work in as any cathedral ever was to worship in,"[9] for

Figure 10.4 Main office space, Johnson Wax Company Administration Building (1936), Racine, Wisconsin. Courtesy Johnson Wax Company.

during the 1930s a job, like religion, was an effective opiate. Both employer and employee, at any rate, applauded Wright's success. The Johnson Company estimated its headquarters to be worth millions of dollars in advertising. Prospective workers were willing to wait a year for a position (even after the Depression), and, once hired, studies showed that their efficiency steadily increased. (Wright attributed it to the architecture.) Many preferred to come early and linger after work rather than return to their unattractive homes. In keeping with the atmosphere of the place and with the philosophy of the owners, the office force began serving tea after it moved into its new quarters in 1939.[10]

The organization of the Johnson Building literally and symbolically recalled preindustrial labor–management relations. The president's suite at the top of the structure rose from the juncture of two oval penthouses containing the other executives. Below them on the mezzanine overlooking the large main room were lesser officers and sub-department heads. Next in the business and social hierarchy came the clerical staff, grouped together on the main floor where their superiors could observe them. And finally, all the services, and the maintenance workers, were directly accessible to the office force from the basement underneath. Since families should play together when labor is done, the recreational aspects of this home away from home were also expressed architecturally with terraces and squash courts on the roof, and a theatre (later a dining room) on the mezzanine. (After Wright's death, the Johnsons hired his business heirs, Taliesin Associated Architects [see Chapter Thirteen], to design a larger movie theatre across the parking lot.)

Since the 1880s, office structures had grown to be tall masonry-encased steel frames with ever larger expanses of fenestration. Wright's "Lieber Meister" Louis Sullivan, in fact, had been the first to clothe the building type in appropriate architectural dress. But Wright chose to ignore the dominant mode of expression by making the Wax Building low and windowless, as if to suggest that Herbert F. Johnson was different from other businessmen. As a result, this unique, marvelously successful, unusually beautiful edifice had little architectural or sociological impact on American commercial design. Land in Racine was not as expensive or scarce as in major metropolitan areas, so the Johnson Company could afford to expand out instead of up. Yet when Wright designed a companion research laboratory in 1946–1947 (see below and Fig. 10.5), he created a fourteen-story tower, which not only reversed the usual order of things (a high-rise office slab with low-rise service buildings, as at the United Nations or the World Trade Center), but was altogether unnecessary, at least in terms of land use. A likely explanation is that Wright wished to state the local prominence of his client with a tower (a modern church with steeple for a business civilization, as Norris Kelly Smith has suggested),[11] and in the complex as a whole imply that, unlike other corporations, Johnson Wax did not debase human relationships by plugging them into the bureaucratic maze of a huge anonymous box.

The Johnson Building was not influential for later corporate architecture (nor was Wright's other office structure, the 1952 Price Tower in Bartlesville, Oklahoma, for reasons to be discussed in Chapter Fourteen), but it did speak reassuringly to contemporary problems. Encouraging a spirit of mutuality in happy surroundings, it was a pleasure to be in, especially during the Depression. It recalled preindustrial working relations by defining everyone's place in an old-fashioned (if disappearing) paternal hierarchy, shunning the impersonal vagaries of the modern corporation. In an age of rapid and uncertain change, it reduced anxiety by stating maxims from simpler days when

Figure 10.5 Research Tower (1946–1947), Johnson Wax Company, Racine, Wisconsin. Courtesy Johnson Wax Company.

social and work life were more easily understood and not so separate from each other. Conditioned by the shared values of architect and client, the Johnson Building was an offspring of hard times and of nineteenth century merchant—not twentieth century industrial—capitalism in a small midwestern city. For the future it was irrelevant, but it helped make work palatable in an organization still somewhat uncommitted to the social relations of modern production.

The Johnson commission also embodied some of Wright's vision for Broadacre City, where business would be locally controlled. Since Johnson Wax was not monopolistic, a public utility, nor yet a major force in production, it met Wright's requirements for private ownership. Its offices and research facilities at least were nonpolluting and were also organic parts of the community whose life in large measure depended on the Johnsons' well-being. It was just the sort of company Wright wanted in Broadacres, and Herbert F. Johnson was just the kind of clear-thinking, middle-scale businessman he had praised in 1910 (see page 147). Tucked away in Racine, Wisconsin, furthermore, Johnson Wax represented decentralization, in a way. It was independent, experimental, and concerned about its workers, representing American capitalism at its best, a model for the humane economy Wright hoped to bring about (discussed in Chapter Eight).

The 1946–1947 research tower was an equally imaginative structure, the first in which floors were cantilevered from a hollow central core containing elevators, stairs, and utilities, a system originally proposed but never executed by Mies van der Rohe around 1920 for skyscrapers in Berlin.[12] Wright sheathed his building with bands of narrow brick spandrels separating two-story spreads of Pyrex tubing. Every other floor was circular, stopping short of the glass portions of the wall hung from the square floors above. The entire building, in fact, seemed to hang in space since only the services reached the ground, while the floors actually began at the second level (Fig. 10.5). The core continued fifty-four feet below grade as a "tap-root" foundation, Wright called it, stabilized by a sixty-foot-diameter annular slab, four feet thick at the center, tapering to ten inches at the edge to transmit the load of 70,000 square feet to the soil, a construction principle Bertrand Goldberg and Associates used in the 1960s for their now famous Marina City in Chicago. Although the Research Tower looked precarious— like a popsicle stuck in the ground—it was exceptionally stable and practical. With centrally positioned elevators, no interior walls, and direct verbal contact between square and circular floors, it facilitated communication among the chemists after it opened in 1950. Because of its high glass-to-masonry ratio, without air conditioning, it was hot to work in, but that could be remedied; and as with many other Wright structures, its uniqueness was discovered to have unforseen advantages.

□ □ □

If during his lifetime Wright had designed only the Johnson Building, Fallingwater, and the Jacobs House—a remarkable ensemble for any architect in a single year—his place in history would have been secure. The three generated an enormous amount of critical acclaim, probably convincing *Architectural Forum* editor and publisher Howard Myers to devote the bulk of his January 1938 issue to some thirty projects by

Wright, who wrote much of the text. *The Forum* reached a professional audience which for the first time in many years saw a striking array of Wright structures actually underway. The general public learned about the new work in the January 17, 1938 issue of *Time*, which illustrated or discussed Fallingwater, the Johnson Building, and the Jacobs House, among others, and in the September 26, 1938 *Life*, featuring a Usonian-type home for $5000–$6000 income families. *Scientific American* analyzed the "Unique Office Structure" in Racine in May 1937, and *Business Week* reported its opening in May 1939. As late as June 1946, *House Beautiful* magazine was still "baffled" by one man producing Fallingwater and the Johnson Building at the same time.

Having recently been consigned to unwelcome retirement, Wright was now acknowledged to be as vital and important as the younger generation. Not since the prairie period had he received so much attention, and then mostly from professionals. When "affinity tangles" and imbroglios in the 1920s made him something of a celebrity, albeit a rather notorious one, newspapers eagerly reported his outspoken comments, outrageous antics, and visionary projects even when he failed to construct them. The less he executed, it seemed, the more famous he became. So when he began to build again, the press was prepared to make this news, especially since he could be counted on for colorful prose and entertaining shenanigans. Most of the stories were favorable, either because of the quality of his work or because among architects he nearly monopolized the media. "There was a time when to call him the greatest architect alive would have started bitter controversy among his professional brethren," *House Beautiful* magazine stated rather typically in June 1946. "Today, not even a pallid debate could get going in the face of his outstanding achievements." After Fallingwater and Johnson Wax, Wright could pretty much rely on laudatory coverage no matter what he built or said.

He obliged by tweaking the public's fancy with a number of unusual structures. There was, for example, the magnificent "Wingspread" (1937), a luxury home in Racine, Wisconsin, for Herbert F. Johnson, president of the wax company (Fig. 10.6). "A tall central brick chimney stack with five fireplaces on four sides," the architect wrote, divided the massive vertical living space into areas for various domestic functions: entry, family living, dining, and reading. Extending from this core were four wings or "zones" for bedrooms, guests and garages, childrens' play, and services. The outdoor quadrants formed by the wings embraced a pool, a terrace, driveways, and gardens. Comparing it favorably with the 1907 Coonley Estate at Riverside, Illinois, Wright called Wingspread "the last prairie house," but thought it "more bold,

Figure 10.6 "Wingspread" (1937), Racine, Wisconsin. Courtesy The Johnson Foundation.

masculine, and direct in form and treatment," with "the best brickwork I have ever seen in my life."[13]

In 1938 he turned out another four eye-catching structures. Taliesin West at Scottsdale, Arizona (discussed in Chapter Eight), was complemented at Spring Green by the Midway Farm Buildings halfway along the road from the Hillside School to Taliesin East. The long, low, multilevel, emphatically horizontal complex seemed to relate the rather abrupt hill behind it to the flat fields in front (Fig. 10.7) with a series of gently descending steps. Tying together old buildings on the estate with new apprentice rooms, tractor sheds, silos, other farm facilities, and cow stalls, it was possibly the most avant-garde bovine domicile in the world. While this was being built, Wright designed a fitting guest house addition on the hill behind Fallingwater, connected to it by a curving walkway with a folded concrete canopy, the inner diameter of which "forms a strong compression ring requiring no support on that side" because the folds matching each step added rigidity.[14] His master plan and individual structures for Florida Southern College at Lakeland (Fig. 10.8) were also approved in 1938. Ground for the Annie Pfeiffer chapel was broken that year, soon followed by

Figure 10.7 Midway Farm Buildings (1938), Taliesin East, Spring Green, Wisconsin. Photo by author.

Figure 10.8 Annie Pfeiffer Chapel (1938), Florida Southern College, Lakeland. Courtesy Florida Southern College News Bureau.

the Walbridge, Carter, and Hawkins Seminar Buildings, and the E. T. Roux Library in 1942. After the war and through the middle-1950s, Wright saw five more buildings to completion in Lakeland, making a total of ten. Some were connected by covered walkways and made from concrete blocks students and faculty laid up themselves. Although designs by other architects were added after Wright's death, Florida Southern is the largest single collection of his work anywhere.[15]

Like the Pfeiffer Chapel, the Community Church (1940) at Kansas City, Missouri, had no steeple or windows. Light from the door and from oddly shaped openings in the roof proved to be more generous than conventional fenestration. Instead of pews the church had upholstered chairs that could be arranged in different groupings or cleared for community activities, twelve dressing rooms for dramatic productions, ground level parking under the sanctuary, and gravity heat. Although it is the least known of Wright's nonresidential work during this period, *Newsweek* ran a rendering and a section-through in its July 1, 1940 issue. Whatever Wright did, it seemed, got publicity.[16]

This was certainly the case with commissions from famous people or for massive ventures, even if not constructed, such as the 1937 projects for Mount Rushmore sculptor Gutson Borglum's Black Hills studio, for pen manufacturer George Parker's garage in Janesville, Wisconsin, and for one hundred all-steel houses in Los Angeles. The Monona Terrace Civic Center (1938) for Madison, Wisconsin, was destined to cause years of public controversy (see Chapters Eleven and Twelve) even though it was never executed. In 1940 Wright designed a $15,000,000, twenty-one unit "Crystal City" complex of hotels, offices, theatres, shops, parking, and 2500 residential apartments for a site on Connecticut Avenue in Washington, D.C., with buildings based on the St. Marks-in-the-Bowery construction principle (see Chapter Seven).[17] And during the war years there was a residence for Federal Works Administration official Clark Foreman, later a high-ranking Democratic Party politico, and a desert spa near Phoenix for cosmetics queen Elizabeth Arden.

Projects such as these went unbuilt but not unnoticed. *The Christian Science Monitor Magazine, The Nation, Time, Life, Newsweek, The New Republic, Scientific American,* and *The New York Times* were among the many nonprofessional publications favorably featuring him and his work during the late 1930s and early 1940s. The expanded version of *An Autobiography* appeared in 1943, followed two years later by *When Democracy Builds* a book about urban problems calling for a Broadacre City solution, discussed very enthusiastically by Ely Jacques Kahn in *Saturday Review*.[18] Wright produced at least twenty-

Figure 10.9 Olgivanna and Frank Lloyd Wright, early 1940s. Courtesy State Historical Society of Wisconsin.

seven interviews and articles between 1936 and 1944 for such widely read newspapers and magazines as *Rotarian, Reader's Digest, Life, The New York Times, Saturday Review, The Herald-Tribune, Christian Century,* and *Scribner's Commentator.* So it came as no surprise when the author of his first entry in *Current Biography* (1941) quoted *Time* to say that his was "as exciting a body of architectural thinking as has come from the brain of anyone since Michelangelo."[19] Wright could not have agreed more, except to leave out the last two words.

Honors accompanied the praise. In June 1937 he accepted an invitation to be the only American representative at an International Congress of Architects in Moscow—where he was elaborately fêted—forcing him to postpone reception of his first honorary degree, from Wesleyan University, until the following year. He showed twenty drawings and photographs of Fallingwater at New York's Museum of Modern Art in January 1938[20] and later in the year launched a two-week tour including an address to one thousand members of the Federal Architects Association in Washington. Construction of the Johnson Wax Building put off his Sir George Watson Lectures of the Sulgrave Manor Board at the University of London from 1938 to 1939, when his week of talks for a £500 honorarium were immediately published as *An Organic Architecture*. He caused a minor sensation in England during a two-month round of dinners, tours, parties, and lectures, and was repeatedly cited as having a "deep influence on European architecture." "The younger half of the profession, certainly," the London *Builder* stated, "is fully aware of what it owes to Mr. Wright."[21] In *The Nation*, critic Talbot Hamlin called the architect's elaborate retrospective of post-1905 work, held at the Museum of Modern Art from November 1940 to January 1941, "a major event," while in *The New Republic*, Bruce Bliven, Jr., added that Wright is "still on his feet, full of bounce and zingo," "the only American architect with a great, worldwide reputation." And in *Magazine of Art*, Frederick Gutheim wrote that his latest buildings were "as fertile in imagination, as shrewd technically, and as satisfying esthetically as those of the classic early period of prairie houses," proof of Wright's "continuing youthful vitality."[22] Meanwhile he was awarded the Gold Medal and made an honorary member of the Royal Institute of British Architects. He was also inducted into the National Academies of Architects in Uruguay and Mexico in 1941 and 1942, respectively.

As Wright crisscrossed the country from lecture to exhibition opening to award ceremony, he continued to debunk, criticizing whatever he pleased, including his audiences. He told the 1937 convention of the Memorial Craftsmens Union that cemeteries were too cramped; each grave, he said, should have more ground with simple horizontal markers instead of grand monuments, so the living could reflect on life, not vaingloriously worship the dead. Aside from Louis Sullivan and himself, he claimed, no one had put any imagination or intelligence into cemetery layout or headstone design.[23] A year and a half later he told the Manhattan Chapter of the National Real Estate Board that skyscrapers were one of the world's worst abominations, that slum clearance was simply slum transferral, and that he pitied anyone living in New York.[24] To an audience of 2500 giving him three minutes of hearty applause when he was introduced to dedicate a new College of Architecture at the University of California in 1940, he declared that he despised Los Angeles: "It is as if you tipped the United States up," he chided, "so that all the commonplace people slid down into Southern California."[25] In Chicago he accused real estate brokers of subordinating health and beauty to profit by chopping up land into tiny house lots. At Colonial Williamsburg he ridiculed historic restoration, in New York told housing officials that projects only institutionalized poverty, and in Washington blasted the District's architecture as "symbols of authority out of a pontifical past."[26]

A typical virtuoso performance began at the Woman's Club in Whitefish Bay, a fashionable suburb north of Milwaukee, when the architect accused his hostesses of inviting him not because he brought them an important message but because he had a reputation for being picturesque, erratic, and peculiar. In America's pervasive mediocrity "you have to be a thriller or a shocker," he declared, as if to explain himself, in order to be noticed. "If people thought your idea meant any actual change in their lives they'd put you in jail. The United States is the least liberal, least inclined for free speech in open forum, least inclined to give an honest man the benefit of the doubt of any nation in the world." Womans' organizations in particular paid little attention to speakers' remarks, he said, present company included. He finished by telling the women that they and their homes were all overdressed and, when he asked their purpose as a club, no one ventured a reply. Wright kept them breathless during his talk, a newspaper reported; some giggled, some gasped, some grinned, some got red in the face, and others walked out when he told a "semi-smutty" story. Wright may not have believed half the things he said, but he obviously enjoyed shocking his listeners. And they, no matter how outrageous his comments, usually invited him back, in part because he was a very good speaker, talking without notes or hesitation in a low-keyed, easy manner, laced with "brilliant and piercing wit," one listener observed. People may have disagreed with what he said, but they loved the way he said it.[27]

□ □ □

Lecturing frequently and pointedly, it was inevitable that Wright would get himself embroiled in political controversy. To accusations in 1936 that he showed too many Soviet films at his Taliesin Playhouse, he replied that they were no more propagandistic than American westerns and that as citizens of the world the Fellowship had an obligation to explore other cultures. While he did not agree with all the Russians were doing, he wrote in a May 1936 newspaper article, he could see the value of many things, and no one was going to prevent him from looking in on anyone's life through the cinema.[28] Much intrigued by the country, he eagerly accepted an invitation to stay in Russia for two weeks in June 1937 as a delegate to the International Congress of Architects. He traveled around a good deal, speaking to officials and ordinary citizens, and liked what he saw.[29] In his speech to "my dear comrades" at the Congress, he criticized "Private Ownership and the Profit System supreme [as] raised to the nth degree" in the United States, pleading with the Russians to decentralize, to avoid the lure of the International Style, and to develop an organic architecture suitable to their own life and culture. When he returned to America he wrote "Architecture and Life in the U.S.S.R." for *Soviet Russia Today* and *The Architectural Record,* an article praising the progress he had seen in agriculture, design, city planning, education, and transportation—"The Moscow subway makes the New York subway look like a sewer"—with only a few reservations.[30]

"If Stalin is 'betraying the revolution,'" he told Madison's *Capital Times* in July 1937, "he's betraying it into the hands of the Russian people." Their new architecture was "far above the level of anything America could show," he wrote, adding that the two nations were the world's best hope for "better life and democracy." If the Soviet Union could benefit from America's industrial techniques, this nation could profit from Russia's sense of dedication, its efforts to abolish private exploitation, its spirit of communalism, and its commitment to the goal of a better life for all. Pointing to the fate of conservatives in the French and American Revolutions, he explained Stalin's purges as the inevitable result of any social upheaval. He praised the Premier as a great leader and said that with economic security repression would subside. The United States and the Soviet Union were natural friends, he insisted, who ought to exchange ideas more freely. He criticized the American press for distorting news from Russia and said that everyone he had met spoke freely, without fear of censorship. "So here's to Russia's America and America's Russia," he toasted optimistically in August 1937. "May both live long and grow together."[31]

Wright endorsed the "sincere Russian experiment" enthusiastically, but was wary of the American Communist Party. "Our so-called Communists," he was quoted as saying, "are mere racketeers, unaware of what is going on in Russia, and they are in reality [its] worst enemies. . . .

They haven't got it straight at all." The Party's Faculty Branch at the University of Wisconsin asked him in print if "a lack of direct acquaintance with American Communists—coupled perhaps with the all too common mistake of confusing [us with] campus bohemians. . .—can be responsible for your statement" that Communists are "racketeers." Wright replied that he had been misquoted, but claimed that among "Trotskyites and campus intelligentsia" as well as labor unions were a number of "racketeers" who were "the worst enemies of Russia," adding rather lamely that any group with "ist" or "ism" after its name was lazy, irrelevant, ambiguous, "corrupted and corrupting."

He then proceeded to lecture the Party on true Russian and American goals, which were, he said: "1. Every man guaranteed the right to work [and] 2. No man able to eat unless he works." "Free ground and a free medium of exchange" was third, "general decentralization" fourth, and finally, "no speculation in natural resources or in the utitlities. . . . No exploitation of earth, water, air, or sky; of. . .oil, gas, coal, common carriers, or radio; no speculation in telephone and telegraph, press, or post; education and medical help to be free." How would this be accomplished in America? Gradually by taxation "and some form of purchase by capitalizing the country itself over and above a fair living for [everyone]—selling the margin back to the people as stock in their own country." He believed, he said, in a "genuine system of private ownership," not communism, or socialism but an arrangement whereby people owned their own land and money.[32] "I believe in a capitalist system," he wrote in 1943; "I only wish I could see it tried sometime."[33]

Anticapitalist views and strong endorsements of Russia, the Racine, Wisconsin, *Journal-Times* editorialized, "are likely to have this country's leading 'Red Hunters' down around his neck. Men have been. . .accused of plotting the overthrow of the American government for saying less." Wright replied that "this 'Red' menace [is]. . .just about as valid as the 'Yellow Peril'. . . . Everyone is getting so damned discreet nowadays that truth. . .has been getting a bad break." Concerning this, Wright continued, "it was bad luck for our citizens when the big corporation newspaper took over. . . . The 'bigs' have given the truth concerning the Russian spirit and what it is doing a bad slant." The newspapers only "conjectured" about life in the Soviet Union, while what "I have said [is] first hand observation." And one thing he saw that he especially liked was "the tenet in Russia's new constitution: 'From every man according to his ability—to every man according to his contribution.'"[34]

The *Journal-Times* was correct. Right-wing professional patriots quickly caught up with the architect. At the unveiling of Abraham Lincoln's head at Mount Rushmore in September 1937, after Senator Edward R. Burke (D.-Neb.), an opponent of Franklin Roosevelt's court-packing plan, used the occasion to condemn the administration's "attack" on the Constitution, Wright criticized him at a press conference, saying the day should have been sculptor Gutzon Borglum's, not the senator's for a political springboard. Wright suggested that the four men on the mountain (Lincoln, Washington, Jefferson, and Theodore Roosevelt) would have been the first to change the Constitution—a tentative, hastily thrown together document, anyway—if they thought it necessary and would have frowned upon propagandists invoking their names for partisan advantage. He could not remember, he claimed dramatically, ever having been so outraged by a politician. Burke retorted that until the sculptor expressed displeasure with the speech, Wright's views did not matter. It was really the condemnation of dictators, especially Stalin, Burke said, not concern for Borglum, that had aroused the architect's ire. And anyway, whatever he said could be dismissed, since his "strong advocacy of communism" was well known, an accusation that would surface frequently during the 1950s.

As his remarks at Mount Rushmore suggest, Wright was an early supporter of Roosevelt and the New Deal. Although the President's recovery measures fell short of the architect's rather naive solution for ending the depression—government-subsidized transportation to country homes so people could grow their own food—Wright was happy to admit that Roosevelt had tried to get some necessary work done, including tentative steps toward the equalization of wealth and power. "I was with him in the early days," he told a Madison, Wisconsin, newspaper editor in June 1941. "I wrote and talked in his defense." But he broke with Roosevelt, he said, when "with only hearsay information, he misjudged the world situation and did universal harm" by getting entangled in the European war.[36]

As late as July 1939, Wright insisted there would be no hostilities between the Axis powers and the West because Adolph Hitler was proud of his achievements in Germany and would not risk them in battle. After years of brutality and murderous power plays, Hitler, like gangster Al Capone, would want peace and respectability. Furthermore, England "holds the whip hand," Wright said, so there would be no war unless England willed it. In May 1941, the architect still believed the United States could coexist with Germany, that its democratic example was the best defense against fascist aggression, that America had at least five years to arm if need be, and that Hitler would not last that long anyway. His opposition to American entry into World War Two was not based on sympathy for the German dictator but on his belief that the European war was "the inevitable result of a policy inspired and desperately upheld by the power-financiers of London and New York."[37]

As he saw it, there were two protagonists in the great struggle: the "visible despotism" of Axis Fascism, and the "invisible despotism" of Anglo-American plutocracy. Average people were caught in the middle, forced to support "the out of date, abstract, big money industry" against what was apparently but not actually a more menacing enemy. The best defense against this double threat—from international fascism and international finance capitalism—was for people to regain control over their lives. In one of the *Taliesin Square-Papers* he began to issue periodically in 1941 he suggested twenty ways to begin the process, including outlawing "the private money power of London and New York," installment buying, interest borrowing, "demurrage" currency, private ownership of the press and radio, military strategists, and conscription, and implementing social credit as a substitute for money credit.[38] Wright believed the nation was being stampeded into a war that would have a short-run yield of huge profits for a handful of arms manufacturers and financiers and the long-run effect of strengthening the grip of international plutocracy, in the process trampling democratic institutions under foot. He feared the United States would grow even more imperialistic in its role as "world savior." In the end, the architect sided with the America First Committee, publicly endorsing Charles A. Lindbergh's isolationist sentiments.[39]

Fears about what the war would do to America, plus an unstated but obvious pacifism, help explain his strong endorsement of conscientious objection. The force of Wright's convictions undoubtedly influenced his apprentices, twenty of whom announced their opposition to conscription in April 1941 to the Wisconsin Committee of the American Peace Mobilization. Claiming it would destroy the Fellowship and its attempt to build an "interior defense," that is, an indigenous democratic way of life as the best weapon against fascism, they said that the draft "violates the deepest concerns of our individual consciences" and asked permission to continue their activities which "may honestly be called national objectives," namely, strengthening the American tradition of hard work and assisting young men to develop their creative abilities by building better buildings, thereby helping construct a true democracy.[40]

The Fellowship's statement aroused little interest until Marcus Weston refused to report for induction late in 1942. Federal Judge Patrick

T. Stone charged Wright with poisoning his students' minds, asked the Federal Bureau of Investigation to see if the architect was obstructing the war effort, ordered Weston to "stay away from that man," and claimed that too many fine boys were being ruined "out there at Taliesin." In an open letter Wright replied that Stone "was another of the things that is the matter with America," suggesting that for the well-being of the nation "such men as yourself should be deprived of any. . .authority whatever. . . ." He had not counseled his apprentices politically, he said, and unlike the judge, respected peoples' rights to their own opinions. To prove this, he noted that nineteen members of the Fellowship were already in the armed services. Nevertheless, he personally believed that conscription had "deprived the young men in America of the honor and privilege of dedicating himself [sic] as a freeman to the service of his country. They were first condemned without a hearing and then enslaved." He would be pleased, he said, to open Taliesin as a refuge for war resisters and claimed that "were I born 40 years later, . . . I too should be a c. o." In private, Wright was even more irate. Stone and men like him, he wrote to author August Derleth, were "yelping maddened animalistic 'patriots.'. . . When the pack runs with blood on its chaps and froth flecking from its chest there is nothing but shame and futility. . . . Democracy's real enemy," he contended, "is not the Axis but Bureaucracy here at home in the War for Gold." Marcus Earl Weston refused noncombatant service, was convicted of draft evasion, and sentenced to three years in a federal penitentiary.[41]

If in evil there is potential for good, there was in war the seeds of a better peace, so Wright thought, at least. Asked to send a 1500-word dispatch on "How I Would Rebuild London" after the blitz to the city's News-Chronicle, Wright replied that "the bombing is not an unmixed evil. Slums and ugliness that would have taken centuries to overcome have been blasted in a few days." The new London, he wrote, should be twenty-five times the area of the old. Based on the Broadacre City plan, the rebuilt metropolis should separate vehicular from pedestrian traffic and elevate railways over warehousing. Homes for rich and poor should vary only in degree, not kind, with both architecturally harmonious. There should be no speculation in money, land, or ideas, and all utilities should be publicly owned. Historic London should be preserved in a great park system and the rest decentralized around nodes of activity with taller buildings pushed to the perimeter of settlement. Housing, industry, recreation, schools, and jobs should be near each other to eliminate material waste and human inconvenience.

"With a new city to build," Wright concluded, Londoners "have a wonderful chance to create something distinctive."[42]

Fearing by 1941 that the American government, poisoned by militarism and greed, had lost concern for the people, Wright proposed a complete restructuring of the nation, something even more distinctive than his London plan. "The United States of North America," as he called the scheme, would be divided into three sections along geographic, economic, and cultural lines: "New England"—also including New York, New Jersey, Pennsylvania, Delaware, and Maryland—the financial and industrial center; "Usonia South," the old Confederacy and staple-producing region; and all the rest (the true America), with a new national capital on the Mississippi River, to be called "Usonia." Each section would elect its own president and congress which in turn would elect a federal congress to choose a federal president. "The United States of North America," Wright claimed, was the only form by which the Founding Fathers' ideals of national independence could be truly realized.

The "tri-state U-S" would allow each region to pursue its own interests. "[New England] mostly remains in power-finance bags of the power-finance system of New York," he insisted, "an alias of the power-finance system of London. Both what we laughingly call the Capitalist System." So New England, which did not have the real interests of the nation at heart, could remain tied to old England as the center of international finance, diplomacy, and cultural traditionalism. The rest of the nation could then go its own way. With the federal capital—also called "Usonia"—at the geographic and spiritual center of American civilization, unhampered by New England and foreign influence, indigenous values and institutions could flourish in relative freedom. Removing the selection of important officials from the people, Wright believed, would improve the quality of government since voters were too easily stampeded into making poor choices, leaving leaders to make dire mistakes, like Roosevelt's foreign policy.[43]

Suspicion about popular wisdom had also characterized Broadacre City. Underneath all Wright's ideas on the liberation of humanity, in fact, was the assumption that people were not to be trusted unless they had autonomous enlightened leaders. But if he doubted the public's ability to look after itself, he had nothing but contempt for most politicians and businessmen. Of course, there were exceptions. Wright endorsed Representative Thomas Amlie, the Wisconsin Progressive Party's candidate for the United States Senate in 1938, and was a staunch supporter of Philip La Follette and Robert M. La Follette,

Jr., Governor and Senator, respectively. He also admired a few businessmen, perhaps because they had chosen him as their architect,
such as Lloyd Lewis, Edgar Kaufmann, Herbert F. Johnson, George
Parker, and one of the biggest plutocrats of all, Solomon R. Guggenheim.[44]

The commission Guggenheim gave to Wright during the war eventually developed into one of the architect's most spectacular and controversial buildings. Guggenheim's intent was to build a suitable home
for his extensive collection of twentieth century paintings, and in 1943
Wright offered three proposals. The first, a variation of which was
later executed, featured a continuous spiral ramp with each turn
smaller than the one above, attached to an apartment for the director
at the north end of the site. The second, recalling the Sugar Loaf
Mountain automobile objective of 1925, inverted the first, placing the
widest turns at the bottom, while the third scheme was composed of
flat hexagonal floors connected by ramps.

The architect unveiled his drawings in New York in July 1945 amidst
much fanfare and the usual Wrightian rhetoric. At a Plaza Hotel luncheon given by Guggenheim, Wright declared that no decent museum
had ever been built but assured the audience that his million-dollar
structure would remedy that. Viewers would be able to see the entire
collection from self-propelled wheel chairs coasting down the ramp,
or watch motion pictures projected on the ceiling from recliner
lounges on the main floor several stories below. If an atomic bomb
hit New York, Wright boasted, with characteristic modesty, the Guggenheim would not be destroyed; it might be thrown in the air, he
conceded, but it would come down in one piece, bounce, and then
settle into place. Last but presumably not least, it would also be "an
inspiring place where great art could be seen to good advantage in
human scale, that is, in the scale. . .it would enjoy were it placed in
the American homes we call modern. . . ."[45] Groundbreaking was
postponed until 1957 (see Chapter Twelve), but from the very beginning Wright conceived of the Guggenheim as a piece of architectural
sculpture expressing human motion, and in many ways it was the most
imaginative structure he ever built.

In 1942, 1943, and 1944, Wright like most other architects executed
nothing, but after the war his practice reached unprecedented dimensions, in part because of Johnson Wax, Fallingwater, the Usonian
House, and the national reputation he had constructed for himself

during the 1930s and 1940s. Soon he would flood the country with his buildings, the press with his comments, the journals with his publications, and the public consciousness with his flamboyant activity. He designed his most lucrative and monumental projects in the 1950s, including a number of engineering marvels and futuristic fantasies, although by then the formative period of his philosophy was long over. During the 1930s he published a number of books representing the full development of his architectural and social ideas, a philosophical swan song carrying him through the remainder of his career.

NOTES

1 "What the Cause of Architecture Needs Most," *The Architectural Review,* 81 (February 1937), 99–100.

2 Wayne Andrews, *Architecture, Ambition and Americans: A Social History of American Architecture* (Glencoe, Ill.: The Free Press, 1964), 243; Vincent Scully, *Frank Lloyd Wright* (New York: George Braziller, 1960), 26–27.

3 Henry-Russell Hitchcock, *In the Nature of Materials: The Buildings of Frank Lloyd Wright, 1887–1941* (New York: Duell, Sloan and Pearce, 1942), 91.

4 *Architectural Forum,* 68 (January 1938), 36.

5 H.-R. Hitchcock, *In The Nature of Materials,* 90.

6 For an early description by an apprentice see Robert K. Mosher, "At Taliesin," *The Capital Times,* January 22, 1937. The best illustrations and most informative accounts are in Bruno Zevi and Edgar Kaufmann, Jr., *La Casa sulla Cascata di F. Ll. Wright* (Milano: ETAS KOMPASS, 1963).

7 The renderings were first published, along with the architect's comments, in *The Racine* (Wis.) *Journal-Times,* December 31, 1936. In *American Building Art: The Twentieth Century* (New York: Oxford University Press, 1961), 172–176, Carl Condit gives an excellent analysis of its technical features, as well as those of the 1946–1947 Johnson research tower (see page 284). The famous demonstration in which Wright proved to the State Industrial Commission that his interior "mushroom" columns could support over sixty tons of dead weight each, though only required to carry from two to twelve, was reported in *The Capital Times,* June 9, 1937, and *The Architectural Record,* 82 (July 1937), 38.

8 Frank Lloyd Wright, *An Autobiography* (New York: Duell, Sloan and Pearce, 1943 ed.), 474; William Wesley Peters first compared the two in *The Capital Times,* March 5, 1937.

9 *The Racine Journal-Times,* December 31, 1936. For a very flattering recent assessment of its many interior design innovations see Monica Geran,

"Frank Lloyd Wright Revisited," *Interior Design*, 46 (November 1975), 96–101.

10 On social life in the building see *The Capital Times*, July 23, 1955, and Wright's "Conversation" with Hugh Downs on NBC–TV, May 17, 1953, in *The Future of Architecture*, 25–26.

11 Norris Kelly Smith, *Frank Lloyd Wright: A Study in Architectural Content* (Englewood Cliffs, N.J.: Prentice-Hall, 1966), 136–148.

12 On the tower see Carl Condit, *American Building Art*, 173–176; *The Capital Times*, March 6, 1946; November 6, 1947; November 8, 1950; *The Architectural Record*, 102 (December 1947), 16, 128; *Architect and Engineer*, 146 (December 1950), 20–24.

13 F. L. Wright, *An Autobiography*, 476–477; William Oliver, "Wingspread," reprinted from *Wisconsin Tales and Trails* (Autumn 1964) as a brochure by the Johnson Foundation.

14 E. Kaufmann, Jr., "Twenty-five Years of the House on the Waterfall," *La Casa sulla Cascata*, 25.

15 Florida Southern College News Bureau, "The Architecture of Frank Lloyd Wright at Florida Southern College," n. d.; "Frank Lloyd Wright's Newest Creation," *Architect and Engineer*, 146 (July 1941), 34–36; *The New York Times*, September 14, 1941; *Architectural Forum*, 88 (January 1948); 94 (January 1951); 95 (September 1952); and "Frank Lloyd Wright," 102 (April 1955), 114–121.

16 Also see *The Capital Times*, July 16, 1940; and *The Chicago Tribune*, January 10, 1942.

17 "Crystal City" received extensive coverage in *The Capital Times*, September 21, 29, 1940; *The Washington Post*, September 25, 1940, a full page spread; and in *Newsweek*, 16 (November 25, 1940), 48.

18 Ely Jacques Kahn, "Realistic Dreams for Tomorrow," *Saturday Review*, 28 (May 19, 1945), 26; Talbot Hamlin wrote a thoughtful review of F. L. Wright, *An Autobiography*, for *The Wisconsin Magazine of History*, 27 (December 1943), 227–229.

19 "Frank Lloyd Wright, American Architect," in Maxine Block, Ed., *Current Biography, 1941* (New York: H. H. Wilson Co., 1941), 938–940.

20 *The New York Times*, January 25, 1938.

21 *The Builder*, 156 (April 28, 1939), 789, and (May 5, 1939), 855. On his whirlwind tour also see *The Architect's Journal*, 89 (May 11, 1939), 756–757; *The Capital Times*, May 23, October 31, 1939; *Baraboo Weekly News*, April 13, June 15, 1939; *The Weekly Home News*, June 15, 1939.

22 Talbot Hamlin, "Frank Lloyd Wright," *The Nation*, 151 (November 30, 1940); Bruce Bliven, Jr., "Frank Lloyd Wright," *The New Republic*, 103 (December 9, 1940), 790–791; F. A. Gutheim, "First Reckon With the Future: Frank Lloyd Wright's Exhibit at the Modern Museum," *Magazine*

of Art, 34 (January 1941), 32–33. For less favorable comments see "A City for the Future," *Time,* 36 (November 25, 1940), 58.

23 The speech, excerpted in "At Taliesin," *The Capital Times,* February 26, 1937, cited the Blue Sky Mausoleum (1928 ?) for the Martin Family in Buffalo as his contribution to humane cemetary design. This project was apparently never built.

24 *The New York Times,* September 15, 1938.

25 Paul Hunter, "Mr. Wright Goes to Los Angeles," *Pencil Points,* 21 (March 1940), 34, 36.

26 *The Capital Times,* June 8, 1938; January 23, 25, 1940; *The Washington Post,* October 26, 1938.

27 *The Milwaukee Journal,* December 6, 1934.

28 *The Capital Times,* May 29, 1936.

29 On the trip to the Soviet Union see *The Capital Times,* June 6, 1937; *The Weekly Home News,* June 17, 1937; F. L. Wright, *An Autobiography,* 541–544; and the sources cited in notes 30 to 34.

30 "Address to the Congress of Architects—Soviet Russia," reprinted in F. L. Wright, *An Autobiography,* 545–548; "Architecture and Life in the U.S.S.R.," *The Architectural Record,* 82 (October 1937), 59–63, reprinted in F. L. Wright, *An Autobiography,* 549–556.

31 *The Capital Times,* July 22, August 1, 1937.

32 *The Capital Times,* July 22, 1937; "An Open Letter to Frank Lloyd Wright," *ibid.,* August 3, 1937, reprinted in F. L. Wright, *An Autobiography,* 557; "Reply to the Faculty Communists of the University of Wisconsin," *The Capital Times,* August 5, 1937, reprinted in F. L. Wright, *An Autobiography,* 558–559.

33 F. L. Wright, *An Autobiography,* 560.

34 "At Taliesin," *The Capital Times,* August 13, 1937.

35 *The Capital Times,* September 19, 21, 1937.

36 *The Capital Times,* October 16, 1939; June 6, 1941.

37 *The Weekly Home News,* July 13, 1939, reprinting *Capital Times* publisher William T. Evjue's column from a few days previously; conversation between Evjue and Wright, May 27, 1941, reprinted in *Taliesin Square-Paper,* May 1941; "To Beat the Enemy," *Taliesin Square-Paper,* No. 5, July 1941.

38 "Defense," *Taliesin Square-Paper,* No. 4, July 1941, reprinted in *The Capital Times,* September 28, 1941.

39 *The Capital Times,* March 29, 1941.

40 *The Capital Times,* April 1, 6, 1941.

41 *The Capital Times,* December 17, 20, 1942; January 14, 1943; Wright to Derleth, December 22, 1942, Derleth Collection, State Historical Society of Wisconsin (SHSW).

42 *Taliesin Square-Paper,* January 1941; "Wright Over London," *Architectural Forum,* 75 (August 1941), 68; *The Capital Times,* January 12, 1941.

43 "Usonia, Usonia South and New England: A Declaration of Independence. . .1941," *Taliesin Square-Paper,* No. 6, August 24, 1941.

44 For his praise of Amlie and certain businessmen see *The Capital Times,* November 23, 1934; July 30, 1937; August 11, 1938; F. L. Wright, *An Autobiography,* 467–478.

45 *The Capital Times,* July 10, 1945; *The New York Times,* July 10, September 21, 1945; "The Modern Gallery," *Architectural Forum,* 84 (January 1946), 81–88; "Optimistic Ziggurat," *Time,* 46 (October 1, 1945), 74; "Museum a la Wright," *Time,* 46 (July 23, 1945), 72; *Life,* 29 (October 8, 1945).

1930–1959

CHAPTER ELEVEN

Organic Architecture

During the last three decades of his life, Frank Lloyd Wright spoke and wrote so frequently for lay and professional audiences that he damaged his credibility. His style obscured his substance: outrageous remarks, esoteric jargon, and abysmal prose fostered misunderstanding and dismissal. He himself wondered if he was making any headway: "Here I am at it again," he confessed in a 1939 lecture, "trying, trying, trying, but what is the use?"[1] His verbal excesses may have obscured the import of his message but his monumental achievements demand that he be taken seriously, that the kernel of his ideas be sifted from the chaff of his rhetoric. With the exception of "The Art and Craft of the Machine" speech, his autobiography, and a handful of books and articles, most of his vast literary output has been ignored, even though his thinking warrants serious attention.

As he grew older he pontificated on everything, diluting his effectiveness when he dealt with subjects he knew best. His belief that success obligated him to dispense wisdom, plus a colossal ego, undoubtedly stimulated the never-ending pronouncements, also motivated by his messianic urge to spread the gospel of "organic architecture," a Hegelian-like overview transcending design to become a philosophy of life. Wright tended to focus at length on one issue at a time: the nature of materials during the 1920s, Broadacre City and political economy in the 1930s, the problems with American life and culture after World War Two. Yet it was uncharacteristic of him to abandon an idea entirely or let one slip from his intellectual storehouse. His organic philosophy, in a word, was cumulative, approaching universality as time passed.

Despite rambling speeches and disorganized prose, his notion of the organic lent a certain consistency and imposed a certain order on everything he said no matter what the topic. "The creative facilities of the human race," he told a student group in 1954, are "intimately linked to the relationship of man to the cosmos." This transcendental belief that the artistic side of humanity represented its divinity led Wright to insist that a kind of structure—a coherent pattern—characterized all life: "Organic architecture feels at home with the ideal of unity," he once remarked.[2] One of the two key words in his philosophical vocabulary, in fact, was "unity," a defining attribute of the second word, "nature," from which everything else flowed. The two became one in organic structure which brought cosmic unity to natural variety and was, Wright believed, a proper basis for all social relations.

□ □ □

So central was "nature" to Wright's thinking that in 1954 he entitled a book *The Natural House.* He used the word in two ways, the first and more familiar referring to the outdoors, "the visible world," or "external" nature. There were at least four ways nature in this sense informed his work, the first being that people should live close to it. During the prairie period he undertook one of the most widely appreciated characteristics of his architecture, namely, its integration with site and environment, when he incorporated the lines of the Midwest's level terrain into his designs. Nestling closer to the ground than their neighbors, they employed outreaching terraces and portes-cochere, casement windows, overhanging eaves, horizontal strips of trim and fenestration, and other devices (discussed in Chapter Three) to associate with the outdoors. Although his houses brought people closer to nature, they were by and large built *on top of* the prairie, failing to reach the ultimate goal of blending architecture with environment, of making indoors and outdoors part of each other.

He came closest on irregular terrain. The W. A. Glasner and Thomas Hardy Houses (both 1905) in Glencoe, Illinois, and Racine, Wisconsin, seemed incomplete without their plummeting sites (see Figs. 3.9 and 3.10). The ravine at the 1911 Sherman Booth project in Glencoe was the *raison d'être* of the design scheme, while his own Taliesin the same year was a virtual outcropping and not a mere acknowledgment of the land itself. His projects during the twenties for Edward Doheny (1921) in California's Sierra Madre Mountains and for the San-Marcos-in-the-Desert resort (1927–1928) near Chandler, Arizona, were defined by hills, streams, woods, and crevices, while the California textile-block homes of the period were interpretive expressions and literal extensions of their rugged hillsides. It was difficult to determine in these kinds of cases, Wright often said, "where the ground leaves off and the building begins. . . ."[3]

By the late 1930s and 1940s, some of his best work appeared on sloping, dropping, or otherwise unusual sites. Fallingwater and the Usonian homes for George Sturges, Ralph Jester, and John C. Pew were worked into uneven land formations (see Fig. 9.6), while houses for Paul Hanna, Gregor Affleck, and several other clients snuggled along gentle grades (see Fig. 9.9). After the war he based a number of commissions on the same principle. Some faithfully reproduced nearby topographical features, the Wyoming Valley Grammar School (1956) near Taliesin East, for example, while others like the Marin County Civic Center (1957–1959) at San Rafael, California, incorporated those features into the design composition. Several more buildings merged so closely into site they could not possibly have been built elsewhere in the same form, for instance, the Roland Reisley House (1951) dropping over a ridge (see Fig. 9.22) at Pleasantville, New York, or the outdoor facilities of the Alvin Miller House (1950) tumbling down the banks of the Cedar River at Charles City, Iowa.

If terrain was insufficiently interesting, Wright sometimes made it so. The second home (1943) for Herbert Jacobs in Middleton, Wisconsin, illustrates the way he manufactured a "natural" site. The berm insulating the rear from northerly winds was made from a shallow circular excavation in front around which the house wraps, serving as a slightly below-grade patio–lawn from which sun reflects off snow during the winter to light and help heat even the upper-level rooms to the rear of the balcony. All this gives the impression that the house projects out of a tiny hill. (Compare Figs. 9.14 and 11.1) And at the partially prefabricated Arnold Jackson House (1957) a few miles away in Madison, he made two small hills with the soil from the excavation, wedging the building lengthwise between, further to enhance the character of a sloping lot already memorable for its distant view of Lake Mendota.

Wright had already perfected the corner window, two sheets of glass mitred directly together without benefit of frame (Fig. 11.2) by cantilevering the roof to eliminate view-impeding posts. Wider, uninterrupted spans were possible with steel beams and plate glass, leading in Usonian homes to living areas with floor-to-ceiling glazed doors and windows for "more open spaces," he wrote, "and a closer relation to nature."[4] With careful landscaping (supervised by Wright), the character of his living rooms depended on the outdoors, were

Figure 11.1 Second house (1943) for Herbert Jacobs, Middleton, Wisconsin. Photo by author.

incomplete without it, were decorated by it, even in winter when massive icicles dropped gracefully from overhanging eaves. Every room, in fact, including kitchens and halls deep inside, looked to the outdoors directly or through others. The prairie house had established the principle of designing according to terrain and environmental features, but the "natural house" did not reach full maturity until the Usonian period.

The architect's insistence on living close to nature may be an area for psychological investigation (akin to the notion that had he been taller than five feet eight and a half inches, his buildings would not have been so low). It may have sprung from his childhood summers on the farm, from the influence of Louis Sullivan, or from his retreat to the suburbs in the 1890s. Whatever the reason, he preferred the country and, in keeping with Broadacre proposals, believed the best thing he could do for clients was move them as far away from the city as possible. In *The Natural House* (1954), he reiterated what he had been saying for over twenty years when he urged his readers to "go way out in the country, . . .and when others follow, . . .move on." Go ten times further out than you think you have to, he often said. (There is a certain irony in the fact that he built only one home for an actual farmer—Robert Muirhead at Plato Center, Illinois, in 1952—although

Figure 11.2 Dining room corner window, Isadore Zimmerman House (1950), Manchester, New Hampshire. Photo by author.

he encouraged his Usonian clients to grow their own food.) In response to television interviewer Mike Wallace's rather pedestrian question, "When you're out in nature, don't you feel small and insignificant?" he stated, in true Whitmanesque fashion, "On the contrary, I feel larger, I feel enlargened and encouraged, intensified, more powerful."[5] Skeptics have claimed that his ode to nature was hypocritical posturing since he so often reveled appreciatively in urban pleasures. The fact remains that, with Thomas Jefferson, Wright was the best known American architect to live and work outside the city.

To help people live naturally close to the great outdoors was

Wright's paramount objective. But nature was also a source of design inspiration, a model for architectural forms and construction principles, a second way in which the architect depended on it. Trees, he said, suggested the "tap-root" foundation of the Johnson Research Tower (1946–1947) in Racine, Wisconsin (see Chapter Ten and Fig. 10.5), wherein the floors were cantilevered like branches from the central "trunk" (of elevators, utilities, and stairs) sunk deep in the ground to stabilize the structure (like a tree above ground and a dandelion below). Wright liked to say that the spiraled, chambered nautilus inspired the Guggenheim Museum (1943–1957) in New York City and that folded hands ("here is the church and here is the steeple. . .") informed the prowlike glass façade of the apse (Fig. 11.3) in the Unitarian Meeting House (1947) at Madison, Wisconsin. The walls of his Midwestern fieldstone houses resembled rock strata in the vicinity of his Spring Green estate, and the way some flowers opened informed the plan of certain prairie homes. There was a wealth of

Figure 11.3 Unitarian Meeting House (1947), Madison, Wisconsin. Photo by Robert W. Giese, 109 Alden Drive, Madison.

information for architects, Wright insisted, if only they would observe nature carefully.

Thirdly, nature taught that the proper way to use materials was to let them be themselves. Wright never painted or turned wood, for example. He might bend it for curved surfaces, stain, smooth, and wax it to bring out the grain, but never cover it over or twist it out of shape. When he used stone in the Midwest, he preferred to cut and lay it up horizontally as it came from fields or from hill outcroppings, leaving exposed edges rough (Fig. 11.4). In the Southwest and Far West, he was apt to mortar together uncut boulders of varying colors and shapes in the same random way he found them on hills or in the desert (Fig. 11.5). It was sometimes easier to locate and use regional stone than regional wood, but he tried to build with local materials if possible to cut shipping costs and to express surroundings. Since each material had its own characteristics, it should never be made to resemble another, the architect taught, nor should it be used in ways negating its essential properties. The same principle applied to fabricated substances. The horizontal jointing of bricks, for example, created a texture most suitable for surfaces where unit lines could repeat and express the shape of the whole composition. Since glass, he said, was

Figure 11.4 Stone work in the Howard Anthony House (1951), St. Joseph, Michigan. Photo by author.

Figure 11.5   Stone work at Robert Berger House (1952), San Anselmo, California. Photo by author.

more beautiful in the shade and shadow than in the sun's glare, it should always be sheltered by overhangs. But since it was also transparent, it should reveal space and volume while uniting compatible entities like indoors and out. Opaque plastic was excellent for capturing or emiting light in dome or roof areas where visual access was unnecessary. Without innate beauty of grain or texture, steel could be spun like webs to make bridges or, because of its strength and plasticity, express span and flow. In combination with concrete it lent itself to continous or curving surfaces. Even synthetic materials, Wright maintained, could be deployed "naturally," that is, in keeping with their defining properties.

A fourth lesson from external nature was to "go *with* the natural climate," he said, rather "than try to fix a special artificial climate." Reyner Banham and John Sergeant are among the few to appreciate fully the ecological sensitivity of Wright's designs. Always concerned with climatic conditions, he sited and organized his homes not only to accommodate family sociology but also for heating, cooling, lighting, and energy conservation. Of course, physical and social comfort were interrelated, supporting Banham's insight that in the Frank J. Baker House (1909) in Wilmette, Illinois, on which he bases his analysis, "hardly any single detail participates in only one function, nor is any single function served by only one item of equipment."[6] In cruciform arrangement, the Baker living room juts at right angle from the main axis, facilitating the open plan. As a semidetached room, it has windows on three sides, opening the interior to the outdoors which vastly increased light and air (see the Isabel Roberts House in Fig. 3.12, built on the same principle). But expanded fenestration also meant heat loss, so Wright increased radiator capacity under the window seats at the largest glazed surfaces, served with hot water pipes concealed in wainscoting around the entire perimeter of the room. Thus, the room is lit and heated on all exposed sides. The expense required to fuel this performance is partly recaptured in summer when open clerestories provide cross currents of air while serving as exhaust vents at the highest point in the house where heat most likely collects. The windows, furthermore, act as a kind of "greenhouse" in winter but their overhangs in summer keep intense sun out. Fresh air from eave vents was warmed in cold weather by passing through grilled light boxes and across hot pipes in roof spaces. Thus, eaves, window seats, lights, wainscoting, glazing, water pipes, and vents all combine in various ways to provide warmth, cooling, view, shade, air circulation, seating, and privacy.

Since Wright did not like mechanical air conditioning even in semitropical climates, he faced his homes south, if possible, so that the afternoon sun in summer did not pour directly in. Long overhangs added shade, for example in the Robie House (Chicago, 1907) where, says Banham, "the shadow of the eaves just kisses the woodwork at the bottom of the glass in the doors to the terrace"[7] at noon in July and August (see Fig. 3.17). Masonry thermal masses were cooling in summer and warm in winter. Gravity heat in Usonians traveled through the floors and up brick walls for even distribution and pleasantly gradual temperature change, while fireplace flue, raised kitchen stack, and living room clerestories cleansed the house with fresh air even in cold weather. These and other features helped residences work with climate to create an atmospherically natural interior. Wright's homes were not energy independent, but they were ecologically intelligent mechanisms for environmental control.

The natural house was intended to maximize people's contact with and utilization of the outdoors. It was often inspired by nature's forms and processes, let its materials retain their natural characteristics, and worked with the climate. But close association with the external world was only one aspect of the "natural" house, for Wright ascribed a second meaning to "nature," a philosophical meaning referring to the essence of what a residence, or any building, was. Only by understanding this second definition can organic architecture be fully appreciated.

□ □ □

This was the concept of "internal" nature. As far back as 1912, he had written in *The Japanese Print* (see Chapter Six) that everything in existence had its own essential reality, its own unique characteristics, its own self-defining features. The internal nature of inanimate objects such as rocks was inherent structure and composition, while in abstract or living phenomena such as ideas or people it was "the working of [organic] principle." By nature study Wright did not mean bird watching or trips to the arboretum, though he advocated them; he meant dedicated probing of essences to discover the particular characteristics making something itself. His attitude was Platonic, that essence existed before perception. After careful investigation, he wrote, "the creative mind sees the basic patterns of construction in the form of whatever is."[8] Taking residences as illustrative, this meant for architecture that there existed an "idea" of a house—its "internal" nature, its defining essence—which the architect could determine and put into form. The nature of a house in this sense did not mean how it looked but what it was. For Wright a house was the embodiment of the nature of the family, of its physical environment, of its culture, its architect, and its construction processes.

All natures or essences had one common characteristic. They were active rather than static; they changed over time. If nature was Platonic, it was also Einsteinian. When the creative mind found the essential "form of whatever is," it invariably turned out to be an "ever-moving, basic inner-rhythm." Although internal structure was eternal in the sense of existing as idea or form forever, it also evolved, and was therefore possible to observe. Thus, a tree was the same and different as time passed. It always had its "treeness," those elements making it a tree and not a log, but its leaves, bark, branches, roots, and everything else changed constantly. "Life itself is a splendid unfolding," Wright went on to say in 1949; "there can be no real *beginning* on this earth. Nor [any]. . .end to be foreseen."[9] Everything was always in the process of becoming.

The implication for architecture was that "no organic building may ever be 'finished.' The complete goal. . .is never reached. Nor need be. What worthwhile ideal is ever reached?" Refinements during planning and construction were always possible, of course, but Wright also meant that even after the client moved in, an edifice continued to be the architect's responsibility. "We must and will see that every building becomes as we intended it to be. . .even if we have to help" the occupant use it correctly. Since structures were always called upon to perform new functions and house new activities, in other words, to *grow*, Wright tried to provide for change in his architecture if he could anticipate its future. Some Usonian residences, for example, were easily added to, especially on the bedroom wing if the family increased, and the large Hanna House was designed for subdivision and rearrangement to meet changing parental needs after the children married and departed. In *The Natural House*, Wright suggested ways to accommodate family growth by preplanning for expansion and alteration without distorting a home's essential character.[10]

Organic buildings not only "grew" from sites as natural consequences of topography, and in form and content as human situations changed, but also as ideas in the mind of the architect. For Wright— and this was one of his most important contributions—a building was enclosed space the reality of which, that is, its nature and essence, was *inside*. The purpose of architecture was therefore to "*un*fold an inner content—[to] express 'life' from the 'within,'" to make space "come through" to the exterior. The outside of a structure was but the expression of interior necessities, a statement about internal functions and events. The architect was thus obliged to conceive a building "from inside out," that is, by visualizing interior spaces, then proceeding to exterior composition, a process in which the design idea "grew" to maturity.[11]

Wright's most illuminating discussion of the way he arrived at building form is his autobiographical account of Unity Temple (see Chapter Four) in Oak Park.[12] The first step in his thinking, he remembered, was to determine the "idea" of the building—its purpose, its philosophy. With this firmly in mind, he worked out the character of the enclosed space, then moved to external articulation. Only then did he begin to sketch, struggling through study after study until the inside and then the outside came true. Drawing the façade was the last step in the conceptual process, the end result of an intellectual exercise from which the "idea"—the nature, the essence—and finally the Temple itself grew "organically." What ultimately separated him from Bauhaus and most other architects, he insisted, was that they settled on the appearance of structure first and then fit interiors to match, while he, on the other hand, proceeded from an idea about spatial provision for human needs to architectural expression.

Just as organic buildings grew in the mind of the architect, so should they also grow from the nature of their culture, from "a whole way of life, material, intellectual, and spiritual," as historian Raymond Williams has defined the term.[13] If the United States was really a democracy, Wright argued, it must have democratic buildings, not bland egalitarian structures of the lowest common denominator but buildings suited to its national institutions, values, and traditions in principle exalting freedom and individualism. And if the United States was really a bold new experiment in human variety, a composite of all the world's nations but the cultural vassal of none, its architecture should be free of historical references to other times and places, as new and different as the nation itself. If America stood for maximum personal liberty and minimal state restraint, residences should assert the importance of privacy, human difference, self-esteem, and unpretentiousness, while state buildings should emphasize citizen participation, not governmental power. The nature of American culture begged for appropriate architectural expression.

The organic building was therefore the physical expression of ideas about people, environment, culture, design, and construction methods synthesized by the architect, all of which were constantly evolving. It hardly seems possible that a structure could be called upon to represent so much and not become a philosophical or aesthetic mishmash. But Wright insisted that continuous change and infinite variety in no way implied disorder, disarray, or chaos. The first principle of organic growth, he maintained, was "perfect correlation," nor was anything "of any great value except as naturally related to the whole." He often said that when the whole is to the part as the part is to the whole, harmony would result and "the *nature* of the entire performance becomes clear as necessity."[14] The means by which growth and variety were integrated into the larger unity of organic architecture was "plasticity" or "continuity," the active stasis resolving the apparent contradiction (not to Wright, however) between Platonic idea and Einsteinian relativity.

From Louis Sullivan, Wright had learned to appreciate design "flow," the idea that a composition should be internally consistent, complete within itself, should develop logically and smoothly without interruption or irrelevancy, in other words, that ornament and skyscraper façades should begin, proceed, and terminate harmoniously. Wright soon discovered—or learned from "Der Lieber Meister"—that natural forms also flowed, or were plastic. Cactus, he frequently noted, "employs cell to cell or continuous tubular or often plastic construction." Human skin sheathed functional workings in a free-flowing material. He reasoned that entire buildings could emanate from this principle. By organizing them horizontally with interpenetrating spaces, uninterrupted lines, extended vistas through and out, long glazed surfaces, and no posts in corner-windows, he achieved the spatial flow, the architectural continuity, and the aesthetic plasticity that make his structures seem to respond to human movement, to change and not to change at the same time.

"Instead of two things," he wrote precisely to this point, let us have "*one* thing. Let walls, ceilings, floors become part of each other, flowing into one another. . .eliminating any constructed feature." Plasticity or continuity meant that "materials are seen 'flowing or growing' into form instead of. . .built. . .out of cut and joined pieces." Plastic forms, he emphasized, are not composed, but "inasmuch as they are produced by a 'growing' process," they are *developed* and *encouraged*. The reality of this for Wright's buildings is that it is difficult to determine where and if one thing ends and another begins. Where exactly is the line between dining room and kitchen, between living room and hall, between inside and outside? The best answer is, wherever the individual wants it. When spaces interpenetrate, when living-room boards and batten continue into the kitchen as storage shelves or window seats move outside as flower planters, the entire structure and the life it expresses become integrated, achieve unity through continuity in natural and inconspicuous ways. Everything in Wright's buildings from hardware to site plan worked toward a consistency of purpose and feeling modeled on the natural world.

Louis Sullivan had also taught that "form follows function," that a building ought to appear appropriate for its purpose. In simple terms related to Sullivan's practice, he meant that contemporary office buildings should have sleek, forthright, soaring forms revealing the power and efficiency of modern corporations. But if function suggested form, there was plenty of room for interpretation, so Wright took his master one better by declaring that "form and function are one," that a building was what it did, implying that there could be only one form for any given function. This seemed to be the case in nature where, for example, the form of a tree—its leaves, branches, trunk, and roots—performed the functions by which it lived and grew. Likewise, a snail shell and a human hand looked the way they looked because of what they did: there could be no alternative. Airplanes, ocean liners, locomotives, automobiles, and the best industrial forms "are perfectly adapted to their function," Wright insisted, and "seem to have a superior beauty of their own." "All features in good building," he said, should "correspond to some necessity for being. . .found in their very purpose."[15] When function became form, structure would be completely unified and harmonious within itself despite the variety of factors calling it into being.

□ □ □

Wright resolutely claimed that all his buildings united form and function, that all expressed and sustained the internal nature of the social group or activity they served. In different ways he said that the Kalita Humphreys Theatre (1955–1956) in Dallas, the Beth Shalom Synagogue (1954) in Elkins Park, Pennsylvania, the Annunciation Greek Orthodox Church (1956) in Wauwatosa, Wisconsin, and the Mercedes-Benz Showroom (1955) in New York City, to mention only four, were ideas about the nature of stage production, Jewish and Greek worship, and automobile merchandising that, given all the relevant conditions of the commission, had found their *only* appropriate form. Another architect's solution, of course, would have been totally wrong. All this smacks of Wright's overdeveloped ego, but there were times when startling results made the theory plausible.

Of all the public buildings Wright designed, the Guggenheim Museum in New York may come closest to reaching the goals of organic architecture. The objective was to show an entire collection and at the same time the development of a painter or an art movement over time, in other words, to express continuity, change, and totality all at once. Conventional museums of fixed rectangular rooms and corridors were unsuited to sequential viewing or the unfolding of artistic maturation. Wright's solution was to twist a quarter-mile-long gallery around a central well into a spiral ramp of three percent grade down which viewers ambled after an elevator ride to the top. Thus it was possible to follow chronological development during a pleasant downhill stroll, to gain perspective on the entire collection by turning to the center, or to leave at midpoint without retracing steps. A huge skylight supplemented by window slits under the ramp provided unusually abundant natural light, while walls sloping away from the floor approximated the angle at which a canvas tilts when painted. With complex engineering he offered a deceptively simple solution to problems that had plagued museums for years.

The Guggenheim façade was a direct expression of its interior space, its spiral form being literally the outside of inside functions (Fig. 11.6). Wright arrived at this solution only after considerable experimenting. His plans for stacked, flat hexagons connected by downramps and for a spiral with the larger turns at the bottom would have made the

Figure 11.6 The Guggenheim Museum (1943–1957) in New York. Courtesy the Solomon R. Guggenheim Museum.

building squat, dull, and oppressively monolithic. But the cone shape with larger spirals at the top left ground space for small sculpture gardens, officials' parking, and an airy entryway, and was structurally quite sound. The skylight works better with larger floors nearer the roof. Entering the museum, viewers do not feel claustrophobic as the space opens overhead, while from the top they are not so inclined to vertigo as the building seems to close in below. Like a coiled spring, the ramp tends to support itself—stabilized by occasional piers—without interior posts, a boon for art lovers. Visitors find that its unusual construction has unexpected practical advantages.

A building so shaped was appropriate only on a flat site that did not compete aesthetically. Although the Guggenheim Museum might have been more visible across the street in Central Park, it would have met strong citizen resistance to encroachment on precious recreational land; but as it stands it can be seen from three sides, as well as from several blocks up and down Fifth Avenue. It added to and helped encourage the location of several museums in its neighborhood and in that sense is part of its immediate cultural environment, while its circular forms accentuate the high-rise setbacks for which the avenue is justifiably famous. Windows are unnecessary in a museum, but Wright provided plenty of natural light, and poured concrete was the only sensible material for such a large, curved surface. The second level that bulges at the southern end of the site to sweep across the front contains the Guggenheim's scattered permanent holdings, which do not require continuous or holistic treatment, while at the northern end the semidetached unit of secondary importance houses facilities for director and staff, bearing an architecturally subservient relationship to the gallery space similar to Unity House and Unity Temple at Oak Park. Given the circumstances, Wright's objectives, and his understanding of a museum's "internal" nature, he would have said there was no alternative for the Guggenheim in terms of form. If enclosed space was to be honestly expressed, the museum could look only the way it did.

The Guggenheim is among the most plastic of Wright's structures. There are no posts and beams, no rectangular rooms, just a few stabilizing columns around the perimeter, and no obvious terminal points, only continuity and rhythm. As the sun moves slowly across its façade, its subtly changing tones with its landscaping and deeply shadowed reveals give a surprisingly mellow texture. Inside, change is its very definition (Fig. 11.7). From every point, viewers are aware of the pervasive ebb and flow of activity, and as they follow the ramp their perspective constantly shifts. From outside the museum is a tone poem of evolving color and frozen change, while inside it is a preserve of human and architectural motion. Yet it is obviously an orderly, solid, and enduring structure. Here, in a single statement, a synthesis of many of his ideas, the architect combined the universal human respect for stability and strength with an equally insistent urge for change and variety. Every element of the Guggenheim has a compelling *raison d'être*, and its form and function are indeed one. Like Fallingwater, it successfully embodies the most important implications of organic architecture.[16]

□ □ □

Frank Lloyd Wright never offered a totally satisfying definition of this famous term, perhaps because he did not have the patience or see the necessity for it, or perhaps because it was such a personal and all-embracing concept. Yet an attempt to put it succinctly seems ap-

Figure 11.7 The Guggenheim Museum (1943–1957) in New York. Courtesy the Solomon R. Guggenheim Museum.

propriate. An organic structure is built according to nature's principles: harmonious in all its parts and with the environment, it expresses and unifies all the factors calling it into being—site, materials, client needs and architect's philosophy, construction methods, its culture, and the nature of the problem. An organic structure defines and prophecies life, grows along with those who use it, states an idea about a social reality, and, by including everything necessary and nothing unnecessary for its purpose, is as unified and economical as nature itself. *"A building can only be functional,"* Wright insisted emphatically, *"when integral with environment and so formed in the nature of materials according to purpose and method* as to be a living entity. . . ."[17] This statement warrants careful attention for it contains snatches of most of his basic ideas. "Organic architecture" is more easily described than defined, in the same way that Wright's buildings are better experienced than explained. What makes so many of them successful are the particulars and intangibles that combine in almost inexplicable ways to nurture human serenity and comfort. Wright's architecture is holistic, almost Zen-like, the outcome of working with "exterior" to express "interior" nature.

□ □ □

Wright justifiably if naively believed that the principles of organic architecture were applicable to personal and social life. Although he may have stretched his ideas too thinly when he tried to adapt them to politics and society, he consciously opposed the intellectual fragmentation that, with the principal exceptions of Hegel and Marx, has characterized modern Western thought. But if he was an idealist, he was also something of an existentialist: "Life is all that can really be trusted," he once said, and it therefore made good sense not to be overly concerned with the past and the future. There was a persistent current of presentism in his thinking. He had once praised Mamah Borthwick for "seiz[ing] the present," for living according to the moment's imperatives. "As far as we can see," he wrote, the future *is* the present, the "evermoving" point in time when tomorrow becomes today, so "it is for us to *act,* now. . . ." "Every day life is the important thing," he wrote his daughter Catherine Baxter in 1921, "not tomorrow or yesterday, but to-day. You won't reach anything better than the 'right-now' if you take it as you ought."[18]

And the best thing about life was the process of becoming. "Human affairs are themselves plastic in spite of. . .man's ill advised endeavors to make them static. . . ." "Does not all live to change?" Life was therefore incompatible with architecture that limited movement and preserved habitual living styles. Boxlike structures composed symmetrically, he contended, virtually dictated rigid patterns of furniture arrangement, room usage, and social life, thus denying the change and "becoming" that defined human existence. That was why organic architecture rejected "every building that would stand in military fashion, . . .something on the right hand and something on the left" in favor of "the reflex, the natural easy attitude, the occult symmetry of grace and rhythm. . . ." Since human life ought to be "a profession of freedom," he told an interviewer in 1953, "there should be free expression in building. The box was merely an inhibition and a restraint," "never intended to serve life [and] mainly an imposition upon it." Architecture would not be free to evolve organically with life itself until it abandoned dependence on the right angle. Then, he said, we will see "entirely new forms of living. . . ."[19]

Shortly before his death Wright asserted that "there is no square in nature—nature knows only circular forms." While not suggesting that all buildings should be without corners, he nevertheless tried to eliminate them whenever he could. During the prairie period he had seized upon the cruciform plan to break the confines of the box and later moved through "zoned," pavilioned, hexagonal, diagonal, and circular arrangements in unending pursuit of spatial freedom. As old age closed in, he may have subconsciously been drawn to symbols of eternity or self-perpetuation, but his use of overlapping or nonrectangular forms was more likely an attempt to escape the limitations that right angles and straight lines imposed on living styles and design possibilities. When we abolished the box, he said, we were "no longer tied to Greek space but were free to enter into the space of Einstein."[20]

Freer expression in design was "simply the human spirit given appropriate architectural form" in which layout, space, and room arrangements were shaped by, but did not themselves shape, the human preferences the architect had carefully ascertained. Every organic building, Wright constantly stressed, "is necessarily expression of the life it is built to serve directly," therefore "a humane and intensely human thing," potentially "the most human of all the expressions of human nature." In his 1901 Hull House speech he had defined architecture—"the principal writing—the universal writing of humanity"—as a people's major artistic and intellectural force. By the 1930s he broadened his definition to mean "life itself taking form."

Wright believed that architecture was life, but then went on to argue that *his* buildings, at least, could *improve* life, that they were psychologically therapeutic and morally uplifting, an extension of the "house beautiful" ideal he had embraced so eagerly in 1896 (see Chapter Two). He reported in 1939 that almost "all my clients have testified to the joy and satisfaction they get from their own particular building." They acquired "a certain dignity and pride in their environment; they see it has a meaning or purpose which they share as a family or feel as individuals." Not only does organic architecture "affect our conduct," he insisted, but it also had a "salutory effect morally." When people knew they were becomingly housed, they found themselves living "according to the higher demands of good society, and of [their] own conscience"; freed from uncertainity they grew rich in spirit. "When you are conscious that the house is right and honestly becoming to you, and feel you are living in it beautifully, you need no longer be concerned about it," Wright assured potential clients. "It is no tax upon your conduct, not a nag upon your self-respect, because it is featuring you as you would like to see yourself." And he was not speaking facetiously when he added that if organic architecture spread over the land, the national divorce rate would drop.[21]

That would be the day when everyone lived in Broadacre City, fulfilling their human natures in a united democratic society. It all seemed simple enough: if his teachings and buildings were universally accepted, America would be better off. But Wright contradicted himself when he explained how the new way of life would actually come into being. Sometimes he said that organic architecture would usher in organic culture: "an architecture upon which true American society will eventually be based. . . . An architecture upon and within which the common man is given freedom to realize his potentialities as an individual. . . ." At other times he argued precisely the opposite: "We cannot have organic architecture," he told a London audience in 1939, "unless we achieve an organic society!" "It is useless to free humanity by way of architecture. . .so long as humanity itself is inorganic." His uncertainty about whether organic architecture would preceed or follow organic culture, however, did not blunt his point that something was terribly wrong with the way Americans lived their individual and social lives. At the very least the principles of organic architecture were a relevant ideal for the nation since "a sense of valid structure in our culture is what we most lack." Wright believed that an entire society, like a building, should be structurally united.[22]

He liked to shock his audiences by saying that the United States was the only nation in history to pass "from barbarism to degeneracy never having known a civilization." Unguided by any national purpose, it copied its culture from others already decaying, leaving itself with "no sense of the whole, nothing of real integrity of concept or structure [with which to] grow its own way of life, and by ways of its own establish a culture belonging to itself. . . ." America's ancient goals had been lost sight of, its promise remaining unfulfilled; it was "losing, completely losing, that dignity and quality of character which was common to our forefathers—the dignity of the individual." Since America had no social or political "forms true to its own nature" which itself was undiscovered, it searched in vain for a commonality upon which to build. Without philosophical or social unity, America had nothing fundamental or valuable to offer its citizens or the world. If archeologists were to excavate the continent a thousand years from now, Wright half seriously told a college audience in 1932, they would find nondegradable bathroom fixtures but very little else, and from them conclude that Americans had been a sanitary lot but probably led empty lives.[23]

In the absence of organic culture, Americans had developed widely applauded but destructive characteristics. Indiscriminate pursuit of private wealth, for one thing, had turned America into a nation of economic "despots" and "wage-slaves," a result not a cause, as he saw it, of cultural disunity. Wright believed that as the most materialistic society since ancient Rome, the United States had reduced the sturdy yeomanry admired by the Founding Fathers into a "mobocracy," brainwashed by governmental bureaucracy and Big Business into thinking that quantity was better than quality, that accumulating goods was life's main objective. The country, he said, had become a "cash-and-carry" nation living by a "Broadway creed" of salesmanship and boosterism.

By worshipping accumulation, Americans placed entirely too much emphasis on ends rather than means. Asking "how" but not "why," they developed a blind and unreasoning love of science, the national substitute for art, religion, and philosophy. In an organic society, Wright claimed, science would be related to creativity as a paint box to an artist—as a tool for human enrichment. But without a social philosophy to adopt and adapt its discoveries, without a sense of the whole in which parts (like science) found meaning, science was socially destructive. Detonation of the first atomic bomb, Wright argued, revealed the fallacy of scientific inquiry without roots in organic social soil. "A ghastly revelation of the failure of our educational, economic and political systems," he lamented in 1947, it has thrown us "completely off our base, undoubtedly making all that we call progress obsolete overnight. Prone to our own destruction, we may be crucified on our own cross!. . . This push-button civilization over which we gloated has suddenly become nameless terror."[24]

Science is applied practically through technology. Always eager to exploit its architectural potential, Wright was nevertheless concerned about its social impact. In terms recalling novelist Frank Norris and others who feared technology's destructive impact on agrarian America, the architect had used his 1901 "Art and Craft of the Machine" speech to warn with mixed metaphor that "this greatest of machines, a great city," is a "monstrous leviathan" whose "fetid breath" reddens the sky. With lights for eyes, streets for veins and arteries, and communications for nervous and sensory systems, the city was like a living organism. At its very heart, industry sent energy to every "tissue and cell" of its "flesh." The city, "this monstrous thing," grew and functioned in "blind obedience to organic law," but whether as technology it would work for humanity's good or ill was unclear. In 1901 he had feared machinery but had also depended on it, and had, in fact, been one of the first to recognize its artistic potential. Thirty years later when he described the city as *"a mechanical conflict of machine resources,"* he seemed to think the industrial metropolis a triumph of evil.[25]

As a creature of technology, the city was inorganic. The reason for air, water, and noise pollution, crowding, crime, poverty, and corruption, the hectic pace, and all the other obvious problems, for "the poles and wires, tracks and sheds, stumpage and dumpage"—the "ugly scaffolding of a civilization" so evident in cities—the reason for all this, Wright thought, was that inorganic culture fostered greed. Cramped and confined by "the landlord's ruse," that is, by buildings jammed together on small lots to extort exorbitant rents, average citizens were denied their own birthright. "Instead of freely going in and out and comfortably round about among the beautiful things to which their lives are related in horizontal lines on top of this green earth," he commiserated, people were marched "six floors up, and up six floors again. And none may know just why they go, so narrowly up, up, to come narrowly down, down. . . ." Superconcentration would eventually destroy urban dwellers because "human motions of the city-inhabitant become daily more and more compact and violent" until the frenetic pace would finally culminate in a great interior collision, an implosion on a gigantic scale. By exploiting the individual's irrational fear of being alone and a misguided belief in the safety of the group, the real estate agent, the landlord, and the politician greedily perpetuated an inhumane arrangement. The epitome of all that was wrong with the city and with misapplied technology, Wright maintained, was the skyscraper, an infinitely reproducible box designed to "pig-pile" people on top of each other for profit, at the same time collectively creating architectural wastelands.

"The modern city," Wright once claimed with typical flamboyance, "is a place for banking and prostitution and very little else," a sort of Jeffersonian antiurban crack that seems more accurate as time passes. On another occasion he said that cities would soon be purely utilitarian, invaded three days a week at ten in the morning and abandoned at four in the afternoon by workers principally employed in financial institutions, commerce, and international trade. The metropolis might eventually become a museum of an abandoned civilization, because someday no one would want to work or be able to live there. This was simply in keeping with the imperatives of social evolution, for the very pursuit of safety and human intercourse that had once made the city desirable now made it obsolete. In an age of nuclear weapons and intercontinental delivery systems, of fast transportation and instantaneous communication, the city was no longer safe or necessary for commercial and social exchange. Salvation from nuclear attack, in fact, now lay in decentralization. Space was becoming more valuable than time, Wright insisted, but with land available only outside the city, urbanism was meaningless.[26]

Wright therefore urged small towns to remain small, to reject the boosterism that encouraged population growth and congestion. The wave of the future, he thought by the 1930s, was away from the city. He was pleased when his reading of the 1930 census showed people already leaving and predicted that by 1940 the trend would be obvious. He pointed to mass communications, highways, and the automobile as advance agents of decentralization, citing the gas station as an embryonic regional distribution center. But "of all the underlying forces working toward emancipation of the city dweller," he wrote in 1958, "most important is the gradual reawakening of the primitive instincts of the agrarian." Like the ancient nomad, future Americans would reject the urban cave for the freedom of the plains to make the natural life a real possibility.[27]

Materialism, misdirected science and technology, and overcentralization were indications of America's cultural insolvency, its lack of national purpose. If organic architecture could improve the quality of life, it followed for Wright that its principles could also benefit society as a whole. Americans would first of all need to discover themselves, to find their true collective nature, then embody it in design, political institutions, cultural forms, and other expressions of a way of life. Lacking an organic or socially unified structure, America wandered at cross-purposes, without goals, direction, or ideals. In order to develop an organic civilization, the country would need visionary statespeople, like Wisconsin's La Follettes or Adlai Stevenson, another Wright favorite, dedicated to democratic individualism. Wright was not enamored with American politicians, but eagerly seized every opportunity to design official buildings, sometimes without being asked, hoping to improve the quality of government by indicating proper relationships between leaders and citizenry.

Wright designed several government projects but built only one. Plans for a state capital and two major civic centers—for Arizona (1957); for Marin County, California (1957–1959); and especially for Madison, Wisconsin (1938), revised three times (1941, 1953, 1956) at an enormous investment of energy—reveal his views on the role of government in a democracy. Wright objected strenuously to traditional symbols of state architecture, particularly to the Renaissance dome which over time had come to represent official hegemony and tired political in-

stitutions, not only in European capitals but also in most local juris-
dictions in the United States, not to mention Washington, D.C. Like
the Pope's mitre, the dome denied citizen input and popular power
and was therefore completely undemocratic.[28] In his architecture
Wright consistently rejected authoritarian imagery as well as materials
such as marble or granite that had come to be associated with government power. But the most startling feature of his designs is how
little they resemble the usual state capitals and county court houses
and how strongly they emphasize citizen participation. He envisioned
the state not as a locus of official power but as the repository of
popular virtue and the coordinator of social harmony, in other words,
as the government of Broadacre City.

Even though the Monona Terrace project for Madison, Wisconsin,
grew more elaborate with each revision, its informing idea remained
the same. (This analysis is based on the final 1956 version.)[29] Approached along a two-block mall from the state capital, the street
level—the roof of the five-story edifice protruding from a bluff over
Lake Monona—was a seven-and-one-half-acre semicircular park with
fountains, gardens, walkways, and benches (Fig. 11.8). But viewed
from the lake below, Monona Terrace was an expanse of concrete and
glass rising out of the water. Wright emphasized its recreational aspects by drawing pleasure craft and excursioners on his numerous
perspectives. The railroad station, a city auditorium, art galleries, a
community center, and other facilities not requiring natural light or
lake views were buried deep inside. Although several municipal agencies—the courts, the jail, law enforcement offices, the mayor and the
council, and others—were given outside exposure, they were not
stated architecturally. Wright's several depictions clearly show that the
civic, not the governmental, aspects of the project were uppermost in
his thinking. First-time visitors happening on Monona Terrace from
downtown Madison would have thought they had discovered an attractive public garden, so well camouflaged were the government
facilities, while from the lake they would never suspect that the airy
glass and concrete semicircle also housed the punitive aspects of local
authority. There was nothing about the place to suggest that the state
coerced as well as served.

Like a doting father expressing his love, Wright drew and redrew
Monona Terrace many more times and from many more angles of
vision than were really necessary. One of these, an astrological "Plan
of Roof Garden,"[30] is a particularly important clue to his thinking. At
midpoint along the chord connecting the ends of the semicircle, that
is, at the most conspicuous point of entry from the street, Wright

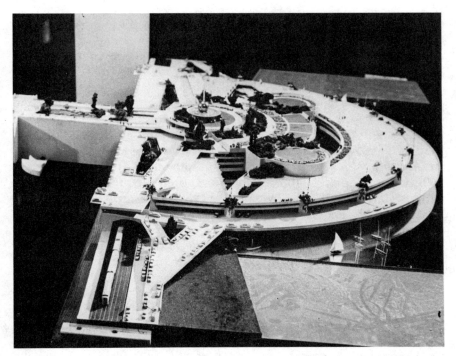

Figure 11.8 Model of the Monona Terrace project (ca. 1956) for Madison, Wisconsin. Photo by Clarence E. Olson, courtesy State Historical Society of Wisconsin.

placed a fountain labeled "earth" which, lighted at night and spraying into space, referred to the four fundamental elements of human life: air, water, fire, and land. Around the circumference next to the lake were twelve smaller fountains for each sign of the zodiac and halfway along the radii between earth and the perimeter at ten and two o'clock were fountains for the moon and sun. Unlike the fourteen stations of the cross which to supplicants denote the humanity of God, Wright's symbols from a pagan age paid tribute to the divinity of humankind. In his plan, the sun, the moon, and the constellations orbited the earth, which he placed at the center of the universe. Centuries before, the Copernican revolution had dealt a crippling metaphysical blow to humanity's ultimate supremacy, undermined even further by industrialization, the corporate economy, and the rise of the modern state. But at Monona Terrace, Wright insisted that people were indeed the measure of all things, that their earth gave meaning to the cosmos. And if people were supreme, of course the state was not.

Wright's "Oasis" plan for the Arizona Capital was captioned "pro bono public."[31] As the youngest state with some of the most beautiful terrain in the world, Arizona would be foolish to build the "already dated New York monstrosity" its politicians had approved. So the architect offered his own plan, a 400-foot-wide hexagonal crenelated canopy of copper-plated concrete ribbing and plastic fenestration supported at the perimeter by a colonnade of onyx duplex columns. The effect was a forest of trees filtering light into an open portico with fountains and plantings; into "Arizona Hall," the great central public space with provision for exhibitions, a kind of crossroads for the state; and into the senate and the house, in plan subdivisions of the great hall of the people. Chambers for the supreme court, the governor, and his staff were in a polliwoglike tail extending from the refectory, flanked at right angles by wings of administrative offices bent around garden and fountain courts like embracing arms. Radio and television transmitting towers rose from the senate and the house which projected through the canopy to accommodate public balconies.

Oasis was clearly intended to be for "the good of the people." Under the canopy the major space was devoted to popular refreshment in the form of gardens, fountains, cultural exhibitions, and dining, capped with radio and television towers for public information. This twentieth century agora (complete with colonnade) dominated and determined the location of representatives who in a republic take their mandate from the people. And like classical Greece, the executive and judicial functions of the state were secondary, finding architectural expression in Arizona as a supplement to the agora, while administrative facilities were clearly intended to service the main building and the people in it. In keeping with Wright's views of the proper nature of democracy, Oasis was a legislative building. "I can see why you, the citizens of Arizona, need to appoint certain men to arrange and look after your mundane affairs," the architect wrote in the text accompanying his design proposals, "just as you need police. But I am totally unable to see why those men should choose the buildings that will characterize your spirit." So he urged Arizonians to select a new capital from three offerings—including his, of course—in public referendum, thereby taking a first step toward instituting the kind of popular government Oasis prophesied in building form.

The Marin County Civic Center at San Rafael, California, embodied a similar philosophy.[32] On 140 hilly and woodsy acres north of San Francisco, Wright laid out a master plan including recreational services, an administration building and a hall of justice, an auditorium, convention and exhibition halls, fairgrounds, a post office, and several other facilities. The major structure—actually two connected buildings

identical in style—is the four-story Administration–Hall of Justice complex, linking hills at either end with a third at the juncture from which
the two branch out at an approximate 120-degree angle. Although the
Administration Building (Fig. 11.9) is 560 feet long and the Hall of
Justice, 850 feet, the fourth floor of the latter is level with the second
floor of the former, the greater height suggesting that service takes
priority over punishment in county government. The Administration
Building spans one roadway, the Hall of Justice, two, hence their
single and double archways leading to parking and other buildings.
The main entrance to the grounds directly serves both structures, but
the Administration Building dominates approach and defines the
premises.

Like Monona Terrace and Oasis, Marin County's symbols and relative importance of parts give clues to its political posture. The visual
and functional focal point of the entire 140-acre scheme is the juncture
of the Hall of Justice and the Administration Building where overhead
soars a 172-foot transmitting tower beneath which is a spacious outdoor terrace with pool, fountain, and garden. Just behind the terrace
where the two buildings actually merge is a shallow-domed circular

Figure 11.9 Marin County Civic Center Administration Building (1957–1959), San Rafael,
California. Photo by author.

library. It was hardly by accident that at the architectural culmination of the project (the first thing motorists see on arrival), Wright made provision for disseminating knowledge, for broadcasting information, and for employee (and public) relaxation. The power and authority of the state, in other words, take root in the wisdom and at the pleasure of the citizenry for whom, in this scheme, the dome houses books and the tower transmits music.

The buildings pay obvious tribute to the Spanish architectural heritage of the region and in shape closely approximate nearby ridges "growing," as Wright would have put it, from their cultural and topographical settings. Unlike most of his designs which terminate rather definitively, although long overhangs can be interpreted as continuations of structure into surroundings, this one flows into the land, seeming not to end at all. In the Administration Building a doorless top-level entrance opens directly onto a patio molded into the hillside (Fig. 11.10). Snuggling into their gentle valleys as bridges between the hills, these very long, low, ground-hugging structures clearly reject the vertical pomposity of traditional government architecture. Courtrooms, the jail, law agencies, sheriff's office, and other instruments of coercion are not articulated on the façade even of the Hall of Justice.

Figure 11.10   Marin County Civic Center Administration Building (1957–1959), San Rafael, California. Photo by author.

Exteriors are made rhythmic by series of arches shading balconies around the outside of the upper three stories, every department having direct access to and an unimpeded view of the outdoors. Inside, Wright strung the offices around central floor-to-roof wells in the manner of the Larkin and Johnson Buildings, but here they were not arranged hierarchically. All officials received the same architectural treatment, implying that none was more important than others. Like its Madison and Arizona counterparts, the Marin County Civic Center anticipated a more egalitarian state, provided stimulating and pleasing working conditions, emphasized the recreational and civic but not the authoritative aspects of government, and advocated citizen participation. By not endorsing official power, the Center anticipated its ultimate abolition.

Wright believed democracy to be the best kind of government, and the American variety potentially the best kind of democracy. When practiced correctly it was "the highest form of aristocracy that the world had ever seen—the aristocracy of the man, the individual. . . . ," a better and purer form of government than one based on lineage or wealth because it allowed people to rise by personal achievement. "Free growth of humane individuality," moreover, was perfectly consistent with social harmony, because in developing self-respect people learned to respect and tolerate others. Natural to true individualism, Wright believed, was the Jeffersonian ideal of government, being best when it governed least. In an organic society "*all* controls" would be corrective, not preventive: "government, therefore, may not institute or lead. . .only execute policy, correct or punish the individual," and only "those matters incapable of individuality—say police powers"—would be entrusted to it. By 1949 Wright was convinced that the Federal Government had become "an enormity." Responding only to the rich and powerful, it was rapidly approaching the "gangsterism" that he now believed characterized the Soviet Union. Already it took "a good one-fifth of [American] society," he complained, "to keep the other four-fifths. . .in order." Wright's was not the "rugged individualism" so highly touted by conservatives, but an individualism made possible by equitable land division and the end of monopoly capitalism. Nor when he criticized the state did he mean educational, welfare, and social services, but oppressive government controlled by developers, "pole- and-wire men," and "political slaves-of-the-Expedient," that is, powerful economic interests. He may have sounded like a conservative at times, but most conservatives found his views uncongenial.[33]

He believed that like organic architecture, cities and governments should be modeled after nature where everything took its proper place, nothing was superfluous, structure was absolutely harmonious, yet where each component asserted individuality, namely, self-expression within an all-encompassing unity. "Internal disorder is architectural disease, if not. . .death," Wright maintained, and so in the proper social state each citizen would enjoy "less government, yet more ordered freedom." Authentic democracy would mean the harmonious integration of truly independent people made possible by universal acceptance of common goals and values. The primary duty of statespeople and of artists was to discover the character—or nature—of a nation, and then fashion a state to preserve the heretofore polar opposites of complete individualism and group harmony. This was obviously an idealistic objective; but Wright, who usually spoke abstractly on social issues, was specific in his assertion that organic architecture could be its model. And he knew what he wanted: "the electric spark of popular curiosity and surprise to come to life again, along the highways and byways and over every acre of the land." Someday, "the salt and savor of individual wit, taste and character. . .will have come into its own and the countryside far and near will be a festival of life—great life."[34] Frank Lloyd Wright's organic philosophy can be faulted for lack of analytical precision, but not for its humanistic objectives.

NOTES

1   F. L. Wright, *Organic Architecture*, reprinted in *The Future of Architecture* (New York: Horizon Press, 1953), 245.

2   Santiago del Campo, "An Afternoon with Frank Lloyd Wright," *Americas*, 6 (April 1954), 11; preface to the 1952 brochure, *Meeting House of the First Unitarian Society of Madison, Wisconsin*.

3   F. L. Wright, *The Living City* (New York: Horizon Press, 1958), 113.

4   F. L. Wright, *The Natural House* (New York: Horizon Press, 1954), 155.

5   *The Natural House*, 139; second interview on "The Mike Wallace Show," Westinghouse Television, reprinted in *The Capital Times*, September 30, 1957.

6   F. L. Wright, *The Natural House*, 178; Reyner Banham, "Frank Lloyd Wright as Environmentalist," *Art and Architecture*, 83 (September 1966), 26–30; and *The Architecture of the Well-Tempered Environment* (Chicago: University of Chicago Press, 1969), 109. On climate control also see John Sergeant, *Frank Lloyd Wright's Usonian Houses: The Case for Organic Architecture* (New York: Watson-Guptill, 1976), Ch. 1 *passim*.

7 R. Banham, *Well-Tempered Environment*, 121. "The house is oriented south by southwest," Robert Llewelyn Wright, the architect's son, remarked about his own 1955 residence. "In the winter the living room and the three bedrooms upstairs are flooded with light. In the summer, because of the overhang, the sun doesn't come in at all. It certainly saves on both heating and air-conditioning." Sarah Booth Conroy, "Living in a Frank Lloyd Wright House," *The Washington Post*, June 2, 1974.

8 In addition to Frank Lloyd Wright, *The Japanese Print: An Interpretation* (Chicago: Ralph Fletcher Seymour Co., 1912), see "Nature," *Taliesin Square-Paper*, No. 9, August 1945; *Modern Architecture* reprinted in *The Future of Architecture*, 91; *An Autobiography* (New York: Duell, Sloan and Pearce, 1943 ed.), 89.

9 Frank Lloyd Wright, *Genius and the Mobocracy* (New York: Duell, Sloan and Pearce, 1949), 28.

10 F. L. Wright, *An Autobiography*, 148, 451; *The Natural House*, 167–168.

11 On interior space as architectural reality see F. L. Wright, *The Natural House*, 31, 220; *Modern Architecture* reprinted in *The Future of Architecture*, 125; "Conversation" in *ibid.*, 12–13; *A Testament* (New York: Horizon Press, 1957), 224; *An Autobiography*, 338–339.

12 On the creation of Unity Temple see F. L. Wright, *An Autobiography*, 153–160.

13 Raymond Williams, *Culture and Society, 1780–1950* (New York: Anchor Books, 1959), xiv.

14 F. L. Wright, *Two Lectures on Architecture*, reprinted in *The Future of Architecture*, 193; "Conversation" in *ibid.*, 12–13; "Recollections—The United States, 1893–1920," *The Architect's Journal* (London), 84 (July 18–August 6, 1936), reprinted in *The Natural House*, 24.

15 F. L. Wright, "Recollections" in *The Natural House*, 20; *An Autobiography*, 146–147; *Two Lectures on Architecture* reprinted in *The Future of Architecture*, 191; *Modern Architecture* reprinted in *ibid.*, 95, 128; *Genius and the Mobocracy*, 109.

16 The Guggenheim Museum has always been controversial. Critics argue that rectangular paintings ought not to be shown against walls that slope backward from the floor and down from left to right. They complain that the ramp hurries patrons along faster than they want to go, that it tires leg muscles, that the lighting is too harsh, that the building is too small, and that viewers cannot get enough distance on larger work for proper perspective. The guard wall for the center well, critics allege, is too low, creating the feeling of danger, thereby forcing people even closer to the paintings. The notion also persists that the Guggenheim is actually Wright's mammoth practical joke on New York and modern art, both of which he is said to have hated.

I find most of these arguments rather specious. It is true that large works are handicapped, but not if the 32-foot-deep top spiral were open

more often. Then the museum could handle *Guernica* or *Water Lillies*
even though it was never intended to compete with the Museum of
Modern Art, only to accommodate relatively small unified exhibits. As for
lighting, it is true the staff supplanted Wright's translucent louvers that
coil under the ramps with artificial lights, but the fact remains that even
if natural light is insufficient for overcast days it is still more generous
than in most museums. Proper viewing distance seems to me a matter of
taste, but in the Guggenheim one can achieve a certain intimacy with the
art, an intimacy enhanced by stabilizing dividers periodically interrupting
the downward slope.

The other criticisms seem to be matters of personal whim, misinfor-
mation, or pettiness. While I would not claim the Guggenheim is flaw-
less—members of the staff complain that the slope and dividers make
hanging a show difficult, although they report that viewers like those
features—I find it after many visits to be a continually fresh and exciting
experience. As interior spaces many museums can be taken for granted,
indeed, forgotten entirely, but in the Guggenheim art lovers get two
shows for the price of one. See the excellent appraisal by John V. Conti,
"The Gallery: Art of Architecture," *Wall Street Journal*, May 7, 1969. For
a completely different assessment see Peter Blake, *Frank Lloyd Wright:
Architecture and Space* (Baltimore: Penguin Books, 1964), 117–122.

17   F. L. Wright, *Genius and the Mobocracy*, 109.
18   F. L. Wright, *Organic Architecture,* reprinted in *The Future of Architecture,*
248–249; "To My Neighbors," *The Weekly Home News*, August 20, 1914;
Wright to Catherine and Kenneth Baxter, February 7, 1921, FLW Collection, Avery Library, Columbia University.
19   F. L. Wright, *An Autobiography*, 366; "Louis H. Sullivan—His Work," *The
Architectural Record*, 56 (July 1924), 30; *Organic Architecture* reprinted in
The Future of Architecture, 225–226, 234; "Frank Lloyd Wright Talks on
His Art," *The New York Times Magazine*, October 4, 1953; *The Living
City*, 138
20   *The Capital Times*, January 1, 1959; F. L. Wright, "Recollections" in *The
Natural House*, 21.
21   F. L. Wright, *The Natural House*, 135–136; *The Living City*, 25–26, 102–104;
Organic Architecture reprinted in *The Future of Architecture*, 225, 288;
The Capital Times, November 2, 1951.
One Wright client described in detailed and moving terms how living
in her 1954 house contributed to her separation from her husband: Rosalie
Robbins Tonkens, "Having a Home Built by Frank Lloyd Wright Changed
Couple's Life," *The New York Times*, February 6, 1972.
22   F. L. Wright, *The Natural House*, 187; *Organic Architecture* reprinted in
The Future of Architecture, 230, 264; *The Taliesin Fellowship* (Spring
Green: Frank Lloyd Wright, 1933); *An Autobiography*, 338.
23   F. L. Wright, *An Autobiography*, 332; *Organic Architecture* reprinted in
The Future of Architecture, 225; *The New York Times*, January 10, 1958;

The Living City, 203; *Modern Architecture* reprinted in *The Future of Architecture,* 127; *The Providence* (R.I.) *Journal,* November 12, 1932.

24 On materialism and science see F. L. Wright, *Two Lectures on Architecture* reprinted in *The Future of Architecture,* 186; *An Autobiography,* 380, 460; *The Living City,* 31–37, 39; "The Architect" in Robert B. Heywood, Ed., *The Works of the Mind* (Chicago: University of Chicago Press, 1947); "Mr. Big," *The Capital Times,* July 18, 1952; Address to the "Planning Man's Physical Environment" Conference at Princeton University in *ibid.,* August 17, 1947.

25 F. L. Wright, "The Art and Craft of the Machine" in Kaufman and Raeburn, Eds., *Frank Lloyd Wright: Writings and Buildings* (Cleveland: World Publishing Co., 1960), 72–73; *Modern Architecture* reprinted in *The Future of Architecture,* 157.

26 For Wright's comments on the city see *An Autobiography,* 325; *Modern Architecture* reprinted in *The Future of Architecture,* 148–182, especially 156, 175; *The Natural House,* 141; *The Living City,* 21–22, 49–50, 60–67; and speeches reported in *The Capital Times,* June 8, 1938; *The New York Times,* November 11, 1940, and November 27, 1956; *The Washington Post,* October 3, 1958.

27 For a speech by Wright urging a small town to stay that way see *The Reedsburg* (Wis.) *Times-Press,* September 24, 1953; also *The New York Times,* November 14, 1931; November 11, 1940; *The Capital Times,* August 17, 1947; *Architectural Forum,* 55 (October 1931), 409; *The Natural House,* 140; *The Living City,* 62; *An Autobiography,* 328–329; *Modern Architecture* reprinted in *The Future of Architecture,* 176–177.

28 F. L. Wright, *Modern Architecture* reprinted in *The Future of Architecture,* 148–149.

29 Published in *The Capital Times,* August 29–31, September 5, 6, 1956.

30 Published as the dust jacket and inside front and back covers of Frank Lloyd Wright, *Architecture: Man in Possession of His Earth* (New York: Doubleday and Co., 1962).

31 "Oasis: Plan for Arizona State Capital Submitted by Frank Lloyd Wright Architect February 17, 1957," a brochure published from Taliesin.

32 The best sources of information are two quite different booklets entitled "Marin County Civic Center," published during the 1960s by the county, and "First Phase of Marin County Center is Completed," *The Architectural Record,* 132 (November 1962), 12.

33 F. L. Wright, *An Autobiography,* 325; *The Living City,* 34–35, 45, 152; *Genius and the Mobocracy,* 65–66, 89; "When Free Men Fear," *The Nation,* 162 (June 2, 1951), 527–528; *The Capital Times,* August 4, 1940; May 11, 1948; September 30, 1957.

34 F. L. Wright, *Two Lectures on Architecture* reprinted in *The Future of Architecture,* 203; *Modern Architecture* in *ibid.,* 178–179.

1946–1959

CHAPTER TWELVE

The Boldest Buildings of His Career

L ike fireworks making their exit in a blaze of glory, Frank Lloyd Wright's performance grew more dazzling as death approached. He designed more buildings than ever, nearly 350 during his last fourteen years, an almost unbelievable output for a man in his eighties. From his unprecedented average of twenty-five annual commissions he executed about ten a year for a total of almost 150 between 1946 and 1959. Among them were some of his grandest residences and an assortment of public structures spectacular enough to amaze admirers and confound his critics. "How do you do it? How do you think of it all?" his sister Maginel Wright Barney asked him near the end. "I can't get it out fast enough," he said.[1]

Many of his buildings were wonderful to behold, each seemingly more amazing than the one before, as if Wright, knowing the end was in sight, seized every opportunity to memorialize himself in brick and mortar. Although a large proportion of his commissions was public buildings—thirty percent from 1952 to 1958 compared to twenty percent overall—and although he built no single dwelling to match the Robie House or Fallingwater, he was still primarily a residential architect. None of his new homes was more luxurious than the Harold C. Price House (1956) in Phoenix, which sold in 1964 for $500,000, and only a few surpassed the Charles F. Glore House (1955) in Lake Forest,

Illinois, on the market the same year for $125,000,[2] although some unexecuted designs were equally elegant. Many were larger and more expensive than Usonian homes, still the principal model for his residential work, because by the 1950s Wright attracted many clients expecting to enhance their reputations by association with him.

But with a kind of compulsiveness he periodically tried his hand at low-cost housing. He had repeatedly said he "would rather solve the small house problem than build anything else I can think of," because it "is not only America's major architectural problem but the problem most difficult for her major architects."[3] In December 1951, he announced that within a year he would be able to build a $5000–$6000 residence better than anything on the market for twice the price. Using nonunion labor and partial prefabrication, he would pour "a few teakettles of grout" over a stack of concrete blocks tied together by steel rods, and presto!—instant beauty. The first "Usonian Automatic" for Benjamin Adelman (1953) near Phoenix had plain hollow blocks, lighter and less expensive than the decorative textile blocks of the 1920s. Construction was simple and comparatively cheap, but unless relieved by trim or plantings the Automatic was rather stark and mechanical, not unlike Bauhaus work on the exterior. Wright was as unrealistic about price as he was in blaming unions for inflated construction costs, for the Adelman residence came in at $25,000, four to five times higher than he had hoped in 1951. Subsequent Automatics were even more expensive if more attractive (Fig. 12.1); and although the hollow block system held potential for self-builders and cost reduction, it was beyond the reach of most of the middle class.[4]

So was the 1700-square-foot exhibition house with Wright's suggestions for "the average American who builds or buys a home." Erected under the supervision of David Henken from the Pleasantville, New York, Usonia, and assembled by a team of Taliesin apprentices, it was linked to a pavilion containing "Sixty Years of Living Architecture: The Work of Frank Lloyd Wright" on the site of the future Guggenheim Museum. Thousands of visitors filed through this "in-line" Usonian after it opened in November 1953 to see the twelve-foot-high, twenty-six-by-thirty-two-foot living–dining area with two bedrooms and other familiar Wrightian features. It probably was "within the reach of many," as the souvenir brochure asserted; but Wright, noting that the 1938 $15,000 price tag for a Usonian was now $35,000, lamented that "times have changed." The model home was the first introduction to the architect's work for most New Yorkers, but it did not seem to stimulate commissions from the area. Considering its amenities, it was a bargain at $35,000, but too expensive to qualify as a low-cost house.[5]

Figure 12.1 Kitchen area of Usonian Automatic (1957) for Toufic H. Kalil, Manchester, New Hampshire. Photo by author.

The same was true of his prefabricated designs. In conjunction with Marshall Erdman Associates, a Madison, Wisconsin, building firm, Wright designed four types of model homes in 1956 and 1957, two of which were built. During the summer of 1956 he produced Pre-Fab Number One (Fig. 12.2) and by October was supervising its construction in Madison. Its 2000 square feet contained three bedrooms at one end of a ninety-six-foot rectangle separated by a squarish sunken dining–living area from a kitchen–utility stack at the other. The slab foundation, extending four inches beyond the house to keep water from the footings, supported two-by-ten joists under a one-inch plywood subfloor over which was laid a hard rubber surface scored to resemble glossy red tile. Walls were framed with two-by-fours and faced inside with four-by-eight sheets of mahogany plywood lined with horizontal battens on sixteen-inch centers. The exterior finish was textured Masonite, battens, and eight-by-eight-by-sixteen standard insulating masonry blocks at the kitchen end, the location of a fireplace, two baths, and a port for two cars.

Pre-Fab Number Two (Fig. 12.3) was first erected in Madison during the fall of 1957 also with three bedrooms, two on a second-level deck projecting into the two-story living area, one sunken slightly below the first floor. The square structure with carport and terrace appended

Figure 12.2 Pre-fab Number One (1956), Madison, Wisconsin. Photo by author.

was built from the same materials as Pre-Fab Number One, although Wright at one point envisioned it entirely in concrete block. Early in 1958 he said he hoped to find at least one client in each state to demonstrate the superiority of these designs; he had already built nine, he said, with ten more awaiting site approval. But *The New York Times* had reported in 1956 that the $30,000–$50,000 price tag for the first pre-fab made it "considerably higher than most standardized

Figure 12.3 Pre-fab Number Two (1957), Madison, Wisconsin. Photo by author.

homes on today's market," and a year later Erdman Associates advertised both models for $40,000–$55,000 depending on shipping distance
and local construction costs.[6] Noting that Wright had "dignified prefabricated housing," Erdman did not add that he was also forced to
price it beyond the reach of those who needed it most. Less expensive
than his custom-built residences, the model homes were purchased
by frustrated Wright lovers who could not otherwise afford him. The
architect himself admitted they were a boon for "upper middle income
groups, [but] not for low cost housing."[7]

Apparently unwilling to admit that working people would never be
able to afford him, he stood before a model of one of his $50,000 pre-
fabs at the Chicago Athletic Club in January 1958 to tell the press that
he could produce a three-bedroom home with a dignified living room
and modern equipment for $15,000. Obviously he wanted to, but he
never managed it. By helping to make prefabrication acceptable to the
upper middle class and to the construction industry serving it, he
damaged the prospects for good lower class housing. Nor did he
recognize that even the middle class found it increasingly difficult to
hire him, that whatever he did to help the less advantaged would be
appropriated for the more affluent. So he kept trying. Another suggestion for cheap housing was certainly provocative and well below
the $15,000 figure but stood little chance of popular dissemination.
For the "Showcase for Better Living" International Home Exposition
at New York's Coliseum in 1957, Wright designed a portable, inflatable
"Air House" of vinyl-coated nylon made by the United States Rubber
Company. Its two units were a thirty-eight-foot-diameter by nineteen-
foot-high living–dining–kitchen space and a twenty-four-by-twelve-
foot bedroom, both supported by a low-pressure heating and air-
conditioning blower. Anchored to the ground by 1750 pounds of sand
in fifteen-inch tubes around the perimeter, the structure could withstand strong winds, a heavy snow load, and someone walking on the
roof. United States Rubber said that air-supported warehouses were
already in use and that Wright's model was intended as a demonstration, not as a substitute for conventional housing. A company in
Lexington, Kentucky, was nevertheless ready to sell comparable
models for $2245, plus $75 for the blower and $100 for the front door.
Weighing 200 pounds (without sand) and capable of storage in a three-
by-five-foot package, the Air House would have been perfect for apprentices living in the Arizona desert.[8]

No one bought a Wright Air House, and only a handful of relatively
well-to-do could afford pre-fabs; but Wright continued to reach out,
to affect or connect with as many people as possible. Always the

missionary for social improvement through design, knowing in his eighties that his time was growing short, he seized every opportunity to broaden his influence. Cynics contended that his lust for fame and glory was insatiable, sympathetic onlookers said that he wanted only to spread his contributions among the people. Perhaps it was a little of both, but there was no doubt during the 1950s that he worked frenetically, hoping to awaken the nation to the benefits of organic architecture, indeed, of the organic way of life. As the decade passed, he increased his attempts at public education, not only by speaking and writing more often, but also by entering a field he had always ridiculed: interior decoration. Convinced of the validity of a new marketing venture late in 1953 by René Carrillo, design director at F. Schumacher & Company, Wright lent his name to lines of fabrics, wallpapers, carpets, and furniture (Fig. 12.4) in October 1955. The "foe of the mass produced," *The Architectural Record* commented, began to mass produce on a lavish scale.

Figure 12.4 Furniture, carpet, and drapery ensemble (1955). Courtesy Henredon Furniture Industries, Morganton, North Carolina.

Designed by Carrillo with Wright's approval, the Taliesin Collection included six printed and seven woven fabrics at $3.40 to $13.50 a yard for upholstery, drapes, and hangings, plus four styles of wallpaper at $5.95 to $7.45 a roll. The Karastan Rug Company produced a companion carpet line, while Virginia Conner Dick, a member of the American Institute of Design, developed furniture mainly in Honduras figured mahogany solids and veneers for the Heritage Henredon Company. Even though Wright admitted having been "black and blue in some spot. . .almost all my life from too intimate contact with my own early furniture,"[9] even though he had always taught that architectural milieu should determine accessory design, and even though he had consistently opposed wallpaper and referred to interior decorators as "inferior desecrators," he enthusiastically endorsed the ventures. Among the rectilinear furniture pieces, the tables and bedframes were quite handsome if heavily trimmed, although chairs were not particularly comfortable. The carpets, fabrics, and wallpapers were especially vivid, with geometrical shapes and abstract patterns strong enough to overpower everything else in their settings. A reporter for *The New York Times* found the ensemble "not too unconventional," explaining perhaps why the National Republican Club chose it for its headquarters. Henredon manufactured one million dollars' worth of furniture in 1955 and 1956 that sold quite well but due to high development and promotional costs was "barely profitable," a spokesperson wrote. This and the violation of some of his most fundamental principles did not seem to bother Wright, who had apparently convinced himself he could spread the gospel of organic architecture through interior design.

But wallpaper and end tables were only sidelines, for as always Wright's major business after World War Two was private homes. From 1946 to 1959 he designed almost 270, or an average of over nineteen a year, of which he built 120, more than eight annually. In 1948 he received thirty residential commissions, over twice as many as the heyday of the prairie or Usonian periods, and in 1950 he executed twenty-one of thirty-eight for a career high. Few if any other architects have ever been so prolific. He built fourteen houses in 1954, and in 1957 as he passed his ninetieth birthday he designed another twenty-seven in his third busiest residential year (with 1950 the busiest—forty commissions, counting nonresidential work). From 1946 through 1950 he produced 120 dwellings, another eighty-two from 1951 to 1955, and a final sixty-five between 1956 and 1959. [10]

This means that with the exception of 1953, Wright worked on at least one and as many as three homes a month from 1946 to 1959. With his burgeoning nonresidential practice (see below), endless speaking and writing commitments, a rather full social life, and other demands on his time, it seems physically impossible to have done so much. Actually, his pace was not as hectic as it looked, for toward the end of his career there were several factors easing his work load. First of all, his innovative days as a residential architect were over. After the war he did not design new houses so much as redesign old ones according to the social philosphy and construction techniques of the Usonian period. He changed plans, programs, and materials, varied size and room shapes, switched geometrical grids, played with trim and details, and put in new devices and equipment to make each dwelling different. But all were fundamentally related members of one family and, more important, they were all variations on a now familiar architectural theme developed in the 1930s.

Wright encouraged his clients to provide him with detailed site photographs if he could not inspect in person. He invited them to Taliesin, often for a stay of several days, interviewing them at length about their families, living styles, hobbies, tastes and preferences, needs and desires, in short, getting to know them as well as he could. During these sessions and in subsequent business relationships (sometimes developing into close friendships) he was perfectly willing, indeed eager to incorporate their suggestions into his designs. Although the notion persists that Wright browbeat his clients into accepting features they did not want, it is more accurate to say that they came to him because they knew in a general way what they would get, but that he was open and receptive to their specific ideas and opinions. Getting to know clients and sites resulted in homes tailored to individual situations but homes of a definite and carefully worked-out type that by 1956 was twenty years old, even if it was, as architect Philip Johnson said, ten years ahead of all its imitators. [11]

The general run of Wright's late residential work was in this sense built from a formula, which is not to say that it was undesirable, for the formula was proven and humane. But since he could apply it to any situation, he did not attend to each house as closely as he used to. His sight, furthermore, began to fail by the mid-fifties, making it difficult to labor at length over the draughting table. So Wright would sit with John Howe, son-in-law William Wesley Peters, a Taliesin Fellow since 1932, or with other experienced staff members, visualize the design in relation to site photos, carefully explain its appearance, then supervise their sketches until they got it right. With the basic conception fixed, Peters or someone else would complete presentation drawings subject to Wright's approval. If the client accepted the plan, Peters and Howe would divide design development among a number of apprentices. At the presentation itself, Wright might dramatically unroll the drawings (signed by him), on occasion hastily adding a tree or penciling in an extra piece of equipment, leading some clients to think that the great man was interested enough in their project to add last-minute improvements right before their very eyes. A little PR among friends never hurt, especially when it was so thrilling.[12]

One scholar has attempted to classify Wright's late homes according to grid systems, but it is still unclear how many were built for which socioeconomic classes. Another has written that "before 1910 it took intelligence to employ Wright, but after 1935 it took only money,"[13] a statement wrong on several counts, not only because it completely dismisses the Usonians, but also because it implies that all the late residences are somehow suspect. Measured by the amount of creative thought invested in each project, they were lesser buildings; but in terms of quality and livability, they were not. After a decade and a half of struggle to perfect a new residential type early in his career, Wright had abandoned the prairie house, beginning a quarter-century search for an adequate replacement. But in the 1950s, after two decades of Usonian and post-Usonian homes, he was unable and unwilling to try something new, in part because he was arrogant enough to think he could not improve upon his accomplishment in any fundamental way, and in part because of age: in his eighties he was simply too old to rethink the single-family residence again for yet a third time. Nor did social conditions demand such an effort. Content to rest on his laurels, to turn out house after excellent house, he produced dozens of dwellings that remain exceptionally desirable.

Still, there were times when dramatic sites, large budgets, or prominent clients stimulated spectacular or especially elegant results or when Wright was inspired to design memorable smaller homes, many of which were reported in newspapers and professional and home-making magazines. *The New York Times* covered several commissions in and out of its region, *House and Home* ran a number of articles during the 1950s, *House Beautiful* devoted an entire issue to Wright in November 1955, *Architectural Forum* featured him regularly, particularly after its special issue in January 1951, and other publications gave him plenty of space. From these and additional sources the public learned about delightful modest dwellings like the exquisite 1946 Melwyn M. Smith House (Fig. 12.5), immaculately executed in Bloomfield Hills, Michigan; the magnificently landscaped, brilliantly detailed Isadore Zimmerman residence (1950), stretching across a subtly depressed site in Manchester, New Hampshire; the semicircular Kenneth Laurent House (1951), nestling into a gentle slope at Rockford, Illinois (Fig. 12.6); the fieldstone home (1952) for Mrs. Clinton Walker, cutting like a prow at high tide into the Pacific Ocean at Carmel, California (Fig. 12.7); the hilltop Quentin Blair residence (1953) with its majestic glass-enclosed living room and building stones from mountains surrounding Cody, Wyoming; the gleaming white-roofed Archie Teeter House (1955) rising like a bird from its plateau near Bliss, Idaho; or the startlingly shadowed, deeply revealed, rectilinear composition (1958–1959) for Robert Sunday in Marshalltown, Iowa (Fig. 12.8).

On the other hand were a number of more luxurious or daring residences. *House and Home* praised the "magnificent coil of. . .concrete block" (1952) for the architect's son David Lloyd near Scottsdale, Arizona, predicting that it would probably be argued over and talked about as no other Wright house since Fallingwater.[14] The multilevel, hexagonal module, brick, wood, and glass home (1956) for

Figure 12.5 Melwyn M. Smith House (1946), Bloomfield Hills, Michigan. Photo by author.

Figure 12.6   Kenneth Laurent House (1951), Rockford, Illinois. Photo by author.

Figure 12.7   Mrs. Clinton Walker House (1952), Carmel, California. Photo by author.

346

Figure 12.8 Robert Sunday House (1958), Marshalltown, Iowa. Photo by author.

Johnson Wax Company executive William Keland in Racine, Wisconsin (Fig. 12.9), was challenged in elegance by the striking 1955 cathedral-roofed structure (Fig. 12.10) for businessman Charles Glore in Lake Forest, Illinois; by the sumptuous brick house (1956) for Oklahoma oilman Harold C. Price, Jr., in Bartlesville; and possibly by the field-stone residence (1954) for Mercedes-Benz distributor Maximilian Hoffman in Rye, New York; but was surpassed by the magnificent concrete block mansion (1956) for Harold C. Price, Sr., in the architect's own Paradise Valley near Phoenix. Although Wright was not the servant of the ruling class—in the sense that Society architect Richard Morris Hunt, the firm of McKim, Meade, and White, or most prominent contemporary architects were and are—endorsing its hegemony and working almost exclusively for its interests, his later dwellings were generally more expensive than Usonians, built for a class of people similar to prairie house clients.

Additional unbuilt residences were for one reason or another especially noteworthy. The 1946 plan for V. C. Morris in San Francisco (for whom he designed a 1948 gift shop discussed below) featured a circular living room cantilevered from concrete retaining walls soaring high above the Pacific Ocean. Supported by a conical, cliff-clinging column shaped like the handle on the Statue of Liberty's torch (making

Figure 12.9 William H. Keland House (1956), Racine, Wisconsin. Photo by author.

Figure 12.10 Charles F. Glore House (1955), Lake Forest, Illinois. Photo by author.

perhaps a comparable symbolic gesture), it was one of Wright's most spectacular conceptions.[15] His plan the same year for Gerald M. Loeb in Redding, Connecticut, an elaboration of the 1938 Ralph Jester project (see Chapter Nine), generated a great deal of discussion, as did his 1947 plan from the same scheme for millionaire Huntington Hartford in the Hollywood Hills, his massive five-story studio home (1947) for novelist–philosopher Ayn Rand in Los Angeles, and his 1957 proposal for playright Arthur Miller and actress Marilyn Monroe near Roxbury, Connecticut.[16] These and others were breath-taking *tours-de-force* made possible by large budgets, some receiving considerable notoriety, others going unnoticed except locally. Many were fresh and innovative, not in social or design philosophy so much as in manner of expression. To anyone knowing architecture there was no mistaking a Frank Lloyd Wright house.

□ □ □

Nor could one ignore his postwar public buildings, of which there were many. During the fifteen years from 1901 to 1915 some thirty-two percent of his commissions and thirty percent of his executions had been nonresidential, dropping to twenty-one and fourteen percent, respectively, in the 1936 to 1941 Usonian period. In the fifteen years from 1945 to 1959, those percentages rose to twenty-three and fifteen, but in the seven years from 1952 to 1958, thirty percent of his commissions and twenty percent of his executions were nondomestic. Although he did not see to completion as many public structures either proportionately on in absolute numbers in his late years as he had in the prairie period, many were especially provocative.

Prior to World War One, his nonresidential work had been closely enough related in grammar and style to his houses to make many of the two visually quite similar, partly because he had intentionally developed an architectural language applicable to many building situations (see Chapter Four). But during the 1950s they were less of a piece. Not only was his public work generally larger in scale and cost, but it was often faced with materials, such as poured concrete, plastics, copper, and colorful trim, he did not ordinarily use and few people expected on dwellings. Nor did his nonresidences as easily lend themselves to imagistic and philosophical references to family life as they had during the prairie years and in the Johnson Wax Building. Although there are similarities between homes for his sons Llewelyn (1955) in Bethesda, Maryland, and David (1952) near Scottsdale, Arizona, on the one hand and the spiral ramps of the Guggenheim

Museum (1943–1957) and the Morris Gift Shop (1948) in San Francisco on the other, or between small buildings such as the Karl Kundert Clinic (1955) in San Luis Obispo, California, and any number of his late houses, resemblances are comparatively infrequent, superficial, co-incidental, or the result of his end-of-career attraction to circles (see below). No longer claiming that a particular mode of expression—the prairie style—was suitable for most architectural problems, Wright now insisted that each building problem called up a particular mode of (organic) expression. All his public structures bore his obvious stylistic stamp, but in the late years they did not so closely resemble each other or his homes in appearance and philosophy as they had before World War One.

Many of his nonresidential designs were magnificent, directly expressing their purpose in clean lines and powerful forms. Among these were the Guggenheim Museum, the Kalita Humphreys Theatre (1955–1956) in Dallas, the Morris Shop, the Unitarian Meeting House (1947) in Madison, the Beth Shalom Synagogue (1954) near Philadelphia, and the Harold C. Price Tower (1952) in Bartlesville, Oklahoma. But despite strong personalities, unique appearances, and functional successes, another group was aesthetically questionable, for example, the Annunciation Greek Orthodox Church (1956) at Wauwatosa, Wisconsin; the Corbin Education Center (1958) at Wichita State University; the Grady Gammage Auditorium (1958–1959) at Arizona State University in Tempe; and the plan and cultural edifices for greater Baghdad (1957–1958). All the public structures were dazzling, daring, or different but not necessarily well conceived.

Several factors contributed to these lapses in and after 1956. First of all, in his eighties Wright succumbed to a kind of "grandomania"— his word—an inclination to build startling, improbable, and flamboyant monuments to himself that no one could ignore, leading in some cases to a notable lack of restraint. Secondly, as his eyesight failed and his energy span shortened, he leaned more heavily on his staff, which in all likelihood was not inclined to criticize the Master. As its influence waxed, design quality waned. A third factor was the emergence of a public building formula. As long as Wright treated each project as a unique problem to be thought through to its own conclusion, the results were outstanding. But around 1956 he began to rely on a circular format in plan and detail not necessarily dictated by the nature of the commission. This may have been stimulated by a subconscious attraction in old age to symbols of infinity, but under the influence of Peters and the staff, the formula became a mannerism applied axiomatically, whether the situation warranted it or not.

As his later independent work shows (see Chapter Fourteen), Peters was particularly taken with circular motifs. Probably because he preferred not to contradict Wright, no one held in check the circles, semicircles, arches, and partial circles that began to proliferate as windows, perforated roof overhangs, colonnades, trim, accessories, ramps, and, as the plan itself, oozing from, dripping over, saturating, and smothering the work. What Wright had once selectively used for certain buildings and details became by 1956 the organizing principle or at least the major feature of a great many designs. Several of Wright's last buildings, moreover, were either on the drawing boards or under construction when he died. Left in charge of completion and execution, Taliesin Associated Architects (TAA, William Wesley Peters Chief Architect), as the staff called itself, made changes as a matter of course that without Wright's flagging sense of restraint were even gaudier and fussier than he might otherwise have permitted. Either because he depended on the Fellows in his last three or four years or because TAA modified designs later, several that are—but should not be—attributed entirely to Wright now compromise his reputation.

It is therefore necessary to sort out what he completed from what he did not, as well as to appraise his late nonresidential efforts. His most famous postwar structure is undoubtedly New York's Guggenheim Museum (see Chapter Eleven and Figs. 11.6 and 11.7) which *Architectural Forum* called "the boldest building of his career."[17] First conceived in 1943, its construction was postponed fourteen years by design changes, objections from municipal authorities, World War Two, the death of Solomon R. Guggenheim in 1949, the slow process of acquiring real estate along Fifth Avenue between 88th and 89th Streets which took until 1951, and by the long wait for leases to expire before demolition began in 1956. When plans were filed in 1952, the Department of Housing and Buildings, deciding a number of codes would be violated, referred the Guggenheim Foundation to the Board of Standards and Appeals, beginning a protracted four-year struggle in which bureaucrats contended that the Museum's six-foot overhang of the sidewalk necessitated a zoning variance they could not grant, that there were too few exits, and that the glass doors and dome were fire hazards. When they scratched heads uncomprehendingly over the whole conception—which after all was quite remarkable—Wright responded with sarcasm, so it was not entirely clear if their reservations represented actual code violations or pique at his arrogance. The architect had a valid point, namely, that bureaucracy was afraid of innovation, but he damaged his own cause with his lack of tact at frequent press conferences.

He was equally insensitive to the twenty-one artists, including Robert Motherwell and Willem de Kooning, who claimed that since paintings could not be properly shown on sloping surfaces the Guggenheim would do them an injustice. Perhaps fearing spectacular surroundings would detract from or overpower their work—a criticism often heard years later—they condemned in architecture the very freedom from traditional forms they cherished for themselves. "I am sufficiently familiar with the incubus of habit that besets your minds," Wright replied rather patronizingly, "to understand that you know all too little of the nature of the mother art—architecture." Painters would produce better pictures, he told an interviewer, if they could count on hanging in his museum.[18] Nor had Wright entirely captivated the potential viewing public. Letters to *Architectural Forum* called an early version of the scheme "a freak building. . .like a cuckoo clock," a Rube Goldberg cartoon, a "monstrosity in a class with Dali's paintings," and the "product of a disordered mind."[19] In the end, Wright agreed to lop thirty inches off the overhang and to make other changes to placate city officials. With everyone apparently reassured, with critics quieted by generally favorable response, with the last of the old buildings demolished, and with removal of the several "obscure reasons" *The New York Times* said had delayed the project, construction began in 1957. Wright kept close watch on proceedings, occasionally scrambling over piles of materials with the press and members of his entourage struggling to keep pace. When the building opened in October 1959, a reviewer for *Industrial Design* called it "thrilling architecture every inch of the way." Wright did not live to hear the praise, but he did see it almost to completion.[20]

A number of other unusual edifices also received extensive press and professional coverage. The Unitarian Society in Madison, Wisconsin, of which Wright was a member and which his father had helped organize in 1879, decided in January 1946 to hire him to design its new meeting house. By the middle of 1947 he came up with a triangular fieldstone central mass, flanked by wings for lobby and classrooms, under a long, sloping, green copper roof uniting chapel, parish hall, and spire in one entity. The roof folded over the auditorium in a gesture of protection for the apse which protruded like hands clasped in prayer from the sleeves of a supplicant's habit (see Fig. 11.3). Rows of removable pews facing each other across the nave for a sense of unity opened the space for social functions (Fig. 12.11). Parishioners hauled 1000 tons of stone for the sixteen- to nineteen-inch walls from a quarry thirty miles distant, plastered the wings and finished the floors and walls themselves, helping to construct a magnificent edifice

Figure 12.11 Unitarian Meeting House (1947), Madison, Wisconsin. Photo by Mary Allen, courtesy Friends of the Meeting House.

for $165,000. "This building is not just a place in which we meet," said a member of the congregation in *Architectural Forum* after the church opened in 1951. "It is a creative participant in all. . .the Society does and is." Perhaps it participated too creatively, for when reporters asked the minister why he resigned that December, he confirmed rumors that because worshippers devoted so much attention to the building they had little left for him.[21]

"Everyone knows," the *Forum* wrote, that a modern store needs a glass façade to reveal its interior and display its wares. But not the 1948 V. C. Morris Shop (Fig. 12.12) on tiny Maiden Lane off San Francisco's Union Square. World-wide repercussions, the journal said, followed its opening in 1949 because Wright had designed a blank brick façade without even the firm's name. Featuring a tunnellike, deeply recessed arched entry, the only other interruptions in the two-story wall were a vertical light slot running from slightly above the sidewalk to the lower of two thin concrete courses spanning the building near the roof line, and a matching wider course at chest level

Figure 12.12 V. C. Morris Shop (1948), San Francisco. Photo by David Roessler.

atop a strip of inset light boxes spaced across the front. Inside, a grand spiral ramp looped to the second floor defining display areas on, under, and above it. The argument over whether a windowless façade would entice people in or shoo them away was quickly resolved to the satisfaction of *Architect's Journal* in London, which said that shop windows had generally gotten boring and, to the benefit of the Morrises who loved it, found it unexpected good advertising and exceptionally popular. (The new owner uses its sketch as her logo in magazine ads.) The Morris Shop was one of the brightest architectural gems in Wright's career.[22]

So, too, was the concrete, copper, and glass tower (1952) for the Harold C. Price Company in Bartlesville, Oklahoma (Fig. 12.13), a building the *Forum* predicted would for its size be one of the costliest but most profitable ever constructed. And, it might have added, one

Figure 12.13   H. C. Price Tower (1952), Bartlesville, Oklahoma. Courtesy H. C. Price Company.

of the most unusual. Based on the 1929 apartment scheme for St. Marks-in-the-Bowery Church in New York (see Chapter Seven), its seventeen floors were cantilevered, as much as twenty feet in some cases, from the central utility core. But unlike the 1946–1947 Johnson Wax Tower, its polygonal plan, essentially a square with diagonal protrusions, was divided into quadrants, three for offices and one for eight duplex apartments. The façades alternated between vertical and horizontal modes of expression, and no two were quite alike. Indeed, with continuous green copper mullions, concrete band spandrels, decorative panels, and projecting sunshades variously arranged to make each side unique, the tower seemed to be an entirely different building from every angle of vision. Totally rejecting the construction and aesthetic principles of steel-frame, curtain-wall skyscrapers that had begun to make their appearance, especially in New York, Price Tower, like the Johnson Wax Administration Building (1936) in Racine, Wisconsin, went against the mainstream of its genre, but because of its practical innovations and daring composition generated its own advertising. Wright called it "the tree that escaped the crowded forest."[23]

Within a year he produced one of the world's most unique synagogue designs (Fig. 12.14) for Congregation Beth Shalom in Elkins Park, a suburb of Philadelphia. A 100-foot blue plastic pyramid sat atop a triangular 175-foot-wide concrete base, from ground level symbolizing Mt. Sinai, from the air forming an abstract Star of David, but also, as Wright said, the open hands of God. Inside was a pillarless, vast yet serene auditorium seating 1000, cooking and dining facilities, a smaller sanctuary, several lounges, and offices. Like the Unitarian Meeting House in Madison, "the seats are wrapped around the pro-

Figure 12.14 Beth Shalom Synagogue (1954), Elkins Park, Pennsylvania. Photo by Jacob Stelman, courtesy Beth Shalom Congregation.

truding pulpit, so that people on one side. . .can see people on the other side. Here is not an audience," the Synagogue's brochure contends; "here is a Congregation where men and women can join in the holy act of worship." The building was also rich in Jewish symbolisms, for Wright had relied on the advice of religious scholars. Ground was broken in November 1954, but construction was held up until May 1956 when the temple found an Oklahoma contractor willing to tackle the avant-garde scheme. Some were irritated by what they considered improbable architecture, while others felt it alien to Jewish traditions. The congregation itself admits its building "requires interpretation," but also insists it is more than "breathtakingly beautiful." Since 1959 when Beth Shalom opened, it has been, its brochure says in terms reminiscent of parishioner response to Oak Park's Unity Temple in 1908, "a place of holiness."[24]

The Kalita Humphreys Theatre (also called the Dallas Theatre Center) was designed in 1955–1956 (Fig. 12.15) and opened in December 1959, but its origins go at least as far back as Wright's "New Theatre Project" of 1932 which surfaced again in 1948 for a Hartford, Connecticut,

Figure 12.15 Kalita Humphreys Theatre (1955–1956), Dallas. Courtesy Dallas Theatre Center.

group that ultimately failed to raise building funds. In Dallas, Wright put normal overhead equipment underground with storage space and workshops, using elevators to get sets on-stage allowing, one architect–writer says, "better control and communication than the conventional layout." The forty-foot revolving center stage, flanked by another forty-five feet at the wings, was one foot above floor level and only three feet from the first row of 440 tiered seats wrapped in a 180-degree arc around it. *New York Times* drama critic Howard Taubman called the theatre "one of Wright's happiest solutions to a practical problem," "in itself justifying a visit to this city." With equipment as "modern as a fan jet," it united players and audience without "excessive formality" or false intimacy. Housed in a poured concrete hexagonal monolith of exceptionally strong forms and bold multilevel roof planes, Kalita Humphreys was one of Wright's most powerful designs. But inside, like his other auditoriums—in the Guggenheim, Beth Shalom, and the Unitarian Meeting House, for example—the uninterrupted space was serene and peaceful.[25]

During the middle years of the decade, Wright produced a number of unique minor buildings. The 1953 Anderton Center in Beverly Hills was a visually and organizationally confusing three-level minimall of shops wrapped around a court crossed in front by cantilevered ramps connecting the two wings, all topped with a functionally unnecessary and aesthetically dubious tower. In 1954 he designed a gallery for an exhibition of his work adjacent to the Barnsdall "Hollyhock House" (1916–1920) in Los Angeles, later preserved as the city's first municipal art center. In his 1955 Mercedes-Benz Showroom on Park Avenue in New York, some cars were lined up on inclines, others on turntables, so sitting or standing customers could inspect the merchandise from all angles as it, not they, circulated. The next year saw a filling station in Cloquet, Minnesota, built from steel and cement blocks, with a thirty-two-foot copper cantilevered canopy holding gas pumps to leave ground space free; a concrete block grammer school (discussed in Chapter Thirteen) for the town of Wyoming, Wisconsin, down the road from Taliesin; and two doctors clinics, one in San Luis Obispo, California, another in Dayton, Ohio.[26]

Beginning in 1956, Wright's larger public structures declined in quality, although in virtually every case there is reason to think he was not entirely responsible. The Annunciation Greek Orthodox Church (Fig. 12.16) that year in Wauwatosa, a suburb of Milwaukee, was a three hundred-foot in diameter concrete bowl containing a 700-seat auditorium sitting on four massive upcurving piers symbolizing an Hellenic cross. Over the bowl an inverted blue-tiled saucer formed the roof.

Figure 12.16 Annunciation Greek Orthodox Church (1956), Wauwatosa, Wisconsin. Photo by author.

The elevated auditorium looked out on an elongated terrace with chapel and meeting hall underground. The entrance lobby, windows, stairwell gates, trim, the perforated sunscreen projecting from below the cornice, and of course the building itself were all circular. Its blatant symbols and obvious heavy-handedness seemed to one critic "curiously antique," especially the gaudy auditorium plastered with goldleaf trim. Construction did not begin until after Wright's death, and the extent to which Peters and TAA were responsible for its aesthetic excesses is unknown. The congregation liked it, but in its ornamental frenzy it was not as gentle or comforting as the synagogue two years before.[27]

Circles and arches also dominated Grady Gammage Auditorium (1958–1959) at Arizona State University in Tempe, the Marin County Civic Center (1957–1959), and the plan for greater Baghdad (1957–1958). The Auditorium (Fig. 12.17) was begun in May 1962, completed by TAA from Wright's unfinished plans, and opened in September 1964. The outer row of columns in the colonnade terminated in arches dripping with elaborately stylized semicircular capitals. Composed of two intersecting circular units—one for workshops, dressing rooms, and stage, the other for auditorium, grand tier, lobbies, and ramps—it looked from the back like a brick hatbox wrapped in a strand of gold

Figure 12.17 Grady Gammage Auditorium (1958–1959) at Arizona State University, Tempe. Courtesy Arizona State University.

braid, from the front like lollipops supporting a carousel. The arched ramp lights can only be described as horrendous. Although it worked very well inside (thanks to Wright), Grady Gammage was an aesthetic disaster compared to Kalita Humphreys.[28]

Ground was broken in 1960 for the Marin County Civic Center Administration Building completed in 1962, five years before construction began at the Hall of Justice which opened in 1969. Wright conceived the two with long series of arches like Roman aqueducts and dome and perforated overhangs similar to the Greek Orthodox Church (see Figs. 11.9 and 11.10). He had apparently developed their plans much further than the rest of the Center, although as executed they were heavily trimmed with circles and balls, probably the work of TAA. The third major structure to open, the Veterans Memorial Theatre in 1971, was essentially done by Peters, TAA, and their Taliesin-trained associate, San Francisco architect Aaron Green. The Theatre emerged as a windowless circle (from Wright's master plan) attached to an unusually drab cylindrical equipment stack (not in the plan) looking like a row of grain elevators.[29] In the case of Grady Gammage, the Greek Church, and Marin County, there is no way of knowing how much the Fellowship influenced Wright's initial designs or to what extent TAA modified them later. But they ended up more ornate than most of Wright's nonresidential work before 1956.

The Plan for Greater Baghdad fell into the same category. For the Isle of Edena and adjacent banks of the Tigris River, Wright laid out a $45 million complex including university buildings, an opera, a civic auditorium, gardens, amusement parks, bridges, and roadways. The auditorium strongly resembled Grady Gammage with a fantastic tower added to the roof. All structures, their grounds, the campus, and its buildings were circles covered with more circles—very elaborate, excessively trimmed. Wright received the commission after a two-week visit to the city late in the spring of 1957, and in March 1958 unveiled the plans at the Iraqi Consulate in New York. A week before Peters was to fly to Baghdad to supervise the first stages of construction, King Faisal was overthrown in a bloodless coup. At first the new government said it would honor the contract, but early in 1959, deeming Wright's plans "rather grandiose," declared that the people needed food, clothing, and shelter more than floating gardens, gold fountains, and a mammoth zoo. The new leaders wanted a university, but decided to look elsewhere for an architect.[30] To them, Wright represented Western imperialism, something of an irony considering his reputation in, and attitude toward, American government. The second irony was that in 1960 Peters landed the commission for, and in subsequent years built, the Pearl Palace for Her Imperial Highness Shams Pahlavi, sister of the Shah of Iran, again a circular design.[31]

The Corbin Education Center (1958) at Wichita State University consisted of two connected structures, one of which was built, of decidedly rectilinear format worked out in intersecting planes (Fig. 12.18). Roof canopies were edged and some terraces draped in drooping semicircles like most of the glazing. The exterior surface was a rough, drab, exposed aggregate, an unattractive material Wright had never used before. Since the design was completed by Peters and TAA which supervised construction until the building opened in June 1964, there is reason to doubt that the choice was Wright's or that the visual effect of a funeral parlor hung in crepe was entirely his responsibility.[32]

Wright's major public structures after 1955 have much of the feeling of Peters about them, especially those for which TAA's chief architect completed plans or supervised construction. But when they were built they were all attributed entirely to Wright, generally given uncritical acclaim, and cited as additional proof—not that any was needed—of his unsurpassed genius. They may have been aesthetically questionable but they were undoubtedly as startling as Wright's many fantastic

Figure 12.18 Corbin Education Center (1958), Wichita, Kansas. Courtesy Wichita State University Public Relations Office.

(and not so fantastic) projects that never saw the light of day: a saucer-shaped resort hotel suspended from a Hollywood hilltop for Hunting-ton Hartford, a floating garden in Florida, a space-age church in Oklahoma, a mushroom wedding chapel on stilts in California, a sports pavilion for New York, a restaurant, a trailer court, a drive-in mortuary, government buildings, art galleries, clinics, theatres, offices, a factory, a motel, a fraternity house, a garage, a bank, a radio station, an airplane hanger, department stores, small shops, bridges, a laundry, and a Christian Science Reading Room—as if Wright wanted to do every kind of structure in every imaginable form while he still had time. It was a marvelous display.

Several generated noisy discussion even when construction was never really possible. The Masieri Memorial (1953), for example, was commissioned by parents of a student admirer of Wright who had lost his life in an auto accident. A vertical three-story row building with concrete balconies projecting over the Grand Canal, it touched off a heated exchange between those who felt it captured the grandeur that was Venice and those who felt it too radical for its "sacred" (read: old) setting. Ernest Hemingway, recuperating in the city from two airplane crashes during an African safari, suggested both sides might be placated if "as soon as it is finished it is burned." The Municipal Building Commission decided the memorial would violate hygienic regulations (which could have meant it was too clean for the area) and that neighbors must agree to it before approval could be granted. When it was finally disallowed by a second commission on grounds of aesthetic incompatibility, Wright declared that tourism had won another victory.[33]

The Masieri Memorial was a believable building provoking a lively controversy, but "Mile High Illinois" was an unbelievable building producing more amusement than anger. He had never been more serious in his life, the architect said, when he announced in 1956 that he was preparing a 528-story edifice for the 100,000 employees of Chicago, Cook County, and the state of Illinois. At a cost of $300 million he would provide 24 million square feet of floor space (later reduced to 13 million at undetermined cost), parking for 15,000 cars, a landing pad for seventy-five helicopters, and nine floors of television studios with a transmitting tower he claimed would reach both coasts. Built on the principle of the Johnson Wax laboratory with a central core sunk 150 feet below grade, it would be pressurized like an airplane and have atomic-powered elevators reaching speeds of a mile a minute. Located in a park along Lake Michigan with its employee hours staggered, "Mile High" would not increase congestion, Wright said, even if it served for the next hundred years. At first he insisted but then denied he had financial backing, saying only he had come up with the scheme after someone came to him with a proposal to build a half-mile-high structure, to which he had scornfully replied: "The hell with that!" No one took the idea very seriously, although buildings now in excess of 100 stories make the notion less improbable, but many were no doubt impressed when he unveiled the drawing, itself twenty-two feet high.[34]

Wright's last design was a small private garden for his wife at Taliesin East, and the last commission he accepted was a tiny $3000 summer cottage for a friend of a friend.[35] Compared to "Mile High Illinois" and the other breathtaking projects of the 1950s, they seem unimportant. But to Wright they were not, for first and foremost he was a residential architect, almost literally to his dying day. And in the years before he died, he lived as flamboyantly as he worked, like a supercharged dynamo, as bold in public as he was in the studio.

NOTES

1 Maginel Wright Barney, *The Valley of the God-Almighty Joneses* (New York: Appleton-Century, 1965), 148.

2 *The New York Times,* April 21, 1963, Sec. 8; June 7, 1964, Sec. 8.

3 Frank Lloyd Wright, "To the Young Man in Architecture—A Challenge," *Architectural Forum,* 68 (January 1938); *An Autobiography* (New York: Duell, Sloan and Pearce, 1943 ed.), 489.

4 "American Landscape III," *Harper's,* 200 (March 1950), 98–100; *The San Francisco Chronicle,* December 7, 1951; *The Capital Times,* December 12, 1951. On the "Usonian Automatic" and the Adelman House see F. L. Wright, *The Natural House* (New York: Horizon Press, 1954), 197–207.

5 "Frank Lloyd Wright builds in the middle of Manhattan," *House and Home,* 4 (November 1953), 118–121; *The New York Times,* October 18, 1953; "The Usonian House: Souvenir of the Exhibition: 60 Years of Living Architecture: The Work of Frank Lloyd Wright," Guggenheim Museum brochure, November 1953.

6 *The New York Times,* October 14, 1956, Sec. 8; "Frank Lloyd Wright Prefabricated Homes," Erdman brochure, no date. Also see *The Milwaukee Journal,* June 21, 1959. The concrete block version is in Frank Lloyd Wright, *The Living City* (New York: Horizon Press, 1958), 70.

7 *The Capital Times,* October 4, 1956. On Pre-fabs Numbers One and Two see *ibid.*, June 10, 12, 1957; January 9, 1958; May 26, 1959; *The New York Times,* December 21, 1956; October 25, 1957, Sec. 6; *The Chicago Tribune,* January 22, 1958; "Here is prefabrication's biggest news for 1957," *House and Home,* 10 (December 1956), 117–121.

8 *The Capital Times,* April 26, 1957; *The New York Times,* February 10, 1957, Sec. 8; "Airhouse," *Domus,* No. 364 (March 1960), 17, including three photographs.

9 F. L. Wright, *An Autobiography,* 145; on furniture, fabrics, and carpets see "Frank Lloyd Wright Collection by Heritage Henredon," a portfolio including photographs; *The New York Times,* October 18, November 18, 1955; "New Era for Wright at 86: The Marketplace Redeemed?," *The Architectural Record,* 118 (October 1955), 20; "Taliesin to the Trade," *Interiors,* 115 (October 1955), 130–133; full page ad in *ibid.*, 114 (July 1955), adv. page 46; speech at Chicago's Merchandise Mart (November ? 1955) at the opening of Henredon's furniture exhibition, copy of tape in author's possession; and Henredon Director of Design Kenneth R. Volz to author, December 11, 1970.

   Wright's other marketing venture did not have time to materialize: "Dome Enterprises," a 1957 partnership with Michael Todd, Sylvester "Pat" Weaver, and Henry J. Kaiser to franchise theatres designed by Wright with Kaiser-made domes' originally developed by Buckminster Fuller. See *The New York Times,* December 11, 1957, and "Wright to design Dome Theatres for Mike Todd," *Architectural Forum*, 108 (February 1958), 61.

10 Figures here and on public buildings discussed below are compiled from Olgivanna Lloyd Wright, *Frank Lloyd Wright: His Life, His Work, His Word* (New York: Horizon Press, 1967), 207–222. In this chapter several designs will be assigned dates differing from this list which, though it purports to be definitive, is actually quite inaccurate. Documentation for revised dates is cited in the notes.

11 "The Frontiersman," *Architectural Review*, 106 (August 1949), 105–110.

12 This design process was described to me by a regular visitor to Taliesin during the 1950s who owned two of Wright's touched-up drawings. Mrs. Robert Sunday of Marshalltown, Iowa, who worked closely with Wright on her 1958 home, remarked on his cataracts and failing vision.

13 Bernard Pyron, "Wright's Diamond Module Houses," *The Art Journal*, 21 (Winter 1961–1962), 92–96; and "Wright's Small Rectangular Houses," *ibid.*, 24 (Fall 1963), 20–23. Reyner Banham, "the wilderness years of Frank Lloyd Wright," *Royal Institute of British Architects Journal*, 76 (December 1969), 514.

14 "Frank Lloyd Wright: This New Desert House for His Son is a Magnificent Coil of. . .Concrete Block," *House and Home*, 3 (June 1953), 99–107.

15 Arthur Drexler, Ed., *The Drawings of Frank Lloyd Wright* (New York: Horizon Press, 1962), plates 184–187.

16 On these projects see A. Drexler, Ed., *Drawings*, plates 220, 233; *The Capital Times*, August 21, 1947; November 5, 1957; on the Loeb House see *The New York Times*, June 19, 1946; "House in Connecticut," *Architectural Forum*, 84 (June 1946), 84–88; "Country House in Connecticut, USA. Designed by Frank Lloyd Wright," *The Architect's Journal* [London], 104 (September 19, 1946), 213–214.

There are simply too many magazine and newspaper articles on Wright houses during the late 1940s and 1950s to list here.

17 "The Modern Gallery," *Architectural Forum*, 84 (January 1946), 82.

18 *The New York Times*, December 22, 1956; Seldon Rodman, *Conversations with Artists* (New York: Devin-Adair, 1957), 73.

19 "Men Against Wright," *Architectural Forum*, 85 (August 1946), 34.

20 George McAuliffe, "The Guggenheim: great architecture, difficult installation," *Industrial Design*, 6 (November 1959), 66. Also see *Architectural Forum*, 96 (April 1952), 141–144; *Life*, 19 (October 8, 1945), 12–13; *New Yorker*, 32 (June 16, 1956), 26–27; and 33 (August 10, 1957), 17; *Newsweek*, 42 (August 10, 1953), 13; and 42 (November 2, 1953), 64; *Saturday Review*, 38 (May 21, 1955), 13; *Interiors*, 69 (December 1959), 88–95, 172; *American Institute of Architects Journal*, 33 (January 1960), 124; *The New York Times*, November 5, 1946; April 17, 1951; March 30, April 4, 1952; July 25, 29, September 3, 1953; May 7, December 12, 1956; October 21, 25, 1959.

21 *The Capital Times,* September 22, 1945; January 26, 1946; July 13, 1947; December 11, 1951; "A Church designed and built in the attitude of prayer," *Architectural Forum* 97 (December 1952), 85–92; Barbara Armstrong, "Frank Lloyd Wright and the Unitarian Meeting House," *The Journal of Historic Madison, Inc. of Wisconsin,* 2 (1976), 14–18.

22 *The Architect's Journal* [London], 110 (November 10, 1949), 512, 516; "China and Gift Shop by Frank Lloyd Wright for V. C. Morris," *Architectural Forum,* 92 (February 1950), 79–85. See the ad for Helga Howie in *The New Yorker,* ca. May 1975.

23 "Frank Lloyd Wright's Concrete and Copper Tower on the Prairie for H. C. Price Company," *Architectural Forum,* 98 (May 1953), 98–105; "Frank Lloyd Wright's Tower," *ibid.,* 104 (February 1956), 106–113; "The H. C. Price Tower," *The Architectural Record,* 119 (February 1956), 153–160, containing Wright's statement, "For the Record;" *The Capital Times,* March 20, 1956; and Wright's book, *The Story of the Tower: The Tree that Escaped the Crowded Forest* (New York: Horizon Press, 1956).

24 "Glass-towered synagogue, Frank Lloyd Wright's first," *Architectural Forum,* 100 (June 1954), 145; *The Architectural Record,* 116 (July 1954), 20; *The New York Times,* November 15, 1954; September 13, 1959; "An Invitation to visit An American Synagogue designed by Frank Lloyd Wright," Beth Shalom brochure, ca. 1963.

25 A. Drexler, Ed., *Drawings,* plates 134–136, and Frank Lloyd Wright, *The Living City* (New York: Horizon Press, 1958), 176–177, for the "New Theatre Project." See *The New York Times,* November 19, 1948; *The Architectural Record,* 105 (May 1949), 156; and Lloyd Lewis, "The New Theatre," *Theatre Arts,* 33 (July 1949), 33–34, for the Hartford plan and on Kalita Humphreys, *The New York Times,* December 25, 1959; "Christmas Present for Dallas: A Theatre By Wright," *Progressive Architecture,* 40 (December 1959), 79; "Frank Lloyd Wright's Dallas Theatre," *Architectural Forum,* 112 (March 1960), 130–135; "A Theatre by Wright," *The Architectural Record,* 127 (March 1960), 161–166; Martin Pawley and Yukio Futagawa, *Frank Lloyd Wright: Public Buildings* (New York: Simon and Schuster, 1970), 123–124; "Dallas Theatre Center" and "The Decennial," booklets published by the Center; and Taubman, "Wright Playhouse Used by Dallas Group," *The New York Times,* July 2, 1963.

26 On the Barnsdall exhibition: Aline Saarinen in *The New York Times,* August 8, 1954, Sec. 2; on Mercedes-Benz: "Frank Lloyd Wright designs a small commercial installation," *Architectural Forum,* 105 (July 1955), 132–133; also Robert C. Wheeler, "Frank Lloyd Wright Filling Station, 1958," *Journal of the Society of Architectural Historians,* 19 (December 1960), 174–175.

27 "Spirit of Byzantium: Frank Lloyd Wright's last church," *Architectural Forum,* 116 (December 1961), 82–97; Pawley and Futagawa, *Public Buildings,* 123.

28 *The New York Times,* July 5, 1959; September 18, 1964; "Frank Lloyd Wright's Legacy: Projects and Sketches," *Architectural Forum,* 117 (July 1962), 9; "Grady Gammage Memorial Auditorium," brochure prepared by the Bureau of Publications, Arizona State University, June 1970; *The Weekly Home News,* June 30, 1960.

29 "Ground is Broken for Wright's Marin County Center," *Progressive Architecture,* 41 (April 1960), 82; "Wright's Ship of State," *ibid.,* 48 (February 1967), 30; "Half a Wright project may be better than none," *Architectural Forum,* 15 (December 1961), 10; *ibid.,* 117 (November 1962), 122–127; "Frank Lloyd Wright's Hall of Justice," *ibid.,* 133 (December 1970), 54–59; *New York Times,* August 3, 1957; February 16, 1960; *The Weekly Home News,* May 4, 1961; *The Capital Times,* June 27, 1957; *The San Francisco Chronicle,* August 1, 3, 1957; "Marin County Civic Center," brochure, ca. 1963.

30 *The New York Times,* January 27, June 7, 8, 1957; May 3, 1958; *The Capital Times,* January 8, 1959; *The Weekly Home News,* July 17, 1958; "Frank Lloyd Wright designs for Baghdad," *Architectural Forum,* 108 (May 1958), 89–102; A. Drexler, Ed., *Drawings,* plates 260–262.

31 William Wesley Peters, "Taliesin in Teheran," *Art in America,* 57 (July–August 1960), 44–51.

32 "Wright designs an elementary school 'teaching laboratory' for Wichita University," *Architectural Forum,* 109 (July 1958), 9; *The Capital Times,* June 25, 29, 1964; *The New York Times,* August 2, 1964, Sec. 8; University of Wichita News Bureau release, June 26, 1964.

33 *The New York Times,* May 26, 1953; March 9, 21, April 22, 1954; November 16, 1955; *The Capital Times,* March 25, 31, 1954.

34 *The Capital Times,* August 27, October 16, December 10, 1956; *The New York Times,* August 26, 1956; *The Chicago Tribune,* October 17, 1956.

35 Olgivanna Lloyd Wright, *Frank Lloyd Wright,* 222; Wright to Willard Jones, April 2, 1959, FLW Collection, Northwestern University Library Special Collections, Evanston, Illinois.

1946–1959

CHAPTER THIRTEEN

A Giant Tree
in a Wide Landscape

During his last years Frank Lloyd Wright was often before the public, his outrageous remarks and irreverence for established institutions enhancing his reputation as an eccentric genius (or crackpot, as detractors preferred to believe). He seemed to thrive on controversy. Nothing escaped his critical attention. As he barnstormed the nation blasting politicians and dominating television interviews, people perceived him as a man of monumental proportions, as a kind of natural resource refusing to be depleted. Honors, awards, praise, and accolades came his way in a torrent, including grudging respect from the same professional colleagues he continually insulted. Home at Taliesin he lived a quieter existence, instructing students and neighbors in the principles of organic living. His death in 1959 two months short of his ninety-second birthday was front-page news. After more than half a century in the public consciousness, many people could not believe he was really gone.

☐ ☐ ☐

The architect disliked the way things were going in postwar America. Distrusting bigness in any form, especially in business and government, he leveled a nonstop fusillade of newspaper articles, books, interviews, and speeches against mass society, corporations, and politicians. He worried about United States power after the end of World War Two, about its international influence, its nuclear weapons, and its economic might. Continued growth of the military establishment and the mushrooming of governmental bureaucracy and of corporate hegemony made him despair for the future of democracy. Fearing that centralized authority manipulating a mass society would crush individual liberties, he interpreted American foreign policy as a cover to advance overseas corporate interests and attacked internal anticommunism as a "smoke-screen" for political consolidation to further selfish partisan gain.

"There is more beneath the present world-situation than is allowed by the 'Haves' to appear on the surface," he wrote in May 1948. "The American dollar was made so almighty by our expert engineering at Bretton Woods [New Hampshire in 1944 where a forty-four-nation conference established the International Monetary Fund and other procedures for stabilizing world currency and organizing postwar economic recovery] that we now have to give it away to foreign nations to enable them to buy anything at all. . . ." The last thing the United Nations wanted, he believed, was human freedom. Listing "no conscription," "no economic conscription," "no tariffs," and "free inter-immigration among all people of the world" as essential for preventing war, he noted that "the Dollar-fight is all that we have seen tried so far to insure Peace of the World." "The U.N.," he added, "has not really been interested in anything but this wrestle for Power."[1]

"The attempt of the nations now to get together is a hopeful sign," he remarked in 1946. But within a year or two he was forced to conclude that internationalism had degenerated into "a tainted commercialism with militarism as its mate." In diplomacy as in architecture "internationalism" turned out to be an antidemocratic imposition on human freedom. "Were we to build a building for the United Nations," he wrote in 1946—meaning not "we" but "I"—it would be "a modern high-spirited place of great repose, an unpretentious building, abandoning all specious symbolism, . . .an example of great faith in humanity. Let the assembly room," he declared, "be a place of light as wide open to the sky as possible—that influence is auspicious—make it no screen to hide ignoble fears or cherish native hypocrisy." Since skyscrapers exploit people, he added the following year, the United Nations should not build one but should buy a 1000-acre relatively isolated tract where in a ground-hugging, generously glazed structure without artificial stimulations or easy recourse to the "flesh-pots," delegates could deliberate the world's situation "naturally," at leisure. Humanity is sick, he diagnosed, and a sick person should not take stimulants. Nor would world recovery be speeded by further urban congestion.[2]

Of course, no one asked him to design the new headquarters, and when an international team of architects headed by American Wallace K. Harrison produced its plan in 1947 it was almost exactly the opposite of Wright's suggestion. The Secretariat was, in fact, a particularly imposing, austere, and monumental high-rise, a symbol not of faith in humanity but of power and might. And the Assembly turned out to be a low stone monolith (with one window wall) with nothing about its shape, its appearance, its position, or its relation to the Secretariat, Lewis Mumford wrote, to indicate it was "the home of what must in time be the most important deliberative body in the world." The UN tower, Mumford thought, should "by its zealous attention to human functions and human needs itself symbolize the great purposes it serves." But it completely failed to do that. Instead, it was "a slick mechanical job," "as obsolete as iron dumbbells." Wright was even more outraged and less verbally restrained. "I think [Harrison] the bellweather architect of it said, 'the slab is the thing.' Well, there isn't a graveyard in the nation which couldn't say Amen to that." To Wright, the UN was indeed "a slab in a graveyard" architecturally and probably politically. "The stone ends are symbols—walls—the world in division." And as a box on stilts, "it's a fascist symbol."[3]

Buildings like it, he added, intimidated people, exactly what politics was doing by 1948. There is "nothing for us to fear from Communism or any other 'ism' on Earth," Wright contended that July. "At bottom Soviet Russia wants what we want but believes in a different way to get it, that's all." The rising tide of anticommunism was a modern instance of the age-old practice of authority frightening the public in order to consolidate its gains. "If you can scare the people you can huddle them where you will. Scare them a little more and they will shoot each other. Scare them enough and they will even go out and shoot themselves." Celebrating his eighty-third birthday in June 1950, Wright said that not only was the Soviet Union not a threat but that the United States should scrap its atomic bombs and sign a treaty outlawing them whether Russia agreed or not. Such a move would reduce the chances of war since "the Russians want peace just as much as we do."[4]

Responding to these and a history of similar remarks (see Chapter Ten) early in 1951, the House Committee on Un-American Activities listed him among hundreds of prominent Americans who had once been affiliated with "Communist front organizations." Wright replied that HUAC "is not only mischievous but un-American itself." And "when a McCarthy can exist in our country," he added in April, "our political system cries out for revision." Applauding Connecticut Republican William Benton's attempt to expel the Wisconsite from the Senate, Wright explained that "if the good American god EXPEDIENT allows such blatant cowards as a McCarthy to flourish on fear in our political system it is partly (if not chiefly) because we now exist as a virulent, conscienceless two-party system degenerate in the struggle for power." The time had obviously come for a new third party "honestly devoted to the Democratic principles of our forebears and the Constitution." The underlying basis for professional anticommunism, Wright believed, was pursuit of partisan political advantage made possible by a national lack of democratic self-confidence causing America to assume a belligerent and preposterous attitude toward the rest of the world.[5] The most convenient means of collective ego-reinforcement during the 1950s was red-baiting, and as far as the architect was concerned the chief baiter was the former county judge from Appleton—that "political pervert"—Wisconsin's own junior Senator, Joseph R. McCarthy.

"Not so long ago," the architect remembered in 1952 of the two Robert M. La Follettes, the father and son who had dominated local and influenced national politics for more than fifty years, "Wisconsin had the reputation of a great and noble state." But now it "is a stench in the nostrils of decency everywhere. . .stand[ing] more for damage to America. . .[than] any other State in the world." Do these fighters of communism "know what communism means? Ask them. Their answers will make you laugh. Do they know what democracy means? Ask them and weep." Wisconsin was no longer "marked by great names of noble statesmen and famed as the home of great individuals, but by inciters of a scared people." What to do about McCarthy? Vote him out, he urged the readers of Madison's *Capital Times* in September 1952. "As an architect," he added, with vitriolic humor,

I submit a simple design for a suitable and perhaps salutary memorial to the chief demagogue. . . .

Here it is: At all principal cross-roads of the State set up, on a solid concrete base, a large cast iron pot of simple but chaste design, say 6 feet in diameter. Pour into it a powerful charge of H_2S or carbon dioxide. On the birthday of the chief demagogue. . .over the entire area of the State light a blaze under every pot and raise such a prodigious stink that the true character of such a "patriot" would be brought to the noses of the voters. . .by their own nausea. This realistic celebration to continue for 24 hours or for long enough to bring to the voters realization of the character of such "patriotism."[6]

In more serious moments Wright advocated reconciliation with the Soviet Union, unilateral disarmament, a one-term limitation on the presidency, and revitalization of local government as ways of restoring power to the people, overcoming anticommunist hysteria, and bringing sanity to the state.

□ □ □

Remarks like these did not win friends in high political places, not that Wright ever had very many. They undoubtedly contributed to his inability to get government contracts and threatened the few he did receive. Aside from the aborted defense workers housing project at Pittsfield, Massachusetts, in 1941 (see Chapter Nine), the federal government never approached the nation's most prominent architect, although in 1954 he desperately wanted it to. Forsaking a lifetime stance as a "lone wolf," he joined with seven other architects in July to form the Kitty Hawk Association, a cabal competing with eighty other firms to design the $125 million Air Force Academy at Colorado Springs, "the commission of my career!" he exclaimed in anticipation. A year later after Kitty Hawk had withdrawn from the bidding, Wright told the House Appropriations Subcommittee that the winning Skidmore, Owings, and Merrill design was a "shocking fiasco," a "half-baked" wayside market "utterly without a soul, utterly without a spirit," "a glassified box on stilts," and suggested that American teenagers could have made a better choice of architects. Political pundit Drew Pearson charged that the brick and stone industries had successfully sold more of their materials to the government as a result of Wright's testimony, overlooking the fact that he was not terribly influential in official circles, and that he had been arguing for a year that the Academy should be built from local stone so as not to disturb the natural beauty and essential character of the site. Pearson also claimed that Wright testified only out of sour grapes at not getting the commission when in fact he was trying to forestall what he believed to be a miserable design. After Wright denied Pearson's allegations, nothing further was heard on the matter.[7] At the height of the flap the architect submitted an unsolicited sketch of a restaurant for Yosemite to the National Park Service. When Director Conrad Wirth dismissed it as "a mushroom type of thing" that would block the view, Wright resigned himself to the fact that "It's politics."[8]

Politics also seemed to influence relations with his adopted state of Arizona, although his own salty personality also played a part. In 1951 he threatened to sell Taliesin West and move away because newly strung electrical lines from Roosevelt Dam through Paradise Valley to a power generator ruined his view of the Superstition Mountains. But neither he nor the wires gave an inch, compounding his outrage in 1956 when the state's Board of Technical Registration announced that Wright would have to obtain an Arizona architect's license or face a misdemeanor prosecution. Of course, it would not be necessary to prove himself qualified, having already met all the requirements to practice, Secretary of the Board Walter A. Biddle said, presumably with a straight face, but there could be no exceptions, and Wright had to follow regulations like everyone else. Obviously miffed, he refused to comply, and the issue was settled only under pressure when the Board decided to grant him and fifteen other architects and engineers their licenses without examination because of their eminence.[9]

Wright got a chance to retaliate in February 1957 when Arizona revealed its plans for a new state capital. Nothing "I've ever seen betokens incompetence as much as this proposed building," the architect claimed with his usual understatement, and in an attempt to embarrass authorities offered his own plan directly to the people (see Chapter Eleven). Endorsed by his friends Henry and Clare Booth Luce and former Senator and Mrs. William Benton—all winter residents there—"Oasis" in a park would cost $5,000,000, Wright said, considerably less than the $9,000,000 Arizona was prepared to pay for its downtown "monstrosity." *The New York Times* found little enthusiasm for Oasis among the public or within the ranks of architects. Wright's suggestion that citizens circumvent the "pole-and-wire" politicians (he had not forgotten the power lines) by selecting their capital at public referendum got nowhere. "Many think of him as an egomaniac, [an] egocentric, [and] a crackpot," an Arizona architect observed, expressing local sentiment rather accurately. Perhaps he has "to be a little of all those things," he added somewhat wistfully, "to be creative and do more than copy the work of others."[10]

Wright's skirmishes with Arizona paled in comparison to those with his native Wisconsin. His outspoken political ideas directly affected the fate of one of his finest projects, the Monona Terrace Civic Center (see Chapter Eleven) in Madison. Originally conceived in 1938, Wright modified it at least three times (1941, 1953, 1956) before William Wesley Peters revised it again in the 1960s. Describing himself as Wisconsin's black sheep in September 1938, Wright criticized Madison's plan for a new city–county building and on November 2 offered his own proposal for a civic center and Lake Monona development. The next day the City–County Board, in part responding to Wright's denunciations of municipal disregard for the waterfront, rejected the original plan, whereupon the architect urged Madisonians to organize citizens' groups to lobby for his Terrace.[11] The issue lapsed until June 1941 when Wright announced the formation of an eighteen-person committee working to build his newly revised design. Arguing that Monona Terrace would significantly increase the city's assessed valuation, attract untold numbers of tourists, utilize the lakefront properly, and provide unparalleled facilities and benefits to residents, Wright identified himself with the "real citizens—the common people—not the politicians or Big Shots." Monona Terrace, he said, would stimulate the growth of democratic architecture, but more important, a citizen movement for its construction would promote the development of democracy itself.[12]

Despite his periodic efforts to awaken it, public interest in the Terrace waned, not to revive again until the fall of 1953 when in the early stages of discussing new city–county facilities Wright offered $20,000 of his own money to hire engineers and contractors to prove that his design could be built for less than $20,000,000 (his 1938 estimate had been $2,750,000). If he were correct, he said, the city and county could go ahead with his proposal or reimburse him, but if he were wrong they would owe him nothing. Publication of the third version in four installments of The Capital Times, plus the architect's several public speeches, inaugurated a year of public debate, settled by referenda in November 1954 when voters agreed overwhelmingly (22,500 to 6300) to float $4 million in bonds to finance a civic center and auditorium, decided convincingly (16,800 to 11,700) to use the Monona Terrace site, and consented reluctantly (15,100 to 13,800) to hire Wright. Many Madisonians had objected to the architect's newspaper article a month before in which he said that the city would be "commonplace" if it did not build his scheme.[13]

With the bonds safely floated, nothing seemed to happen. Through 1955 and into 1956 Wright spoke out for his project, made a model available for public display, criticized the decision to go ahead with a city–county office building near the Monona Terrace site, and blasted the city for foot-dragging. Finally, some sixteen months after the referenda, in July 1956, he signed a contract with the city of Madison, even though he later said it was one of the worst he ever concluded. Stipulating a low fee, severe budgetary limitations, constant review, and inadequate planning time, the contract also included a seemingly innocuous provision that later came back to haunt him: he would not be paid for preliminary work if the Terrace were prohibited by state law. When revised plans (see Fig. 11.8) were unveiled in August 1956, an issue was transformed into a controversy. Right-wing "Wrightophobes," as *Capital Times* editor William T. Evjue called them, did everything possible to stop the project. Motivated by the architect's history of marital irregularities, controversy, outspokenness, pacifism, sympathy for the Soviet Union, anti-anticommunism, and who knows what else, they cut the budget, nitpicked over design details, criticized Wright in public, refused to pay him, constantly demanded changes, secured court injunctions, and tried to invalidate the contract. By March 1957, an angry Wright was saying he did not "know of a stupider city in the United States" than Madison. Comments like that, of course, only generated further opposition.

One of its leaders, Carroll Metzner, a conservative Republican Assemblyman, finally thwarted Wright altogether in September 1957 by securing passage of a state law prohibiting construction of anything on the Terrace site over twenty feet tall, thereby halting the project and denying the architect some $650,000 in fees. *Architectural Forum* correctly called it a "spite bill," noting that Governor Vernon Thompson, a Republican foe of Wright's, was only too happy to sign it. Carrying his opposition to extraordinary lengths, Metzner had turned up unexpectedly in August 1957 at a public hearing in San Rafael, California, during a "vacation" to lobby against Wright as the architect for the Marin County Civic Center. Claiming to have proof of his "incapacities" for the job, Metzner made no specific public accusations, but coincidently one of the five county supervisors released a document prepared by former HUAC Staff Director J. B. Matthews purporting to show that Wright had given "active and extensive support" to Communist enterprises. The architect's disgusted reply—"Oh rats!"—apparently mirrored the general consensus, for the Board of Supervisors voted four to one to hire him, and Wright went on to design his only executed government structure. Disappointed Metzner took some solace in the fact that his Wisconsin law remained in force until March 1959, a month before the architect's death, denying Madison the Civic Center it voted for.

Wright had meanwhile continued to push the project by again designing a temporary structure for its model in downtown Madison and by speaking frequently on its behalf, sometimes in ways virtually guaranteed to keep opposing factions at loggerheads. He advised the city how to vote on referenda, campaigned against an anti-Terrace mayor, then said he was "ashamed" of his boyhood town. Few other architects ever identified themselves so closely with civic virtue to build one of their own structures. Wright did it not for money—in the end he was never paid—but because he thought Madison offered an unusual topographic occasion to do something really special, because the city meant a great deal to him personally, and because he deeply believed that citizens should control the decision-making processes affecting their lives (and especially their physical environment) as he had plainly stated in the Arizona "Oasis" incident. Since history has shown that his buildings do generate tourists and revenue, Madison missed a singular opportunity to enhance its income while beautifying itself. Many of its residents have never forgiven Carroll Metzner and his associates.[14]

The Monona Terrace controversy was unusually long and loud but only one of several with his native state during the late 1940s and 1950s that contributed to his undeserved reputation as an irresponsible troublemaker. In the fall of 1947, with the solid support of Spring Green, he asked the State Highway Commission to replace a steel-truss bridge scheduled for demolition with one of his concrete butterfly designs (a single row of piers fanning out to form the underside of the roadway) and to consider his area highway rerouting and landscaping scheme that would have located the town in the northeast corner of a square formed by four river level roads that could remain open all winter to the benefit of rural residents. The Commission wanted to skirt the village altogether, but Wright suggested linking it to U.S. 14 with an alternate city route. Connecting Spring Green to the highway system with bypasses would necessitate replacing two other ugly and unsafe steel-truss bridges with his own butterflies, but he assured everyone that they could be built much more cheaply and would be stronger, longer-lasting, easier to construct, and aesthetically more pleasing than the standard issue. No one seemed to notice that Wright had organized local transportation routes according to his Broadacre City model by removing them to the periphery of town.

In his first public address to his neighbors—some 600, possibly the largest audience in Spring Green's history—he advocated regular citizen meetings for discussing mutual problems and coping with bureaucracy when it failed to act in the public interest. Despite enthusiastic support for Wright's proposal—some 400 signatures on a petition to the governor and local editorial endorsement—the highway plan failed. The state let a contract for a steel-truss bridge on Route 14 cutting close to the edge of town, and nothing was done to improve the back roads for winter passage or to landscape crossings over the Wisconsin River. Highway Commissioner James R. Law, a traditionalist architect and former Madison mayor who disliked Wright and his work intensely, stated flatly that nothing in the plan had ever been taken seriously. Wright immediately fired off "Bureaucracy Jumps the Gun," an indignant editorial accusing the state of neglecting popular will while knuckling under to "interests," but failed to secure an injunction halting bridge construction.[15]

Four years later in 1951, Wright renewed his offer to build a butterfly bridge, this time free of charge at the state's most famous tourist spot, the Wisconsin Dells. Claiming that no one this side of Switzerland designed decent bridges but that his would preserve the area's beauty as well as be a work of art, he wanted to locate the span at scenic Echo Point, thereby provoking a confrontation with businessmen looking for a feeder into the town of Wisconsin Dells, half a mile away. Governor Walter J. Kohler and the Sauk County Board of Supervisors endorsed Wright's plan and site, but met stiff opposition from Highway Commissioner Raymond Jensen—"We are not looking for beauty"—and Columbia County officials representing the merchants. Wright also wanted assurances he could serve as contractor so the bridge would be properly built and landscaped. The Highway Commission, hiding behind the stipulation that the Federal Bureau of Roads had final say because it dispensed matching funds, endorsed the scenically inferior but commercially superior site chosen by the businessmen. When Wright said flatly he would not do a bridge except at Echo Point, Commissioner James R. Law replied that if Wright designed it there would be no bridge. So the architect withdrew his offer and Wisconsin lost another opportunity to be the first state to commission him.[16]

Another encounter with Wisconsin had been festering ever since he opened the Taliesin Fellowship in 1932. Contending that part of his estate, that is, the Hillside School, eighty agricultural acres, and later the Midway Farm Buildings, were used for educational purposes and should therefore be tax exempt, in 1937 and 1939 he had protested his local real estate levies which he usually left in arrears but eventually paid. (In May 1939, for example, he discharged his obligations from 1933 through 1937.) Under threat from Iowa County officials of property confiscation, he apparently kept reasonably up to date for several years, for nothing further was heard about the issue until the Frank Lloyd Wright Foundation (incorporated in 1940) renewed the claim to exemption in 1950, the next year arguing in circuit court that $3642 in taxes accrued since 1942 should be dismissed because eighty of Wright's 373 acres were used for architectural education. By the time the case came to trial in June 1953, Iowa County and the town of Wyoming alleged that Wright, who had meanwhile acquired more land, owed $13,477.67 in taxes, penalties, and interest for the last eleven years.[17]

Circuit Judge Arthur Kopp denied the Foundation's request in his September decision. After studying Taliesin's financial records which revealed that Wright's fees since 1942 averaged $80,000 to $100,000 a year, that apprentice tuition came to $18,000 to $36,000, and that farm income ranged from $4000 to $12,000, leaving an annual profit anywhere from $20,000 to $40,000, Kopp decided the architect's operation was in fact a business, not an educational venture. Wright might have accepted the verdict and paid up had not the Governor's Educational Advisory Committee less than a month later approved Taliesin as an architectural school for veterans, granting exemption on part of the estate for Wisconsin taxes as the Internal Revenue Service had already done at the Federal level. Wright immediately petitioned for a new trial which Kopp denied on grounds that the Advisory Committee's decision was not retroactive. Now owing county and town well over $14,000, Wright decided to appeal to the State Supreme Court.[18]

When the case came up in September 1954, Wyoming Township argued that since Wright used his apprentices to reduce expenses, Taliesin was primarily a business, while he on the other hand claimed that architecture was not a business at all, that he spent much of his time teaching, and that his method involved learning by doing. Speaking for a unanimous court agreeing with Wyoming, Chief Justice Edward Fairchild decided in November that the Foundation "is completely dominated in every detail of its life by Frank Lloyd Wright, the individual," and that apprentice training was incidental to "the main purpose of continuing [his] architectural business." Fairchild ordered Wright immediately to pay Wyoming $886 covering 1944 through 1948 when the tax law changed somewhat, leaving the remainder for further determination, and added that Taliesin did not qualify either as an educational or as a fine arts institution.[19]

On November 10, 1954, the day of the Supreme Court decision, Wright phoned Madison's *Capital Times* from New York to announce he would leave the state, taking his practice with him. Considering all he had done—bridges for Spring Green and the Dells, and the Monona Terrace project, all gifts to the people, he said, plus paying taxes on hundreds of acres, not to mention his professional and personal example—he was extremely upset to discover how little Wisconsin appreciated him. It was not the $14,000 which he could easily afford that mattered, he insisted, but the minimal value seemingly placed on what he did. Rather than try to sell Taliesin or give it away, he would burn it to the ground and move to Arizona, or to New York or Illinois where governors, he claimed, had invited him to relocate. Telling *The New York Times* he planned to live at the Plaza Hotel for the next year, he revealed that his entire income went directly into the Frank Lloyd Wright Foundation for training young architects, that he lived on an expense account and could probably not even write a ten-dollar check without borrowing to cover it. William Wesley Peters disclosed that since Taliesin buildings were assessed at one million dollars, Wright could never retrieve their full value if he sold (or burned!) them.[20]

"The hometown folks don't want him to leave," wrote the editor of Spring Green's *Weekly Home News*. "The local citizen will take no pride in directing tourists to ruins. We hope we'll always have a Taliesin." But his neighbors need not have worried, for a few days later Wright confided to his friend William T. Evjue of *The Capital Times* that he would probably not follow through on his theatrics. He did not have as much money as people thought, he said, and if state and federal authorities decided on the basis of the supreme court's decision to revoke their tax-exempt educational institution charters and demand back taxes themselves, he would be unable to pay. This would force him to leave and to make a memorial to his forefathers out of his buildings' foundations. Evjue was nonetheless left with the clear impression that Wright would neither leave the state nor destroy his home. But rather than give further assurances, the architect flew off to Chicago to discuss plans for a new University of Illinois, to Philadelphia for groundbreaking at the Beth Shalom Synagogue in Elkins Park, and to New York to see if he could make things happen on the Guggenheim Museum, as if to indicate that he could do without Wisconsin.[21]

Without probing his intentions or his financial situation, a group of Wright's admirers, deciding the time had come honor him, organized a testimonial dinner at the University of Wisconsin's Memorial Union in February 1955. Three hundred seventy well-wishers from around the nation paid $25 a plate to hear featured speaker New York architect Ralph Walker extol Wright and to see him hand the guest of honor a $10,000 check for his taxes. "After the demonstration of feeling and affection last night," the architect commented the next morning, "I don't think it will be possible for me to leave my native state." The guests and many others unable to attend may not have known and probably would not have cared that ten days before the banquet in the face of writs of attachment, Wright had sent Wyoming $2000 for 1944 through 1952 (he had previously paid 1953, and 1954 was not yet due) and $5000 to Iowa County. But with $12,000 still outstanding to the county, he was as glad to accept the check as his well-wishers were to give it, for they were as eager to honor him as he was to receive adulation. What he had wanted more than money, and what he got, was an expression of concern, public recognition that he was indeed Wisconsin's leading citizen. In almost half a century of residence, the state had never commissioned a building, given him an honorary degree, consulted him professionally, or acknowledged his presence except by spurning his design offers and battling him over taxes, morals, and politics. As if to corroborate the point, neither Wisconsin nor its university sent an *official* representative to the testimonial. But the situation was somewhat alleviated when state senator Gaylord Nelson cosponsored a bill to grant full tax exemption to the Wright Foundation. At a legislative hearing in May, the architect confided that he had gotten everything out of life he wanted "except the respect of my neighbors" but then confessed he never went out of his way to get it.[22]

This was not entirely true. A footnote to this lengthy imbroglio was that in 1956 the village of Wyoming hired him to design a consolidated school. Wright completed the plans in October before it came out that he had purchased two and one half acres and given it to the town as a site, designed the building free of charge, and donated $7000 for an assembly room dedicated to his mother Anna and his aunts Ellen and Jane Lloyd Jones. His only rural schoolhouse (Fig. 13.1) consisted of two classrooms separated from the gymnasium–cafeteria–assembly hall by a clerestoried central corridor under a forest of crossed beams. Its roof line almost exactly reproduced hill contours in its bucolic setting, a fitting and simple expression of organic architecture. Most of the 1200 people at the dedication in January 1958 agreed it would be nice to study in such a fine building. The favorable reaction was reminiscent of response to the equally unorthodox Hillside Home School more than half a century before, underscoring the point that Wright's work was not unappealing to the artistically unschooled in rural America. Although the two buildings were only a few minutes apart down a quiet country road, they were separated by half a lifetime of tumult. But in the end, Wright again became his people's architect.[23]

□ □ □

The Wyoming Valley Grammer School appeared in Wright's views of Broadacre City,[24] and in retrospect it seems that as his relations with his neighbors improved during his last few years he tried to influence their development along his model's lines. Some examples: two years after Spring Green failed to secure his highway and bridge

Figure 13.1 Wyoming Valley Grammar School (1956), Wyoming, Wisconsin. Photo by author.

relocation, its Businessmen's Association accepted his design in 1949 of a fieldstone and wood sign for a landscaped piece of state land on Highway 14 calling attention to the town and (by its singular appearance) to the seat of modern architecture. The Highway Commission did not approve. In 1952 when the local fire department put out a blaze at Taliesin, Wright thanked it with a $100 check, suggesting the men blow it on a good time. (They bought new equipment instead.) Then in 1953 he purchased a lunchroom overlooking the bridge in sight of Taliesin leading into Spring Green, announcing he would build a restaurant with a small bar and a terrace cantilevered from the hillside toward the river for outside dining. As a handsome gateway to Wyoming Township and an added attraction to the Spring Green area, it would also be, Wright said, his "gift to the people."[25]

His 1956 design for a Spring Green post office was discarded because the government said it would exceed by $8000 the $16,000 limit on a facility for the town. Backers of a small medical building the next year sought financing by the entire community but could not complete the project until William Wesley Peters did it after Wright died. The general sentiment was to have him build something, village President Archie Fleming stated in July 1957, but his plan for a civic auditorium in 1958 never came to fruition. Nor did the spectacular 1957–1958 revival of the highway marker scheme. This version called for a ninety-foot light shaft at the intersection of Highways 14 and 23 rising from a landscaped base with three fountains spilling into pools representing a spring. Someone suggested adding "teaser" markers all the way to Madison (forty miles) and an equal distance to the west. Trees the village gave Wright in 1957 that he planted along public roadways and in a little park he was developing at the site of the light shaft were later cut down without warning by the State Highway Commission which probably would not have approved Spring Green's attempt to advertise itself. Wright's plan died with him and just as well, since it was little more than high-class boosterism, much too grandiose for such a small community. The light shaft (in Broadacres "a totem and a beacon to the lost tribes of a continent") was intended to stimulate local commerce, but its unique design and the American Automobile Association's guidebooks would have inevitably made it an advertisement for Taliesin as well, linking the destinies of home and community in a way Wright would have approved.[26]

The high point of good relations between the architect and his neighbors came between 1957 and 1959. Eager to honor its most prominent citizen, thankful for the long hours donated by members of the Fellowship to planning Spring Green's centennial in 1957, the town decided to hold a Frank Lloyd Wright Day during the celebration and to dedicate to him its commemorative booklet the cover of which was designed by Wright's secretary, Eugene Masselink. Taliesin held open house every afternoon from June 27th to the 29th, sponsored an architectural exhibition at the High School, and gave a concert, while on his day, the 29th, Wright was fêted at a luncheon and was guest of honor at a pageant on Spring Green's history. The next day he and Olgivanna led a parade. "Nothing is ever sweeter or rarer," he said, "than such a tribute from neighbors." Things went so well with so much input from the Fellows that the town decided to make the festival an annual event—Wright foresaw yearly celebrations in Broadacre City—and there was talk of his designing a civic center or a summer theatre. (He said he would do a theatre and Fellows would help with productions if the plays were really high quality.) Eugene Masselink and William Wesley Peters (as chairman) were included on the four-person planning committee for 1958, symbolizing the kind of working relationship with his neighbors the architect had long envisioned. When he said he was "eager to put every effort into building Spring Green's future," the newspaper editor noted that Wright had always hoped town and Fellowship might collaborate, a hope, he added, now being realized. "It's no longer a friendship between Taliesin and Spring Green," an enthusiastic apprentice observed after the successful three-day 1958 festival, "It's a love affair."[27]

Wright died before Peters and Masselink could organize a third event, and slowly the bonds between Spring Green and Taliesin withered away. His many attempts to design something for it, free of charge if need be, show his strong commitment to the town's future, his desire to make it "an ideal community in which to live," he said in 1958,[28] to bring it closer to his Broadacre City standard. But Spring Green did not take advantage of its opportunities. Just down the road and across the river from America's most famous architect with his international group of apprentices, it was actually in another world. His life style was not its residents', nor was his art something they really wanted: respected, perhaps, and admired, but not something they were determined to have. Spring Green never got a Frank Lloyd Wright building. The restaurant finally opened in 1967, but as a TAA-designed private venture across the river and out of town. In the village proper there are only a handful of second-rate structures to memorialize his name—a medical building, a cocktail lounge, a theatre façade, and a bank—also done after his death by TAA. Of course, there are the usual drugstore postcards and souvenirs in the Dutch Kitchen giftshop, and a highway motel and a scattering of buildings in the countryside by former members of his staff who settled nearby. Everyone knows the way to Taliesin and can repeat apocryphal stories about the Master. Spring Green tends the Wright legend and trades on his name, but it failed to reap the most lasting benefit of all.[29]

Nevertheless, more than any other community in the state it paid tribute to Wright during his last few years when many organizations and institutions outside Wisconsin were also honoring him. Few who could have done so failed to, it seemed. Responding to pressure from "progressives" within its ranks, the American Institute of Architects, the establishment of the profession he had attacked so many times, awarded Wright its Gold Medal in 1949, long after several others of comparatively limited achievement had received it. Between 1947 and 1953 he accepted citations from the National Academy of Arts and Letters, Cooper Union, the American Academy of Arts and Letters, the National Academy of Design, the American Institute of Arts and Letters, Franklin Institute, the National Academy of Finland, and the Royal Academy of Fine Arts in Stockholm. He received Italy's Star of Solidarity in 1951, and honorary doctorates from Princeton University

(1947), Florida Southern (1950), Yale (1954), the University of Wisconsin, and the Technical Institutes of Darmstadt, Germany, and Zurich, Switzerland (all in 1955), the University of Wales (1956), and from Sarah Lawrence in 1958.[30] A photographic exhibition of both Taliesins by Ezra Stoller at the Museum of Modern Art in New York in 1947 was far surpassed in scale and splendor by "Sixty Years of Living Architecture: The Work of Frank Lloyd Wright" which opened at Gimbel's in Philadelphia in January 1951 and for the next three years toured the United States and the major capitals of Europe. Chicago held a Frank Lloyd Wright Day on October 17, 1956, and labeled the Robie House an official landmark, shortly after *The Architectural Record* selected it as "one of the seven most notable residences ever built in America."[31]

Wright, it seemed, could do no wrong. *Time* magazine ran at least seventeen stories about him between 1945 and 1957, usually treating him as an Olympian figure whose pronouncements deserved to be engraved on stone tablets. *Life,* another of his friend Henry Luce's publications, presented him in a similar manner. Reviewers in *Saturday Review, The Nation,* and even Hilton Kramer in *The New Republic* praised *An American Architecture,* a profusely illustrated anthology of his writings published in 1955.[32] *Newsweek* and *The New Yorker* were also generous with space, the latter interviewing him on his periodic trips to the city, the former commenting favorably whenever he announced another monumental design. Even Hollywood paid its respects. Warner Brothers asked him to design sets for *The Fountainhead* (1949) based on Ayn Rand's novel by the same name, but when Wright demanded $250,000 for the job—he did not want it—negotiatons ended. Supposedly based on Wright's life, although some saw touches of Louis Sullivan in it, the film was an architectural (and cinematic) disaster, hardly a fitting depiction of the man (or men) it allegedly portrayed.[33]

Basking in his glory, having conquered the mass media, Wright might have been more generous toward other architects. Occasionally he had a kind word—Edward Durrell Stone was "honest" (perhaps because his early residences were very Wrightian) and the Mormon Tabernacle in Salt Lake City was "a remarkable structure with an original and harmonious expression"—but generally he was uncivil. "He is a highbrow," he said of Philip Johnson. "A highbrow is a man educated beyond his capacity." Mies van der Rohe was "very nice" but an architectural reactionary wasting his time trying to modernize the nineteenth-century steel-frame skyscraper. Skidmore, Owings, and Merrill (SOM) he ridiculed as "Skiddings, Own-More, and Sterile," and as for "the Whisky Building, the Soap Building, and the

Bank"—translation: the Seagram Building (1958) by van der Rohe and Johnson, the Lever House (1952) by SOM, and the Manufacturer's Hanover Trust (1954) by SOM, all landmarks of the modern movement—"they are just extensive. . .cages. . . .rusting at the joints, [with] facades like posters." The Whisky Building was the best of the lot, he insisted, but they were all outdated.[34]

Corbusier? "Why do you link me with that man?" he demanded of an interviewer. "I think Corbusier should have been a painter. He was a bad one but should have kept on. No painter can understand architecture." He did not even acknowledge that he got his ideas from me! "The little geometrical shapes my mother gave me to play with," Wright twitted, Corbusier now calls "Modular." Indeed, most contemporary work was a "betrayal" of his own innovations.

Like those awful UN buildings. Or that Corbusier thing in Marseilles. Massacre on the waterfront, I call that. Or any of those skinny glass boxes. Why, I wouldn't walk on the same side of the street with them. Fool things might explode. There! That's from a fellow who knew what architecture was when the glass-box boys were just so many diapers hanging on the line.[35]

"Do you like Henry Moore?" he was asked in London in 1956. "He has some of your qualities." Then "he must," retorted Wright, "be a very great man."[36]

His ego knew no bounds. "I defy anyone to name a single aspect of the best contemporary architecture," he asserted hotly and sincerely in 1953, "that wasn't first done by me." A guest on an NBC radio program remarked, "I don't think you could find a building constructed anywhere in the United States today, even a lunch stand, that doesn't show in some degree the influence of his architectural ideas." And Wright, who was also on the broadcast, nodded approvingly. "Once, after her husband had agreed on the witness stand that he was the world's greatest architect," *Look* magazine reported, "Mrs. Wright protested, 'Frank, you should be more modest.' 'You forget, Olgivanna,' he replied quickly, 'I was under oath.'" His son John, also an architect, was a bit more objective. "My father, whose colossal ego is matched only by his towering ability, would be the first to agree that anyone who would choose the son when he could have the master ought to have his head examined. In fact, I once heard him say to one of MY clients, 'Why fool around with the coupon when you can have the genuine bond?'" And Wright *was* the genuine article:

Figure 13.2   Frank Lloyd Wright, September 14, 1955, at Chicago Merchandise Mart. Courtesy Henredon Furniture Industries, Morganton, North Carolina.

"an American original," a friend called him. He lived life to the fullest, "at its central current," never wasting a moment, his sister Maginel commented. "If I felt any better," the architect declared, a month before his 89th birthday in 1956, "I couldn't stand it."[37]

By the fifties, Wright was a familiar figure appearing frequently on national radio and television, giving scores of interviews, lecturing and publishing constantly. Often in the news, he was a reliable fount of quotable quotes. "A great showman and cut-up," his friend Bruce Barton remarked, he "loves to say things that make headlines."[38] Though he mixed his bombshells with cogent analysis, the outrageous attracted more attention. Some rose to take issue but most were overpowered by the force of his personality. He liked to play with audiences, relishing the repartee of question and answer (Fig. 13.2). A typical exchange at the University of Michigan School of Architecture and Design in 1954 illustrates his self-assurance, his questionable humility, and his amused tolerance of the lesser mortals before him. One member of the audience had understood Wright to say that people were products of their environment. No, he replied:

FLW   Our environment is a dreadful byproduct of ourselves. We got just exactly what we earned and what we deserved.

AUDIENCE   I happen to like it, as far as that is concerned.

FLW   You are welcome.

AUDIENCE   But I would also like to live in one of your homes.

FLW   You are not entitled to it, I'm afraid, if you like what you are in now.

AUDIENCE   I'm in life right now, and I happen to like it. I would like one of your homes; I would appreciate it very much. However, if I can't have it. . .I am not going to drop dead over it.

FLW   I don't think you need to. I think you have to makeshift, poor fellow. I'd like to help you but I can't.

*　*　*

AUDIENCE   That is a difference of opinion, I happen to think it is.

FLW   Good.

AUDIENCE   And I'd like to see everybody—not who deserves it, but everybody who feels for it—to be able to take advantage of [your architecture].

FLW   I wouldn't.

AUDIENCE   That is another difference of opinion.

FLW   I think you have to earn these things.[39]

So effectively had he mesmerized the public that he could, for example, barge unchallenged into board meetings or other private gatherings at New York's Plaza Hotel, where he kept a permanent suite with furnishings of his own design, and with his malacca cane point out flaws in the decor. Or he would stride down Fifth Avenue from the Guggenheim construction site, entourage hurrying to keep pace, acerbatingly criticizing buildings en route. The Plaza itself, of course, escaped his venom: built by "the Astors, Astorists, Astorites,

Plasterbilts and Whoeverbilts, who wanted to dress up and parade," spoiled in large part by "inferior desecrators," it still had "human sense." But the rest of New York upset him: after each visit, he claimed, he was "turned inside out, shaken," and emptied. He could get around faster by walking over the tops of taxis, he sneered, than by riding in them. Yet he loved the city, especially his Plaza suite which, he told visitors, had once belonged to Diamond Jim Brady. "It's the best part of New York," he proudly proclaimed.[40]

In many ways the comparison was a good one, for there were obvious similarities between the gambler and the architect. Both lived high, wide, and handsome, unrestrained by fetters binding average people. There was a drama and a flair to Wright's life: contact with celebrities and headliners, praise and adulation, television appearances, flashy automobiles, globehopping and much, much more. Even his parties at Taliesin were newsworthy events: a small affair might feature Alexander Woollcott, Adlai E. Stevenson, or Carl Sandburg among the hundred or so guests, replicas of Egyptian barques floating in the lake, hundreds of Japanese lanterns bobbing in the breeze, supper on the lawn, and after dinner outdoor dancing.[41] His life was a whirlwind of activity. When he was not off speaking somewhere, he was turning out buildings at a furious pace, if anything picking up steam as he entered his tenth decade. As he passed his ninetieth birthday in 1957 he accepted a career high of forty commissions, followed by another twenty as he turned ninety-one. With his five books and fifty or more lesser publications during the 1950s he made many a younger person wonder how he did it.

□ □ □

Underneath this supercharged veneer was a quieter man, hardly the Diamond Jim known to the public, a man cherishing his moments of relaxation and privacy. There was about him "none of the efficiency, the snap, the sense of speed and high-pressure salesmanship of the era he has endeavored to express in steel and stone," one interviewer noted after being alone with Wright. He was something of an anachronism, another reported, with his alpaca suit, white collar, and black string tie, "that turn-of-the-century ensemble of the romantic and aesthetic rebel." And within the walls of Taliesin he was even less flamboyant. On a typical day he arose at seven-thirty, took breakfast in his quarters (Fig. 13.3) with Olgivanna, then read and sketched until ten, when he strolled the three quarters of a mile over his land to visit the apprentices in their draughting room at the old Hillside School,

Figure 13.3 Wright's private balcony off his bedroom at Taliesin East. Photo by author.

returning to his office an hour or so later. After lunch he napped until three o'clock tea, then held a staff meeting followed by an Old Bushmill and water chaser to whet his appetite for dinner. In the evening he usually read, perhaps James Thurber, O. Henry, or Ralph Waldo Emerson's essays, maybe watched some television, and talked with Olgivanna before bed at ten. On weekends he might indulge himself with an Irish whisky nightcap.

The routine varied a little on Saturdays and Sundays. When he was home on the Sabbath he liked to preach a "sermon" at the tiny Unity Chapel he had helped his aunts and uncles build seventy years before, an hour or two talk to the Fellowship on whatever concerned him. Sometimes guests or apprentices substituted, but the service was always homey and simple. After evening dinner with the Fellowship on Saturdays, there would be a film, and on Sundays, a musicale, followed in either case by refreshments and discussion. Taliesin was "a special kind of oasis," one visitor recalled, "in which the raw and hostile forces of surrounding life had somehow been reorganized into a landscape of blessed peace and plenty." Wright could have said the same thing when he built the place for Mamah Borthwick forty-five years before.[42]

At age ninety-one, he seemed a permanent part of the American scene, as much a fixture as an historic landmark. He was rarely sick, always active, vigorous, and very conspicuous. As March turned into April 1959, he accepted another commission, granted another interview, continued work on the Marin County Civic Center and several other projects, and fired off an indignant letter denouncing Monona Terrace opponents: everything business as usual. At Taliesin West he and Olgivanna celebrated Easter with the Fellowship as was their custom. "Arm and arm we walked back to our rooms to talk," she remembered, "to be in each other's presence."[43]

It was their last Easter together. On April 4, Wright complained of abdominal pains and was rushed to Saint Joseph's Hospital in Phoenix where he underwent emergency surgery for an intestinal tract obstruction and related hemorrhaging. For the next few days he recuperated nicely, apparently on the way to full recovery. Doctors marveled at his strength and resiliency. Then fifteen minutes after his nurse checked him, on April 9 at 4:45 A.M., having developed a coronary thrombosis, he "just sighed and died.[44]

His body was driven the 2000 miles to Spring Green in a panel truck and placed in front of the stone fireplace in Taliesin's living room. Hundreds of red clay pots with blue, pink, and purple petunias were scattered about. As the sun set at five o'clock on April 12, some forty relatives and close friends followed the flower-draped, horse-drawn farm wagon (Fig. 13.4) driven by William Wesley Peters and Eugene Masselink down the dirt road to Unity Chapel where 200 Taliesin and Spring Green residents—the only mourners Olgivanna permitted—gathered to hear Reverend Max Gaebler of Madison's Unitarian Society deliver the eulogy. As it grew dark, Wright was lowered into an unmarked grave lined with soft green pine boughs a few feet away from a small fieldstone bearing the simple inscription, "Mamah Cheney."[45]

Well-spoken, well-placed people from around the world offered eloquent regrets, too many for one architecture journal to publish in a single issue. Mies van der Rohe's may have been the most appro-

Figure 13.4 Funeral of Frank Lloyd Wright, April 12, 1959, Taliesin East in background. Photo by John Ahlhauser, courtesy State Historical Society of Wisconsin.

priate: "In his undiminished power he resembles a giant tree in a wide landscape which year after year attains a more noble crown." But the most poignant tributes came from Spring Green, almost overlooked in the eulogizing. "We are much diminished in his passing," the newspaper editor wrote; we have "suffered a great loss." It won't be the same with Mr. Wright gone, a bank cashier remarked; "we always got a thrill when he came walking in here. . . ." But the drugstore owner's wife said it best: "I just can't believe it. He was the kind of man you thought would live forever."[46]

NOTES

1 "Frank Lloyd Wright Sees Hypocrisy As a Taint In All American Life," *The Capital Times*, May 11, 1948.

2 "Wright Calls for Organic Architecture to Match Growth of Democracy," *The Capital Times*, November 10, 1946; "U.N. Stands Like Slab in a Graveyard," *ibid.*, July 13, 1953; *The New York Times*, April 20, 1947, Sec. 6.

3 Lewis Mumford, "A Disoriented Symbol," *The New Yorker* (1951) and "United Nations Assembly," *ibid.* (1953) reprinted in *From the Ground Up* (New York: Harcourt, Brace & World, 1956), 51, 53; F. L. Wright, "Culture and Education," *The Capital Times*, October 30, 1952.

4 "Hypocrisy As a Taint," *The Capital Times*, May 11, 1948; "Harum-Scarum," *Taliesin Square-Paper*, No. 12 (July 1948); *The New York Times*, June 9, 1950.

5 *The Weekly Home News*, April 12, 1951; "Reply of FLW to House Un-American Activities Group Charge," *The Capital Times*, April 21, 1951; "Frank Lloyd Wright Hits McCarthyism: Sees Need For a New Third Party," *ibid.*, August 21, 1951.

6 "Wake Up Wisconsin," *The Capital Times*, September 22, 1952.

7 Drew Pearson column, *The Capital Times*, October 17, 1955; "Answers Drew Pearson: Wright Denies Air Academy Criticism Link to 'Interests,'" *ibid.*, October 21, 1955; *The Denver Post*, July 2, 1954; *The Washington Post*, July 8, 1955; *The New York Times*, July 16, 1955. Also see *ibid.*, July 8, 1955; *The Denver Post*, May 29, 1955; *The Capital Times*, May 27, 1955; "FLW Explains His Views on Academy Design," *ibid.*, August 16, 1955; "Wright Replies to Architectural Record Article," *ibid.*, September 6, 1955.

8 *The New York Times*, December 1, 1954; "Frank Lloyd Wright on Restaurant Architecture," *Food Services Magazine* (November 1958).

9 *The Capital Times*, April 23, 1951; July 23, 1956; *The New York Times*, July 22, September 28, 1956.

10 *The Capital Times*, February 24, April 7, 1957; "Wright Picks a Fight in Arizona," *Life*, 42 (May 13, 1957), 59.

11 Herbert Jacobs, "Wright Pleads for Civic Center on Lake Monona, Warns City to 'Wake Up,'" *The Capital Times*, September 28, 1938; "FLW Offers Lake Monona Development Plan for Public Buildings," *ibid.*, November 2, 1938; *ibid.*, November 3, December 5, 1938.

12 "FLW's Revised Monona Development," *The Capital Times*, June 4, 1941; "Civic Center Project Needs Youth Group for Success: Wright," *ibid.*, October 15, 1941.

13 "Wright Envisions Huge Civic Center on Monona," *The Capital Times*, May 31, 1946; *ibid.*, July 7–10 (showing plans), August 25, September 15, 21, 1954; May 27, July 10, ("Madison to be Commonplace") October 4, November 3, 1954.

14 For the remainder of the Monona Terrace controversy see *The Capital Times*, February 7, 8, April 21, August 12, 1955; May 23, July 6, August 17, 25, 29–31, September 5, 6, 1956; March 19, May 3, September 27, 1957; June 18, July 19, 1958; January 21, March 11, April 6, 1959; *Architectural Forum*, 102 (April 1955); 107 (August 1957), 7; "Wisconsin governor signs spite bill that kills FLW's Madison Civic Center," 107 (November 1957), 7, 9; and for its San Rafael spin-off *The New York Times* and *The San Francisco Chronicle*, August 3, 1957.

15 "General Plan of Highway and Bridge Relocation as Proposed by the Frank Lloyd Wright Foundation," *The Weekly Home News*, October 9, 1947; also *ibid.*, October 2, 16, 23, 1947; *The Capital Times*, October 12, 25, 31, 1947. Wright may have been prompted to suggest these improvements by the deaths of stepdaughter Svetlana and his grandson Daniel in a Spring Green highway accident: *ibid.*, September 30, 1946. But he continued to be especially concerned about bridge safety: *ibid.*, November 25, 1948.

16 *The Capital Times*, August 1, 15, 24, 28, September 1, 6, 7, 1951; *The Weekly Home News*, August 2, 16, September 6, 1951; October 2, 1952. He also proposed a Broadacre City highway rerouting scheme for the Dells similar to the one for Spring Green: *The Capital Times*, September 10, 1951. For a butterfly bridge see Arthur Drexler, Ed., *The Drawings of Frank Lloyd Wright* (New York: Horizon Press, 1962), plate 232.

17 *The Weekly Home News*, May 4, 1939; November 30, 1950; August 16, 1951; June 4, 1953; *Baraboo Weekly News*, March 18, 1937.

18 *The Weekly Home News*, September 17, 24, December 10, 17, 1953; *The Capital Times*, September 24, October 16, December 14, 1953.

19 *The Capital Times*, November 9, 10, 20, 1954; *The Weekly Home News*, September 2, November 11, 1954; *The New York Times*, September 9, November 10, 1954.

20 *The New York Times*, November 12, 1954; *The Capital Times*, November 11, 15, 16, 1954; "Wright's Exodus," *Newsweek* 44 (November 22, 1954), 63.

21 Vernon E. Hill, "They Want Him to Stay," *The Weekly Home News*,

November 18, 1954; William T. Evjue, "Wright Will Not Leave State and Will Not Destroy Taliesin," *The Capital Times,* November 23, 1954.

22 *The Capital Times,* February 1, 11, 17, May 18, 1955; *The Weekly Home News,* November 25, 1954; January 27, February 3, 17, May 19, 1955; *The New York Times,* February 12, 1955.

23 *The New York Times,* August 3, 1957; *The Weekly Home News,* October 25, November 1, 1956; January 30, 1958; *The Capital Times,* October 17, 1957; April 7, 1959.

24 Frank Lloyd Wright, *The Living City* (New York: Horizon Press, 1958), 128–130.

25 *The Weekly Home News,* November 3, 10, 1949; August 7, 1952; July 23, August 13, 1953.

26 *The Weekly Home News,* January 31, July 25, September 12, December 5, 12, 19, 1957; May 15, 1958. The beacon reference is on the fold-out map of Broadacres in *The Living City.*

27 *The Weekly Home News,* March 14, 28, May 16, June 27, July 4, August 22, September 26, October 31, November 7, 1957; January 23, June 30, July 3, August 7, 1958; *Centennial Spring Green: The First Hundred Years, 1857–1957* (Baraboo, Wisconsin: Sauk City Publishing Co., 1957), 3–7 especially.

28 *The Weekly Home News,* January 23, 1958.

29 There was another monument to Wright in Spring Green, surely an unappreciated one. At the intersection of Highways 14 and 23, at the outskirts of town on the triangular plot he planned to use for his markers, landscape and give as a gift to the town, there stood upright for several years a large fieldstone slab, once intended to point the way to Taliesin. It was unmarked and its purpose virtually forgotten, a sad symbol of Wright's ultimate impact on Spring Green. By 1972 it had been removed.
    Wright unwittingly revealed some of the reasons for, and captured some of the flavor of, the lack of cultural rapport between town and Taliesin in a news item he placed in the February 22, 1934, *Weekly Home News:*

Are the village people uncomfortable in our playhouse. . . ? Perhaps we are highbrows or something. . . ? Groups of people drive out every Sunday. . .from Madison. . .to our shows but the village just sits.

. . .one might safely suppose a community would be interested. . .to encourage the superior way in its own interest. But you know how it is. . . .

Anyhow, the folks are missing something. . .they can't get for love or money anywhere else.

If we knew who these were who would [come] but couldn't we might help.

30 Most of these are listed in Olgivanna Lloyd Wright, *Frank Lloyd Wright: His Life, His Work, His Word* (New York: Horizon Press, 1967), 217–221, although she omitted Sarah Lawrence; see *The New York Times*, May 31, 1958, and *The New Yorker*, 34 (June 14, 1958), 26–27.

31 On the exhibition see *The New York Times*, January 26, 1951 and October 23, 1953; "Business and Culture," *Newsweek*, 37 (February 5, 1951), 76. On Wright's Day in Chicago, *The Capital Times*, October 18, 1956, and *Architectural Forum*, 105 (November 1956), 21.

32 Hilton Kramer, "Architecture and Rhetoric," *The New Republic*, 133 (December 26, 1955), 20; Elizabeth Pokorny, "Use, Form, and Art," *The Nation*, 192 (January 14, 1956), 35–36; Peter Blake, "Our Elder Statesman," *Saturday Review*, 39 (August 5, 1956), 22.

33 George Nelson, "Mr. Roark Goes to Washington. . . ," *Interiors* 108 (April 1949), 106–111.

34 Olgivanna Lloyd Wright, *The Shining Brow: Frank Lloyd Wright* (New York: Horizon Press, 1960), 242; *Desert News* (Salt Lake City, Utah), April 27, 1953; Seldon Rodman, *Conversations With Artists* (New York: Devin-Adair, 1957), 58, 74; *The Capital Times*, June 3, 1957; Aline Saarinen, "Tour With Mr. Wright," *The New York Times Magazine*, September 22, 1957.

35 "Outside the Profession," *The New Yorker*, 29 (September 26, 1953), 27.

36 "From Taliesin to Shepherd's Bush," *The Architect's Journal* [London], 125 (July 26, 1956), 110–111.

37 *The New Yorker*, 29 (September 26, 1953), 27; text of NBC radio's "Biography in Sound" in *The Weekly Home News*, August 6, 1956; "A Visit With Frank Lloyd Wright," *Look*, 21 (September 17, 1957), 31; Merle Armitage, "Frank Lloyd Wright: An American Original," *Texas Quarterly*, 5 (Spring 1962); Barney, *Valley*, 148; *The Capital Times*, May 5, 1956; January 8, 1958.

38 Bruce Barton to Otto McFeeley, February 20, 1956, Barton Collection, SHSW.

39 "By FLW," *Monthly Bulletin, Michigan Society of Architects*, 28 (June 1954), 10.

40 "The Wright Word," *Time*, 64 (August 2, 1954), 61; "Talk With Mr. Wright," *The New York Times*, November 1, 1953; "Wright Revisited," *The New Yorker*, 32 (June 16, 1956), 26–27.

41 For descriptions of two see *The Weekly Home News*, August 1, 1946 and *The Capital Times*, June 9, 1956.

42 *The New York Times*, January 17, 1932, Sec. 5; July 24, 1949, Sec. 7; June 22, 1958; *The New Yorker*, 32 (June 16, 1956); editors, "Frank Lloyd Wright, 1869–1969," *Architectural Forum*, 110 (May 1959), 112.

43 O. L. Wright, *The Shining Brow*, 119.

44 *The Capital Times*, April 7, 9, 1959; *The New York Times*, April 8, 10, 1959.

45 *The New York Times,* April 13, 1959; Rosalie Robbins Tonkens, "Wright's Funeral: A Remembrance," *ibid.,* April 9, 1972.

46 *Architectural Forum,* 110 (May 1959); Vernon E. Hill, "Frank Lloyd Wright is Gone," *The Weekly Home News,* April 9, 1959; for neighbor comments see *The Capital Times,* April 10, 1959.

After 1959

CHAPTER FOURTEEN

How Do You Speak to a Divinity?

Even before his death several significant Frank Lloyd Wright buildings were destroyed. After more than a decade of abuse, Midway Gardens (1913–1914) in Chicago was demolished in 1929, a year after his 1893 boathouse for Madison, Wisconsin, one of his first commissions in independent practice, was torn down. The Larkin Administration Building (1904) in Buffalo, a major early work, perished in 1949, followed the next year by his very first design, the original Hillside Home School (1887) on the Taliesin estate at Spring Green. Others were lost after 1959. The innovative residence for Allison Harlan (1892) in Chicago burned in 1963 just before its scheduled restoration. Among more recent fatalities were the 1911 Lake Geneva (Wisconsin) Hotel; the Munkwitz Apartments (1916) in Milwaukee; the Francis and Francisco Terrace Apartments (both 1895) in Chicago; and "Northome" (1913) for Francis Little in Wayzata, Minnesota, the living room of which was preserved by the Metropolitan Museum of Art in New York City. The most publicized demolition was the Imperial Hotel (1913–1922) in Tokyo. After withstanding 400 incendiaries gutting an entire wing during Allied bombing in 1945 and repeated attempts to secure its choice location, the hotel finally succumbed to "progress" in 1967, to be replaced in 1969 by a seventeen-story, $60 million "New Imperial."[1] At the time of Wright's death, some 300 of his structures remained, several dozen less than he built.

On the other hand, the growing movement to preserve and restore architectural landmarks and structurally sound lesser buildings benefited Wright's legacy. His own 1889–1895 Oak Park quarters, for example, were purchased by a dedicated middle-aged couple who completed major renovations from proceeds of guided tours before selling to the newly organized Frank Lloyd Wright Home and Studio Foundation. The Darwin C. Martin House (1904) in Buffalo was refurbished as a presidential residence by the local branch of the State University of New York too late, unfortunately, to salvage its one-hundred-foot pergola or any of its furnishings.[2] Periodic public outcries saved the 1907 Robie House from repeated attempts by the University of Chicago to tear it down, leading in 1964 to its registration as a National Historic Landmark and in 1966 to its complete rehabilitation as the Adlai E. Stevenson Institute for International Affairs. Public pressure forced Interior Secretary Stuart Udall to intervene in 1964 and help move the Loren Pope House (1940) in Falls Church, Virginia, from the path of highway bulldozers.[3] Especially in and around Chicago a number of Wright residences were purchased and with considerable dedication and sacrifice renovated by admirers.[4] Many early homes had been well maintained over the years, but extensive efforts and funds were expended to return others to their rightful condition, for example, the 1908 Boynton House, beautifully restored at great expense during the 1970s by Joan and Louis Clark in Rochester, New York.

In addition to stimulating causes célèbres and personal crusades, Wright's architecture entered the cultural mainstream in several other ways. Some of his public buildings were opened to scheduled tours, among them the Hillside Home School at Spring Green and Taliesin West in Arizona, Unity Temple in Oak Park, the Johnson Wax Building in Racine, the Beth Shalom Synagogue, the Annunciation Greek Orthodox Church, and the Unitarian Meeting House in Madison. By their nature a number of others are usually open: his shops, clinics, and theatres, the Guggenheim Museum, Marin County Civic Center, his university buildings, and so on. Several residences are more or less available to the public. In 1963 Edgar Kaufmann, Jr., donated his father's Fallingwater at Bear Run, along with $500,000 and 500 acres, to the Western Pennsylvania Conservancy, and since it opened in 1964, over 500,000 people have gone considerably out of their way to see it.[5] Others are the presidential Martin House in Buffalo; the Hanna House (1936) in Palo Alto, California, donated by its owners to Stamford University in 1975; the 1952 Arthur Matthews residence in Atherton, California, now a behavioral studies institute; the Robie House; the 1900 Bradley residence in Kankakee, Illinois, tastefully transformed into a restaurant; Aline Barnsdall's "Hollyhock" (1916–1920), part of the Los Angeles Municipal Art Museum; Herbert F. Johnson's "Wingspread," location of the Johnson Foundation; Wright's own Oak Park home and studio; and undoubtedly a few more.

Owners of lived-in residences, on the other hand, find themselves on the horns of a dilemma, caught between a natural inclination to show off what they have and the need to preserve some semblance of privacy. With the publication of lists and maps of their locations, Wright homes are increasingly besieged by visitors, especially in or near metropolitan areas. Some owners have retreated behind electric fences and guard dogs, opening their doors to no one except occasionally by appointment, but many more welcome anyone no matter the day or hour at considerable personal sacrifice. The most gracious are undaunted by film wrappers on the lawn, trampled flowers, strangers popping out from behind bushes, or even in one celebrated case in Arizona by a man and his horse peering in the bedroom window as the startled woman of the house awoke. Common courtesy, of course, suggests that interested parties make prior arrangements before invading personal privacy. In a society based on "free" enterprise, most works of art are not in public trust, but the best way to have them reasonably available is to respect the rights of those who currently care for them.

By the 1960s Wright's once controversial and mind-boggling designs were so familiar to many Americans that major corporations could appropriate them to hawk their wares. Goodyear advertised its Neothane synthetic rubber coating in a dramatic two-page photograph of the Marin County Civic Center roof in the July 14, 1969 Newsweek. Atlantic-Richfield identified itself with good taste by publishing a picture of Fallingwater in the September 3, 1973 Time] Mobil Oil used a shot of the Guggenheim in the August 21, 1977 New York Times to notify the city of its financial support for cultural events. And General Motors pushed its 1969 Luxury 98 Oldsmobile by driving it and a leggy, fur-draped model to the Annunciation Greek Orthodox Church and publishing the photo in a spread in the November 3, 1968 Milwaukee Journal. Lesser businesses also found Wright good for sales. The Arizona Biltmore depicted itself in The New York Times, Helga Howie boutique used a logo of "the celebrated shop designed [for the Morrises] by Frank Lloyd Wright" in The New Yorker, and the Comsky Gallery in the Anderton Court Center in Beverly Hills did the same in Art in America.

The New York fashion industry ran an inspired ad in The Times (August 29, 1976) showing a model on a skateboard sailing down the ramp of the Guggenheim, an ad that had actually been topped two weeks earlier by an August 13 New Yorker cartoon in which a small boy on his own skateboard—presumably starting at the top—comes roaring hell-bent-for-leather out the Museum's front door. The "Wizard of Id" comic strip once joked about the noted Japanese architect "Flank Roydd Light"; and the Nichiren Shoshu Academy, a pseudo-Buddhist organization, had a story in its October 31, 1975 *World Tribune* on the man whose "name is almost a household word." (Their using it helped prove the point.) When Wright's 1953 design for the Riverview Terrace Restaurant was finally executed by TAA in 1967, Ladybird Johnson, the President's wife, officiated at the dedication.[6] On June 8, 1966, his ninety-ninth birthday, the Post Office issued a two-cent stamp, the first to commemorate an American architect (excluding Thomas Jefferson); and in 1969 Chicago and Oak Park collaborated on a five-week celebration of his supposed centennial.

Exhibitions of Wright furniture and stained glass have been held from time to time (the latest and most elaborate in 1978 by the Smithsonian Institution in Washington), collectors scramble for exorbitantly priced artifacts from his early buildings, innumerable books by and about him have been issued and reissued, a jazz program was televised from Fallingwater and a documentary from the Johnson Wax Building, rock duo Simon and Garfunkel included "So long, Frank Lloyd Wright," in their 1970 *Bridge Over Troubled Water* album, his name is used on real estate pages to sell houses he did not design, in 1974 an Aspen, Colorado, firm tried to market "Indian Memorial" sculptures made from a 1924 sketch, *Frank Lloyd Wright on Record* appeared from Caedmon in 1961, and in 1976 V.O.P. Productions of Oklahoma City sold a one-hour tape of a 1952 Wright lecture—a "true collector's item [it said], strictly limited edition, one of a kind, timely, educational, act now, there are no plans to repeat this offer"—for $32.50 (postpaid).[7] Once considered a rebel, Frank Lloyd Wright is now harnessed for all sorts of mundane purposes.

Demolition of his buildings has in part been offset by others erected after his death. Some he left under construction including Beth Shalom, the Guggenheim, the Kalita Humphreys Theatre, Riverview Restaurant, and about fifteen private homes. Several more for which ground had not been broken were completed even later, among them portions of the Marin County Civic Center, the Annunciation Greek Orthodox Church, Grady Gammage Auditorium, the Corbin Education Center, and the Southwestern Christian Seminary in Phoenix modified from a 1950 design by Taliesin Associated Architects for 1972 completion. The forty to fifty buildings, mostly houses, in various stages of planning and construction were supervised after Wright's death by his widow Olgivanna and by his son-in-law William Wesley Peters, president and vice-president, respectively, of the Frank Lloyd Wright Foundation. Founded in 1940, this parent organization created two subdivisions in 1959: Taliesin Associated Architects, a firm composed of Wright's staff and former apprentices, and the Frank Lloyd Wright School of Architecture, drawing its faculty primarily from TAA. The Taliesin Fellowship passed out of existence, but the name continued to be applied informally to the corps of architectural trainees.

It was inevitable, of course, that without Wright significant changes would occur at Taliesin. Despite his insistence that organic buildings could be conceived only by an independent architect working alone, TAA followed the general trend in the profession to become a firm even though Peters usually signed the renderings. A second change was away from Wright's notion that architecture should be taught by the apprenticeship system and on-the-job training. TAA introduced a formal array of mandatory and recommended courses at the School of Architecture predictably including "The Art and Philosophy of Frank Lloyd Wright," later changed to "Principles of Organic Architecture." The adoption of modern pedagogy may have been a tacit admission that Wright's methods had been deficient or could not be passed on to his disciples, but abandoning the apprenticeship system as the major means of instruction was clearly a significant departure from the Master's preferences. Thirdly, the Foundation scaled down its attempts at "organic" living, preferring to purchase rather than grow its own food, and to contract rather than perform much of the repairs and maintenance, especially at Taliesin East, although students are still required to work on construction sites. And finally, the Foundation began to summer in Switzerland and to spend eight months a year at Taliesin West (Wright had stayed for five or six) where the climate was less rigorous, allowing Taliesin East to become quite dilapidated.[8] Only after plans for a TAA-designed resort complex for the Spring Green area were announced in 1967 (see below) did it return to Wisconsin during the summers to make minimal repairs on its property.

The Frank Lloyd Wright School of Architecture continued some of the more objectionable features of the Fellowship. Incoming students are screened during a one-year probationary period and may expect to remain "eight or more years" even if they enter with college degrees. Classes meet all twelve months, eight hours a day, six days a week. Work permitting, a student may take fourteen days a year leave but otherwise may not go off "campus" without permission. Since "social development and ability to move in any social group are considered a necessary feature in the training of any Architect," the application brochure explains, "participation is required of each student in the weekly formal occasions and traditional social activities." "Any student failing to live up to the high standards of moral, ethical or social conduct, and appropriate personal appearance established by the Foundation," furthermore, "will be dismissed upon due examination." Attendance is checked every day at 6:30 A.M. breakfast where *each student's presence is mandatory*," lights are out at 10:30 P.M., emergency absences—death in the family, illness, or jury duty, for example—are deducted from the fourteen-day annual leave, and students must abide by a dress code. To be sure they do, the Foundation mails applicants *two* descriptions of proper attire: women may not wear slacks in the draughting room; men must don jacket and tie, and women dresses, for dinner; "town wear" is specified; and for the required weekly "occasions" men must have dark tuxedos, with "white formal shirt, studs, cuff links, bow tie, cummerbund, black formal shoes," optional dinner jackets and turtle necks "occasionally," women long and cocktail-length dresses. Little is left to the imagination or to the discretion of individuals.[9] (One may wonder if there are any individuals in this military school atmosphere.)

The nonspontaneous quality of life at Taliesin is reflected in TAA's architecture. Even while it was executing Wright's unfinished designs, it began to solicit new clients. Perhaps the continuing demand for "Wright" buildings was sufficient to justify this action, perhaps Olgivanna's desire to perpetuate the gospel of organic architecture was the primary motivation, or perhaps the architects were simply shrewd enough to trade on Wright's name rather than try to make it on their own. By 1963 they had accepted more than fifty new commissions, less than half as many as he had during the comparable four-and-one-half-year period from 1955 until his death, but obviously enough to stay in business.[10] TAA's work can be divided into three categories: execution of Wright's uncompleted designs; new commissions calling for additions to older Wright buildings; and third, new commissions for entirely new projects.

Since the first category has already been discussed (above and in Chapter Thirteen), it remains to be said only that in completing Wright's unfinished work, TAA's products were so fussy and elaborate that he may not have approved. The second category can also be disposed of quickly. TAA built additions to the Unitarian Meeting House in Madison, the Johnson buildings in Racine, and to a number of other Wright structures by duplicating and extending the originals so faithfully that it is difficult to tell the new and the old apart. At the Guggenheim Museum, on the other hand, it based its 89th Street curatorial quarters on a 1949 Wright sketch.[11] When it relied on the

Master's drawings or when in lieu of them the character of the structure dictated the addition, TAA's work was reasonably good. The firm was at its best, in other words, when creative imagination was not required.

The third category—entirely new commissions—overlaps the second somewhat because in a few cases TAA simply built old Wright designs. In 1972, for example, Foundation Archivist Bruce Brooks Pfeiffer reproduced, with a garage and a few minor alterations, Wright's 1938 Ralph Jester project (see Chapter Nine) as a residence for himself at Taliesin West.[12] And for a Country Club House near Spring Green (more on this below), TAA decided to use Wright's 1924 Madison Nakoma Country Club project, making only a tiny, insignificant change on a side terrace.[13] Obviously, most clients would not be content with forty- or fifty-year-old resurrections, so TAA usually tried to strike out on its own. But elements of Wright's work invariably crept in. The Lescohier House in Madison, for example, horizontally oriented but propped up as it pulled away from its sloping site by the Corbusier-type poles Wright had railed against, culminated in triangular corner windows under a cathedral roof very much like the Unitarian Meeting House a few miles away and, with its fieldstone chimney, concrete block walls, orange panels, and vertical brown trim, was a kaleido-scope of garish materials and elements ineffectively borrowed from several of the Master's designs. Despite removal of the more rigorous aspects of life under Wright, his presence lingered everywhere at Taliesin, especially in the draughting room.

When it could not borrow directly from the Master, TAA relied on the device of dressing up structures with excessively elaborate trim, substituting flashy technique for creative content. The 1962 Lincoln Income Life Insurance Company (Fig. 14.1) in Louisville, Kentucky, for example, took a spectacular engineering concept from Wright—its fifteen floors are cantilevered from a deeply sunk utility spine without touching the ground—but is so completely smothered with a lacework grille of gold-anodized aluminum set in front of plastic panels that the windows cannot be seen, an entirely inappropriate treatment for a high-rise monolith, and an embarrassing architectural blunder.[14] From the very beginning TAA lapsed into a style which Wright may or may not have condemned since it was more or less his style. But by treating façades as applications of surface rather than as expressions of interior events, his followers opened themselves, perhaps with even more justification, to the very criticisms Wright had leveled against the Prairie School and the Internationalists years before. As TAA moved away from Wright in point of time, it grew more and more enamoured of

Figure 14.1 Lincoln Income Life Insurance Company (1962) by Taliesin Associated Architects in Louisville, Kentucky. Courtesy Lincoln Income Company.

the circular modes of expression—in plan and detail—that had characterized his last three or four years, circles covered with circles dripping with more circles (Fig. 14.2). It had found its cliché.

One of TAA's largest projects illustrates the detrimental consequences of its inability to establish architectural independence. In 1967 it announced plans to construct an all-season "Spring Green" resort based, it misleadingly said, on Wright's own ideas for the region.[15] Referring to the Broadacre City model, William Wesley Peters and associates laid out a 4000-acre project along a four-mile stretch of the Wisconsin River for William Keland, president of the Wisconsin River Development Corporation, former executive of the Johnson Wax Company, and once a Wright client. Along with The Springs, a golf

Figure 14.2 The Spring Green (Wisconsin) Bank (ca. 1972) by Taliesin Associated Architects. Photo by author.

course by Robert Trent Jones, the scheme also included a club house, a three-hundred-room hotel with convention facilities, a ski run and lodge called The Wintergreen, a marina, a fishing village, other recreational features, shopping and crafts areas, and summer and year-round homes. TAA has design control over every detail, and a newspaper report gave the impression that the project evolved from a plan Wright had drawn especially for the locale.

The roots of the development can indeed be found in Wright's ideas, not one of such monumental proportions, but in the 1953 Riverview Terrace Restaurant, his "gift to the people," that the Fellowship began to construct in 1957, continued in the summer of 1958, but failed to resume after Wright's death. Eight years later when TAA modified the original design, it changed the name to "The Spring Green," opening it not as a gift but as the first stage in Keland's Wisconsin River Development. The restaurant (Fig. 14.3) is itself a measure of TAA's progress since 1959. Its several units are clumsily forced together, and its cantilevered entrance canopy and octagonal tea house are much too singular and ostentatious for the rest of the building, serving basically as nonfunctional, showy eye-catchers. Not only is The Spring Green an unresolved assortment of Wrightian forms, but all the major buildings in the proposed development were

Figure 14.3 The Spring Green Restaurant, completed in 1967 by Taliesin Associated Architects from Wright's 1953 design for the Riverview Terrace Restaurant. Photo by author.

either based directly on forty-year-old plans or are abysmal variations on their themes. The resurrected 1924 Nakoma Golf Club House was accompanied by private dwellings based on an Indian tepee motif Wright had developed for cabins at Lake Tahoe in the 1920s. The restaurant tower, duplicating another just out of sight at Taliesin's 1938 Midway Farm Buildings, had also appeared on the 1953 Anderton Court Center in Beverly Hills. And the Wintergreen Ski Lodge, an hexagonal structure with rooms protruding in lateral setbacks covered with a heavily articulated diamond module concrete surface, was surpassed in ugliness only by its gatehouse (Fig. 14.4), surfaced with a course pebble concrete aggregate occasionally overlaid with diamond and diagonal strips of trim.

According to Peters, the Wisconsin River Development "represents the realization of a dream Frank Lloyd Wright envisioned—the creation of an organic community with all facilities for recreation and resort living in the Wisconsin he loved so well." Not only does this contain an obvious contradiction as well as a basic misunderstanding of Broadacre City, to which Peters was alluding, namely, that a vacation retreat can be an organic community, but it also assumes that Wright would have accepted a colony of transients commercializing his relatively unspoiled countryside. Far from improving the lives of the local population in any significant way, it will simply be an unusual resort, ministering to the whims of affluent pleasure seekers for a season, but

Figure 14.4 Gatehouse for The Wintergreen ski lodge (ca. 1967) by Taliesin Associated Architects at Spring Green, Wisconsin. Photo by author.

largely unavailable to the host community except for jobs. Built with out-of-town money, it will turn Spring Green into an employment agency, a labor pool dependent on the vicissitudes of distant financiers. Close architectural supervision, especially of questionable quality, will not ensure the kind of social integration Wright knew could only evolve organically. Although there will be permanent homes in the development, it is unlikely that this minority of residents will be easily absorbed into Spring Green. They are more apt to have a disruptive impact similar to that of New Yorkers who fled to the once stable villages of Long Island and southwestern Connecticut.

This project and TAA's work in general shows it has absorbed little more than the superficialities of Wright's teachings. Two decades after the Master's death, its designs are still derivative and distinctly second-rate, relying on unorthodox or elaborate devices for interest. It is quite possible, of course, that like many great artists, Wright's concepts were so personal, so much the product of a supremely creative mind, that they cannot be taught either to or by his successors, and it is also understandable if those close to him were unable to emerge from his overpowering influence. But TAA goes blithley about claiming to carry on his work. It has not and can not. No one can. What it has done is confuse architectural appearance with philosophical substance, institutional continuity with creative generation. Sculptor James Seawright once remarked that "the best ideas grow out of an understanding of processes being used, rather than out of a preconceived notion of the effects to be achieved."[16] TAA never learned that lesson.

Nor did it fulfill two specific obligations to Wright it undertook at his death. It did not build "Unity Temple," a thirty-foot-square glass and fieldstone chamber of meditation he designed for himself and his family as a final resting place at the site of Silsbee's 1886 Unity Chapel across the road from Taliesin. Neither did it erect the air-conditioned, fireproof vault and museum to house the architect's papers and 8000 drawings at Taliesin East.[17] Perhaps these failures are blessings in disguise for where TAA altered the Taliesins, the results were disappointing. At Spring Green it placed a rather flashy swimming pool (Wright preferred the river), with round metal doors cut through a fieldstone wall decorated with ornament taken from demolished Louis Sullivan buildings, in such a way that the green sunshield throws up a glare ruining the southern broadside view of the building. And in order to air condition Taliesin West, which Wright would never have approved, TAA replaced the canvas roof and sideflaps and the magnificent redwood beams in the draughting room with translucent plastic panels and steel girders painted red, destroying the ambience of one of his finest conceptions. But if his disciples have failed him architecturally, they have more than fulfilled his expectations in public relations.

Under the aegis of Olgivanna Wright, the Foundation has performed one task with utmost fidelity. Perpetuating the myths and legends the architect originated about himself, and the flattering self-evaluations he broadcast, Mrs. Wright and her minions have stoked the furnaces of mystique to full capacity. Since his death she has published four books about her late husband: *Our House* (1959), selections from her column by the same name that ran for several years in Madison's *Capital Times*; *The Shining Brow: Frank Lloyd Wright* (1960), biography, anecdotes, and recollections; *The Roots of Life* (1963), addresses (some to the Fellowship) and "thoughts"; and *Frank Lloyd Wright: His Life, His Work, His Word* (1967), a "biography" based largely on *An Autobiography* and other oft-quoted sources. She also assisted in the posthumous preparation of Wright's *Architecture: Man in Possession of His Earth* (1962), featuring a "biography" by their daughter Iovanna.[18]

These 1200 pages do little more than reproduce writings and photographs that were reproduced before and, although they add to the storehouse of apocryphal Wright stories and remarks, they belabor the redundant. Except for what can be recognized from prior publications, the material in these anthologies is largely unidentified; the

numerous talks to the Fellowship, for example, and long private conversations supposedly repeated verbatim—complete with quotation
marks—are generally undated, thereby diminishing their utility and
making their authenticity questionable. By refusing to locate her husband's comments in time and place, Mrs. Wright elevates them to
eternal verities as if reluctant to concede his death. But her childlike
adoration for even his most banal observations and offhand remarks
is ludicrous and embarrassing. She embalms his conscious levity in a
reverential formaldehyde, draining off his life juices and reducing him
to High Camp. She never questions his absurdities or corrects his
mistakes but enshrines his every word as if it were Absolute Truth.

Nevertheless, Olgivanna's prodigiousness has the singular merit of
preserving and fleshing out the "official" interpretation of the architect's life. From his and her writings one learns that two crucial factors
shaped his career: continuous confrontation with obstacles, and the
certainty of predestined greatness, the first a legacy from his father,
the second from his mother. Anna Wright determined his destiny, so
the story goes, when she willed her unborn son to be a famous
architect, relieving him of any responsibility in the matter. But assur-
ance of ultimate success did little to ease his way, for when William
Wright deserted the family and left it impoverished, his son found
himself a modern-day Ulysses, a secular pilgrim condemned to struggle for his own birthright. As he matured, his obvious talents added
complexity to the paradox of inescapable hardship and inevitable
triumph: he could speed down the broad road to money and prestige
by doing conventional work, a chimeric victory at best, or he could
labor along the narrow path of integrity and innovation to unassailable
greatness in the long run. Choosing the difficult course determined
major turning points in his life: leaving the university allegedly one
term short of a degree, refusing to design in the accepted styles,
leaving his wife and children when they interfered with his creativity,
and refusing to bend to yellow journalism, social ostracism, professional hostility, and government harrassment—all in the name of principle. His work was maligned, ridiculed, misunderstood, and purposefully ignored. The cause for which he fought was as unpopular as
cavalry at Little Bighorn, and Wright certainly believed himself a target
for the slings and arrows of outrageous fortune.

When after many years the material and intangible benefits of his
work were finally recognized, the legend continues, inferior architects
claimed them as their own; first the Prairie School and then the Internationalists parlayed his innovations into wealth and fame without
giving him credit. But he took consolation from the fact that he alone

(sometimes he included Louis Sullivan) had developed modern architecture. "When Sullivan and I came to architecture," he told an interviewer in 1953, "it had been slumbering for five hundred years. We woke it up. We gave it a fresh start." To reverse its decline since the Renaissance, he had had to fight the profession every inch of the way. "I was entirely contrary to everything they believed in," he said, "and if I were right, they were wrong. . . . It was a question at one time, I suppose, of their survival or mine."[19] But when the archenemy, the American Institute of Architects, awarded him its Gold Medal in 1949, it confirmed what he already knew, that he had won the ultimate victory: recognition of his birthright, his predestined greatness. In the architect's own eyes and in his wife's he was a kind of superman, defying belief with fantastic accomplishments.

If Wright had somehow conquered human limitations, if he was really like Jesus Christ as Olgivanna has implied, then she was entirely correct to label the Guggenheim "The Miracle on Fifth Avenue." Not to be outdone, the minister of the Annunciation Greek Orthodox Church once remarked with questionable theology, "How do you speak to a divinity? I mean, I do that when I pray, but what about on earth? That's the way I felt about him." And Wright's son John, with a certain immodesty of his own, referred to "my father who is on earth."[20] This flighty rhetoric is all very flattering, but it obscures the man. Wright can hardly be congratulated for his accomplishments if he was predestined to greatness, if he possessed superhuman abilities. Awarding him honors would be like giving God a medal for designing the Grand Canyon. It is much more gratifying to presume that Wright was human—and there is evidence to suggest that he was very human indeed—for then his achievements stand as monuments to humanity's greatness. The more Wright is demythologized, the more satisfying he becomes.

□ □ □

How then is this man, this Frank Lloyd Wright, to be evaluated? Was he a conservative, a radical, a romantic, a modernist? Was he immoral, as many believe, or did he have unusual, almost compulsive, integrity? Why did such a successful artist need to construct legends applauding himself? Why did he need to trumpet his own achievements when he accomplished far more than most people dare to hope?

The most important early documents in the development of Wright's embattled and superhuman persona are the 1914 "In the Cause of Architecture, II" article, and *An Autobiography*, first published in 1932.

Both were written during very trying times for Wright: in 1914 when he was the object of public condemnation for living with a woman not his wife, also a period of his own architectural uncertainty, and in the late 1920s, during years of financial hardship and cacophonous battles with Miriam Noel. Adversity undoubtedly influenced his self-interpretation. Clearly he felt personally threatened and socially intimidated, and both these literary works depend on a spirited offense as the best defense. Blaming others for all his difficulties, they claim purity of motive for his every action. In them he constructed a more pleasant world, one in which he controlled his own destiny. When people were reluctant to purchase his services, these writings exaggerated his greatness; when the future seemed bleak, they reminded him of monumental obstacles he had already surmounted. In 1932 Wright was sixty-five, too old to change his analysis of events, his fixed convictions, or his self-image. He had been playing the role of harrassed genius since at least 1914, and it became increasingly difficult to separate role from reality. What began as a defense mechanism slowly and imperceptibly evolved into an enjoyable performance and then a way of life.

It has not generally been realized that his major obstacles were largely self-created. His popularity waned only when he followed architectural detours (in the 1920s, for example) or when he flaunted social conventions, most notably from the moment he abandoned his family and practice in 1909 until he finally resolved his marital difficulties before developing the Usonian house in the 1930s. Wright's major difficulties during the prairie period were not lack of clients, critical hostility, or colleague rejection, as he claimed, but were on the contrary the by-products of his own struggle for architectural perfection. In 1909 he walked away from a successful practice based on a popular house type, and in 1923 because of personal problems failed to take advantage of the international acclaim stemming from publicity surrounding the Imperial Hotel. Since his 1920s buildings were as antisocial as his life style, it is little wonder the public was leary. By choosing professional and personal unorthodoxy, he denied himself continuing success. But the choice was his own. His insistence on reading public disapproval of his personal life as rejection of his architecture was a way to avoid confronting the implications of his own design and personal decisions, a way to absolve himself of responsibility for the consequences of his own actions.

Wright's tendency to project the root of his difficulties onto other people suggests that his ego may have been as fragile as it was overdeveloped. To protect himself from criticism and from recognizing his own responsibility for it, he transformed trivial encounters into cosmic clashes and mild critics into determined combatants. To assure himself that "they" and not he was at fault when he violated convention he depicted himself as a besieged genius—ridiculed, exploited, and unrecognized—who ultimately prevailed over rivals, thieves, governments, skeptics, the ignorant, and the envious. The irony, of course, is that his life was more triumph than tragedy. Fame and fortune more than outweighed a periodically hostile public or an aloof architectural establishment both of which Wright had offended anyway. Toward the end of his life he surrounded himself with impressionable young admirers (including a wife, thirty years his junior) willing to believe the myths, supply the necessary ego gratification, and perpetuate the legends after his death. Olgivanna Wright and the Taliesin Fellowship have more than kept the faith, but their supercilious attempts to ensure his immortality have detracted from his name and tarnished his legacy.

Despite his own hyperbole and his disciples' cultlike efforts to canonize him in a religion of their own making, the fact remains that in building matters Wright was an eminently practical man. To the extent that he was an experimenter, inventing or popularizing many new architectural devices, he was also a radical, willing to rethink his medium "from the roots," to introduce thorough-going change when necessary. He is generally acknowledged to be responsible for corner windows, early developments in air conditioning and fireproofing, several types of prefabrication, radiant heating in moderately priced homes, eliminating cellars and attics, innovations in the use of poured and blocked concrete, expanded fenestration, and the modern open plan with bedroom zone. He was also among the first to utilize casement windows, cantilevering in house construction, plate glass and other materials, horizontally oriented façades, far overhanging eaves, minimal decoration, slab roofs, carports, and nonrectangular modules. These are only partial lists, but they indicate that in matters of implementation and technique he was an uncompromising progressive.

He was also in the vanguard in matters of design philosophy, challenging conventional wisdom on the shape, aesthetics, organization, and content of structure. Provision for merging interior spaces, for greater contact between indoors and outdoors, and for uniting architecture with site features required innovations in form and appearance. Consequently, prairie and Usonian houses simply did not look like their neighbors and for their times were radical new departures. The fantastic cantilevers in the Robie House (1907) made possible by 100-foot welded steel channel beams recently developed in the Chicago shipyards showed how Wright's up-to-date technical knowledge influenced his aesthetic daringness.[21] He believed in change, in new-ness, in experimentation, in challenging the status quo, not for their own sakes, but to make things better. He tore down and rebuilt portions of Taliesin, for example, more times than can be recorded, always trying to improve it, and one of his very last designs was for yet another alteration. The way he conceived his buildings, his manner of execution, and the appearance of the finished product challenged prevailing assumptions.

Despite their radical aspects most of his residences were purchased by solid citizens of conservative mold—architecture, after all, is the province of the well-to-do—who found them congenial to their com-fortable life styles. His buildings militated against certain twentieth-century trends by resisting the destructive tendencies of urbanization. By uniting the family in happy surroundings Wright hoped to coun-teract the centrifugal nature of city life, the absence of fathers from home, the takeover of familial functions by society at large, in essence, the tendency of industrial capitalism to weaken traditional kinship ties. The "natural," close-knit, mutually dependent, socially independent family of warm stove and glowing hearth he tried architecturally to sustain may never have existed in pure form, the Lloyd Joneses not-withstanding, but it is noteworthy that Wright invariably put fireplaces at the physical "heart" of his houses and after the 1930s located kitch-ens ("work-spaces") so their influence could permeate the whole, thereby referring to the congenial nineteenth-century farmhouse he remembered fondly. Recalling a simpler and more virtuous America his clients also cherished, especially during periods of rapid social change and economic dislocation, Wright's residences used advanced technology and avant-garde aesthetics in what historian Norris Kelly Smith and the architect himself affirmed as "a cause conservative."[22]

But if his political views are taken into consideration, Wright appears to be more of a true populist, a romantic anarchist, or at least a Jeffersonian-type laissez-faire democrat, than a twentieth-century con-servative. Always a staunch opponent of centralization, be it in cities, in the economy, or in government, he opposed authority in ways conservatives dared not. In matters of national defense and internal security, for example, he was unwilling to consign the powers to the state that they thought proper. Although he believed in private enter-prise, he opposed monopoly capitalism, considering it as dangerous to human freedom as fascism or any other oppressive system. Advo-cating universal ownership of land and the means of production bro-ken down into small units—a kind of updated Jeffersonian dream—he held a much more optimistic view of human nature than conservatives for he truly believed that with enlightened leaders people could care for themselves if freed from the debilitating burdens of corporate hegemony and governmental bureaucracy. He insisted that the way to human liberation was not through state action but by a reawakening of popular consciousness brought about by the development of an organic culture through the vehicle of organic design.

Wright did not mean to banish government altogether, only to remove all but its police and service functions. Until people discovered their true individualities and their innate sense of social relatedness, possible only in an organic milieu like Broadacre City, his buildings would have to serve as examples of the therapeutic environmentalism he envisioned. He therefore regarded his Larkin and Johnson offices in particular not only as assets to owners and workers but also as models for furture social organization. Built around the concept of the work force as an extended family, they attempted to reinforce group harmony as well as recall precorporate hierarchical relationships. They combatted business impersonality, bureaucratic compartmentaliza-tion, sterile working conditions, and humanity's alienation from its labor by encouraging a sense of participation and mutual endeavor, not simply to increase productivity, but because Wright believed that purposeful work was beneficial, that positive environment mattered, that capitalism could be made humane, and that the preindustrial family ought to be the basis of laboring as well as home life. His office buildings were without influence in corporate America because they implied disapproval of the social relations of production.

Another office structure, the H. C. Price Tower (1952) in Bartlesville, Oklahoma (see Chapter Twelve and Fig. 12.13), illustrates Wright's deeply ingrained romanticism, his preference for the preindustrial union of work and residence, and his insistence that architecture ought to express human individuality, that it should proclaim peoples' feelings and spirit as well as their intellect. The Price Tower is a seventeen-story polygon divided into quadrants, three for offices and one for eight two-floor apartments. By completely rejecting steel-frame, curtain-wall construction, it is unlike most modern skyscrapers. With its soaring roof fins and multidirectional façades, it asserts human aspiration by breaking traditional forms, by symbolically refusing to contain or be contained. Its visual complexity would be too stimulating for an urban setting where it could not be fully seen or appreciated and where it would clash with neighbors. A street lined with Price Towers would be aesthetically disastrous, and that is really the point, for the building was not meant to be copied. Proclaiming itself a bulwark of individuality and the foe of uniformity, Price Tower was

not offered as a remedy for urban ills, or as a model for other architects, but as a *tour de force* of human singularity.

As the only high-rise in Bartlesville (population 27,000 in 1960), it
could be seen from miles away in any direction, asserting Wright's
notion that as works of art tall buildings (like any other) should be as
accessible to viewing as paintings in a museum. To be fully appreciated
and to permit inhabitants to see something other than their counterparts looking back at them from similar structures, skyscrapers should
have space enough to cast their shadows on the ground, as Wright
put it, in parks or in small towns, but certainly not in rows on city
streets. From a commercial standpoint, of course, this was absolute
nonsense, but to environmentalists and to architects concerned with
design visibility, it made good sense. By including apartments in Price
Tower, furthermore—certainly a boon for company officials wishing
to cut commuting time but hardly necessary in Bartlesville—Wright
probably meant to suggest that people need not be separated from
their work, that office staffs could really be extended families, and
that life functions should not be compartmentalized. There are other
multiuse high-rises, but they are usually segregated by floors or groups
of floors, and rarely so closely integrated as the Price Tower.

The tower also rejected technological and bureaucratic "fascism,"
Wright called it, by refusing to plug people into identical rooms in
homogenous, characterless monoliths. Van der Rohe's high-rises have
been praised as expressions of neoclassical rationalism, so carefully
were their façade proportions determined. Wright admired Mies' per-
fectionism, but he struggled to achieve a "heart-felt simplicity instead
of a *head-made* simplicity," in other words, to capture in architecture
certain truths about life that can only be described as instinctual.
"Without this essential *heart* beating in it," he proclaimed in language
the modernist movement unfortunately ignored, architecture "would
degenerate to a box merely to *contain*. . .objects it should itself create
and *maintain*." "True romanticism in art is. . .the result of an inner
experience," he explained, "and is the essential poetry of the creative
artist that his exploring brother, tabulating the sciences, seems never
quite able to understand nor wholly respect." Whoever condemns
romance, Wright affirmed, "is only a foolish reactionary."[23] Price
Tower also warned that architectural homogeneity was spiritual death.

As this language attests, Wright was in many ways a nineteenth-
century man using twentieth-century methods, or, to put it more
accurately perhaps, he was a preindustrial man using the latest technology to construct nonmechanistic living environments. Ever since
his "Art and Craft of the Machine" speech in 1901 he had accepted

technology as humanity's great liberator. Later he often claimed that it had enslaved people—he did not mean wage slavery in factories so much as misplaced dependence on machinery—but his own use of it belied the assertion. "I believe that romance—the quality of the *heart,* the essential joy we have in living. . .can be brought to life again in modern industry," he declared in 1930.[24] Wright used technology to increase peoples' contact with the outdoors, thereby strengthening their essential selves. Organic architecture meant after all that buildings should be built and function according to the principles of nature. But as Fallingwater and other designs demonstrated, Wright also believed that art could improve nature, that the relationship was reciprocal. His description of Price Tower as "the tree that escaped the crowded forest" indicates that natural fecundity sometimes required intelligent pruning.

His emphasis on nature's benevolence was particularly American, but in the first third of the twentieth century he was as highly regarded in parts of Europe as its own architects and perhaps admired there even more than here. His work and his year on the Continent, from September 1909 to September 1910, were crucial for its artistic development. Even before he visited Berlin in 1910 to supervise publication of his two Wasmuth retrospectives, the city's leading architect Peter Behrens had paid him tribute by quoting the 1904 Larkin Building in his local turbine factory (1908–1909). Of Behrens' three most promising employees in 1910—Corbusier, van der Rohe, and Walter Gropius—the latter was most immediately influenced by Wright, whose City National Bank (1909) in Mason City, Iowa, clearly presaged the German's model factory (1914) for the Werkbund Exhibition. There is no evidence that Wright met the trio or its employer in 1910—his introduction to Gropius and van der Rohe was in 1937, the year they arrived in America—but they probably pored over his German publications which by all accounts were profoundly liberating for the younger Europeans. The *de Stijl* movement, cubism, constructivism, neo-plasticism, and the International Style were all in some way indebted to Wright, and by 1930 most critics agreed that his Continental impact had been enormous.

Despite his warm European reception, and the simultaneous social hostility at home, he never seriously contemplated expatriation because he was unabashedly American, glorying in its virtues, anxious about its faults. His heroes were Jefferson, Thoreau, Whitman, and Emerson whose 1858 essay on "Farming" he partially reproduced as the appendix to his last book, *The Living City,* exactly one hundred years later, and whose work he read and reread. Throughout his life

Wright continually proclaimed America the greatest nation in human history. He insulted it, criticized and condemned it, but always out of love, hoping to stem its drift toward conformity, mediocrity, and materialism. In his expansiveness, his faith in technology to solve problems, his optimism about human nature, his strange blend of practicality and idealism, his individualism, his ingenuity, his distrust of government, his restlessness, and his disrespect for authority, in all this and more he was typically American. But he was *not* a modern man. He was as unlike Moses Herzog, Rabbit Angstrom, and similar literary figures as Theodore Roosevelt, whose "strenuous life" he exemplified. He was not introspective or self-analytical; he did not examine his own existence. But he believed in himself as strongly as can be imagined. He was an uncompromising individualist in a mass society, an authentic human being in a formica landscape.

By preference he was also a Midwesterner, a fact that shaped certain of his prejudices, themselves part of the national character. "If English travelers want to see America as it really is," he told a London audience in 1939, they must ignore the East. "America begins *west* of Buffalo. The greatest and most nearly beautiful city of our young nation," he continued, "is probably Chicago. Eventually I think that Chicago will be the most beautiful great city left in the modern world." Why? asked someone, probably not the only skeptic in the group. Because, Wright said, it has the greatest park system on earth, a properly developed waterfront, "a life of its own," and because it "takes pride in building things in a big substantial broad way."[25] His regional loyalties seem to have influenced the location of his architecture. Only fifteen of his 135 executed structures from 1894 to 1914 and twenty-nine of his 230 projects were outside the Middle West, and even when he was nationally known the pattern remained almost unchanged. One hundred sixty-eight of the 300 or more buildings still standing at his death were in three states—thirty-seven in Michigan, forty-three in Wisconsin, and eighty-eight in Illinois. And with eleven in Ohio, ten in Minnesota, nine in Iowa, and eleven scattered elsewhere, the Midwest could claim 209, or roughly two thirds of his entire output. With an additional twenty-five structures in California, nine in Arizona, and twelve in other states, fully 255, or approximately eighty percent of his executed commissions, were in the West. (He built only five houses in New England, all after 1940.) But like William Faulkner, another famous regionalist, Wright invariably spoke to universal human concerns.

Like Faulkner's Yoknapatawpha County, Wright's Broadacre City was a world of his own making, its geography as fixed in the architect's mind as the author's was in his. In 1958 Wright completed a final series of Broadacre studies, in effect, an abbreviated catalog of his life's work. Scattered around his fictional countryside in one perspective drawing were a segment of the Doheny Ranch (1921), the Ennis House (1924), the Gordon Strong Planetarium and automobile objective (1925), a St. Mark's tower (1929), the Rogers Lacy Hotel (1946), the Pittsburgh Community Center, the Huntington Hartford Hotel, a self-service garage, and a butterfly bridge (all 1947), the Beth Shalom Synagogue (1954), and a portion of the Marin County Civic Center (1957–1959), altogether a startling furturistic montage. The drawing represents Wright's last attempt at synthesis, his final depiction of America as he would have planned it. One observer was entirely correct to conclude that Wright "could well have furnished the countryside with some of the most dazzling buildings ever seen."[26]

But the comment and the drawing also suggest that some of Wright's work may have been too forceful for the architectural integration he envisioned. If he had actually assembled his buildings in one place, if he had lined New York's Park Avenue with Price Towers or designed Spring Green *in toto*, the effect might have been overpowering, a mind-blowing collage too stimulating for his own purposes. Unlike his houses which individually or in groups (like the Usonias or in Oak Park) achieved the sought-for repose, and unlike his master plans (like Florida Southern College or Marin County Civic Center) designed as single entities, his defiantly vigorous and assertive larger projects, reflecting his own "absolute inability to endure confinement of any sort,"[27] as one observer put it, did not always go well together. Many were *tours de force*, visual and emotional challenges to the public, uncompromising expressions of his own untrammeled individualism. By extolling human variety so energetically, he may have unintentionally negated the possibility of communality in an environment too lively, too electric, in the end too exhausting for leisurely sensory experience and relaxing social life. Indeed, the suspicion lingers that even Frank Lloyd Wright himself might not have lived comfortably in some landscapes of his own design.

But this assessment is incomplete, for beyond his life-long commitment to organic communities, he was first of all a residential architect. In an age of energy shortages and environmental crises, he left models of how to build *with* nature, not against it. His cooperatives, quadruples blocks and homes, and his Usonias remain pregnant with suggestions for ecologically minded individuals seeking social connectedness. Years later, his houses still startle, not just because they are beautiful and make common sense, but also because they are transcendent. They are—at the risk of sounding sentimental—enriching, as people who live in them consistently attest. Other major architects built residences as if they were design exercises, as though it were an obligation at some point in their careers—like penance—to show what they could do before moving on to where the money was. But Frank Lloyd Wright designed houses, hundreds of them, because he wanted people to live better. No matter that America was culturally retarded: he would do for it what he could. And when he was finished, he had done more than most.

NOTES

1 On the demise of the Imperial Hotel see *The New York Times,* August 9, 23, 1964; September 2, 1969; March 11, 1970; *The Milwaukee Journal,* October 23, November 7, 16, December 1, 1967; February 16, 1969; Frank Riley, "Deathwatch in Tokyo," *Saturday Review* (December 16, 1967), 40–41; Karl Kamrath, "The Stubborn Hotel is Shaking," *American Institute of Architects Journal,* 48 (November 1967), 70; *Architectural Forum,* 127 (December 1967), 23–24; *Inland Architect* (December 1967), 12–13.

2 "Strangers Keep Ringing the Bell, Wanting to Look," *The New York Times,* September 17, 1968.

3 "Udall Aids Frank Lloyd Wright Landmarks," *Architectural Forum,* 120 (May 1964), 7.

4 See for example, "Chicagoans Battle to Save Wright Heritage," *The Capital Times,* July 9, 1964.

5 *The New York Times,* September 7, 1963; *The Architectural Record,* 134 (October 1963), 24; *Carnegie Magazine,* 38 (September 1964), 237–241; "Frank Lloyd Wright's Fallingwater," Western Pennsylvania Conservancy brochure, n.d.

6 *The Capital Times,* September 20, 1967; *Newsweek* (October 13, 1967), 78.

7 "V.O.P. Productions Presents Frank Lloyd Wright" (1976), an advertising mailer.

8 A day spent wandering over the entire Spring Green estate in April 1968 revealed its appalling condition. The Midway Farm complex, including a round tracter shed, a remodeled non-Wright cottage, the main building with wing, and a few minor structures, was literally crumbling, as were the Romeo and Juliet Windmill and "Tanyderi," the Andrew T. Porter House. The Porter garage was almost beyond repair. Two nearby apprentice cabins were open to the weather. The Hillside Home School, the only building seen by the public, was in reasonably good condition. Silsbee's Unity Chapel across the highway was bare and filthy, but has since been repaired. Most of the farmland had gone to seed, and the dam was

breaking up. It was also clear that at Taliesin itself, maintenance crews could not keep pace with deterioration. Hillsides under some of the most dramatic cantilevering were eroding, leaving glaring, unsightly gashes. Peripheral service quarters were faring quite badly, much of the wood was rotting, and the place generally showed signs of better days. The resident in charge asked visitors not to photograph boarded-up windows which he described as "winter precautions."

9 The Frank Lloyd Wright School of Architecture "Bulletin," January 6, 1975, and accompanying material for applicants. For descriptions of life at the Taliesins since Wright's death see: Wolf von Eckardt, "The Wright Idolators," *The Washington Post,* May 8, 1966; Loudon Wainwright, "Guardian of a Great Legacy," *Life,* 70 (June 11, 1971); and Tom Hall, "If you would be an architect, grab a hammer," *Chicago Tribune Magazine,* November 16, 1975.

10 On Wright's leftover and TAA's early work see *The Capital Times,* January 16, 1959; August 3, 1960; "Mr. Wright and His Successors" and "Taliesin Today," *The Western Architect and Engineer,* 221 (March 1961), 20–33, and 34–39; *The New York Times,* October 20, 1963, Sec. 8; and "The Living Heritage of Frank Lloyd Wright," *Arizona Highways,* 38 (April 1962), 2–8.

11 Arthur Drexler, Ed., *The Drawings of Frank Lloyd Wright* (New York: Horizon Press, 1962), plate 197.

12 *L'Architecture d'Aujourd hui,* No. 168 (July–August 1973), lxxi–lxxii; "Casa Pfeiffer a Taliesin West, Scottsdale, Arizona," *L' Architecttura,* 20 (August 1974), 240–246.

13 Compare A. Drexler, Ed., *Drawings,* plate 104, with rendering in *The Spring Green,* the Wisconsin River Development Corporation's promotional booklet, n.d.

14 Also see "Taliesin in Kentucky," *Architectural Forum,* 117 (October 1962), 55; and *The Capital Times,* March 15, 1966.

Even though William Wesley Peters is presumably a skilled engineer, there are also doubts about TAA's technical abilities. Early in 1977 a San Mateo County Superior Court judge ordered Peters, TAA, the Wright Foundation, their associate Aaron Green, and two engineering firms to reimburse the city of San Jose, California, $1.5 million of a $2 million settlement for the ceiling of the Performing Arts Center which collapsed in 1972 "because of substantial structural and design defects." *Building Design & Construction* (April 1977), 22.

15 On this project see *The Spring Green,* booklet cited in note 13; *The Capital Times,* September 20, 1967; March 26, 1968.

16 Quoted by Stanley Kaufmann in *The New Republic,* 163 (November 21, 1970), 22.

17 *The Capital Times,* April 13, 1959; *The Weekly Home News,* April 16, 1959; and *The New York Times,* April 19, 1959.

18 Except for *Architecture*, a Doubleday book, the publisher in every instance has been Horizon Press. Mrs. Wright has also elaborated her own philosophy in *The Struggle Within* (1955) and in portions of *The Roots of Life*.

One reviewer called called *Frank Lloyd Wright: His Life, His Work, His Word* (1967) "another work of piety," adding "nothing of any importance to the well-known story": *The Times Literary Supplement,* April 9, 1971.

19 "Outside the Profession," *The New Yorker,* 29 (September 26, 1953), 27; "Conversation" in F. L. Wright, *The Future of Architecture* (New York: Horizon Press, 1953) 29.

20 Olgivanna Wright, Address to the Phoenix Art Museum League, in *The Roots of Life,* and "The Miracle on Fifth Avenue," a chapter in *Frank Lloyd Wright. My Father Who Is on Earth* is the title of John Lloyd Wright's book (New York: G. P. Putnam's Sons, 1946) and Reverend Emanuel N. Vergis' comment is in "Teacup Dome," *Time,* 78 (August 18, 1961), 50.

21 Fred C. Robie, Jr., "Mr. Robie Knew What He Wanted," *Architectural Forum,* 109 (October 1958), 126–127, 206, 210.

22 "In the Cause of Architecture," *The Architectural Record,* 23 (March 1908); Norris Kelly Smith, *Frank Lloyd Wright: A Study in Architectural Content* (Englewood Cliffs, N.J.: Prentice-Hall, 1966), Chapter 1.

23 F. L. Wright, *Modern Architecture* reprinted in *The Future of Architecture,* 103, 106.

24 F. L. Wright, *Modern Architecture* reprinted in *The Future of Architecture,* 107.

25 F. L. Wright, *An Organic Architecture* reprinted in *The Future of Architecture,* 260, 268.

26 A. Drexler, Ed., *Drawings,* plate 267, and comment on page 315.

27 Winthrop Sergeant, *Geniuses, Goddesses and People* (New York: E. P. Dutton, 1949), 229.

Author's Comments
on the Drawings

David Roessler's four drawings in this book—one each of the Cheney and Jacobs houses, two of the Willitts residence—establish a new standard of accuracy for those dwellings.

From photos in *Global Interiors #9* Roessler was able to clarify the details around the fireplace and correct errors at the entry of the Cheney House as shown in Wright's Wasmuth portfolio and Hitchcock's *In the Nature of Materials*.

From his own photographs Roessler determined that the Jacobs plan in the January 1938 *Architectural Forum* was more nearly correct than those in Wright's *The Natural House* or Sergeant's *Usonian Houses*. The architect broke into the 4-foot grid system at the hall end of the dining table with a 2-foot extension of the bedroom wing's floor mat. In plan, this clarifies ambiguities in previous publications at the building's "elbow."

Plans for the Willitts House as built are here drawn correctly for the first time from Roessler's photographs, and thanks to assistance from the current owner, architect Skip Altay, and Susan B. Benjamin of Highland Park, Illinois.

Bibliography

The following includes as complete a list as possible of Frank Lloyd Wright's published works. Secondary sources have been cited in the footnotes.

Books by Frank Lloyd Wright

The House Beautiful (River Forest, Ill.: Auvergne Press, 1896–1897), text by William C. Gannett, page decorations by the architect. Privately published.

Ausgeführte Bauten und Entwürfe von Frank Lloyd Wright (Berlin: Ernst Wasmuth, 1910), a portfolio of drawings with the architect's introduction.

Frank Lloyd Wright Ausgeführte Bauten (Berlin: Ernst Wasmuth, 1911), photographs introduced by W. R. Ashbee.

The Japanese Print: An Interpretation (Chicago: Ralph Fletcher Seymour Co., 1912).

Love and Ethics by Ellen Key (Chicago: Ralph Fletcher Seymour Co., 1912), translated by Mamah Bouton Borthwick and the architect.

Two Lectures on Architecture (Chicago: The Art Institute, 1931), containing "In the Realm of Ideas" and "To the Young Man in Architecture."

Modern Architecture: Being the Kahn Lectures for 1930 (Princeton, N.J.: Princeton University Press, 1931).

The Disappearing City (New York: William Farquar Payson, 1932).

An Autobiography (New York: Longmans, Green, and Co., 1932) containing three books: "Family-Fellowship," "Work," and "Freedom." In 1943 Wright published an expanded edition (New York: Duell, Sloan and Pearce) dividing the original Book One in two ("Family" and "Fellowship") and adding a fifth book, "Form." Subsequent printings included Book Six, "Broadacre City," originally published separately as *An Autobiography: Book Six, Broadacre City* (Spring Green, Wis.: A Taliesin Publication, 1943). Except for changes in paragraphing, the text of the two editions and later printings are the same. A third edition including Wright's later revisions was published posthumously by Horizon Press (New York) in 1977.

Architecture and Modern Life (New York: Harper & Brothers, 1938), with Baker Brownell.

An Organic Architecture: The Architecture of Democracy (London: Lund, Humphries & Co., 1939), the Sir George Watson Lectures of the Sulgrave Manor Board for 1939.

When Democracy Builds (Chicago: University of Chicago Press, 1945), an expanded version of *The Disappearing City.*

Genius and the Mobocracy (New York: Duell, Sloan and Pearce, 1949), a biography of Louis H. Sullivan.

The Future of Architecture (New York: Horizon Press, 1953), containing "A Conversation" with Hugh Downs, NBC–TV, May 17, 1953; *Modern Architecture; Two Lectures on Architecture; An Organic Architecture; Architecture and Modern Life,* Chs. 2, 4; "The Language of Organic Architecture," *Architectural Forum,* 98 (May 1953).

The Natural House (New York: Horizon Press, 1954), containing "Recollections—The United States, 1893–1920," *The Architect's Journal* (London), 84 (July 16–August 6, 1936); preface to "Sixty Years of Living Architecture: The Work of Frank Lloyd Wright," exhibition brochure, Guggenheim Museum, November 1953; sections from *An Autobiography;* and new material.

The Story of the Tower: The Tree that Escaped the Crowded Forest (New York: Horizon Press, 1956) on the Price Tower in Bartlesville, Oklahoma.

A Testament (New York: Horizon Press, 1957), additional autobiographical material.

The Living City (New York: Horizon Press, 1958), an expanded version of *When Democracy Builds.*

Architecture: Man in Possession of His Earth (New York: Doubleday and Co., 1962), a reformulation of the 1927–1928 "In the Cause of Architecture" series from *The Architectural Record* (listed below) with a biography by the architect's daughter Iovanna.

Frank Lloyd Wright Anthologies

Gutheim, Frederick, Ed., *Frank Lloyd Wright on Architecture: Selected Writings, 1894–1940* (New York: Duell, Sloan and Pearce, 1941).

Kaufmann, Edgar, Jr., Ed., *Taliesin Drawings: Recent Architecture of Frank Lloyd Wright, Selected from his Drawings* (New York: Wittenborn, Schultz, Inc., 1952).

Kaufmann, Edgar, Jr., Ed., *An American Architecture: Frank Lloyd Wright* (New York: Horizon Press, 1955).

Drawings for a Living Architecture (New York: Horizon Press, 1959).

Kaufmann, Edgar, Jr., and Raeburn, Ben, Eds., *Frank Lloyd Wright: Writings and Buildings* (Cleveland: World Publishing Co., 1960).

Drexler, Arthur, Ed., *The Drawings of Frank Lloyd Wright* (New York: Horizon Press, 1962).

Wright, Olgivanna, Ed., *Frank Lloyd Wright: His Life, His Work, His Word* (New York: Horizon Press, 1967).

Gutheim, Frederick, Ed., *In the Cause of Architecture: Frank Lloyd Wright* (New York: McGraw-Hill, 1975), containing Wright's articles for *The Architectural Record* from 1908 to 1952.

Frank Lloyd Wright's Articles, Reviews, Speeches, Interviews, and Published Letters

Letter to George R. Dean, "'Progress Before Precedent,'" *The Brickbuilder*, 9 (May 1900).

"The Architect," *ibid.*, 9 (June 1900), address to the Second Annual Convention of the Architectural League of America.

"A Home in a Prairie Town," *The Ladies Home Journal*, 18 (February 1901).

"The Art and Craft of the Machine," *Chicago Architectural Club Catalogue of the 14th Annual Exhibition* (1901), also in *Brush and Pencil*, 8 (May 1901).

"A Small House with 'Lots of Room in It,'" *The Ladies Home Journal*, 18 (July 1901).

"The 'Village Bank' Series. V," *The Brickbuilder*, 10 (August 1901).

"Ten Letters from Frank Lloyd Wright to Charles Robert Ashbee [1902–1939]," *Architectural History*, 13 (1970).

Three letters to Mrs. Harvey P. Sutton, July 9, 30, 1906, April 9, 1907, in Don L. Morgan and the Editors, "A Wright House on the Prairie," *The Prairie School Review*, 2 (Third Quarter 1965).

"The New Larkin Administration Building," *The Larkin Idea* (November 1906), reprinted in *The Prairie School Review*, 7 (First Quarter 1970).

"A Fireproof House for $5,000," *The Ladies Home Journal*, 24 (April 1907).

"Tribute" to actor Donald Robertson, *Oak Leaves* (Oak Park, Ill.), December 14, 1907.

"In the Cause of Architecture," *The Architectural Record*, 23 (March 1908).

"Ethics of Ornament," *Oak Leaves*, February 16, 1909, reprinted in *The Prairie School Review*, 4 (First Quarter 1967).

Press statements regarding Mamah Borthwick in *The Chicago Tribune*, December 26–31, 1911; January 4, 1912.

Letter to the Editor, *The Weekly Home News* (Spring Green, Wis.), January 4, 1912.

Eulogy for Daniel Burnham in *The Architectural Record*, 32 (August 1912).

"In the Cause of Architecture, II," *ibid.*, 34 (May 1914).

"To My Neighbors," *The Weekly Home News*, August 20, 1914.

Interview with Henry Blackman Sell, "Interpretation not Imitation: The Work of Frank Lloyd Wright," *The International Studio*, 55 (May 1915).

Interview with Walter Noble Burns, "Love Truce at Wright Cote; Live in Fear," *The Chicago Tribune*, November 8, 1915.

Statements regarding Miriam Noel in *The Chicago Herald*, November 11, 1915.

Speech on his "American System" houses in *The Western Architect*, 24 (September 1916).

"Non-Competitive Plan for Development of Quarter Section of Land" in Alfred B. Yeomans, Ed., *City Residential Land Development. Competitive Plans for Subdividing a Typical Quarter Section of Land in the Outskirts of Chicago* (Chicago: University of Chicago Press, 1916), reprinted in *The Western Architect*, 25 (January 1917).

"The New Imperial Hotel in Tokyo, A Message from the Architect, Tokyo, March 24, 1922," *Kagaku Chishiki* (Tokyo), April 1922.

"In the Cause of Architecture: The New Imperial Hotel, Tokyo," *The Western Architect*, 32 (April 1923).

"In the Cause of Architecture: In the Wake of the Quake, Concerning the Imperial Hotel, Tokio," *ibid.*, 32 (November 1923); 33 (February 1924).

"Louis H. Sullivan: Beloved Master," *ibid.*, 33 (June 1924).

"Louis H. Sullivan—His Work," *The Architectural Record,* 56 (July 1924).

Statement on American commercial architecture, *Baraboo Weekly News* (Baraboo, Wis.), December 4, 1924.

Speech to Baraboo Kiwanis Club in *ibid.*

"To the Countryside," *The Weekly Home News,* June 10, 1926.

"Frank Lloyd Wright Tells Story of Life: Years of Work, Love, and Despair," *The Capital Times* (Madison, Wis.), November 1, 1926.

"In the Cause of Architecture: I. The Architect and the Machine," *The Architectural Record,* 61 (May 1927).

"In the Cause of Architecture: II. Standardization, the Soul of the Machine," *ibid.*, 61 (June 1927).

"In the Cause of Architecture: Part III. Steel," *ibid.*, 62 (August 1927).

"In the Cause of Architecture: Part IV. Fabrication and the Imagination," *ibid.*, 62 (October 1927).

"In the Cause of Architecture: Part V. The New World," *ibid.*, 62 (October 1927).

"Why the Japanese Earthquake Did Not Destroy the Imperial Hotel," *Liberty,* December 3, 1927.

Letter to the Editor, *The Weekly Home News,* December 15, 1927.

"In the Cause of Architecture: I. The Logic of the Plan," *The Architectural Record,* 63 (January 1928).

"In the Cause of Architecture: II. What 'Styles' Mean to the Architect," *ibid.*, 63 (February 1928).

"In the Cause of Architecture: III. The Meaning of Materials—Stone," *ibid.*, 63 (April 1928).

"In the Cause of Architecture: IV. The Meaning of Materials—Wood," *ibid.*, 63 (May 1928).

"In the Cause of Architecture: V. The Meaning of Materials—The Kiln," *ibid.*, 63 (June 1928).

"In the Cause of Architecture: VI. The Meaning of Materials—Glass," *ibid.*, 64 (July 1928).

"In the Cause of Architecture: VII. The Meaning of Materials—Concrete," *ibid.*, 64 (August 1928).

"In the Cause of Architecture: VIII. Sheet Metal and a Modern Instance," *ibid.*, 64 (October 1928).

"In the Cause of Architecture: IX. The Terms," *ibid.*, 64 (December 1928).

"Fiske Kimball's New Book," *ibid.*, 64 (August 1928).

"'Towards a New Architecture,'" *World Unity,* September 1928.

"Taliesin: The Chronicle of a House with a Heart," *Liberty,* March 23, 1929, later included in *An Autobiography.*

"American Architecture: Correspondence of Walter Pach, Paul Cret, Frank Lloyd Wright and Erich Mendelsohn with Fiske Kimball," *The Architectural Record,* 65 (May 1929).

"A Building Adventure in Modernism: A Successful Adventure in Concrete," *Country Life*, 56 (May 1929), on "La Miniatura," later included in *An Autobiography*.

"Surface and Mass—Again," *The Architectural Record*, 56 (July 1929).

"The Logic of Contemporary Architecture as an Expression of this Age," *Architectural Forum*, 52 (May 1930).

"Frank Lloyd Wright and Hugh Ferris Discuss the Modern Architect," *ibid.*, 53 (November 1930).

"Architecture as a Profession is Wrong," *The American Architect*, 138 (December 1930).

"Principles of Design," *Annual of American Design* (1931).

"To the Young Architect in America," *The Architect's Journal* (London), 74 (July 8, 1931), excerpted from *Two Lectures on Architecture*.

"Highlights" of a speech to the Michigan Architectural Society in *Architectural Forum*, 55 (October 1931),

"Advice to the Young Architect," *The Architectural Record*, 70 (August 1931), excerpted from *Two Lectures on Architecture*.

Interview in *The New York Times*, January 17, 1932.

"For All May Raise the Flowers Now For All Have Got the Seed," *The T-Square Journal*, 2 (February 1932).

Letter to the Editor, *ibid.*

"'Broadacre City': An Architect's Vision," *The New York Times Magazine*, March 20, 1932.

"Why the Great Earthquake Did Not Destroy the Imperial Hotel," *Creative Art*, 10 (April 1932), also in *An Autobiography*.

"Of Thee I Sing," *Shelter*, 2 (April 1932).

"America Tomorrow," *The American Architect*, 141 (May 1932).

"A Treatise on Ornament," *The Saturday Review of Literature*, 8 (May 21, 1932).

"The House of the Future," *National Real Estate Journal*, 33 (July 1932).

"Caravel or Motorship?" *Architectural Forum*, 57 (August 1932).

"What Does the Machine Mean to Life in a Democracy?" *Pictorial Review* (September 1932).

"To the Students of the Beaux-Arts Institute of Design, All Departments," *Architecture*, 66 (October 1932), also in *An Autobiography*.

"Why I Love Wisconsin," in Gutheim, Ed., *Selected Writings*, 157–160, was not published in *Wisconsin Magazine*, as he says.

"Another Pseudo," *Architectural Forum*, 59 (July 1933).

"The Chicago World's Fair," *The Architect's Journal*, 78 (July 13, 1933).

"In the Show Window at Macy's," *Architectural Forum*, 59 (November 1933).

"Why Prod the Prexy, Is Wright's Defense of [University of Wisconsin President Glenn] Frank," letter to the Editor, *The Capital Times*, February 6, 1934, reprinted in *The Weekly Home News*, February 22, 1934.

"Opinion in American Architecture 1. Architecture of Individualism," *Trend*, 2 (March–April 1934).

"True Architecture Seeks Greater Unity: Wright," *The Capital Times*, May 3, 1934.

"What is the Modern Idea?" *Physical Culture* (June 24, 1934).

"At Taliesin," sometimes called "Taliesin," was a sporadic weekly column written by Wright and his apprentices for four Wisconsin newspapers: *The Capital Times* and the *Wisconsin State Journal* in Madison from February 2, 1934 to October 1937; *The Weekly Home News* in Spring Green from March 1934 to July 1935; and *The Iowa County Democrat* in Mineral Point from May 20 to September 30 and December 2, 1937. All of Wright's articles appeared in *The Capital Times*:

    1934: February 13, July 13, 20, August 26, November 23, December 14;

    1935: April 26, August 9, October 4, 11, 18, November 7;

    1936: May 29, July 11, 31, September 18, November 20, December 18;

    1937: January 3, February 26, April 2, July 30, August 13, September 17, 24, October 1.

"Louis Sullivan's Words and Work," *The Architectural Review*, 77 (March 1935).

"Broadacre City: A New Community Plan," *The Architectural Record*, 77 (April 1935).

"Broadacre City," *The American Architect*, 146 (May 1935).

"Form and Function," *The Saturday Review*, 13 (December 14, 1935).

"Skyscrapers Doomed? Yes!" *The Rotarian* (March 1936).

"Taliesin: Our Cause," *Professional Arts Quarterly* (March 1936).

"Recollections—The United States, 1893–1920," *The Architect's Journal*, 84 (July 16–August 6, 1936).

"Apprentice-Training for the Architect," *The Architectural Record*, 80 (September 1936).

"What the Cause of Architecture Needs Most," *The Architectural Review*, 81 (March 1937).

"Wright Regrets Russia Is Using US as Model for Architecture. Raps Communists of University as Racketeers after Trip," *The Capital Times*, July 22, 1937.

"US, USSR are the Two Greatest Hopes for Better Life and Democracy, FLW Declares," *ibid.*, August 1, 1937.

"Wright Lists 'Testament' of Beliefs After Visit to Russia; Lauds Stalin," *ibid.*, August 3, 1937.

"Wright Denies He Said Communists Racketeers," *ibid.*, August 5, 1937.

"Building Against Doomsday," *The Reader's Digest*, 31 (September 1937), on the Imperial Hotel, also in *An Autobiography*.

"Architecture and Life in the U.S.S.R.," *Architectural Forum*, 82 (October 1937), originally published in *Soviet Russia Today* and included in *An Autobiography*.

"The Man St. Peter Liked," *Coronet* (December 1937), on tree planting.

"To the Young Man in Architecture—A Challenge," *Architectural Forum*, 68 (January 1938).

"Architect Wright Boosts Tom Amlie for Senate: Calls Him 'Like FDR,'" *The Capital Times*, August 11, 1938.

"Ideas for the Future," *The Saturday Review*, 18 (September 17, 1938).

"A Little Private Club," *Life*, 5 (September 26, 1938), reprinted in *Architectural Forum*, 69 (November 1938).

Letter to the Blackburn family in "Houses for $5,000–$6,000," *ibid*.

"FLW Offers Lake Monona Development Plan for Public Buildings," *The Capital Times*, November 2, 1938.

"Williamsburg as a Museum Piece," *New York Herald Tribune*, November 6, 1938.

"Frank Lloyd Wright Again," *Architect and Engineer*, 136 (March 1939).

Address to the Architectural Association School in *Architectural Association Journal*, 54 (May 1939), reprinted in *Architectural Association Quarterly*, 5 (January–March 1973).

"Organic Architecture," *The Builder* (London), 156 (May 5, 12, 19, 1939), later published as *An Organic Architecture*.

"To the 58th," *Journal of the Royal Institute of British Architects*, October 16, 1939.

"Let's Discover America," *The Capital Times*, August 4, 1940.

"Chicago's Auditorium is Fifty Years Old," *Architectural Forum*, 73 (September 1940).

"From Frank Lloyd Wright," *The Christian Century*, 57 (November 13, 1940).

"Louis Sullivan and the Chicago Auditorium: Frank Lloyd Wright's Reminiscences," *The Builder*, 159 (December 27, 1940).

"FLW Hits Conscription; Says U.S. Has Five Years to Build Defense Machine," *The Capital Times*, June 6, 1941.

"The American Quality," *Scribner's Commentator*, 10 (October 1941).

"FLW Denounces Stone for Judgment Hearsay," *The Capital Times*, December 20, 1942.

"FLW in Tribute to Will—and Sally [Allen White]," *ibid.*, February 1, 1944.

"To the Mole," *Magazine of Art*, 37 (December 1944), a reply, which *The Times* declined to print, to an article by Robert Moses in *The New York Times Magazine* (June 18, 1944).

"On Organic Architecture," *Weekly Bulletin, Michigan Society of Architects*, 19 (April 10, 1945).

"The Modern Gallery: For the Solomon R. Guggenheim Foundation: New York City," *Magazine of Art*, 39 (January 1946).

Speech to the newspaper's Forum in the *New York Herald Tribune*, November 10, 1946.

"On the Right to Be One's Self," *Marg* (Bombay), 1 (January 1947).

"We Must Shape True Inspiration," *The New York Times Magazine* (April 20, 1947).

"Frank Lloyd Wright Replies: . . .to Robert Moses' Attack on 'Functionalism,'" *New York Herald Tribune*, June 30, 1947.

"Let Us Go Now and Mimic No More," speech at Princeton University, in *The Capital Times*, August 7, 1947.

Comments on the United Nations Secretariat in *The Architect's Journal*, 106 (August 28, 1947).

"Bureaucracy Jumps the Gun," *The Weekly Home News*, October 30, 1947.

"The Architect," a lecture at the University of Chicago, in Robert B. Heywood, Ed., *The Works of the Mind* (Chicago: University of Chicago Press, 1947).

"FLW Sees Hypocrisy as a Taint in All American Life," *The Capital Times*, May 11, 1948.

"Frank Lloyd Wright on Hospital Design," *Modern Hospital*, 71 (September 1948).

"Begin with a Hoe: An Interview with Frank Lloyd Wright," *The Nation's Schools*, 42 (November 1948).

"State Road Commissioner's Use of High-Truss Steel Bridges Flayed by Wright," *The Capital Times*, November 25, 1948.

"Acceptance Speech of Frank Lloyd Wright," *Journal of the American Institute of Architects*, 11 (May 1949).

"Sullivan Against the World," *Architectural Review*, 105 (June 1949), a chapter from *Genius and the Mobocracy*.

"Talk with Frank Lloyd Wright," *The New York Times*, Sec. 7, July 24, 1949.

Memorial to Lloyd Lewis in Lloyd Lewis, "The New Theatre," *Theatre Arts,* 33 (July 1949).

"Frank Lloyd Wright Speaks on Hardware," *Weekly Bulletin, Michigan Society of Architects,* 23 (August 16, 1949).

"Chairs Designed for Sitting," interview in *The New York Times,* Sec. 6, August 21, 1949.

"To Arizona," *Arizona Highways,* 25 (October 1949), 10–11.

"Living in the Desert," *ibid.,* 12–15.

"A Birthday Message," *The Capital Times,* June 10, 1950.

"Frank Lloyd Wright," speech at the Architectural Association School, *The Architect's Journal,* 112 (July 27, 1950) and in *Architectural Association Journal,* 66 (August–September 1950).

Speech at a dinner in his honor, *ibid.*

"Cities: Medieval or Modern," *Architectural Forum,* 105 (August 1950), conversation between Wright and William Zeckendorf on NBC television.

"An Adventure in the Human Spirit," address at Florida Southern College, in *Motive,* journal of the Methodist Student Movement (November 1950).

"Force is a Heresy," *Wisconsin Athenaean,* 11 (Spring 1951).

"Reply of FLW to House Un-American Activities Group Charge," *The Capital Times,* April 21, 1951, reprinted as "When Free Men Fear," *The Nation,* 167 (June 2, 1951).

Listen to. . .Frank Lloyd Wright," interview in *Collier's,* 138 (August 3, 1951).

"FLW Hits McCarthyism: Sees Need for a New Third Party," *The Capital Times,* August 21, 1951.

"Unitarian Building 'Makes Music—Is Itself a Form of Prayer,' Wright Says," *ibid.,* August 22, 1951.

"Wright Asks US Build Truck Routes Along Rail Lines as Safety Measure," open letter to Wisconsin Highway Commission, in *ibid.,* September 10, 1951.

Statement on the Guggenheim Museum and organic architecture, *The New York Times,* March 30, 1952.

"Organic Architecture Looks at Modern Architecture," *The Architectural Record,* 119 (June 1952).

Address at Meeting of Student Members, AIA, June 25, 1952, in William A. Coles and Henry Hope Reed, Eds., *Architecture in America: A Battle of Styles* (New York: Appleton-Century-Crofts, 1961).

"Nautilus's Prune," interview in *The New Yorker,* 28 (July 12, 1952).

"Mr. Big," *The Capital Times,* July 18, 1952.

"Wake Up Wisconsin," *ibid.,* September 22, 1952.

Comments on Florida Southern College in *Architectural Forum,* 97 (September 1952).

Contributor to "The Future: Four Views," *The New York Times,* Sec. 6, Part 2, February 1, 1953.

Interview in *New York Herald Tribune,* May 14, 1953.

"The Language of Organic Architecture," *Architectural Forum,* 98 (May 1953).

"Against the Steamroller," *The Architectural Review,* 113 (May 1953).

"Frank Lloyd Wright Speaks Up," *House Beautiful,* 95 (July 1953).

"U.N. Stands Like Slab in a Graveyard," *The Capital Times,* July 13, 1953.

"Wright Now Ashamed of Town of his Boyhood," *ibid.*, August 25, 1953.

Letter to the Editor, *ibid.*, September 22, 1953.

"FLW Protests Court Rule on Tax Exemption," *ibid.*, September 24, 1953.

"A Letter from Frank Lloyd Wright," *The Weekly Home News*, September 24, 1953.

"Outside the Profession," interview in *The New Yorker*, 29 (September 26, 1953).

Letter and editorial in *Monthly Bulletin, Michigan Society of Architects*, 27 (October 1953).

"Frank Lloyd Wright Talks of His Art," *The New York Times Magazine* (October 4, 1953).

"Wright, Continued," interview in *The New Yorker*, 29 (October 21, 1953).

"Talk with Mr. Wright," *The New York Times*, Sec. 7, November 1, 1953.

"By Frank Lloyd Wright," *Monthly Bulletin, Michigan Society of Architects*, 28 (June 1954).

"Frank Lloyd Wright Talks About Photography," *Photography*, 34 (February 1954).

"A New Debate in Old Venice," *The New York Times*, Sec. 6, Part 1, March 21, 1954.

Santiago del Campo, "An Afternoon with Frank Lloyd Wright," *Americas*, 6 (April 1954).

"Man," *Journal of the American Institute of Architects*, 28 (April 1954).

"FLW Discusses Plan for New Civic Center," *The Capital Times*, May 27, 1954.

"Madison to be Commonplace?" *ibid.*, October 4, 1954.

"Wright Tells the Capital Times What He Had in Mind for Taliesin," *ibid.*, November 20, 1954.

Interview in *The Diplomat* (March, April 1955) reprinted in U.S. Congress, *Congressional Record*, 84th Cong., 1st Sess. (1955) 101, Part 4.

"Wright Says Civic Auditorium Can Be Built in 2 Years," *The Captial Times*, April 21, 1955.

Letter to the editor, Colorado Springs *Free Press*, May 27, 1955, reprinted in *The Denver Post*, May 29, 1955, and in U.S. Congress, *Congressional Record*, 84th Cong., 1st Sess. (1955) 101, Part 7.

"The Future of the City," *The Saturday Review*, 32 (May 21, 1955).

"FLW Explains His Views on [Air Force] Academy Design," *The Capital Times*, August 16, 1955.

"Wright Replies to Architectural Record Article [on Air Academy]," *ibid.*, September 6, 1955.

"Wright Denies Air Academy Link to 'Interests,'" *ibid.*, October 21, 1955.

"I Believe a House is More a Home by Being a Work of Art," *House Beautiful*, 97 (November 1955).

"Faith in Your Own Individuality," *ibid.*

"Architecture: Organic Expression of the Nature of Architecture," *Arizona Highways*, 32 (February 1956).

"For the Record" on the H. C. Price Tower, *The Architectural Record*, 119 (February 1956).

"Wright Revisited," interview in *The New Yorker*, 32 (June 16, 1956).

Two interviews in *The Capital Times*, August 27, 28, 1956.

"Milestones and Memoranda on the Work of Frank Lloyd Wright," picture captions by

Wright for his exhibition in Chicago, October 16–18, 1956, in *Land Economics*, 32 (November 1956).

Three interviews in Seldon Rodman, *Conversations with Artists* (New York: The Devin-Adair Co., 1957).

"U.S. Architecture to be Greatest in World—Wright," *The Wisconsin Architect* (February 1957).

"Meeting of the Titans: Frank Lloyd Wright, Carl Sandburg Talk of Life, Work, Happiness," *The Capital Times*, June 3, 1957.

Partial transcript of the Mike Wallace Show, Westinghouse TV, in *ibid.*, September 2, 1957.

"A Visit with Frank Lloyd Wright," *Look*, 21 (September 17, 1957).

Aline B. Saarinen, "Tour with Mr. Wright," *The New York Times Magazine* (September 22, 1957).

"Wright Asks Court Test of Metzner Law's Validity," *The Capital Times*, September 27, 1957.

"Architecture and Music," *The Saturday Review*, 40 (September 28, 1957).

Complete transcript of the second interview on the Mike Wallace Show, Westinghouse TV, in *The Capital Times*, September 30, 1957.

"Frank Lloyd Wright Town Hall Lecture, Ford Auditorium, Detroit, October 21, 1957," *Monthly Bulletin, Michigan Society of Architects*, 31 (December 1957).

"Education and Art in Behalf of Life," interview in *Arts in Society*, 1 (January 1958).

"America's Foremost Architect Speaks on Prefabrication," *House & Home*, 13 (April 1958).

Letter to the University of Wichita in Olgivanna Lloyd Wright, *The Shining Brow: Frank Lloyd Wright* (New York: Horizon Press, 1960).

"A Conversation with Frank Lloyd Wright: 'Flat on Our Faces,'" *The New Republic*, 139 (September 8, 1958).

"Frank Lloyd Wright and the Toronto City Hall," interview in *The Builder*, 195 (October 10, 1958).

"Frank Lloyd Wright on Restaurant Architecture: An Exclusive Interview of the Month," *Food Services Magazine* (November 1958).

Interview with representative of NBC-TV's "Wide, Wide World" in Olgivanna Lloyd Wright, "Our House," *The Capital Times*, January 19, 1959.

Letter to the editor, *ibid.*, February 12, 1959.

"Frank Lloyd Wright's Last Interview: Why People Create," April 3, 1959, in *School Arts*, 58 (June 1959).

"Wright Replies to Group Seeking to Stall on Terrace," *The Capital Times*, April 6, 1959.

Frank Lloyd Wright's Pamphlets, Catalogues, Brochures, and Booklets

Hiroshige: An Exhibition of Colour Prints from the Collection of Frank Lloyd Wright (Chicago: The Art Institue, 1906).

Antique Color Prints (Chicago: The Art Club, 1917).

Experimenting with Human Lives (Los Angeles: The Fine Arts Society, 1923), on the Imperial Hotel.

The Frank Lloyd Wright Collection of Japanese Prints (New York: The Anderson Galleries, 1927).

The Hillside Home School of the Allied Arts. Why We Want This School (Spring Green, Wis., October 1931).

"An Extension of the Work in Architecture at Taliesin to Include Apprenticeship in Residence," circular letter, Summer 1932, reprinted in *An Autobiography.*

The Taliesin Fellowship (Spring Green, Wis, 1933), descriptive pamphlet and application brochure.

Taliesin (Spring Green, Wis., 1934, 1935), the only two issues of a twenty-eight-page magazine.

Taliesin: The Taliesin Fellowship Publication (Spring Green, Wis., October 1940, February 1941), the only two issues of a projected quarterly.

A Taliesin Square-Paper: A Non-Political Voice from Our Democratic Minority (Spring Green, Wis.: Taliesin Press, 1941–1951), a quarter-fold sheet, unnumbered through three, then numbered through fifteen, appearing occasionally from January 1941 to January 1951.

Sixty Years of Living Architecture: The Work of Frank Lloyd Wright (exhibition brochure, 1951 to 1953), contents varying slightly from city to city.

Wright also wrote fliers for a number of projects, for example, "Oasis" (1957) for the Arizona State Capital.

Miscellaneous Sources

The several versions of the Monona Terrace Civic Center in Madison were published in *The Capital Times*, November 2, 1938; June 4, 1941; July 7–10, 1953; August 29–31, September 5, 6, 1956; September 18, 1967 (1938 rendering).

"General Plan of Highway and Bridge Relocation" for the Spring Green area in *The Weekly Home News*, October 9, 1947.

A May 1952 lecture made available on tape in 1976 from V.O.P. Productions, Oklahoma City.

November 1955 lecture in Chicago at opening of Henredon furniture display, tapes in author's and company's possession.

A June 1956 recording, *Frank Lloyd Wright on Record* (New York: Caedmon Records, 1961).

Manuscript Collections

Although William Wesley Peters has publicly stated that researchers are welcome, the Frank Lloyd Wright Foundation continues to deny access to the architect's voluminous files stored at Taliesin West except for approved scholars willing to pay a $40 an hour fee.

There are a few Wright letters in the public domain. The largest collection, some forty-odd pieces at the Northwestern University Library, is of limited interest since it deals mostly with efforts during the 1930s and 1940s to interest Wright in designing mobile homes. The Frank Lloyd Wright and John Lloyd Wright Papers at Avery Library, Columbia University, are much more important. Other letters are scattered around the country in possession of clients or their heirs; in several collections at the Archives of American Art, New York City; in the Claude Bragdon and William C. Gannett Papers in the University of Rochester Library; in the American Council for Judaism, Jane Lloyd Jones, Bruce Barton, and the (restricted) August Derleth Collections at the State Historical Society of Wisconsin; and at the Burnham Library, The Art Institute, Chicago. There are four excellent letters in the Harriet Monroe Poetry Collection, University of Chicago Library. In all, there seem to be little more than one hundred unpublished Wright letters available for scholarly research.

A Note on Newspapers

For Wright's Oak Park years, *The Reporter, The Vindicator,* and the *Argus* (all weeklies) were surpassed in quality and extent of coverage when *Oak Leaves* began in 1902. *The Weekly Home News* is indispensable for any Wright biographer, and along with its Spring Green predecessors was researched for the years 1879–1968. Other Wisconsin weeklies—particularly *The Sauk County Democrat* (Baraboo), *The Iowa County Democrat* (Mineral Point), and the *Baraboo Weekly News*—were most useful from 1911 into the 1930s. From 1909 to 1915 *The Chicago Tribune* is a valuable source. *The New York Times,* which in Wright's case did not print all the fit news, was consistently the most inaccurate newspaper, but beginning in the 1920s was useful as an index to his national reputation and as a chronical of his more conspicuous activities. The best and most important press coverage came from *The Capital Times* in Madison whose editor, William T. Evjue, interviewed Wright upon his final return from Japan in 1922, which began a warm friendship that lasted until the architect's death. Evjue opened his pages to Wright (and his wife) whenever he had something to say and published news of many of the architect's most trivial activities.

A Note on Iconographic Collections

A number of research institutions now have extensive collections of photographs of Frank Lloyd Wright and his buildings. Among the best are the Public Library and the Frank Lloyd Wright Home and Studio Foundation in Oak Park, Illinois; the State Historical Society of Wisconsin; the Kenneth Spencer Research Library at the University of Kansas, Lawrence; the Burnham Architectural Library at the Chicago Art Institute; and the Avery Architectural Library, Columbia University, New York.

Index